A Complete Guide to
Premises Security Litigation

ALAN KAMINSKY

TORT TRIAL & INSURANCE PRACTICE SECTION

Defending Liberty
Pursuing Justice

Cover design by ABA Publishing.

12 11 10 9 8   5 4 3 2 1

Library of Congress Cataloging-in-Publication Data

Kaminsky, Alan, 1958-
    A complete guide to premises security litigation / by Alan Kaminsky.—
3rd ed.
        p. cm.
    Includes index.
    ISBN 978-1-59031-941-3
        1. Premises liability—United States. 2. Actions and defenses—United
States. I. Title.
    KF1287.K35 2007
    346.7303'2—dc22

                                                                2007041374

Discounts are available for books ordered in bulk. Special consideration is given to state bars, CLE programs, and other bar-related organizations. Inquire at Book Publishing, ABA Publishing, American Bar Association, 321 N. Clark, Chicago, Illinois 60610.

www.ababooks.org

ACKNOWLEDGMENTS

Premises security is a fascinating area of law, one which I have enjoyed specializing in for the past 20 years. To be successful in litigating these cases, you need a solid team of attorneys working with you, you need the support of some of the top experts in the world, you need the backing of one of the country's leading firms, and you need the support and trust of your clients.

Toward that end, I thank all the members of Lewis Brisbois Bisgaard & Smith General Liability Practice Team, headed by Dirk Haarhoff, that helped update the research for this book.

I also thank the leadership of Lewis Brisbois Bisgaard & Smith for affording me the opportunity to work with such an extraordinarily gifted group of attorneys, here in our New York office as well as in our offices across the country, and for entrusting me to serve along with Doug Lewis as co-chairs of our General Liability Practice Team.

A special thanks is owed to Dennis Alonzo, Andy Barberis, David Crowe, Aaron Doynow, John Graham, Ed Kennelly, Bruce McCarthy, Bob Mooney, Jane Motyka, Jim Parr, Charlie Patitucci, Barry Reiber, Jim Siessel, Marco Spadacenta, Howard Tripolski, Sean Upton, and Barbara Zuckerman. We have tried and defended some extremely high profile cases together, and I am grateful for the opportunities you have given me and the trust you have shown in me.

And, under the category of giving credit where credit is due, acknowledgment is given to Harvey Weitz, Peter Grenier, Bob Sullivan, Howard Borowick, and Leslei Kelmachter, some of the most talented plaintiffs' lawyers you will ever find.

Thanks also to Lou Eckert, Mark Cipolla, and Shadena Morant for joining me at our new firm, and thanks to my partners Karen Campbell and George Catlett for coming on board. Thanks especially to my partner and friend, John Doody, who made all of this possible. I owe you bigtime.

In addition, I want to give a special thanks to Bob Smith, Bob

Lewis, Richard George, and Jody Jackson for the warm welcome my team and I received upon joining Lewis Brisbois Bisgaard & Smith.

And a special thanks to my parents and my family for a lifetime of love, support, and encouragement.

To my children, Joseph, Anna, and Robert, with much love

CONTENTS

INTRODUCTION

Until the last several years, when insurance companies issued standard general liability policies for commercial and residential landlords and business owners, the last thing they contemplated was potential multi-million-dollar exposure presented by lawsuits brought on behalf of crime victims who were assaulted, injured, raped, and/or killed during the commission of a crime within buildings the carriers insured. Instead of claims for tens of thousands of dollars on behalf of plaintiffs who may have broken an arm tripping over a cracked staircase, carriers began facing claims for millions of dollars on behalf of plaintiffs who were brutally assaulted and injured as the result of intentional criminal acts.

Understandably, this was not what the insurance industry anticipated when it actively sought business from the public and private landlords it now insures. As recently as the mid-1980s, personal injury actions against landlords for crimes committed within their buildings were virtually unheard of. Yet today, these high-exposure cases constitute a large percentage of the caseloads of most state courts located in urban areas.

How did this transformation come about? How has an entire genre of cases that until recently was virtually nonexistent so quickly come to the forefront of personal injury lawsuits? Several reasons come to mind. Crime victims, once hesitant to publicize the facts concerning their victimization, are now eager to seek redress for their injuries through the justice system. The plaintiffs' bar, recognizing the potential for large recoveries presented by these cases, now actively advertises for and recruits crime victims as clients in civil actions. Also, the average citizens who serve on juries are anxious to vent their frustration with the inordinate amount of crime that is plaguing the country, and appear eager to hold landlords responsible for "allowing" crimes to occur in their hotels, stores, and buildings.

Perhaps a team of socioeconomic experts could write a companion text to this book to explain in greater detail how various sociological, economic, and other such factors have combined to produce crime victims more willing to come forward about their victimization, and jurors more willing to award damages in favor of those victims. (The motives for the plaintiffs' bar to recruit these cases actively is easy enough to understand.) However, we in the legal, insurance, and real estate professions cannot afford the luxury of waiting for a scientific and/or philosophical analysis providing various rationales for these lawsuits. For the lawyer who is about to defend a building owner against a claim brought by an assault victim, for the claims examiner who must decide whether to settle or proceed to trial with a multimillion-dollar lawsuit against an insured, and for the landlord who is trying to understand legal obligations to provide protection from crime in his or her buildings, answers to important questions are needed now. This book addresses those questions.

Part One of the book discusses the various components of premises security claims, and sets forth strategies for defending such claims. Part Two consists of a case study focusing on a plaintiff's and defendant's efforts in handling a multimillion-dollar lawsuit on behalf of a rape victim against her landlord. Part Three contains a state-by-state analysis of important court decisions in the area of premises security law, and provides an overview regarding how these cases are decided in different jurisdictions.

Using a step-by-step method, this book analyzes the proper handling of a premises security action. We hope it assists you in your endeavors.

PART I

Guide for Handling Premises Security Actions

♔ CHAPTER 1

Statistical Information and Elements of a Premises Security Claim

Statistical Information

What Is a Premises Security Lawsuit?

A premises security lawsuit (also known as a negligent security lawsuit) is a claim for damages brought in civil court on behalf of a crime victim, usually against the owner of the premises where the crime occurred. The victim of a crime such as a mugging, assault, or rape seeks to hold the landowner responsible for the injuries—usually both physical and psychological—that the victim sustained, contending that the crime was "caused" by the landowner's failure to provide sufficient security to protect persons from criminal occurrences at the location.

Within those parameters, a premises security claim can be commenced against virtually any landlord or business owner when a crime has been committed within their premises. Crime victims have commenced lawsuits against obvious parties, such as hotels, apartment complexes, and office buildings, and also against less likely defendants, including libraries, restaurants, and dormitories.

Defendants in premises security lawsuits are often confronted with emotional testimony of a crime victim, whose psychological damages are often more serious than the physical injuries suffered in the crime. Although these defendants face no criminal liability, crime victims contend that landowners who do not actually commit the crime should nevertheless be held civilly liable for it and compensate the crime victim for his or her damages.

Average Settlements and Verdicts

Crime pays. A quick glance at the average verdicts for premises security cases shows that, in many cases, crime does pay. However, the business and land owners, rather than the assailants, often must satisfy the large settlements and verdicts awarded to crime victims.

Available information from the early to mid 1990s suggests that the average reported verdict against a landlord in favor of an assault victim was over $1 million. The average verdict in favor of a rape victim was over $1.8 million. The typical verdict in favor of an estate in a wrongful death claim was $2.1 million. Even settlement amounts in premises security cases are staggering. The average reported settlement amount for premises security lawsuits is over $500,000. More-over, premises security lawsuits are not limited to certain jurisdictions

Average Settlements and Verdicts in Premises Security Cases

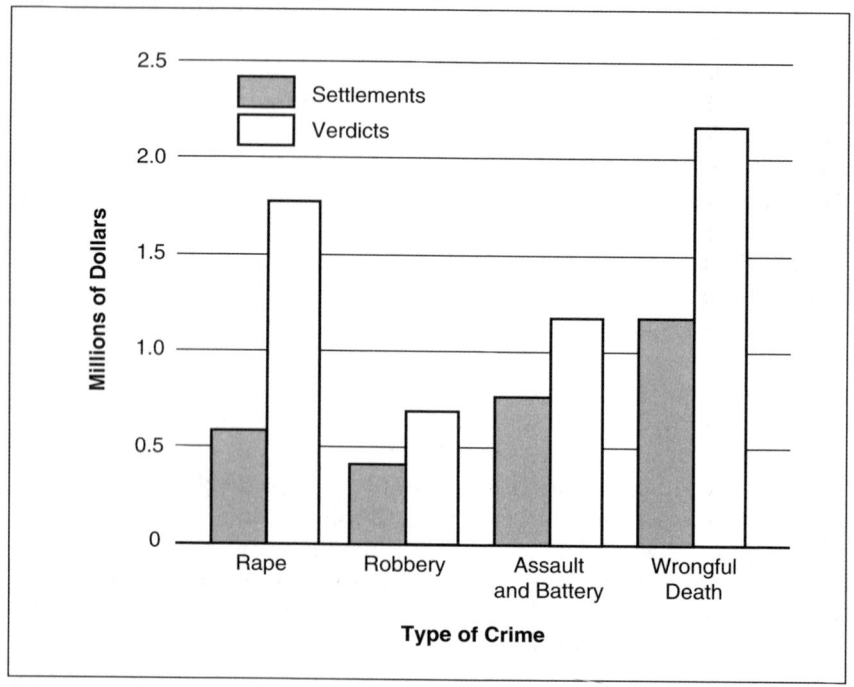

Source: Liability Consultants, Inc. (Reprinted by permission.)

or certain industries; claims have been commenced across the country against every conceivable type of landlord or business owner.

Given this background, it is important to recognize that any land-lord, landowner, business owner, or business establishment faces the potential for enormous exposure in a premises security case.

Typical Costs Incurred in Defending a Premises Security Action

Not only are the average reported settlements and verdicts in premises security actions exceptionally high, the expenses incurred in defending such claims can also be quite substantial, as suggested by the following typical lawsuit.

FACTS: A sixty-five-year-old woman is mugged as she is about to enter her car, after she has finished shopping in a shopping mall. As a result of the assault, during which her bags were grabbed from her and she was thrown to the ground, the woman fractured her ankle and four ribs and developed heart palpitations, allegedly shortening her life expectancy.

The lawsuit alleges that the shopping mall owners failed to provide adequate security to protect their patrons from criminal attacks within their outdoor lot; that the parking lot was dimly lit, affording predators a place to congregate; and that the security patrols took an unduly long time responding to the woman's calls for help, resulting in a worsening of her heart condition. The complaint seeks $3 million in damages.

The chart on page 6 describes the anticipated costs for defending the lawsuit.

Premises Security Cases on the Rise

Less than a decade ago, the number of lawsuits pending nationwide on behalf of crime victims against landlords was negligible. Today, premises security lawsuits are among the fastest growing segment of personal injury lawsuits. Some have estimated that early in this century, claims alleging inadequate security will be second only to general negligence/slip-and-fall cases as the most common lawsuit brought against residential landlords. Moreover, owners of residential property are not alone in being targeted as defendants in premises security cases. Claims against hospitals, colleges, day care centers, and especially shopping malls are also increasing dramatically.

Anticipated Costs for Defending Lawsuit

Before Trial

Investigation (securing incident reports and statements of responding security personnel, obtaining reports of prior incidents in parking lot, photographing scene, interviewing police detectives assigned to case)

Cost: $3,000-$5,000

Legal Expenses (responsive pleadings, research, depositions, discovery, witness meetings, motion practice)

Cost: $10,000-$20,000

Experts (medical expert and security expert for initial review, examinations, and consultation)

Cost: $5,000

Total Expenses Before Trial: $18,000-$30,000

Through Trial

Continued Investigation (conducting surveillance, locating witnesses, interviewing mall personnel, subpoenaing documents and witnesses)

Cost: $5,000-$7,000

Legal Expenses (preparing for and conducting two-week trial)

Cost: At least $20,000

Experts (medical and security experts' time testifying at trial)

Cost: $7,500

Miscellaneous Expenses (documents, court fees, reporters' fees, records)

Cost: $2,500

Total Trial Expenses: At least $35,000

TOTAL EXPENSES FROM INCEPTION THROUGH VERDICT: At least $53,000

Average Costs by Industry

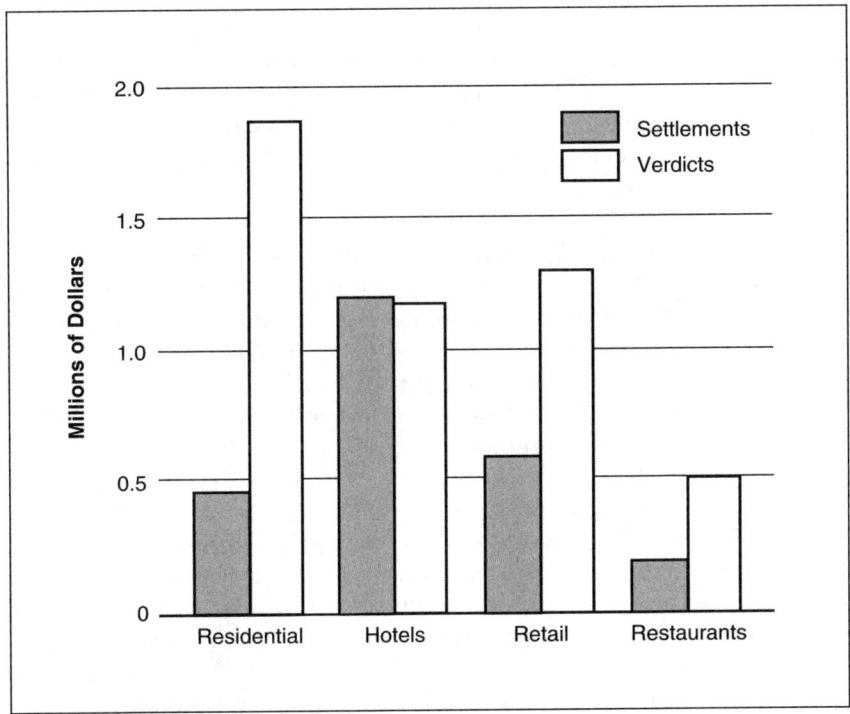

Source: Liability Consultants, Inc. (Reprinted by permission.)

Elements of a Premises Security Claim

Plaintiff's Theory of the Case

To maintain a viable negligent security action against a landlord or business owner, a plaintiff must establish that

- the defendant owed a duty to protect the injured crime victim;
- the defendant breached that duty; and
- the breach of the duty was a proximate cause of the criminal act and the victim's injuries.

As simple as that criteria may appear, establishing it is a difficult task. Each element of the alleged negligence—duty, breach of duty, and proximate cause—is subject to intense legal scrutiny that, without impeccable evidence, could result in the dismissal of a potential million-dollar claim.

Accordingly, the prosecution of a premises security case must begin with a thorough understanding of the nature of the evidence required to document the existence of a duty, to establish that the defendant breached the owed duty, and to demonstrate that the breach of the owed duty was a proximate cause of the underlying crime and the victim's alleged injuries.

DUTY. Initially, it must be recognized that the true culprit in a premises security action is not the landlord or business owner who operated the premises where the crime occurred; the responsible party is the person who actually committed the crime. Given that consideration, a fair number of court decisions have held that a landlord does not have a duty to protect individuals from the intervening criminal acts of third persons. Those decisions refuse to impose an affirmative duty of protection on a landlord or business owner, and hold that the intentional intervening act of a third person breaks any causal connection between the alleged acts of negligence and the injuries deliberately inflicted by an assailant upon a plaintiff. In recent years, however, such definitive decisions have given way to the realities of urban and suburban crime, and courts are now inclined to acknowledge that, in certain circumstances, landlords or business owners owe a duty to protect tenants, patrons, or guests from criminal acts committed within their premises.

The essential factors that often determine whether a duty to provide protection exists in a specific case are the nature of the relationship between the parties and the concept of "foreseeability."

Relationship Between the Parties. Many jurisdictions have specifically enumerated the types of relationships, often called "special relationships," that give rise to a duty on behalf of a defendant to protect a plaintiff from criminal acts. These special relationships have included innkeepers and their guests, common carriers and their passengers, and school districts and their students. Courts have continually expanded the special relationship concept, which began as a very narrow exception to the long-standing proposition that a landowner cannot be held liable for the criminal acts of third persons. Now most courts regard the nature of the relationship between a landlord and tenant, or business owner and patron, sufficient to find that a duty to provide protection may exist.

Courts may also consider commercial and residential leases, to the extent they make representations concerning security issues, to decide whether a duty exists. Some jurisdictions have analyzed lease provisions containing references to security under a "warranty of habitability" theory. Similarly, state statutes and local ordinances may support the existence of obligations concerning required levels of security, or possibly negate any owed duty under a grant of immunity to governmental agencies.

Also, in many instances, courts may find that a landowner has voluntarily assumed a duty to provide protection that did not otherwise exist. For example, landowners may place guards in their place of business or in a parking lot they do not own but that is used by their patrons. Courts may find such acts to be a voluntary assumption of a duty to provide protection and, if done negligently, may expose the landowner to liability.

Foreseeability. "Without foreseeability, there is no duty" is a quote that can be taken from many of the hundreds of decisions that have granted a defendant's motion for summary judgment in premises security cases. To establish that a crime was or should have been foreseen by the defendant, the plaintiff must show that the defendant knew or should have known that the criminal act was likely to occur. Strategies for establishing foreseeability include presenting evidence of prior crimes within the building or surrounding neighborhood, evidence that the building is in a high-crime area, and evidence that the condition of the building itself attracts criminal activity.

Importantly, many jurisdictions have relaxed the nature of evidence required to demonstrate foreseeability. In certain cases, courts will consider a crime foreseeable even if it was the first crime reported to have occurred in the building. Similarly, courts may consider a crime foreseeable even if reported prior crimes are dissimilar in nature, or occurred blocks away from the defendant's premises.

Generally, the specific crime committed upon a particular plaintiff need not have been foreseen by the defendant. Rather, the likelihood of almost any variety of criminal activity occurring in the building is usually deemed sufficient to find a specific crime as foreseeable. Several states, however, still require a plaintiff to present evidence that the defendant knew or should have known that the specific crime in a particular case was going to be committed—a virtually impossible criterion for a plaintiff to establish.

BREACH OF DUTY. Once the existence of a duty to provide protection is demonstrated, a plaintiff must then establish that the defendant breached that duty.

Generally, a landowner owes a duty to provide reasonable security measures to protect a person from criminal acts. Those measures may include working door locks and intercom systems, or more elaborate safety features such as security guards and surveillance equipment, depending on the circumstances of a particular case.

A plaintiff must demonstrate, then, that the landlord or business owner failed to provide the required level of security. Claims of broken door locks and faulty intercom systems constitute the largest percentage of premises security cases. Security guards alleged as having been negligently hired or trained, or as having left their post when a crime was committed, also are the focus of a large number of these cases. Many crimes are committed in darkened parking lots; hence, claims of inadequate or insufficient lighting are also quite common.

The mere commission of a crime does not mean that a defendant breached its duty to provide security to the plaintiff. Expert testimony, therefore, is a virtual prerequisite for demonstrating such allegations.

PROXIMATE CAUSE. Just as it must be understood that the real culprit in a premises case is the assailant and not the landlord, it must also be recognized that the true cause of a crime victim's injuries are the intentional acts of the criminal, and not the security features (or lack thereof) of a building. Nevertheless, courts in virtually all jurisdictions will entertain evidence that a defendant's breach of a duty to provide security contributed to the criminal occurrence.

Depending on the nature of the crime, the security features of a building may be relevant to the commission of the criminal act. The assailant's means of entry into the building is, therefore, of vital concern and could have a definitive impact on the issue of proximate cause. Any potential relationship between the assailant and the victim must also be explored. While past associations or knowledge of the victim's identity may have no bearing on the assailant's guilt or innocence, those factors could have a dramatic impact on whether an alleged breached duty to provide security was a proximate cause of the crime.

A plaintiff can anticipate having an affirmative obligation to present evidence that enhanced security features could have deterred the underlying crime, or that security lapses at the building contributed to the occurrence of the criminal act. Without such evidence, the case most likely will not withstand a challenge by the defense on the issue of proximate cause.

Defendant's Theory of the Case

A defendant can contest a plaintiff's claim of negligent security on one or more issues: by denying a duty was owed to protect the plaintiff; by challenging allegations that any owed duty was breached; or by disputing contentions that any breach of an owed duty was a proximate cause of the crime.

DUTY. In raising the argument that a defendant did not owe a duty to the plaintiff, the issues of the nature of the parties' relationship and foreseeability must again be addressed.

Relationship Between the Parties. Ironically, the nature of the relationship between the crime victim and landowner is fairly insignificant in most cases, as most jurisdictions no longer make distinctions in a plaintiff's status as a trespasser, licensee, or invitee.

However, while the nature of the relationship between the crime victim and the landowner alone may be inconsequential, coupled with one or more other factors, such as the location of the crime or relations to other persons, the relationship between the parties may take on added significance. In many instances, defendants will not owe a duty to protect plaintiffs from criminal acts that occur off-premises or in non-common areas. Hence, a duty to provide protection may not exist for a crime committed in a parking facility not controlled by a defendant though adjacent to the defendant's premises, or for a crime committed within the specific confines of a tenant's apartment.

The relationship between a victim and an assailant, and even between an assailant and a defendant, may also negate the existence of a duty. For example, a landlord may be under no duty to protect a tenant from crimes committed by another tenant, or from crimes that are inter-household in nature.

Foreseeability. The most common method for denying the existence of a duty to provide protection from crime is to raise the issue of foreseeability. In most instances, a defendant will not owe a duty to protect a person against criminal activity if the defendant could not have reasonably anticipated and acted upon the crime.

The absence of prior crimes on the premises, while not dispositive, is a vital element to a defense that uses the issue of foreseeability to challenge a landlord's duty to provide protection to a plaintiff. The nature of the specific crime is also of great importance. The foreseeability defense has greater credibility when a particular crime is either highly unusual or spontaneous in nature, rendering it less likely to have been reasonably anticipated or acted upon by the defendant.

Businesses Most Often Sued in Premises Security Cases

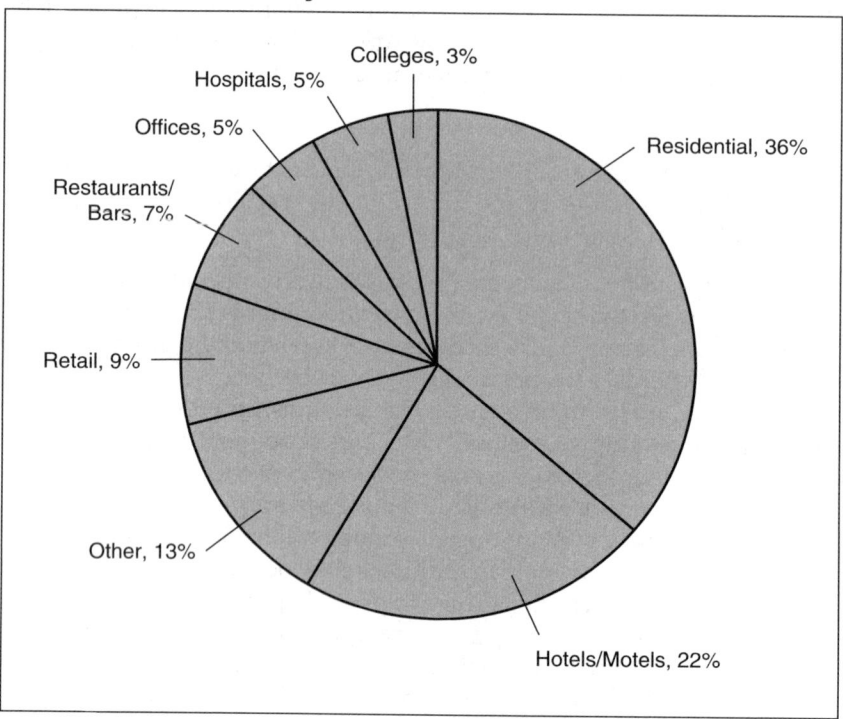

Colleges, 3%

Hospitals, 5%

Offices, 5%

Residential, 36%

Restaurants/ Bars, 7%

Retail, 9%

Other, 13%

Hotels/Motels, 22%

Source: Liability Consultants, Inc. (Reprinted by permission.)

Many courts now hold, however, that the defendant need not have foreseen the specific crime committed, and that it is sufficient for a plaintiff to simply establish that the defendant should have foreseen criminal activity of a more general nature.

SATISFACTION OF DUTY. Leading appellate decisions across the country reiterate the proposition that "landlords are not insurers of public safety." Even in buildings replete with extensive criminal history, arguments can be raised that the landowner provided the required level of security. Accordingly, a defendant must document every security feature present within the premises to establish that the duty to provide the required level of protection against a criminal occurrence has been satisfied.

Top Ten Crime Claim States

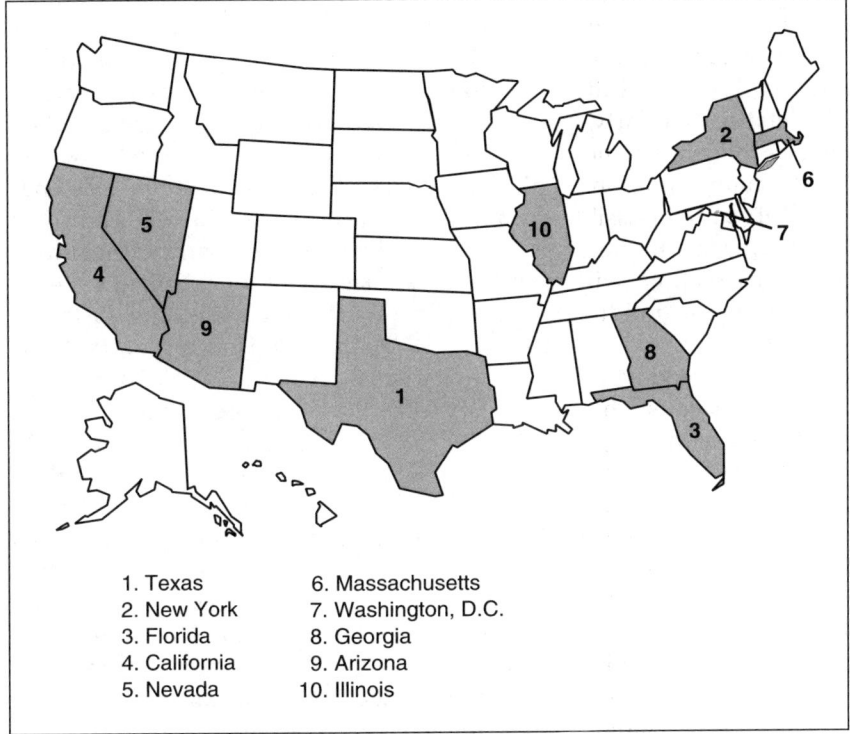

1. Texas
2. New York
3. Florida
4. California
5. Nevada
6. Massachusetts
7. Washington, D.C.
8. Georgia
9. Arizona
10. Illinois

Source: Liability Consultants, Inc. (Reprinted by permission.)

In many jurisdictions, courts have found that working front and rear door locks and intercom systems satisfy the required level of security a landowner must provide. In other states, necessary security features are determined by what is reasonable under the circumstances.

As is the case for plaintiffs, defendants require expert testimony on the issue of an alleged breach of duty.

PROXIMATE CAUSE. Even in a case where a defendant owes a duty of protection, and evidence suggests a breach of that duty, a case can still be defended by showing that the building's security features (or lack thereof) were not a cause of the particular crime.

As the prominent factor in this defense is often the assailant's method of entry into the building, a defendant must undertake all reasonable efforts to determine that manner of entry.

For example, if either the victim or someone authorized to be in the building invited the assailant into the premises, the defendant can raise a viable defense based upon proximate cause. If the rear entrance is shown to have been defective, but the evidence suggests the assailant entered through a different entrance, proximate cause is again a credible defense. Similarly, proximate cause will be an issue if the assailant simply followed someone into the premises.

In many situations, a plaintiff will be able to establish the existence of a duty and a possible breach of the required level of protection, but the assailant's manner of entry into the premises will be uncertain. Some jurisdictions will permit an inference about the assailant's means of entering the building from circumstantial evidence; other courts will not allow for such speculation. Without definitive proof that the assailant entered a building due to inadequate security, a plaintiff may be unable to satisfy his burden of proof on the issue of proximate cause.

States with the greatest incidence of reported crime are likely to have the largest number of premises security cases commenced in their jurisdiction. However, other important considerations affect the number of premises security cases that have been and will be commenced in each state. Most significantly, appellate court decisions regarding landowners' obligations toward crime victims—which vary greatly from state to state—influence the number of lawsuits filed. While some courts have adopted conservative positions that seem to protect landlords from liability, others have espoused liberal positions that almost ensure a crime victim's ability to recover damages.

A state-by-state analysis of premises security law is presented in Part Three of this book.

CHAPTER 2

The Importance of Investigation: Proper Investigative Techniques for Ensuring Favorable Results

The key to successful prosecution or defense of a premises security case can be summed up in one word: investigation. Whereas diligent investigation is important in all premises liability actions, it is essential in a security case.

Due to the nature of these actions, retired police officers and detectives are best suited for obtaining valuable investigative results. Lawyers must remain focused, however, about the objective of the investigation, as their job is not to solve the underlying crimes. Rather, their task is to demonstrate whether a building was equipped with the required level of security and, if not, whether the lack of such security was a cause of the criminal act.

An example of a typical security case follows: A young woman is shot by an unknown assailant as she enters the lobby of a multiple dwelling. Based upon only those generic facts, how should lawyers begin their investigation of the case?

Defendant's Investigation

Defense investigation of a premises security case should begin the moment reports of a serious crime occurring in a client's building are received. Beginning investigative efforts before the start of a lawsuit is imperative. Many jurisdictions have a three-year statute of limitation for negligence actions, and thus conducting a meaningful investigation will be virtually impossible if it does not begin until the first notice of a lawsuit, perhaps years after the crime occurred. The expenses associated with conducting a prompt investigation will be more than offset by the potential savings on exposure realized as a result of the investigation.

In many jurisdictions, prompt investigative efforts will also have the desired effect of rendering privileged the fruits of the investigation, as such investigation is being conducted in anticipation of litigation.

Additionally, the sooner the investigation begins after the crime, the greater the likelihood of helpful information being uncovered. For example:

- Photographs of working door locks taken within several days of an occurrence may be admissible at trial, whereas the same photographs taken months later would arguably be deemed irrelevant.
- A videotape of an entranceway opening and closing properly and taken the day of the incident could unilaterally provide for a successful defense.
- Building residents interviewed promptly after the crime is committed may specifically recall working door locks during relevant time periods.
- Building personnel interviewed near the time of the occurrence are apt to have stronger recollections of any inspections they performed that day.

The defense should also undertake the following efforts at the earliest opportunity.

Inspect the Premises

In addition to videotaping and photographing all entranceways, the defense must preserve evidence of all other security features. Elevators should be confirmed as working properly, lighting in all strategic locations must be established as adequate, and the activities of any lobby attendants or security guards must be documented. Also, emergency exits, surveillance cameras, intercom systems, and alarms must be tested, inspected, and confirmed to be working satisfactorily.

Preserve Records

All landlords keep a variety of records, many of which can prove most helpful in defending a security case. The investigator's job is to secure all such records before they become either misplaced or irretrievable.

Copies of all tenant complaints—whether received in person, by phone, or in writing—must be obtained, and any complaint related to security must be confirmed as having been addressed. Work-order tickets to support any completed tasks must also be obtained. In addition, the following documents must be secured: janitorial inspection logs and reports, time cards and attendance records for all employees on duty during relevant time periods, all management communications to tenants related to security issues, communications or reports about prior criminal occurrences and related correspondence with the local police department, records of inspections by city or local agencies, contracts with any outside security or maintenance providers, and sign-in sheets for any visitors or guests.

Interview Building Personnel

Of course, maintenance, management, and security personnel must be interviewed about their knowledge of the occurrence. Equally important, all employees must be questioned about their understanding of the building's security features and their knowledge of any prior criminal activity within the premises. Such interviews may reveal a maintenance worker who explains that he personally checks entrance door locks each time he enters and exits the building, a manager who discloses that a large percentage of rental income is allocated for security concerns, or a security guard who says very few prior criminal acts have been committed in the building.

Building employees can also assist in establishing security features of the building that are not readily apparent. For example, a lobby designed to provide extra sunlight could be a security feature. Regular elevator inspections could also qualify as overlooked security. A manager who visits the premises on a daily basis and simply walks through the building may also unwittingly provide security.

Often, maintenance employees will be candid about prior criminal occurrences within their knowledge. It is important to obtain the facts pertaining to those occurrences so they can be distinguished from the crime in the security case and their relevance can be challenged. Building employees can also provide insights about tenants identified as potential witnesses by the plaintiff. Occasionally, an alleged notice witness will have a history of difficulty with building management that may affect the witness's credibility. Tenant folders may also prove to be a source of valuable information.

Obtain Witnesses

The police can provide information about any eyewitnesses to the crime. However, the investigator must locate non-eyewitnesses who can also provide assistance with the defense. For example, longtime building residents who express satisfaction with building security are viable witnesses. Similarly, residents who can attest to management's efficiency in removing loiterers are also legitimate witnesses, as are persons who can recall that locks and intercoms were working during relevant time periods. Tenants who participate in a tenant's group, such as a tenants association, may also prove to be important defense witnesses.

When warranted, the entire building should be canvassed, with each resident interviewed, so that the witnesses with the most favorable accounts of building security can be disclosed for trial. As potential witnesses will often "side" with the party who makes first contact with them, defense investigators should not be hesitant about speaking to all residents.

Investigate the Plaintiff

As sympathetic a witness as a crime victim may be, a thorough investigation into the plaintiff's own actions must be conducted. A recent study from the United States Justice Department confirms that many victims of serious crimes are assaulted by known acquaintances. While the fact that an assault was committed by a known perpetrator may not imply any wrongdoing by the plaintiff, such a scenario could result in a successful defense to a claim of negligent security. Accordingly, the defense must undertake all efforts to determine whether the assailant knew the victim, including the following:

- The plaintiff's actions on the day of the crime must be retraced. Was anyone known to have been stalking the plaintiff?
- Neighbors should be interviewed, as should coworkers. Did anyone notice anything unusual in the plaintiff's behavior?
- Is it conceivable that the plaintiff himself or herself was involved in illicit activity? Were drugs possibly involved? Does the plaintiff have a criminal record?
- If the crime occurred in a high-crime area, what is the plaintiff's explanation for being there? Is the story credible?
- Anyone who accompanied or spoke with the plaintiff on the day of the crime should be questioned.

Quite often, the investigation will uncover information that presents the plaintiff in a light contrary to that of an innocent crime victim.

Obtain Ambulance Reports,
Medical Records, and 911 Call Reports

These documents should also be scrutinized for any inconsistencies the plaintiff may have given about the facts and circumstances of the crime. Does the account the plaintiff provided to ambulance workers coincide with current allegations regarding the facts surrounding the crime? Do the reports or records provide any clues about the manner in which the assailant entered the premises or the assailant's identity?

Often these records contain entries that suggest the plaintiff may suspect a certain individual of committing the crime, or they may contain the names of witnesses with whom the plaintiff had contact on the day of the crime.

Interview the Responding and Investigating
Police Officers and Obtain Police Records

Responding police officers are often valuable sources for documenting the presence or absence of locks on an entranceway at the time of an incident. Lawyers should be certain to question police officers about their usual custom and practice for recording such information in their records. In addition to reviewing official police reports that are prepared following all reported crimes, lawyers should be certain to obtain copies of each officer's handwritten memo books, as they routinely contain vital information that can help the case. For instance, a police officer may have recorded in a log book that entry into the building was delayed because the officer had to wait for someone to let him or her into the building. Similarly, an officer may have noted that the door was locked upon his or her arrival.

An often overlooked source of information is the investigation conducted by the police department's crime scene unit. In serious criminal cases, it is not unusual for a special unit of the detective bureau to conduct its own investigation of the crime. These investigations routinely include photographs of the crime scene, and may include photographs of a locked door as well. A thorough investigation involves securing all relevant police documents, including the personal notes of all responding officers and detectives involved with the case, as well as the records from every police unit, bureau, or department involved in investigating the case.

Aside from the information contained in these materials, the police records and detective files may also provide essential information for later use by an appropriate expert. The assailant's modus operandi will be a valuable key for ultimate opinion testimony by a criminologist or other liability expert concerning the manner in which the assailant entered the premises, the apparent randomness of the crime, and the causation between the building's security and the criminal act.

Acquire Crime Statistics and Incident Reports

The records concerning prior criminal activity within the premises are as important as the records about the specific crime in the case. Every time a crime is reported to the police an incident report, which contains relevant information about that particular crime, is generated. These reports are a readily available source for documenting prior criminal activity (or the lack thereof) within the very building where the plaintiff was assaulted.

Many jurisdictions do not require proof of prior crimes within a specific building or location before allowing a crime victim to recover. In a large number of jurisdictions, a plaintiff may establish foreseeability of criminal activity by showing prior criminal activity within the immediate and surrounding neighborhoods. A proper investigation, therefore, should secure incident reports for the entire precinct in which the particular building is located, so that an expert can properly analyze such reports.

The crime statistics for the overall precinct are also important for comparison with the statistics for a particular building. For instance, the number of reported crimes in the building at issue can be extrapolated on a per resident basis, and the resulting figure may show that the number of crimes reported in the building compare favorably with the number reported on a per capita basis in the surrounding area. Through appropriate expert testimony, crime statistics can be used to show that, at least on the surface, the location of the underlying criminal act was arguably as safe as neighboring buildings, including buildings equipped with enhanced security devices.

Importance of Thorough Investigation— An Example Case

The following case, which was defended at trial by the author, makes clear how a thorough investigation affects the outcome of a trial. The claim against the defendant was that a young girl had been brutally raped by an unknown assailant, after the assailant gained entry to her apartment building through an unlocked rear door, grabbed her, dragged her up several flights of stairs, and forced her out on the roof.

During trial, the plaintiff presented crime scene photographs clearly depicting a broken frame on the rear door that prevented the door from locking and provided unrestricted access to the premises by unauthorized persons. The plaintiff also presented unchallenged evidence that the building had been the scene of numerous prior criminal acts, and that the rear door had been reported to be in a state of disrepair for a significant period of time before this particular occurrence.

To complicate matters for the defendant, the rape occurred after the plaintiff had returned home from church, and the medical evidence suggested that she was suffering from acute post-traumatic rape disorder, which was significantly affecting her lifestyle. Understandably, the plaintiff's settlement demand had been in excess of $1 million.

However, the defendants remained confident. Before trial, the defendants conducted an exhaustive investigation and, as a result, located two witnesses who happened to be standing in the lobby of the building on the date of the incident. The witnesses were disclosed to the plaintiff, and subsequently called to testify by the defendant. During trial, both witnesses confirmed that they observed the alleged assailant enter the building through the front door, rendering all allegations of a defective rear door irrelevant.

The jury dismissed the case.

♠ CHAPTER 3

Defending a Premises Security Action: Important Strategies for Successfully Defending a Landlord or Business Owner

Multimillion-dollar verdicts or settlements in favor of crime victims against residential and commercial building owners are no longer newsworthy. They have become so common, they are almost expected. Virtually any claim on behalf of a seriously injured crime victim is regarded as presenting the potential for enormous exposure. Consequently, following consultation with carriers and lawyers, defendants often make "business decisions" to settle these cases at almost any cost rather than risk a runaway verdict at trial.

But are all of those large settlements appropriate? Should defense lawyers, whose assessment on liability and exposure is sought by their clients, be readily recommending high-priced settlements of premises security cases?

The first item that must be addressed is how to evaluate a premises security case. If a dozen lawyers were polled and asked to assess a claim brought on behalf of a thirty-year-old plaintiff who fell down a defective flight of stairs and fractured her wrist, the odds are that after asking a couple of questions about her recovery, about the nature of the defect and how long the dangerous condition was present, and about comparative negligence issues, each lawyer would come up with a valuation within a few thousand dollars of each other in assessing the case. But what is the value of a case where that same thirty-year-old woman, instead of falling down a flight of stairs and breaking her wrist, is dragged from the staircase and onto the roof of her building where she is brutally raped? $500,000? $800,000? What is the value of a case where a young man is stabbed or shot in an elevator and will have permanent residual injuries for the rest of his life? $750,000? $1 million? More? What is the value of a case where a young businesswoman opens the door to her motel room, expecting someone from the maintenance department, only to be confronted by three men who ransack the room and then proceed to sexually assault her over the course of thirty minutes? Again, $1 million? Perhaps even higher?

What about the issue of comparative negligence? In virtually all personal injury actions, a defendant can almost always establish a certain amount of comparative negligence to offset damages. If a plaintiff trips and falls on a raised sidewalk, perhaps she was 30 percent comparatively negligent for not observing the defect. If a plaintiff sustains a herniated disk to his lower back in an automobile accident, perhaps he contributed to his injuries by not wearing a seat belt. However, in a premises security case, comparative negligence is a virtual nonissue. Rarely will comparative negligence even be charged to a jury. The issue of damages therefore must be considered at full value.

So before starting a plan of defense, the first task is to put into perspective a premises security action.

Components of a Premises Security Action

Ultimately, a premises security lawsuit has five components: the plaintiff, the landlord or business owner, the jury, the judge, and the nature of the crime itself.

The Plaintiff

As far as the plaintiff is concerned, no one would doubt the sympathetic nature of a crime victim's testimony. Imagine how enraged a jury will feel when it hears the testimony of a crime victim and observes her in court day after day. The jurors establish a bond with her. They are "rooting" for her to win. They feel for her. The plaintiff is, truly, the victim, and jurors have an understandable desire to want to compensate the plaintiff for the ordeal she has endured.

A plaintiff's recounting the nature of the crime and the specifics of an attack can be riveting and emotional. The jury watches the plaintiff's every move and listens astutely to every word. Jurors seem to relive the crime with the plaintiff as it is described in detail.

Accordingly, the defense must anticipate that a crime victim's testimony will be well received by a jury.

Landlords or Business Owners

Conversely, often the most that can be expected from a landlord's or business owner's testimony is that it will not offend the jury. Landlords are often perceived as uncaring and oblivious to security problems within their buildings, and business owners are viewed as caring only about profits. Nearly everyone who serves as a juror has had an unpleasant experience with a landlord. Although prospective jurors will give assurances that any ill feelings they may have toward their own landlords will not affect their impartiality, landlords and business owners are often no match for a plaintiff's testimony.

Defense lawyers must, therefore, personalize landlords and business owners. Even the largest landowners have "hands-on" maintenance personnel who can explain their various undertakings to ensure proper security at the premises. While such personalization is essential, defense lawyers must be aware that they are entering a trial with jurors inherently biased against their client.

Juries

How do jurors view premises security cases? Recent public opinion surveys show that crime is perceived as one of the most pressing problems in the country. A local newscast in New York airs a daily tally of the number of persons murdered in the city for the calendar year to date. Elderly seniors choose to live in barricaded developments, sealing themselves off from the outside world, because they are so afraid of becoming crime victims. Metal detectors are common at schools, nightclubs, and auditoriums. In fact, jurors often must pass through a metal detector simply to enter a courthouse. It is the average citizen who rates crime as perhaps the number one problem in the country who will be serving as a juror for these cases. It is the average citizen who spends thousands of dollars to secure his own residence and equip his own car with advanced alarm systems who will decide the issues in the case. It is the average citizen who himself or whose family member has probably been a crime victim who will decide the fate of the defense lawyer's client.

Suffice it to say that a jury cannot be expected to condone inadequate security features at a building.

Judges

In most personal injury cases, judges tend to go to great lengths to allow a case to be submitted to the jury. Successful dispositive motions in routine slip-and-fall or automobile accident cases are uncommon. As questions of fact are routinely found to exist, the overwhelming number of motions for summary judgment are denied.

Premises liability actions, however, are appropriate for dispositive motion practice. As numerous courts have held, issues of foreseeability and duty are often questions of law in premises security cases. Therefore, these cases are suitable for summary judgment consideration and judges will not hesitate to grant summary judgment motions when appropriate.

The Nature of the Crime

The final factor that the defense must consider is the nature of the crime itself. Most premises security cases involve shootings, stabbings, or violent assaults. Often, the victims' physical injuries pale in comparison to the emotional trauma they sustain.

As a general rule, the more violent the crime, the more impassioned the jury, and the greater the deference defense lawyers should show to the plaintiff, particularly during cross-examination.

Defense lawyers should also undertake efforts to preclude particularly explicit evidence such as crime scene photographs or certain accounts of the incident, on the grounds that such photographs or testimony would be inflammatory and grossly prejudicial.

Given these various components of a premises security case, defendants must prepare their defense on two fronts: the facts, and the law.

Preparing the Defense

Upon learning that a claim of negligent security is being brought against a landowner, defense lawyers should immediately conduct the following actions.

Inspect the Building

Defense lawyers should personally inspect and assess all elements of building security. It is imperative that lawyers get their own sense of the building's security.

Meet with Building Manager

Lawyers should promptly confer with building representatives to establish rapport with them, and to ensure their cooperation as the case progresses. Management should provide an explanation of all security features that were in place on the date the crime occurred.

Secure Records

All maintenance reports should be immediately obtained. Defense lawyers should also secure copies of any incident reports, as well as log books, inspection records, and attendance reports for all building personnel.

Preserve Evidence

Photographs of entranceways and videotapes of working door locks must be secured.

To ensure that these actions provide as much valuable information as possible, the checklists shown at the end of this chapter should be used for reference during each undertaking.

Upon completing the essential investigation, defense lawyers should proceed with the actual litigation of the case. The most important item in the defense of a premises security action is the pretrial examination of the plaintiff. The preliminary investigation must be completed before conducting the plaintiff's deposition. Defense lawyers should not feel pressured by their adversaries to depose the plaintiff until they are ready to proceed.

Plaintiff's Deposition

When conducting the plaintiff's deposition, the defense lawyer must be certain to elicit testimony that addresses all issues from both a legal and factual approach. For example, did the plaintiff know her assailant? Does she know how he gained access into the building? Was she ever previously at the building? Is the plaintiff aware of any prior crime within the premises? What was the plaintiff's purpose for being present at the location that day? Did she have any contact or conversation with the assailant prior to the crime?

Information obtained at the plaintiff's deposition will often affect the outcome of a case. Lawyers should consider the following outline for deposing a crime victim.

I. Background Information
  A. Residential history
  B. Scholastic history
  C. Employment history
  D. Social history
    1. Family relationships
    2. Boyfriend/girlfriend relationships
    3. Names of close friends and associates

E. Medical history
  1. Prior medical concerns
  2. Prior counseling/therapy
  3. Prescription medications
  F. Date of birth, social security number, driver's license
II. Experiences at Building
  A. Guest, tenant, visitor
  B. Prior visits to the building
    1. Description of any prior problems
    2. Description of complaints given to management; copies of any written complaints
    3. Knowledge of complaints given by others
    4. Knowledge of any prior criminal acts in building; description of such crimes
    5. Knowledge of any prior crimes in neighborhood; description of all such crimes
    6. Purpose and number of prior visits to building
    7. Names of all persons known by plaintiff in building
    8. Prior observations of security features
    9. Plaintiff's possession of a key to the building
    10. Means of entry into the building on previous occasions
III. Date of Incident
  A. Recapitulation of the day's earlier events
    1. Names of all places visited
    2. Names and addresses of all persons accompanying the plaintiff that day
    3. Names and addresses of all persons called on phone or spoken to
    4. Whether the day's events were scheduled or unplanned
    5. Day of week incident occurred
      a. Plaintiff's regular routine for that day
      b. Persons usually visited or seen that day
      c. Places usually visited that day
      d. Persons who know the plaintiff's schedule for that day
    6. Unusual occurrences or observations
      a. Unusual phone calls
      b. Unusual conversations
      c. Any indication of pending danger
IV. The Crime
  A. Date and time crime was committed
  B. Exact location of crime
    1. Where crime commenced

    2. Where crime concluded
    3. Duration of crime
C. Recapitulation of events immediately before the crime
    1. Place from which the plaintiff was coming
    2. Persons with the plaintiff
    3. Route taken by the plaintiff
    4. Plaintiff's ultimate destination
    5. Reason for visiting location where crime occurred
    6. Persons observed following the plaintiff
    7. Last person with whom plaintiff spoke before occurrence
D. Plaintiff's arrival at building
    1. Date and exact time of arrival at building
    2. Means of transportation to building
    3. Means of entering building
        a. Front, rear, or other door
        b. Plaintiff's use of key to open door
        c. Whether door was locked
        d. Any locks observed on door
        e. Other doors observed by plaintiff upon entering
    4. Description of door, door frame, locks
    5. Use of intercom system
        a. Whether plaintiff used intercom system
        b. Whether plaintiff knew if the building was equipped with an intercom system
E. Observations upon entering building
    1. Lighting conditions
    2. Weather conditions
    3. Maintenance conditions
    4. Whether plaintiff observed any persons in lobby; description of all such persons
    5. Whether plaintiff observed any persons entering the building
        a. Means of entry
        b. Description of all such persons
    6. Whether plaintiff noticed any building employees in lobby
    7. Any maintenance being performed
    8. Any unusual occurrences or suspicious individuals; complete description of such occurrences or individuals
    9. Names and addresses of all persons with whom the plaintiff spoke in building
F. Plaintiff's actions upon entering the building
    1. All steps taken by plaintiff upon entering premises

2. Plaintiff's first observation of assailant
   a. Any conversation with assailant
   b. Complete description of assailant
   c. Knowledge of assailant's identity
   d. Knowledge of how assailant entered building
3. All of plaintiff's actions upon observation of assailant
4. All of assailant's actions
5. Anyone else accompanying assailant
6. Whether assailant mentioned anyone's name

G. Complete description of the crime
   1. Thorough recounting of assailant's actions
   2. Thorough recounting of plaintiff's actions
   3. Whether assailant used any physical force
   4. Whether assailant used or brandished any weapons
   5. Whether assailant made any threats
   6. Efforts by plaintiff to resist
   7. Witnesses to any aspect of the crime

H. Assailant's actions after crime
   1. Method of escape
   2. Path of escape
   3. Assailant's comments to plaintiff
   4. Personal property taken

I. Plaintiff's actions after crime
   1. Retrace plaintiff's actions
   2. First persons to whom plaintiff spoke and nature of conversations
   3. Time frame of all activities

J. Police/ambulance response
   1. Time of response
   2. Names of reporting personnel or officers
   3. Names of persons present during interview
   4. Names of all persons to whom plaintiff described crime

K. Lawyer involvement
   1. Date lawyer first consulted
   2. Date lawyer first retained

L. Medical chronology
   1. All treating doctors and dates of treatment
   2. All hospitals and dates of admission
   3. All other treating medical personnel and dates of treatment
   4. Names of all counselors or therapists
   5. Names of any prescription medications
   6. Documentation of all medical expenses

7. Symptomology of damages
   a. Nature of orthopedic injuries
   b. Nature of neurological injuries
   c. Nature of physical injuries
   d. Nature of emotional injuries
   e. Lost work days and verification of lost earnings
   f. Effect on family and social relationships
   g. Effect on day-to-day activities
   h. Effect on sexual relationships

The pretrial examination of the plaintiff is the defense lawyer's best opportunity to conduct a thorough "cross-examination" of the witness, as he or she may be unable to question the plaintiff at length during trial for fear of alienating the jury. Hence, the deposition may provide the only opportunity to thoroughly question the plaintiff and to conduct a "cross-examination" without adverse repercussions.

The Assailant

What makes premises security cases so dangerous is the anger a jury feels when it hears about the brutalization of a crime victim. Jurors want to punish someone for the crime, and because the landlord is often the only defendant in the lawsuit, that anger—that desire to punish—is directed at the landlord. Therefore, defense lawyers must try to deflect that anger. While the landlord may not have had infallible security at the building, the landlord is not the person who committed the crime. The real villain in these cases is the mugger, or the assailant, or the rapist. Defense counsel must divert the jurors' anger away from the landlord and place it on the assailant, where it rightfully belongs.

In roughly 50 to 60 percent of premises security cases, the assailant is arrested and, very often, the criminal case is resolved while the civil action is still in discovery. Possibly, while the civil case is still pending, the assailant will have been confined to a penitentiary. Defense lawyers should seek court orders that instruct the director of the correctional facility where the assailant is confined to produce the inmate for a deposition. Courts routinely issue such orders.

The lawyer should question the assailant about his familiarity with the building. Had he ever been there before? Why did he choose that building? How did he get into the building? Does he know the plaintiff? Why did he choose the plaintiff as his victim? Would he have been deterred by additional security features? Did the plaintiff precipitate the crime in any way? Most often, lawyers will obtain information from the assailant that will support defense contentions. However, when the elicited information is not favorable, lawyers should consider bringing a third-party action against the assailant for indemnification or contribution. Obviously, the plaintiff will not sue the assailant directly because the assailant probably cannot satisfy a judgment. Nevertheless, the defense should vehemently contest the plaintiff's efforts to have a landlord or business owner satisfy a judgment on his or her behalf.

Even if an arrest has not been made, someone may still have been identified as a suspect. That person should be interviewed and, if appropriate, he or she should be considered for an impleader action. The defense may seek indemnification or contribution from a suspect as a potential third-party defendant, even if the suspect has not been arrested and convicted.

Naming the assailant as a party to the lawsuit—even if he defaults and does not participate in the trial—is a tremendous benefit to a landowner. The assailant's involvement, even if in name only, affords the jury an opportunity to find in favor of the plaintiff without finding liability on behalf of the landowner. The assailant's participation in the lawsuit may lead to other unexpected benefits for a defendant, such as versions of events that differ from those presented by the plaintiff, and suggestions of a prior relationship between the assailant and the crime victim.

If the assailant is unknown, the defense should consider bringing a third-party action against "John Doe." Some states will allow the jury to apportion liability between the landowner and the assailant, thus limiting a landowner's liability for damages to the percentage of negligence apportioned against him or her.

Holding Plaintiffs to Their Burden of Proof

Even though many recent court decisions have expanded landlords' obligations to provide security within their premises, a plaintiff still has a substantial burden to overcome before liability can be established. Generally, a plaintiff is under an affirmative burden to establish each of the following:

- That the crime was foreseeable by the defendant
- That the defendant owed a duty to protect the plaintiff
- That the defendant breached its duty to provide protective measures

- That the defendant's breach of duty was a proximate cause of the crime committed

The defense must vehemently challenge each assertion.

Foreseeability of Crime

How does the defense challenge a plaintiff's claim that a particular crime was foreseeable? To support their argument, plaintiffs undoubtedly will introduce evidence of prior crimes committed on the premises. What defense lawyers must do, then, is challenge that evidence. The defense should consider the following:

- Did the prior crimes occur in different parts of the building? If the crime in the case occurred in an elevator, how many of the earlier crimes can be discounted because they occurred in lobbies or stairwells?
- Are the prior crimes similar to the crime in the case? Did some of the prior crimes involve property damage or vandalism rather than violence?
- What is the nature of the specific crime? The more bizarre or unusual the crime, the less likely the crime could be considered foreseeable.
- Did the prior reported crimes actually occur, or are the reports unsubstantiated?
- At what times of day and on which days of the week did the prior crimes occur?
- How many of the earlier crimes were drug related and not necessarily comparable with an assault or other similar crime?
- How close is the building to a highway or subway station, making it more susceptible to crime? The further the building from public transportation, the less foreseeable the crime.
- Was the plaintiff the specific victim of a stalker or someone following him or her, rather than a random victim of a crime?

At first glance, it may appear that because many incidents of prior crime occurred in the building, the plaintiff can support a foreseeability argument. However, after closer evaluation, the defense may distinguish many of those crimes from the one in the case, and eliminate them from a court's consideration of foreseeability.

Existence of a Duty to Provide Security

In many jurisdictions, a plaintiff must establish a "special relationship" between the plaintiff and defendant to give rise to a duty to provide protection. What qualifies as a special relationship is open to interpretation by the respective court. However, in all cases, defense lawyers should assess the nature of the relationship between the crime victim and the defendant to determine whether the relationship imposes a duty on the defendant to protect the plaintiff from criminal activity.

The defense must also consider the various relationships between and among the plaintiff, the defendant, and the assailant to determine whether any of those relationships impose or specifically exclude a duty of protection.

Consider the following scenarios:

- Did the crime originate off the premises? Landlords may not owe a duty to protect against crimes that begin off their premises, even if the criminal act carries over onto the premises.
- Was the plaintiff on the premises lawfully? Does any evidence suggest that the plaintiff was not an innocent bystander?
- Did the crime occur on property that the landlord did not own or control, regardless of whether the property was used by the landlord's patrons?
- Did another tenant commit the crime? Landlords generally do not owe a duty to protect tenants from each other.
- Was a domestic dispute involved? Landlords may not be responsible for crimes resulting from domestic disputes.

Satisfaction of Duty to Provide Security

Should it be established that the landowner did owe a duty of protection to the plaintiff, defense counsel must then seek to document that the client satisfied the owed duty. The mere occurrence of a crime does not mean that the defendant automatically failed to provide the level of security he or she was required to so provide. Accordingly, defense lawyers must undertake all efforts to show that the landlord satisfied any owed duty.

In assessing whether the defendant provided the required level of security, the defense should consider the following:

- Are the entranceways to the building equipped with locks?
- Does the building have an intercom system?
- Does the building have security patrols?
- Does the building have a tenants organization or a neighborhood watch group?
- Do the maintenance workers report any suspicious activity?
- What do other tenants say about security features at the building?
- Does the building have surveillance cameras?

By documenting all security features of the premises, defense counsel can argue that the landowner was not negligent, in that the landowner duly provided the level of security he or she was obligated to provide to protect the crime victim from the underlying criminal act.

This author has had the pleasure of defending the largest cooperative development in the country against premises security lawsuits. By documenting the development's existing security features, the defense successfully impressed upon the appellate court that a claim of inadequate security on behalf of a plaintiff who was stabbed on the premises must be dismissed. The court agreed that the cooperative development had provided the required level of security to protect the plaintiff against reasonably foreseeable criminal acts.

In many jurisdictions, a plaintiff must prove not only that a duty was breached, but that he or she relied on the defendant to provide the required level of security. Therefore, the defense should also consider the following:

- Does any evidence suggest that the plaintiff actually relied on the security? Did the plaintiff previously visit the building, or know about its security features?
- Was the building's security modified during the times the plaintiff previously visited the premises?

Proximate Cause

Is it correct to assume that any criminal occurrence within a building was proximately caused by the defendant's alleged failure to provide security measures? Very often, as a case progresses, it will become apparent that the assailant

- knew the victim;
- had been given keys to the building;
- gained entry into the building because someone let him or her in; or
- would not have been deterred from committing the crime by enhanced security.

Any one of these factors can help establish the absence of proximate cause.

In almost all cases, plaintiffs are unable to present direct evidence about how the assailant entered the premises. They are forced to rely on circumstantial evidence to support their theories of negligence.

The assailant's means of entering the building, once known, may provide the defense an opportunity to challenge—as a matter of law—

any allegations of broken locks, faulty intercom systems, or other inadequate security as being the proximate cause of the crime. Therefore, all avenues for securing that information must be explored.

For instance, a plaintiff, who presently claims to have no idea how the assailant got into the building, may have originally told police that she opened the door and the assailant followed her inside. Or, the defense may discover that an attack originated outside the premises. The defense should also question ambulance personnel about any statement the plaintiff may have given when medical personnel arrived.

Issues of proximate cause are often appropriate for assessment by experts. For example, in a case where a crime occurred in a building that had no front-door locks, an expert might use crime statistics to show that criminal activity in the building was no greater than crime in the overall precinct—including buildings that had considerable security devices.

If a plaintiff was assaulted by someone who may have been stalking him or her, the defense should secure an appropriate expert to testify that the crime was not the type of random criminal act that might have been deterred by enhanced security. The assailant may have been a "career criminal" whose commission of the crime was not influenced by the building's security features. This argument is also appropriate for expert analysis.

Depending on the specific circumstances, it may be appropriate to retain a criminologist, an expert in socioeconomics, or a detective to assist in challenging the issues of foreseeability, duty, and proximate cause.

Defense lawyers should also interview the police officers who were directly or indirectly involved in the criminal investigation of the case, to discover whether the officers were able to ascertain the manner in which the assailant entered the building, or whether they suspected a possible relationship between the assailant and the victim. Obviously, the police officers are concentrating on solving the crime. Because the lawyers' interests are different, they can obtain information helpful to the defense without needing an arrest or solved crime. Instead, a successful defense may lie in a few paragraphs of handwritten notes maintained by a police officer.

Miscellaneous Considerations

It is well documented that the majority of violent crimes are committed by assailants who know their victims. For instance, an overwhelming number of murders and rapes are committed by the victims' family members or acquaintances. There is no reason to suspect that these statistics do not hold true in premises security cases as well.

Neither an extra door lock nor an enhanced intercom system will prevent such crimes. Because it is doubtful that a building's security features are a factor in the commission of such crimes, credible defenses on the issue of proximate cause can be pursued when the evidence suggests that the plaintiff was victimized by a known assailant.

The defense should remember that the plaintiff has the extraordinary burden of establishing duty, breach of duty, and proximate cause. The defendant must successfully challenge only one of those elements to resolve the case in its favor. Accordingly, the defense should

- confirm whether the defendant owed the plaintiff a duty to provide protection;
- challenge the allegation that the crime was foreseeable;
- document the security provided at the premises;
- contest allegations that the conditions of the building were a cause of the crime;
- pursue theories of indemnification and an apportionment of liability against the assailant; and
- verify the reason for the plaintiff's presence at the location.

In premises security actions, defense lawyers are obliged to hold plaintiffs to their burden of proof on each issue that establishes negligence on behalf of landlords or business owners.

A. CHECKLIST FOR BUILDING INSPECTION

Exterior of Building

Lighting (Indicate adequacy/inadequacy)
Shrubbery (Does shrubbery provide hiding opportunities?)
General maintenance (Are grounds well kept?)
Proximity to public transportation (Does building provide
    escape routes?)
Nature of surrounding neighborhood (Residential or
    commercial)
Visibility (Hidden or in clear view)
Adjacent buildings (Banks, liquor stores, or other likely crime
    targets)
Parking facilities (Is parking lot well lit and secure?)
Walkways (Are walkways well lit and properly maintained?)
Exterior security features (Fences, gates, or other barricades)
Means of access to building (Broken windows)

Entranceways to Building

Front Entranceway:
Door locks (working?)
Exact types of locks
Self-closing mechanisms
Intercom system
Vestibule area
Artificial lighting
Observations of door (Glass panels? Door composition?)
Surveillance equipment
Warning signs or notices

Access to Front Door:
Keys and key control
Intercom system

Rear Entranceway:
Type of door (Fire exit?)
Manner of access control (Self-closing, pushbar?)
Locking mechanisms (Key control and accountability)
Alarms
Signs/warnings regarding use of rear entrance

Rear door (Where does it lead? Is it commonly used? Is its use restricted in any way?)

Other Entrances:
Entrances for building personnel only
Ground floor windows (Window guards or bars?)
Side entrances (Manner of ingress and egress)

Interior of Building

Number of apartments
Number of families and residents
Vacancy rate
Elevators (Passenger or freight)
Internal staircases (Lighting and general maintenance)
Fire escapes
Roof landing
Basement (Means of access to basement and subbasement)

Security Observations

Perimeter security
Interior security provided by landlord (Doorman, lobby patrol, security guards)
Other possible security features (Tenant patrols, neighborhood crime watch, police presence, tenant groups and associations, security bulletins and advisories)
Maintenance (On-premises superintendent, janitors, caretakers)

Overall Impressions

General neighborhood
Immediate vicinity
Surrounding buildings
Particular premises

B. CHECKLIST FOR MEETING WITH BUILDING MANAGEMENT

Prior Crimes

Knowledge of prior crime in building
Records of complaints filed with police department
Police responses to prior crimes
Complaints of prior crimes by tenants
Remedial action in response to prior criminal acts

Safety Features

Door locks
Intercom system
Surveillance cameras
Security guards/doorman
Key allocation and key control
Self-closing and self-regulating fire exits
Budget allocation for safety features
Tenant involvement and advisors

Maintenance Features

On-premises superintendent or maintenance personnel
Nature of building inspections
Artificial lighting
Elevator inspections
Procedures for lock repairs

Security Enhancements

Recent efforts to increase security
Specific responses to prior crimes
Tenant advisors
Communications with law enforcement agencies
Security related expenditures

C. CHECKLIST FOR SECURING RECORDS

Maintenance Records

Inspections of door locks—daily and monthly reports
Reports of vandalism
Requisitions for new door locks and lock repairs
Work-order tickets for lock repairs
Invoices for lock purchases
Records for key allocation and key replacement
Frequency of lock changes
Tenant complaints and responses

Inspection Reports

Daily attendance records of building employees
Log books to support daily activity
Schedules for daily responsibilities
Weekly and/or monthly inspection reports
Inspections by outside agencies (Building code inspectors, fire
    code inspectors, engineers)
Compliance with applicable ordinances

Security Records

Attendance records of security guards
Patrol records
Reports of any unusual occurrences
Tour-of-duty reports
Log books

Incident Reports

Records of previously reported crimes
Records pertaining to specific incident

D. CHECKLIST FOR PRESERVATION OF EVIDENCE

Photographs

Videotape depicting door locks in proper working condition
Surveillance cameras documenting absence of unusual activity
Photographs of entranceways to building
Photographs of door locks
Photographs of door closure regulators

Police Reports

Obtain all police reports
Secure crime scene analysis
Obtain police photographs
Obtain results of police interviews
Ensure production of ambulance records
Obtain transcripts of 911 calls

Crime Statistics

Secure crime statistics for precinct
Obtain complaint records for all reported crimes in building

Miscellaneous

Obtain original copies of any surveillance video
Obtain copies of inspection reports by local building inspectors

♨ CHAPTER 4

Proper Use of Experts in Premises Security Cases

For a plaintiff, the use of a liability expert to establish negligence is a virtual necessity. Depending on the nature of the criminal act involved, it may be necessary to use one expert to document a breach of security and another to explain how that breach caused or permitted the crime to occur. For a defendant, an appropriate expert will shift the focus of the trial from the allegations of negligence against the landlord or business owner to the actions of the criminal.

Although a security expert remains the most vital expert in a premises liability action, lawyers have been successfully using other kinds of experts to support their claims. As these cases develop, courts are qualifying additional types of experts to testify in security cases. An explanation of experts appropriate for premises security actions follows.

Security Experts

In many jurisdictions, the use of a security expert is not optional. Without appropriate expert testimony about the building's security features and lapses, a case may not be presented to a jury. Many consulting companies have been formed specifically to analyze these cases and provide expert testimony at trial.

In selecting an expert, the defense should choose an expert with an appropriate background. Some experts are more suitable for assessing security issues at commercial establishments, while others have better credentials for working on cases concerning residential premises. Some experts consult primarily for hotels, others for restaurants, and yet others for banks.

Ideally, the defense should choose an expert with an extensive background and employment history in the geographic area related to the case, and with prior experience with the type of premise involved. Also, the expert should have reached a high rank in a major police department, taught security courses at various colleges or universities, and authored publications on the topic of security.

The security expert should be able to provide the following information:

1. An assessment of crime conditions for the surrounding neighborhood, supported by crime statistics
   - Population statistics
   - Number of new and closed businesses
2. A breakdown of reported crimes, by type, for the surrounding neighborhood
3. An overall assessment of the safety of the building in the case
   - Detailed compilation of each security feature present at the premises
   - Detailed list of security shortfalls, and a projection about the costs associated with each item
4. An analysis of crime statistics to determine patterns of criminal activity in the neighborhood
5. A plan for effectively responding to crime trends
6. An evaluation of the building's compliance with applicable codes and regulations
7. Societal and economic considerations of the neighborhood and the residents of the building
8. A comparison of per capita crime committed in the building with that committed in surrounding buildings
9. An assessment of the effectiveness of any security personnel at the premises
10. An analysis of the training methods employed for any security personnel
11. A physical inspection of the premises for security matters not readily noticeable
    - Proximity to public transportation
    - Outside illumination
    - Parking facilities
12. Cost-benefit analysis of specific security features
    - Likelihood of specific features deterring specific crimes
13. Specific reasons for concluding that the crime committed against the plaintiff was or was not foreseeable by the landlord

14. Conditions within the building that render it susceptible to crime
    - Average age of residents
    - Number of senior citizens
    - Number of women living alone

A security expert must be qualified to render an opinion, with a reasonable degree of "security expertise," about whether the particular building was equipped with reasonable security features, and whether its security features were a cause of the crime in the case.

Criminologist

In an appropriate case, a criminologist can be an invaluable witness. Criminology is a subdivision of behavioral science. A criminologist specializes in the study of criminal behavior and, oftentimes, works with police departments and governmental agencies to formulate and implement strategies for combating crime. A criminologist will study a criminal's behavior, assessing his or her reaction to various circumstances.

A criminologist can almost be compared to an accident reconstructionist. By studying all of the known evidence pertaining to the crime, a criminologist can render an opinion about whether the crime was random or deliberate, and whether the assailant was a "professional" who could overcome additional security measures or an opportunist who might have been deterred by increased security.

A criminologist can be helpful in the following cases:

- When relying on circumstantial evidence to establish that an assailant knew the victim
- When trying to establish that an assailant was a "professional" criminal
- When trying to establish that an assailant was an "insider" who had access to the building
- When contending that enhanced security would not have prevented the specific crime
- When an assailant is apprehended, and/or his identity is known

A criminologist can also provide valuable testimony concerning the assailant's prior criminal record, if any. Based on the nature and types of prior crimes an assailant committed, a criminologist could determine whether the crime in the case would have been avoided by additional security measures.

Criminology has become a recognized field of scientific study, and courts are now allowing criminologists considerable leeway in rendering opinion testimony in a wide array of areas. An additional advantage to using criminologists is that their field of study is intriguing, and their testimony often has a dramatic impact on a jury.

Criminal Profile Expert

When attempting to solve a crime, local, state, and federal authorities often prepare a criminal profile based on the criminal's method of operation, the physical evidence, and psychological assessments. While the primary purpose of such a profile is to apprehend the assailant, a criminal profile prepared by an appropriate expert could be of considerable value in handling a premises security action.

Criminal profile experts should be considered for retention in the following cases:

- When contending that the assailant's methods of operation were such that security issues were not a factor
- When the criminal's behavior suggests he or she would not be deterred by security
- When the criminal's profile suggests the crimes committed were precalculated and the victims were specifically targeted

A criminal profile expert may be able to successfully isolate the specific crime, based on a comparison with other crimes reported in the surrounding vicinities. If there are no reported crimes with similar characteristics, the expert may deduce that the isolated nature of the crime indicates the assailant knew the victim.

Many of the leading criminal profile experts are retired Federal Bureau of Investigation (FBI) agents with years of special training. Given their impressive credentials, such persons could have a dramatic impact on the outcome of a trial.

Victimologist

An evolving, and somewhat controversial, area of expertise is victimology. Here, almost always on behalf of a defendant, a behavioral science expert with a specialization in victim behavior studies the victim's actions and assesses whether the victim acted in a way that either caused or contributed to the crime.

A victimologist could prove helpful in the following situations:

- When the defense suspects the plaintiff was involved in criminal activity
- When the crime may have emanated from a drug transaction involving the plaintiff
- When the plaintiff's behavior is considered unusual

The defense should limit its use of victimologists to cases in which it has a good-faith basis to believe that the plaintiff, somehow, caused or contributed to the criminal occurrence. Without such a foundation, unsupported opinions from a victimologist will serve only to inflame a jury.

Authoritative Sources

Numerous federal and state agencies, including the FBI and the U.S. Justice Department, occasionally publish studies on the relationship between crime victims and assailants. In the overwhelming number of violent crimes, especially homicides and rapes, the assailant was a family member, an acquaintance, or someone known to the victim. These studies, which courts routinely recognize as authoritative sources, are valuable tools to either impeach or verify testimony from experts.

Local governmental agencies also conduct studies about trends in criminal activity in different locales. These reports could serve to confirm or dispute contentions that a particular building is located in a high-crime area, or that the building's security features are appropriate or inappropriate for deterring the types of crimes most commonly committed in the area.

"Freedom of Information" requests directed to various governmental agencies are often the easiest means of obtaining valuable information for a premises security case.

Police Officers

Perhaps the most obvious source for expert testimony, yet often the most overlooked, is the police officer or detective assigned to the particular crime.

Because police officers are concerned with solving crimes and not with testifying during civil trials in exchange for expert fees, their testimony is often the strongest and most influential during a trial. Such testimony is particularly helpful when the plaintiff's credibility is an issue, such as when the crime was not reported to the police, or was reported well after the incident.

It is incumbent upon any lawyer handling a premises liability action to speak with the appropriate police representative to obtain the following information:

- Statements made by the plaintiff about the underlying event
- Statements made by the plaintiff about whether he or she observed the manner in which the assailant entered the premises
- The officer's observations of the building's security features upon his or her arrival at the premises
- The officer's conclusions concerning whether the assailant knew the victim
- The officer's opinion about whether the building's security features were a factor in the crime
- Identity of any suspects
- Identity of any witnesses
- Whether the plaintiff fully cooperated during the investigation
- Prior incidents of crime reported in the building
- Copies of all notes and reports prepared by the police
- Names of emergency or other medical personnel who responded to the crime

Often, the responding and investigating police officers are in the best position to know whether the assailant knew the victim, and whether the building's security features could be considered a possible cause of the criminal act. Depending on the particular officer's own experience, a court may or may not allow the officer to render expert opinion testimony at trial.

Psychiatrists

In many cases, psychiatrists are used to provide expert analysis regarding a plaintiff's medical condition and prognosis for recovery. However, psychiatrists tend to be overlooked as a source for expert testimony on liability issues.

Whereas an orthopedic surgeon or a neurologist would be precluded from offering opinion testimony on most liability issues, a psychiatrist, after evaluating the plaintiff, might be able to conclude that the plaintiff either did or did not know the assailant. Similarly, a psychiatrist may be able to opine that the victim somehow contributed to the crime or bears a certain amount of responsibility for allowing the incident to occur.

Psychiatrists should be consulted as potential experts on liability in the following cases:

- When the defense suspects that the crime was committed by a known assailant
- When a question exists about whether the victim somehow contributed to the occurrence

Engineers

In many cases, the issue of adequate lighting becomes a central matter in assessing security. Consequently, the defense should consider consulting with an engineer who can verify whether the lighting complied with industry standards. A general security expert may lack the specific qualifications to render an opinion about the technical aspects of the building's illumination features.

♟ CHAPTER 5

Contesting Psychological and Emotional Injuries of a Crime Victim: Post-Traumatic Stress Disorders

PAUL BOTTARI, Esq.

Long after the physical injuries have healed, many crime victims continue to experience emotional and psychiatric trauma attributable to the crime. Post-Traumatic Stress Disorder (PTSD) is the generic classification used to categorize the intrusive thoughts, anxiety, and fear that crime victims may experience for decades following a serious physical criminal act.

While PTSD has been specifically defined in the *Diagnostic and Statistical Manual of Mental Disorders, IV* (DSM-IV), it is a diagnosis often misapplied. PTSD is as common an alleged injury in security cases as herniated disks in automobile accident cases and carpal tunnel syndrome in wrist injury cases. Accordingly, defense lawyers must be able to readily discern the crime victim who has escaped the emotional and psychiatric trauma that afflicts true victims of PTSD.

This chapter will review the history of PTSD, define its current criteria, differentiate actual and questionable cases of PTSD, suggest preliminary information necessary for litigation, and provide areas to be explored during cross-examination of the crime victim and the victim's expert witnesses.

History of Post-Traumatic Stress Disorder

While the term "post-traumatic stress disorder" first appeared in the *Diagnostic and Statistical Manual of Mental Disorders, III* (DSM-III), the concept of this disorder is significantly older in origin. The background of this diagnosis is closely tied to warfare, and as early as 1871 the

American Journal of Medical Sciences characterized chest pain, dizziness, and palpitations as "irritable heart."

Clinicians thought certain victims of World War I were suffering from "shell shock," and as clinicians developed their theories more fully, both physical and psychological traits were applied to this syndrome. Alexandra Adler was one of the first to describe what we now call PTSD, after examining the victims of the Coconut Grove disaster in Los Angeles, California, where more than forty people perished in a fire. Adler found anxiety, depression, autonomic arousal, and apathy as responses to the physical and emotional aspects of the traumatic event. Other clinicians described similar findings in a variety of circumstances. In fact, in 1952, after a number of World War II combat veterans were diagnosed with "combat neurosis" or variations thereof, the initial edition of the *Diagnostic and Statistical Manual of Mental Disorders* included a category called "gross stress reaction." This gross stress reaction was thought to occur when an unusual stressor would invoke a normal reaction of fear in the general population.

Definition and Current Criteria

The medically accepted definition of PTSD has progressed through a number of refinements, evolving into the presently recognized definition as accepted by the American Psychiatric Association. The following definitions of PTSD clarify this evolution. DSM-III defines PTSD as follows:

> The essential feature is the development of characteristic symptoms after the experiencing of a psychologically traumatic event or events outside the range of human experience usually considered to be normal. The characteristic symptoms involve reexperiencing the traumatic event; numbing of responsiveness to, or involvement with, the external world; and a variety of other autonomic, dysphoric, or cognitive symptoms. The characteristic autonomic, dysphoric, and cognitive symptoms include such phenomena as exaggerated startle response, difficulty concentrating, memory impairment, guilt feelings, and sleep difficulties.

The *Diagnostic and Statistical Manual of Mental Disorders Revised* (DSM-III-R), issued in 1987, contains the following definition of PTSD:

> The essential feature of this disorder is the development of characteristic symptoms following a psychologically distressing event that is outside the range of usual human experience (i.e., outside

the range of such common experiences as simple bereavement, chronic illness, business losses, and marital conflict). The stressor producing this syndrome would be markedly distressing to almost anyone, and is usually experienced with intense fear, terror, and helplessness. The characteristic symptoms involve reexperiencing the traumatic event, avoidance of stimuli associated with the event or numbing of general responsiveness, and increased arousal. The diagnosis is not made if the disturbance lasts less than one month. . . .

DSM-IV, issued in 1994, defines PTSD as follows:

The essential feature of post traumatic stress disorder is the development of characteristic symptoms following exposure to an extreme traumatic stressor involving direct personal experience of an event that involves actual or threatened death or serious injury or other threat to one's physical integrity; or witnessing an event that involved death, injury or a threat to the physical integrity of another person; or learning about unexpected or violent death, serious harm or threat of death or injury experienced by a family member or other close associate (criterion A1). The person's response to the event must involve intense fear, helplessness, or horror, (or in children, the response must involve disorganized or agitated behavior) (criterion A2). The characteristic symptoms resulting from the exposure to the extreme trauma include persistent re-experiencing of the traumatic event (criterion B), persistent avoidance of stimuli associated with the trauma and numbing of general responsiveness (criterion C), and persistent symptoms of increased arousal (criterion D). The full symptom picture must be present for more than one month (criterion E), and the disturbance must cause clinically significant distress or impairment in social, occupational, or other important areas of functioning (criterion F). . . .

DSM-IV classifies a PTSD diagnosis as acute when the duration of symptoms is less than three months, as chronic when the symptoms last three months or longer, or as delayed onset when the symptoms do not occur for at least six months after the traumatic event has been experienced.

As can be seen from the evolution of the definitions, the current definition of PTSD is an attempt to "tighten up" the diagnosis. With the kind permission of the American Psychiatric Association, the diagnostic criteria for 309.81 PTSD is reproduced in full on pages 52–53.

Diagnostic Criteria for 309.81
Posttraumatic Stress Disorder

A. The person has been exposed to a traumatic event in which both of the following were present:
1. the person experienced, witnessed, or was confronted with an event or events that involved actual or threatened death or serious injury, or a threat to the physical integrity of self or others
2. the person's response involved intense fear, helplessness, or horror. **Note:** In children, this may be expressed instead by disorganized or agitated behavior.
B. The traumatic event is persistently reexperienced in one (or more) of the following ways:
1. recurrent and intrusive distressing recollections of the event, including images, thoughts, or perceptions. **Note:** In young children, repetitive play may occur in which themes or aspects of the trauma are expressed.
2. recurrent distressing dreams of the event. **Note:** In children, there may be frightening dreams without recognizable content.
3. acting or feeling as if the traumatic event were recurring (includes a sense of reliving the experience, illusions, hallucinations, and dissociative flashback episodes, including those that occur on awakening or when intoxicated). **Note:** In young children, trauma-specific reenactment may occur.
4. intense psychological distress at exposure to internal or external cues that symbolize or resemble an aspect of the traumatic event
5. physiological reactivity on exposure to internal or external cues that symbolize or resemble an aspect of the traumatic event

(continued on next page)

Actual vs. Questionable Cases

DSM-IV's treatment of this diagnosis offers new insights that the experienced litigator can use to challenge both the nature and extent of PTSD claims and give an alternate explanation or "differential diagnosis" for a number of similar but different symptoms. The entire DSM-IV section on PTSD should be read, as the subsections entitled "associated features and disorders," "prevalence," "course of the symptoms," and "differential diagnosis" all contain significant information that the skillful cross-examiner can use to his or her benefit.

(Continued from previous page)

C. Persistent avoidance of stimuli associated with the trauma and numbing of general responsiveness (not present before the trauma), as indicated by three (or more) of the following:
   1. efforts to avoid thoughts, feelings, or conversations associated with the trauma
   2. efforts to avoid activities, places, or people that arouse recollections of the trauma
   3. inability to recall an important aspect of the trauma
   4. markedly diminished interest or participation in significant activities
   5. feeling of detachment or estrangement from others
   6. restricted range of affect (e.g., unable to have loving feelings)
   7. sense of a foreshortened future (e.g., does not expect to have a career, marriage, children, or a normal life span)
D. Persistent symptoms of increased arousal (not present before the trauma), as indicated by two (or more) of the following:
   1. difficulty falling or staying asleep
   2. irritability or outbursts of anger
   3. difficulty concentrating
   4. hypervigilance
   5. exaggerated startle response
E. Duration of the disturbance (symptoms in Criteria B, C, and D) is more than one month
F. The disturbance causes clinically significant distress or impairment in social, occupational, or other important areas of functioning.

Specify if:
   Acute: if duration of symptoms is less than 3 months

Specifically, in the differential diagnosis section, DSM-IV indicates that malingering "should not be ruled out in those situations in which financial remuneration, benefit eligibility, and forensic determinations play a role." This new addition, which is not contained in DSM-III or DSM-III-R, essentially mandates that the medical provider consider malingering in his or her diagnosis. Malingering is defined in DSM-IV, Section V65.2 as follows:

The essential feature of malingering is the intentional production of false or grossly exaggerated physical or psychological symptoms, motivated by external incentives such as avoiding military duty, avoiding work, obtaining financial compensation, evading criminal prosecution, or obtaining drugs. Under some circumstances, malingering may represent adaptive behavior—for example, feigning illness while a captive of the enemy during wartime.

DSM-IV, at p. 683, states the following:

Malingering should be strongly suspected if any combination of the following is noted:

1. Medicolegal context of presentation (e.g., the person is referred by an attorney to the clinician for examination)
2. Marked discrepancy between the person's claimed stress or disability and objective findings
3. Lack of cooperation during the diagnostic evaluation and in complying with the prescribed treatment regimen
4. The presence of Antisocial Personality Disorder

Thus, DSM-IV gives the defense lawyer a powerful tool when the plaintiff has been referred to a psychologist or a psychiatrist for treatment, and there is medical evidence in the form of hospital records and/or prior medical opinions that do not confirm the allegations of PTSD. The presence of malingering as a differential diagnosis in DSM-IV cannot be overemphasized. The defense should always consider using a combination of the new diagnostic criteria, as well as the definition of malingering, in an attempt to defeat a marginal post-traumatic stress claim.

Preliminary Information Necessary for Litigation

The starting point for any defense of post-traumatic stress is a complete investigation and analysis of both the relevant event and the corresponding medical and hospital records. In this regard, the plaintiff's deposition is critical because it lays the foundation for both subsequent impeachment and a change in circumstances. The plaintiff's prior history must be explored in detail, including the following areas: whether any mental disorders existed prior to the incident; whether the plaintiff has a lifelong personality disorder; whether any physical disorders could cause the psychological symptoms now present; whether any drug or alcohol problems existed prior to the incident; whether the plaintiff's family has a history of mental disorders; whether the plaintiff was suffering from another major stressor unrelated to the incident; whether the plaintiff had any previous disciplinary problems; and whether the plaintiff had any developmental problems in school prior to the incident.

In a case involving a minor, all school records, including school medical records, have obvious and extreme importance because they usually predate litigation and have diagnoses independent of the traumatic event. Furthermore, they almost always note whether certain family members have problems of substance, which becomes significant where courts do not allow the lawyers to obtain independent family member medical records. In those cases, notations in the school records can be extremely helpful, particularly if they show family members with psychiatric problems or stressful home situations that the plaintiff subsequently denies during deposition or trial. Information about all past counseling and psychological treatment, as well as all records from medical providers, are an absolute necessity to a proper defense.

Areas of Questioning for Cross-Examination

To rebut plaintiff's treating and/or expert witnesses, defense lawyers should pose questions regarding any failure to

- take adequate history from the plaintiff;
- obtain all appropriate medical and school records;
- consider psychological conditions that may be preexisting;
- conduct adequate interviews with parents, teachers, and other medical providers;
- rule out malingering and/or secondary gain;
- take into account various forms of medical treatment and/or medications;
- offer differential diagnosis or recognize adequacy of differential diagnosis;
- perform, and/or recognize need for, psychological testing;
- base opinions on adequate medical foundation;
- properly score and interpret tests;
- use multiaxial diagnostic system with explanation (defense should make certain expert is fully prepared to diagnose plaintiff using multiaxial diagnostic system, both at the current time and for previous <u>twelve</u> months);
- admit that certain areas of treatment (group therapy and/or counseling) could be helpful.

Additionally, because PTSD results from an event that will at least partially, if not totally, remit in most individuals, a number of queries should be used as defense strategies. Specifically, defense lawyers should discover whether

- the incident was sufficient to cause PTSD (for example, most car accidents do not meet the criteria);
- the incident was outside the range of human experience and thus would not be markedly distressing to the average individual, as required by DSM-IV;
- the alleged nightmares relate to a specific event;
- the nightmares result from other life stressors, such as a previous trauma or a subsequent stressor;
- the avoidance behaviors and other alleged sequelae relate to events separate and apart from the incident;
- the increased arousal, hypervigilance, and recurring nightmares result from the litigation, and in all likelihood will subside markedly at the conclusion of the litigation (meaning that perhaps the plaintiff has only an adjustment disorder rather than PTSD);
- the plaintiff's allegations are mostly subjective and neither verifiable by standard tests nor observed by the defendant's experts (meaning that perhaps the plaintiff's symptoms result from prior personality disorders and not the incident in the case);
- even though the plaintiff had symptoms for several months, the current symptoms are not sufficient for PTSD;
- various treatments have not been used, including medications;
- the plaintiff has disregarded medical advice to seek counseling and/or medications;
- various other life stressors, either alone or in conjunction with the trauma, are exacerbating whatever minimal anxiety exists (for example, a history of depression in the family could lead to a number of these anxiety symptoms);
- the symptoms are a side effect of any medication the plaintiff takes.

The etiology of PTSD has been described as follows:

The etiology of post traumatic stress disorder is probably multifactorial. By definition, the disorder is caused by a stressor so severe that it is likely to produce psychological trauma in most normal individuals. The role of the stressor in post traumatic stress disorder may be compared to the role of force in producing a broken leg.

It is normal for a leg to break if enough force is applied, although a broken leg is a pathological condition. Individual legs vary, however, in the amount of force that is required to produce a break, the amount of time required for healing, and the degree of residual pathology that may remain. In most individuals experiencing post traumatic stress disorder, the stressor is a necessary but not sufficient cause, because even the most severe stressors do not produce post traumatic stress disorder in all individuals experiencing the stressor. A variety of psychological, physical, genetic and social factors may contribute to the pathogenesis of this disorder. (Dr. Nancy Andreasen, Neurotic Disorder, "Post Traumatic Stress Disorder.")

The defense's awareness of the foregoing information is imperative. Armed with analyses from defense experts, defense lawyers should probe into whether the plaintiff's expert will admit that the bulk of people with PTSD—even those with severe cases (from rape, for example)—are essentially symptom-free four to six years after the event. While a plaintiff's lawyer can argue that his or her client is in the group that will not recover, various other factors can mitigate the damage exposure, particularly if the plaintiff has abandoned therapy or not sought medical help.

Defense lawyers should also note the general consensus that very young children and persons of advanced age appear to have more difficulty coping with trauma than people of other ages. Also, the disorder is more likely to occur in persons who are single, divorced, widowed, or otherwise experiencing social difficulties. Most clinicians agree, however, that with a good foundation of social support, the degree and severity of PTSD are lessened. Thus, a defense lawyer should focus on social supports from family, friends, and medical personnel when discussing the development, duration, and severity of any post-traumatic stress claims.

In sum, to refute claims of PTSD, defense experts must be extremely well prepared and must have prior medical records and expert diagnoses before being placed on the witness stand. Otherwise, the nature of their testimony and their credibility are both subject to attack. Furthermore, the element of differential diagnosis must be addressed from both the claimant's perspective and the defendant's point of view.

PTSD will continue to be a favorite allegation of the sophisticated lawyer. Obviously, a legitimate case of PTSD with sequelae continuing for years may warrant surveillance, in addition to expert opinion, to confirm an alleged restricted lifestyle. Confirmation of PTSD, coupled with an unfavorable liability position, may warrant settlement. However, in the marginal PTSD case, in which the required criteria are not met, other life stressors exist, or other medical or lifestyle conditions could account for the claimed symptoms, a thorough investigation and medical expert advice can go a long way toward explaining why the alleged symptoms have little, if anything, to do with the traumatic event.

Lawyers must remember to be thorough, but to keep the case simple and most important, understandable. Those who do so will have a better chance of convincing the judge or jury of the merits of their client's position, and will not get bogged down by psychiatric verbiage. While the foregoing efforts will not guarantee a successful result, they will help mitigate sympathy and establish the trial record for appellate review.

♠ CHAPTER 6

How Jurors View
Premises Security Claims

A good way to gain an understanding of how jurors view premises security actions is to talk with members of a jury after a trial whenever possible. This author has gained much insight about those views through conversations with jurors who presided over premises security cases.

Jurors' Observations

Whether the particular building where the underlying crime occurred had nominal security, or whether the premises were replete with security forces, a common refrain echoed by numerous jurors was that "the landlord should have done more." If there was one security guard, jurors felt there should have been two. If locks were checked daily, jurors felt they should have been checked hourly. If police officers conducted regular patrols of buildings, jurors felt patrols should have been more frequent. While jurors would not specifically declare it a landlord's responsibility to prevent all crime within the premises, the jurors' message was quite clear: "Increase the security."

Surprisingly, many jurors nevertheless were quick to place some of the responsibility for the crime on the victim. "She should not have been there" or "she should have been more careful" were comments routinely made by jurors who served on extremely serious rape cases, even though there was no direct evidence of any wrongdoing by the plaintiff. In one case, the court did not even charge comparative negligence, yet the jurors still regarded the plaintiff as being partly at fault.

The jurors stated that their reduced damages award reflected their suspicion that the plaintiff contributed to her injuries.

Jurors also expressed dissatisfaction with the credibility of certain experts. When experts testified about liability, jurors took offense to unsupported opinions from security experts that buildings were "safe" when crime statistics readily documented extensive criminal activity within the building. When experts analyzed damages, jurors were overwhelmingly more impressed with testimony offered by treating medical personnel than blanket assessments rendered by nontreating consultants. However, jurors were "intrigued" by testimony from criminologists.

Ironically, jurors who themselves had been crime victims seemed less sympathetic to a plaintiff's plight than jurors who had never been the victim of a crime. Sample comments ranged from "I never got any money when I was robbed" to "I got over my injuries, and so will she." However, when the underlying crime was more serious than a simple robbery or minor assault, virtually all jurors—crime victims and nonvictims alike—expressed considerable sympathy for the plaintiff.

Many jurors drew conclusions about a case from their personal knowledge of the respective neighborhoods where the crimes occurred. Although the jurors may have never been to the particular buildings involved, they had their own general impressions of a neighborhood, and relied heavily upon their own experiences in assessing issues such as the foreseeability of a crime.

Similarly, many jurors reached conclusions about the events surrounding the crime by relying on their own common sense. Quite often, jurors concluded that the crime resulted from a drug transaction that may have involved the plaintiff. Even when a plaintiff presented an apparently reasonable explanation for his or her presence at a building, jurors immediately suspected drugs as somehow being involved.

Jurors who were tenants were receptive to arguments that tenants are aware of a building's security features when they sign a lease, and can elect to live in a safer building by paying more rent elsewhere.

Although many jurors indicated a distrust of police officers, jurors nevertheless seemed impressed with testimony provided by police officers, particularly high-ranking officers and decorated detectives.

Men, overwhelmingly, were more conservative in their damage awards than women. Men were much more critical of claims for future lost earnings and future expenses than were women. Similarly, men were less inclined to award excessive damages for pain and suffering. Surprisingly, however, while men tend to be more conservative in awarding damages, women tend to be more skeptical of allegations of negligence.

As stated earlier, the overall theme expressed by virtually all jurors was clear: "Increase the security." Accordingly, lawyers can anticipate that jurors will not be receptive to general arguments that adequate security was provided when, in fact, building security had not been enhanced for considerable periods of time. As crime becomes more prevalent, jurors expect landlords to respond to the increase in crime by similarly increasing their buildings' security. Landlords must be proactive in implementing security measures at their buildings, or jurors will be inclined to find against them at trial.

Tips for Jury Selection

Lawyers should question prospective jurors about their expectations for security in their own residences, as well as any knowledge they may have about prior criminal occurrences in either their homes or places of employment.

Jurors who are nonchalant about their own personal security tend to be more pro-defendant than jurors who always put safety first. Lawyers should question jurors about personal safety measures, including whether they carry firearms, whether they have installed security features in their homes, whether they use automatic teller machines at night, or even whether they wear seat belts. Jurors who tend to follow all safety precautions strictly tend to hold landowners liable for crimes committed within their premises.

During jury selection, lawyers should be sure to address—from their own perspectives—the fact that the defendant did not commit the underlying crime, and the defendant's liability, if any, is civil and not criminal in nature.

♠ CHAPTER 7

Special Concerns for Landlords and Business Owners: Important Tactics for Guarding against Premises Security Claims

It is sad commentary, but it can be said in this day and age, anyone can foresee or expect that a crime will be committed at any time and at any place.

The above observation, from a recent California court decision, reflects the understanding of most judges and nonjudges alike—that no building is immune from crime. Accordingly, the mere fact that a crime occurs within a specific building does not mean that the landowner will ultimately face civil liability. Landowners are neither obligated nor expected to render their buildings "crime-proof." Rather, landlords are generally expected to provide reasonable security features at their premises, to guard against reasonably foreseeable criminal acts.

Nearly all multiple dwellings are equipped with front-door locks. Therefore, plaintiffs in most premises liability lawsuits concede that the doors were equipped with locks, but allege that the locks were not working properly on the day of the underlying crime. Similarly, as the presence of intercom systems or surveillance cameras is easy to verify, the issue in the case becomes whether that equipment was functioning properly during relevant time periods.

In sum, the critical issue in most security cases is not whether landlords provided required security measures at the building, as most often they have. Instead, the primary issue is whether the existing features were working properly. Providing reasonable security features will protect tenants, guests, or patrons from criminal occurrences within a building or store; documenting that the security features were working properly will help protect the landowner from liability once an inevitable crime is committed.

Reasonable Security Features

Two of the most simple security measures landlords can implement involve front-door locks and keys. Suggestions related to each follow.

Front-Door Locks

Building personnel should be instructed to inspect the door locks daily, upon entering and exiting the building, and to keep a written record of all such inspections.

Generally, cases do not proceed to trial until several years after a crime has occurred, and it is nearly inconceivable that a building employee will have an independent recollection of inspecting a front-door lock on a specific date several years earlier. Written documentation of such inspections is therefore essential. The defense must also recognize that a janitor or superintendent who maintained the premises and verified the proper working condition of the door locks may not be available to testify at the time of trial. In those cases, inspection reports will become even more significant.

The form used to document the inspection is often as important as the inspection itself. Frequently, inspection reports address only maintenance issues and are devoid of meaningful information concerning security. A simple form that verifies working door locks at the time of inspection could bolster the defense to a premises security lawsuit. A proposed form is shown on page 64.

In addition, a log book documenting all repairs to, or replacements of, door locks is essential. Even if the plaintiff establishes that a crime occurred during a period when an entranceway lock was broken, the defendant can still present a viable defense if it can show that it made efforts to repair the lock promptly upon ascertaining the need for repair.

Generally, a landlord is entitled to a reasonable period of time to correct a defective condition after having received notice of the defect. Therefore, to help confirm the elapsed time, landlords should keep records that report when they received notification of the need for repairs and when all repairs were made.

Sample Inspection Form

Weekly Inspection Report for Week Ending ___(Date)_____

Location of Building _____(Address)_____

Inspection Completed by ___(Name and Title)_____

	Satisfactory	Unsatisfactory
Exterior of Premises		
Outside lighting	____	____
Walkways	____	____
Interior of Premises		
Lobby	____	____
Front entrance and locks	____	____
Elevator	____	____
Staircases	____	____
Fire exits	____	____
Rear entrance and locks	____	____
Intercom system	____	____

	Yes	No
Personal Observations		
Front entrance door lock in proper working condition	____	____
Rear entrance door lock in proper working condition	____	____

Comments: _____

_____

_____

Key Control

Landlords have been found liable in premises security actions even when the undisputed evidence confirms that the door locks and intercom systems were working properly on the date of the crime. One theory of negligence that plaintiffs have pursued in such cases is called negligent key control. A plaintiff could apply this theory in a case involving the following facts.

Each family in a thirty-unit residential building is issued one replacement key to the front door over the course of each year. If the front-door locks have not been changed in five years, then there are 150 missing keys that could readily provide access to the building. A jury could infer that a particular assailant simply found one of the many missing keys and used it to gain access to the building.

Negligent key control is a common theory of liability in hotel security cases. By simply issuing keys without room numbers and otherwise enhancing the privacy of room numbers, defendants can help contest allegations of negligent key control.

Sources of Information for Defense

Tenant Complaints

Ironically, tenant complaints are often an asset in defending security cases. At one time or another, most large apartment complexes have been subject to a rent strike or at least a threatened rent strike. In the overwhelming number of cases, rent strikes and threatened rent strikes are precipitated by concerns unrelated to security. Building maintenance and elevator efficiency are predominant causes of such tenant actions. In such cases, an apparently negative occurrence (tenant strikes) can effectively be used to suggest that although tenants were unhappy with maintenance, they never raised concerns of security within the building as grounds for a rent strike.

Tenants also create formal and informal organizations, often under the generic heading of "tenants associations." Landlords should encourage such groups, and seek to participate in their meetings. Minutes of all such meetings should be kept, so that when a crime occurs in the building and tenants suddenly express dissatisfaction with building security, the minutes might establish that building security was not even addressed at tenant gatherings.

Local police departments will often arrange to meet with tenant groups to address their concerns. In addition to mitigating crime, meetings with police representatives can be considered a legitimate security feature of a building. Also, an attendance sheet from such a meeting might document that a plaintiff did not attend, displaying a lack of concern about the building's security.

Tenant groups are often overlooked as a source of information about a plaintiff's relationship, if any, with his or her assailant. Whenever a significant crime occurs in a residential building, tenants will talk among themselves about who may have committed the crime and why. Residents may indicate "off-the-record" that a crime victim was involved in a drug transaction, or an assault victim had been known to associate with the assailant. Tenants may be unwilling to provide this information to police officers or investigators, but they certainly are willing to discuss such situations among themselves.

Tenant Folders

A wealth of information about a crime victim may be found in that person's tenant folder. It is a virtual certainty that a crime victim who has resided in a building for a period of time before the crime occurred will allege that he or she routinely complained to management about security lapses. However, the tenant folder will probably be devoid of such complaints and will be a useful tool for impeachment. Most likely, the tenant folder will suggest that the plaintiff's only contact with management was to request that a room be painted, or such other innocuous matters.

Tenant folders also contain important information such as social security numbers, birth dates, employment histories, and other data that can help propel ongoing investigations.

Security Consultants

Of course, after litigation begins, security experts can be hired to help prepare the defense of a case. Much more valuable, however, is a security consultant who is hired to canvass the building before the underlying crime even occurs.

A routine inspection of a building (sort of a security "checkup") could result in an expert report that documents security features existing before the particular crime occurs. If the "checkup" occurs within a reasonable period of time before the crime, the security consultant who performed the inspection may prove to be the trial's star witness, as he or she can testify from firsthand knowledge that certain security features were undeniably in place at the location near the time of the crime. Equally important, the mere fact that a security consultant was retained to perform a security evaluation will help to impress upon a court and jury that the landlord was concerned about tenants' safety.

Even though a security consultant will be forced to concede that the building's security was not foolproof and could be improved, he or she can help convince the court or jury that existing security, though not perfect, was legally sufficient.

Moreover, an expert who performs a security evaluation before litigation commences has much more credibility with a jury than one who does so later. It is easy enough for either party to retain an expert to testify at trial; retaining a security expert before litigation begins is an effective option available exclusively to the landlord.

Employee Records

Building and business owners must maintain thorough records regarding the hiring, training, and employment of all personnel. Several of these employees may ultimately be called as witnesses during trial, on behalf of either the defendant or the plaintiff. Well-documented employee files will help support the employees' testimony.

Business owners should also recognize that many lawsuits against landlords and business owners involve criminal acts committed by their own employees. Claims of negligent hiring and negligent supervision of employees can be best defended with a thoroughly documented employment folder confirming that appropriate efforts were undertaken to verify an employee's background and ensure proper training, and that no complaints were ever received about the employee's behavior.

Conclusion

Landlords and business owners must understand that, while they are not ensurers of the public's safety, they may have a duty to protect persons lawfully on their premises from reasonably foreseeable criminal actions of third persons. Because the trial will focus extensively on the security features provided by the landlord at the time of the criminal occurrence, it is essential that those security features be properly documented.

♨ C H A P T E R   8

How Hotels, Motels, Restaurants, Hospitals, and Shopping Centers Can Guard against Liability in Premises Security Lawsuits

In assessing landlord liability in premises security litigation, courts examine where, how, when, and why the underlying criminal activity that led to the lawsuit occurred, as well as the status of the victim, the landowner, and the perpetrator. The examination of these elements generally establishes the nature and level of the duty the landowner owed to the victim and will most likely determine the liability of the landowner.

The type of premises where the underlying incident occurs determines the duty or level of care that the landowner owes to the victim. In practice, the owner of a hotel owes a different level of duty to a guest than a multiple dwelling owner or the owner of a two-family house owes to his or her tenants. The status of the victim and the perpetrator also dictate the level of care or duty owed to the victim, as do the manner of and reason for the criminal act, and these elements together have a tremendous impact on the likelihood of success in defending a premises security claim.

This chapter will discuss liability issues facing hotels, motels, hospitals, and shopping centers, and review security measures that would enable them to reduce occurrences of underlying criminal acts, prevent criminal acts from generating claims, and increase the likelihood of a defense verdict when a claim results in litigation.

Innkeeper Liability

Innkeepers are held to the highest standard of care of all landlords, as amply established by an entire body of law that dates back to the nineteenth century. Hence, when a guest at a hotel or motel is the victim of a crime, the landowner is confronted with a very difficult lawsuit.

Aside from the elevated standard of care issue, there is something inherently frightening about crimes committed in a hotel or motel; victims are often hundreds of miles from home—often on business trips to an unfamiliar city—and they have put their safety in the hands of the innkeeper. Jurors can easily relate to this scenario, and the defense should expect that jurors will have little tolerance for crimes committed in hotels or motels.

This is not to say that premises security cases against innkeepers cannot be defended successfully. However, defending inadequate or negligent security claims against hotels and motels is inherently difficult and fraught with danger.

In recent years, a mini-industry has developed as dozens of specialty companies and thousands of consultants have performed and provided security analyses exclusively for hotels. In addition, hotel owners and administrators have formed associations to address enhancement of security measures and other security issues within their premises. Numerous television exposés have also heightened awareness of the potential for crime against which hotel management must guard.

Computer and other technological advances have benefited hotel owners and managers by permitting significant improvements in a wide variety of hotel security features designed to address the security deficits highlighted by these various studies, including—but not limited to—the following:

- Many large hotel and motel chains have replaced standard room keys with coded card keys.
- Guest room door lock codes are changed whenever a guest requests a replacement key or checks out of the hotel or motel.
- Improved door, lock, and safety-chain designs better prevent unauthorized room access.
- Identification cards issued to hotel and motel personnel are more difficult to counterfeit.
- Most large hotel and motel chains routinely employ video surveillance of their premises, many placing cameras even in elevator interiors and stairwells.
- In conjunction with the use of video equipment, improved recording media, such as digital videotapes and discs, are employed to capture clear images of illegal activity.
- Hotels and motels now routinely broadcast safety awareness tips to guests on in-room closed circuit television channels.

- Registration forms and other documents no longer include room information.

Even where such technology is not available, the following types of simple security measures are being, or should be, implemented:

- Most large hotel and motel chains no longer utilize keys (standard or coded) that display guest room numbers.
- Guest room numbers are no longer provided to anyone other than the guests.
- Upon request, many hotels and motels provide guests with escorts to and from on-premises parking facilities.
- Guests are instructed to immediately call the front desk to verify the identity of anyone who comes to their doors claiming to be housekeeping or other hotel personnel.
- Additional security personnel are being employed to patrol the premises, both interior and exterior.
- Hotel or motel operators will not forward a call to a guest's room unless the caller is able to provide the guest's name and the guest's room number.
- Many hotels and motels, especially the large chains, no longer keep key return boxes in unattended locations.

Of course, even with technological advances and other security improvements, hotels and motels—like other commercial premises—are not immune from crime. Studies have shown that a common criminal modus operandi is for an assailant to gain access to a guest's room simply by finding and using discarded or returned keys. Strict key control, which helps to prevent keys from falling into the wrong hands, is an essential element of proper and defensible innkeeper security. The widespread move away from keys that display guest room numbers will reduce the potential for this type of unauthorized access into guest rooms.

Simply hiring additional security personnel is not sufficient to increase the innkeeper's chances of success in defending a premises security action. Hotel and motel owners must be cautious in the hiring and deployment of additional security forces, ensuring that the personnel hired are properly screened, receive appropriate training, and are deployed in such a manner that they are not viewed as merely protecting the hotel's property.

When a premises security claim is brought against a hotel or motel, management must immediately secure all relevant documentation and other materials that could aid defense preparations, including security and maintenance logs, incident reports, surveillance tapes, witness names and statements, guest registrations, and phone logs. Defense lawyers should promptly retain an investigator and a security expert with a specialty in hotel safety to review all available information and, where possible, to help formulate a viable defense.

Given the heightened duty of care imposed on innkeepers, the defense of a premises security action against a hotel or motel will often focus on a causation argument.

Through appropriate expert testimony, strong evidence can be presented that the security features of the hotel—or lack thereof—were not a factor in causing the crime. The defense must consider the possibility that an assailant who victimized a guest followed the victim back to the room after encountering him or her elsewhere. There will be many instances when criminals readily spot out-of-state visitors, either in tourist areas or other locations, and target them at that time.

In such cases, where the assailant targets the guest at a different location through no fault of the hotel or motel and simply follows the target back to the premises, the defense should raise the issue of causation. Many jurisdictions deem such directed attacks as intervening and/or superseding events that break the causal chain between the landowner's alleged—and often actual—negligence and the attack on the victim.

Other scenarios where the causation defense should be raised include when the assailant stalks the victim prior to the attack or the victim knows the assailant and invited him or her onto the premises.

Though hotels and motels have a duty to provide security, innkeepers cannot prevent all crimes from occurring on their premises, despite their best efforts. Neither are they ensurers of the safety of people on their premises. If there is adequate lighting, working locks, properly trained and deployed security officers, video surveillance, and other security measures or some combination of these in place, the chances of a favorable defense verdict in a premises security case are significantly increased. On the other hand, if any of these security measures are lacking or improperly implemented, the chances of an adverse outcome are heightened.

Preferably, the landowner can demonstrate that it either owed the claimant no duty or had implemented sufficient security measures to satisfy its duty such that the landowner can dispose of the case by seeking and obtaining summary relief. A comprehensive security plan that is properly implemented and documented is therefore an integral element of a successful defense if a guest, who unfortunately becomes the victim of a crime on its premises, brings a premises security lawsuit against an innkeeper. Defense lawyers and claims personnel must be able to determine which cases are defensible and which cases present the possibility of unfavorable liability. Innkeepers should aggressively defend the cases where liability is favorable, and probably just as vigorously pursue settlement negotiations where cases present the probability of an unfavorable outcome.

Restaurant Liability

Premises security cases against restaurants are generally defensible. The usual scenario out of which a premises security claim against a restaurant arises involves a dispute that develops between two or more patrons. The patrons exchange words, an altercation ensues, someone is injured, and the injured party brings a lawsuit against the restaurant owner. Discovery often results in information sufficient to posture these lawsuits for a favorable defense.

In many jurisdictions, restaurant owners owe a duty to keep their premises in a reasonably safe condition and to guard against occurrences that are reasonably foreseeable. Hence, with the exception of certain nightclubs where altercations occur on a regular basis, most restaurants can challenge allegations of negligent or inadequate security by raising the issue of foreseeability.

Restaurants are also in a strong defense posture when one patron commits an attack upon another patron. The occurrence is usually spontaneous, thus offering the restaurant owner little time to undertake any action to control the assailant or to otherwise prevent the assault. Liability may be somewhat more questionable in instances where patrons act unruly for lengthy periods of time and management fails to take any action to evict or otherwise control the unruly customers.

Tavern owners face added risks of exposure to liability when alcohol plays a role in assaults on their premises. If a victim who brings an action against a tavern owner alleges that a tavern's bartenders served alcohol to an intoxicated patron who subsequently assaults the victim, liability may be established against the tavern owner on a dramshop theory of negligence, rather than a premises security theory.

Ironically, a substantial percentage of premises security claims against nightclubs and bars involve allegations that the establishments' bouncers assaulted the plaintiffs. Here, liability may attach under a negligent hiring theory, rather than under a premises security theory.

Restaurant owners should therefore screen and monitor employees and potential employees, especially bouncers and security personnel, for violent or criminal behavior. They should also implement a security plan that provides the number of bouncers and other security personnel required to safely manage the number of patrons present in their establishments. Monitoring of rest room facilities and other isolated areas should also be considered as part of a comprehensive security plan for restaurants, taverns, and nightclubs.

Hospital Liability

Hospitals, which are often operated as for-profit businesses, are held to the same standards as other landlords, including the duty to keep their premises in a reasonably safe condition and protect people there from foreseeable incidents. Hospital owners and administrators are faced with the unique problem that the nature of their operations permit many unknown and unidentified persons to enter their premises at all hours of the day and night. As with other landlords, however, hospitals can protect themselves from premises security claims by implementing security measures specifically designed to prevent reasonably foreseeable acts that may occur on their property.

Requiring employees to wear identification at all times, posting security guards at unlocked doors, requiring visitors to register, prominently posting signs prohibiting unauthorized personnel from entering nonpublic spaces, proper lighting, and video surveillance are all integral—but nonexclusive—elements of a well-designed security plan for a hospital. The clear demarcation of areas as off-limits to the general public is important because many jurisdictions hold landowners to a lesser duty toward claimants who are injured after venturing into restricted areas.

The most vulnerable area of a hospital is usually the parking lot. Victims of attacks in parking lots who bring premises security claims against the landlord hospital can often prove their prima facie case more easily than claimants who were attacked in the hospital buildings. Records and reports of prior criminal acts in the parking lot are usually more readily available and may establish the foreseeability of the underlying event. If the hospital has not implemented sufficient security to prevent the criminal act, or at least to satisfy its level of duty to protect the victim, then its chances of being held liable have increased.

The most common problem with hospital parking lots is inadequate lighting. A hospital's chances of obtaining a favorable outcome in a premises liability action involving a parking lot, therefore, is significantly increased if the hospital implements and maintains proper illumination of the lot.

Controlling access to the lot would also provide the hospital better chances of a favorable outcome in defending claims brought by victims of criminal acts in the lot. Reasonable measures that the hospital could implement to control access to the lot include, for example, placing a fence around the lot, posting security guards at the entrances and exits, and/or requiring that users present a parking ticket before permitting them to exit.

Shopping Center Liability

While automobile theft and shoplifting remain the most common types of security-related problems for shopping centers, incidents of carjackings, assaults—and worse—are being reported at shopping centers across the country.

Major shopping centers now routinely employ fully staffed security departments. Neighborhood "strip malls" have also intensified their efforts to enhance security features.

One of the most significant issues relative to shopping center security is lighting. As with hospitals, the overwhelming majority of premises security cases against shopping centers involves incidents that occur in parking areas, and claimants generally allege negligence due to inadequate illumination. Criminals are known to look for dark places in which to confront and attack their victims. Consequently, courts will often allow expert testimony on the issue of whether or not the parking area was properly illuminated. A common practice at many shopping centers is to wait until a fair number of outdoor lights need replacing before changing bulbs. A better practice may be to immediately replace all blown bulbs.

Shopping center security forces are often trained that the focus of their job is to deter shoplifting, rather than to protect individual patrons. Training programs, hiring procedures, and supervision of employees are all topics that will be scrutinized in a premises security lawsuit. Courts often review job description manuals and are likely to permit them to be presented as evidence to the jurors for their consideration during deliberation.

A noticeable trend has been for shopping centers to employ off-duty local police officers to patrol their premises. Statistics have shown that the presence of off-duty police officers has not only produced a decrease in criminal activity, it has also been good for business! Such innovative and commonsense measures reduce the liability exposure of landowners and increase their chances of success in defending premises security claims.

Conclusion

In a criminal court of law, an assailant who attacks an acquaintance may be just as guilty as an assailant who attacks a stranger. But in the civil trial of a premises security claim, the victim's status as a stranger or acquaintance can be the difference between a multimillion-dollar judgment for the plaintiff and a verdict for the defense. Therefore, if the defense can demonstrate that an assailant gained entry into the victim's room as a result of the victim's invitation—regardless of how innocent the victim's intentions were—the defense will have gone a long way toward winning a favorable verdict.

Hotels, motels, restaurants, hospitals, and shopping centers can raise successful defenses by arguing, in appropriate cases, that they cannot be expected to prevent attacks upon individuals by assailants known to those individuals. Therefore, the defense should make every effort to document the nature of any relationship between a crime victim and his or her assailant, especially when it suspects the victim may have invited the assailant onto the premises.

In the absence of such a relationship, the defense must demonstrate that the attack was not foreseeable and there was therefore no duty to protect the claimant from it. If a duty *is* found, the defense must establish that the landowner had implemented sufficient security measures to satisfy its duty to the claimant or that the criminal act was an intervening or superseding event. If the landowner had implemented a comprehensive security plan including all or some of the various security features discussed in this chapter, and its defense counsel and claim examiner prepare the defense as set forth throughout, then the chances of the defense achieving a favorable outcome would have been significantly increased.

♠ CHAPTER 9

Suggestions for Claims Personnel: How to Obtain Favorable Resolutions in Premises Security Cases

Claims personnel must often contend with the issues involved in premises security cases as frequently as lawyers and business owners. This chapter offers claims personnel several suggestions for addressing those issues.

Resist Early Settlement

Settle or defend?

As difficult as that question always is, it becomes even more problematic in a security case, where the potential for an enormous adverse verdict routinely exists. Accordingly, the temptation to pursue settlement negotiations, at almost any cost, is great. The plaintiffs' bar is certainly aware of that anxiety.

Early in the litigation, perhaps before a lawsuit is even initiated, claims personnel can expect to receive a phone call from the plaintiff's lawyer, who will broach the topic of settlement negotiations. The lawyer may say a client was raped in the insured's building, the locks on the front door were inoperable, and the building has a history of prior criminal occurrences. Because the lawyer has not yet expended a lot of time on this case, he or she is willing to settle the case "cheaply" for, say, $400,000. The claims person has read the verdict reports and realizes the case presents exposure in excess of $1 million, and so considers the demand conducive to further negotiations. Because a settlement may be imminent, the claims person curtails further investigative efforts as a means of keeping costs down, and contemplates the possibility of maybe, just maybe, getting the demand reduced to a figure under $300,000, and then ultimately wrapping up the case for about $200,000 or $225,000.

The claims person can imagine the accolades, as the supervisor commends her brilliant negotiating skills and the entire claims department marvels at her uncanny ability to settle such dangerous cases so favorably. What the claims person does not hear, however, is the plaintiff's lawyer's sigh of relief, as he pats himself on the back for obtaining such an extravagant settlement for a "no-liability" case.

An investigation costing a few thousand dollars may uncover the fact that another tenant invited the plaintiff's assailant into the building; or that the plaintiff was assaulted by her former boyfriend, to whom she previously had given a key to the building; or that some other evidence exists that supports defendability of the case.

Claims personnel should allow significant time for the defense to formulate. Unlike most personal injury cases that are best handled with prompt settlements, before nominal injuries are magically transformed into major impairments, the defense of security cases takes time to develop. The primary tactic for claims personnel to implement in handling premises security cases is to resist the temptation to settle cases early in the litigation.

Seek a Dismissal

Every effort should be made to have a security case dismissed by dispositive motions. Claims personnel should work closely with defense lawyers to secure appropriate documentation to support such a motion, and should not be deterred from proceeding based on prior experience in other personal injury cases. Security cases, due to the nature of controlling court decisions, are very susceptible to motions for dismissal.

Remain Focused

It is easy to be intimidated into settling a security case when considering the trauma and possible psychological damage sustained by a plaintiff who is the victim of a brutal crime. Similarly, it is cause for concern that an assailant has not been apprehended, and therefore a jury will focus solely on the actions of the insured. However, claims personnel must always recognize that the insured is not the party who committed the crime. The insurer represents the building owner, not the criminal. Claims personnel must therefore evaluate the case from the perspective of the landowner, not the perpetrator.

Use Experienced Counsel

Yes, there are innumerable defense lawyers who will handle personal injury cases at favorable hourly rates. Claims personnel must be certain, however, to retain defense lawyers who have expertise in defending premises cases. Within weeks of assigning a premises security case to defense lawyers, claims personnel should request a meeting with the lawyers to ensure that they are comfortable with the lawyers' assessment of the case and proposed defense strategy.

If there is a legitimate defense to the case, claims personnel should make certain they are confident their lawyers will find the defense, and will be able to present the defense persuasively to the court and jury.

Claims personnel should also feel free to interview prospective lawyers, asking them about their trial experiences in premises security cases, including how many convicted felons they have deposed in prisons throughout the state. Claims personnel must remember they bear ultimate accountability for the case, and must be certain they are entrusting the defense of the case to appropriate lawyers.

Visit the Building

Claims personnel will learn more from a one-hour visit to the crime scene than from reading hundreds of pages of reports and investigative materials. They should take the time to go to the premises and assess the building, the building's security features, and the surrounding neighborhood.

Claims personnel can use themselves as an example of how jurors may ultimately feel. If they are uncomfortable while visiting the building, that will tell them how jurors might view the case. Conversely, if they are impressed with the building's security features, that too may be readily apparent to jurors. Claims personnel must remember that a landlord has an obligation to provide only reasonable security measures. The building does not have to be "crime-proof."

Understand the Law

Claims personnel should understand how the courts in their jurisdiction determine foreseeability. For example, does the state require evidence of prior crimes committed in the specific building, or is it sufficient that there were prior crimes in the neighborhood?

It is imperative that claims personnel familiarize themselves with the controlling case law, so that an appropriate assessment of liability can be made. If they are fortunate enough to be in a jurisdiction with strict limitations on a landowner's liability for criminal activities, they should capitalize on the legal hurdles the courts have placed on the plaintiff's case.

Investigate the Case

Premises security cases are no place to cut back on investigative expenditures. Claims personnel must allow the investigator full reign in conducting the investigation of the case. A successful investigation will dramatically curtail loss exposure. Because there are so many areas that can be explored, a strong likelihood exists that a vigorous investigation will produce favorable results.

All potential witnesses must be interviewed. Even the most seemingly innocuous witness may possess information that can alter the outcome of a case.

Understand the Defense

Claims personnel are not trying to solve the crime—they should leave that to the detectives. They must simply try to establish that the building owner satisfied the obligation to provide a certain level of security.

Whether the crime was ever solved is virtually irrelevant to the existence of security features. Claims personnel should understand the elements of the defense and not be concerned with irrelevant factors, regardless of how significant they may appear.

Negotiate from Strength

The highlight of a plaintiff's case is the actual commission of a crime. The plaintiff is seriously injured, and the crime was committed in the insured's building. The plaintiff's lawyer has a very sympathetic client and a building prone to criminal activity. From there, however, the plaintiff's case can only go down.

Claims personnel should never negotiate at the high point of a plaintiff's case. They should delay any settlement discussions until the investigation is underway. They should also amass evidence of working door locks and intercoms, secure crime statistics that document an absence of prior criminal activity, and read a recent court decision that limits a landlord's liability.

Then, and only then, should negotiations begin. Plaintiffs' lawyers are as concerned about their cases as the defense. They are fully aware of their cases' weaknesses. Once they recognize that the defense has uncovered some of those weaknesses, their usual outlandish settlement demands may be reduced precipitously.

Compile the Best Team

In addition to selecting properly qualified defense lawyers, claims personnel must also retain appropriate experts, doctors, investigators, and other individuals to constitute their defense team.

Claims personnel should keep track of all experts who have testified in premises security cases in their jurisdiction, and should similarly maintain a list of all medical experts who have worked both with and against their company on similar cases.

The retention of a well-qualified expert on liability can dramatically affect the outcome of the case. Curricula vitae for all potential experts should be requested and carefully reviewed with defense lawyers. In addition, the "best" investigators should be saved to work on premises cases.

One Final Thought

By their very nature, premises security cases often involve claims of horrific physical and emotional injuries suffered by the victim. However, claims personnel must remember that premises security cases are among the most difficult cases for a plaintiff to prove. As concerned as claims personnel may be about the exposure presented by the plaintiff's injuries, the plaintiff's lawyer is equally concerned about the very real likelihood of not being able to establish proximate cause and the landowner's negligence.

♟ C H A P T E R 1 0

Liability of Security Companies for the Actions/Inactions of Their Employees

For as long as security companies have been hired to protect persons and property, the actions of frontline security guards with regard to third parties, whether innocent or guilty, have been the subject of litigation, the nature of which varies from the use of excessive force to taking steps far beyond the security guard's role.

In an early decision, which is actually a textbook tort case, *Bird v. Jones*, 115 Eng. Rep. 688 (1845), an action was brought by a plaintiff on the theory of false imprisonment when he was not permitted access to a public highway that was temporarily closed for use as a grandstand during a boat race. Later, the plaintiff climbed over the barricade, which blocked the street where the grandstand stood. At that point, guards prohibited the interloper from moving any closer to the grandstand. However, he was not physically placed under arrest, and was still free to return over the barricade and move in any other direction.

The court held that since the plaintiff was not within a fixed boundary, and therefore was not imprisoned, he was not wrongfully imprisoned. This is one of the earliest reported cases regarding the tort of false imprisonment, which gave rise to the false arrest/false imprisonment cases being brought today against security companies and their principals by persons apprehended under suspicion of criminal activity such as shoplifting.

The Doctrine of the Shopkeeper's Privilege

The doctrine of the "shopkeeper's privilege" expressly grants shopkeepers or their agents (such as security guards) the authority under law to detain persons who are reasonably believed to have stolen merchandise, so long as the manner in which the persons being detained and the duration of the detention are reasonable under the circumstances.

In many states this doctrine has been codified in statutory form to provide merchants or their agents with absolute immunity from civil liability for intentional torts such as assault and battery, negligence, false arrest, and intentional infliction of emotional distress, which may occur during the apprehension and detention of a customer suspected of shoplifting. *See* Virginia Code Section 18.2-105; Florida Statutes Section 812.015; and Texas Civil Practice Code §124.001 for examples of codified variation of the shopkeeper's privilege.

Although this legal doctrine has been codified, its breadth has been explored through case law. For example, in *Jury v. Giant of Maryland, Inc.*, 491 S.E.2d 718 (Supreme Court of Virginia 1997), the court held that a merchant's immunity from civil liability for acts done in connection with detention of a suspected shoplifter is not absolute. In the *Jury* case, the plaintiff was shopping in Giant Food to purchase various items. When she was at the cash register getting ready to check out, she was approached by a store security guard who grabbed her by the arm and told her to accompany him. When Ms. Jury refused to go, the security guard struck her in the chest causing her to fall to the floor. At that point, the store manager came to the scene and, with the security guard, took Ms. Jury to a storage area in the back of the store. On the way back to the security area, the security guard twisted Ms. Jury's arm behind her back and proceeded to shove her.

As the three reached the back of the store, Ms. Jury was kicked in the back of the leg by one of the two men, and fell to the floor. The store manager then lifted her by her hair and stomped on her foot. While being detained in the back of the store, Ms. Jury was prohibited from using a bathroom or checking on her children, whom she had left in a car in the store's parking lot. Ms. Jury was then handcuffed and held until the police arrived, at which time she was arrested and brought to the police station. Ms. Jury was subsequently convicted of concealment of merchandise, though the conviction was reversed on appeal.

Later, Ms. Jury brought a civil action against Giant and the security guard involved in her detention in the supermarket. The court initially dismissed Ms. Jury's assault and battery and negligence claim citing to Virginia's "merchant's privilege" under Virginia Code Section 18.2-105. Ms. Jury's intentional infliction of emotional distress claim was eventually stricken under the same statute after all evidence at trial was heard.

The Supreme Court of Virginia reversed the trial court's determination. Although the court acknowledged that merchants and their agents are shielded from civil liability for actions reasonably necessary to protect the owners' property by detaining suspected shoplifters, the court held that where a tort was committed in a willful, wanton, and otherwise unreasonable or excessive manner, such immunity could not be extended. Citing to principles behind the shopkeeper's privilege codification, the court indicated that the purpose of the statute was to "strike a balance between one man's property rights and another man's personal right. In this case, it was apparent that Ms. Jury's personal rights were trammeled by the defendant during the course of protecting the defendant's property."

The *Jury* case was significant insofar as it lead to a case-by-case analysis as to whether or not the methods used to detain shoplifters are reasonable. The court felt that to hold otherwise could lead to irrational consequences such as those found in the *Jury* case.

In *Rivers v. Dillards Department Store*, 698 So. 2d 1328 (Fla. Dist. Ct. of App. 1997), an issue of fact was found that prevented dismissal of a false imprisonment claim by plaintiffs who had been detained by security guards working in defendant's store. In this case, four store patrons were detained on suspicion of shoplifting and warned that they could be arrested for trespassing if they ever returned to the store. Before being released, attempts were made to photograph the patrons so that their photographs could be placed on a "wall of shame" within the store, thereby alerting store workers that they were suspected shoplifters.

The court refused to permit the defendant store and security company to invoke the shopkeeper's privilege doctrine as codified by the State of Florida because on this occasion, the detention of the patrons was simply to warn them not to return to the store, not to recover property that had been stolen. Thus, the court remanded the matter for determination as to whether or not the method and duration of detention was reasonable under the circumstances.

In another false imprisonment case, *Wal-Mart Stores, Inc. v. Resendez*, 962 S.W.2d 539 (Sup. Ct. of Texas, 1998), plaintiffs sued Wal-Mart claiming that the ten to fifteen minute period of time that she was detained by Wal-Mart security until she was arrested by a police officer was unreasonable, and caused her to suffer emotional distress.

Ms. Resendez entered the Wal-Mart store and asked where the store kept its peanuts. Shortly thereafter, Ms. Resendez was seen walking around the store, eating a bag of peanuts bearing a Wal-Mart price tag. Ms. Resendez disposed of the peanut bag within the store, purchased various items at the check-out counter, and left the store. After confirming that Ms. Resendez had not paid for the peanuts, a Wal-Mart security guard followed her to the parking lot, accused her of stealing the peanuts, and asked her to accompany him back to the store. Although Ms. Resendez objected to returning to the store, she accompanied the guard. Ten to fifteen minutes later, she was arrested, and later convicted of misdemeanor theft. The court of appeals eventually overturned the conviction due to a defect in the charging instrument.

Ms. Resendez sued Wal-Mart for malicious prosecution, false arrest, and intentional infliction of emotional distress. The court held that since the alleged detention was performed within the authority of law, a false imprisonment could not have occurred. The court cited to Texas's version of the shopkeeper's privilege, which expressly grants an employee or security guard the authority to detain a customer to investigate the ownership of property. Such authority requires that the detention be done in a reasonable manner and for a reasonable period of time, and that there be a reasonable belief that the customer had stolen property or was attempting to steal property. In the *Resendez* case, since Ms. Resendez was only detained for a period of ten to fifteen minutes, as a matter of law, the detention was not for an unreasonable period of time.

Once the period of time that Ms. Resendez was held was determined to be reasonable, the court analyzed whether or not there was probable cause to suspect that she had stolen store property. Interestingly, in this regard, the court held that since the security guard initiated criminal proceedings against Ms. Resendez by calling the police in the first place, it was obviously his belief that Resendez stole the peanuts. This satisfied the security guard's burden of establishing probable cause to detain Ms. Resendez.

Injuries to Third Parties When Suspected Shoplifters Are Detained

As noted above, store owners and their agents, including security guards, have the right to detain anyone reasonably suspected of shoplifting. From the exercise of this right has stemmed an interesting body of case law involving innocent third parties bringing actions against store owners and security companies for injuries sustained as a result of a shoplifter's escape from a detention by a security guard or in avoiding such detention.

In *Giant Food, Inc. v. Mitchell*, 334 Md. 633, 640 A.2d 1134 (Md. 1994), plaintiff was injured when she was knocked over by a fleeing shoplifter. Ms. Mitchell brought suit against Giant Food for her personal injuries, contending that Giant had negligently confronted the shoplifter and that this was the proximate cause of her injuries.

In deciding the case, the court took a close look at the manner in which Giant Food attempted to detain the shoplifter. No verbal announcement was made to the shoplifter. He was followed out of the store, and when he was between two sets of doors, a store representative attempted to grab the bag of merchandise that had apparently been stolen. Upon realizing that an attempt was being made to detain him, the shoplifter fled and collided with the plaintiff causing her to sustain injury. Plaintiff alleged that the store was negligent in its attempt to apprehend the shoplifter in that it would be foreseeable that he would flee in an attempt at detention and could cause injuries such as those sustained by the plaintiff.

The court held that as a result of the shoplifter's actions, it would be unreasonable for Giant to expect that the shoplifter would have abided by any requests at detention and, therefore, the store was within its right to attempt to simply grab the stolen merchandise rather than attempt to capture the shoplifter.

The court, in acknowledging the defendant's right to apprehend the shoplifter, held that each such case must be dealt with on its own facts, and that there were no hard and fast rules to determine whether or not attempts at apprehension were reasonable. However, under the facts of this case, since the repossession attempt took place between two sets of doors that were, in essence, an isolation chamber, the acts were reasonable. Therefore, liability could not be found as against Giant.

In *Colombo v. Wal-Mart Stores, Inc.*, 709 N.E.2d 301 (Ill. Court of Appeals 1999), a shoplifter apprehended by Wal-Mart security fled the store after being under the control of the security office. The court held that it is reasonably foreseeable that a suspect who previously fled the scene would flee again after being apprehended. Therefore, the court held that once security personnel undertook a duty to detain the suspect and escort him back to the store, they had a duty to use reasonable care in keeping him detained. A failed attempt to detain the suspect, thereby preventing injuries to those in the zone of his escape, was adequately plead by plaintiff. Therefore, the case could not be dismissed as a matter of law.

Respondiat Superior

Unfortunately, despite all the training in the world, it is nearly impossible to prevent security guards from occasionally committing crimes against the people and property that they are hired to protect. However, the doctrine of respondiat superior, which normally makes employers responsible for the tortuous acts of an employee, can likewise shield a security company from liability for the acts of its employees where they are found to be committed beyond the scope of their employment.

In *Kensington Associates v. West*, 362 S.E.2d 900 (Sup. Ct. of Virginia, 1987), Kensington hired a security guard to provide security services at a construction site and to prevent vandalism at the building. As part of its security measures, Kensington provided the security guard with a firearm. The security guard was also directed not to get involved with the construction workers being housed at the building he was hired to protect. Despite these directives the security guard engaged in a playful relationship with one of the construction workers, which frequently involved brandishing the firearm provided to him by Kensington. In one incident, the security guard went to the construction workers' recreation room, where he was expressly informed not to go, to horse around with one of the construction workers. When he arrived at the room, the security guard, who had also been under the influence of alcohol (another breach of company policy) brandished his firearm, and upon placing it back in its holster, accidentally shot one of the construction workers in the foot.

The construction worker brought suit against Kensington Associates based upon the negligent actions of the security guard. The court held that since the shooting incident occurred during horseplay and in an attempt to socialize with the construction workers, while the security guard was under the influence of alcohol, it was clear that the security guard acted beyond the scope of his employment. The court held that the security guard's acts were reckless and were of such an unusual deviation from Kensington's business that he clearly acted outside the scope of his employment and, therefore, liability could not be held against Kensington.

In another case, *Kirkman v. Astoria General Hospital*, 204 A.D.2d 401 (N.Y. Sup. Ct., Appellate Div. 1994), a security guard raped a minor who was an admitted patient to the hospital. After the rape, the minor initiated suit against the hospital and the private security company retained by the hospital. The court held that neither the hospital nor the security company could be held vicariously liable for the security guard's actions since the security guard's criminal actions were intentional, done solely for his personal motives, and unrelated to the furtherance of the security company's business. Obviously, the rape of the infant patient was not in furtherance of the security company's business and was clearly a departure from any normal security personnel duties. Therefore, the court held that liability in this regard could not be held as against the employer.

Aside from the above theory of liability, the plaintiffs claim that the security company should be held liable for negligence in the hiring of the security guard. However, since a routine pre-employment background check of the assailant confirmed that he had no prior criminal history, the security company could not be charged with negligent hiring.

In another negligent hiring case, *Carter v. Skokie Valley Detective Agency*, 628 N.E.2d 602 (Appellate Court of Illinois 1993), a rape and murder victim's mother sued the security company that employed the perpetrator as a guard alleging that the perpetrator was negligently hired.

The security guard was stationed to work at a gas station where the victim also worked as a cashier. On a day that the security guard was not scheduled to work, he nevertheless appeared at the gas station, informed the cashier that he was not scheduled to work, and requested that she give him a ride to another location. On the following day, the cashier's body was found raped and murdered.

The basis of the claim against the security company was that although the security guard had previously worked for one of the company's subsidiaries, he left that employment and did not return for nearly a year. However, during the one-year period he had been arrested on several occasions for unlawful weapon possession and aggravated assault. Despite these arrests, no background check was conducted and the security guard was nevertheless rehired.

Interestingly, the security company acknowledged that it was negligent in its rehiring of the assailant, although it argued that its negligence was not the proximate cause of the victim's rape and murder. Specifically, it was alleged that since the assault occurred while the security guard was off-duty and off-premises, the security company could not be held liable. The victim's family argued that but for the security company negligently rehiring the guard and placing him in the gasoline station, the victim never would have known him.

In dismissing the action, the court held it was not the security company's employment of the guard itself that created the situation where the rape and assault occurred. The court noted that it was not the fact the assailant was a security guard that got him into the victim's car and thereafter caused the victim's injuries and death, it was the fact that the victim trusted the assailant because she had known him through her employment. Under these circumstances, the court held that liability could not be found as against the security company insofar as proximate cause could not be extended as far as plaintiff would suggest. The court went on to note that should proximate cause be extended as far as plaintiff would wish, an employer would, in essence, be an ensurer of the safety of every person who came into contact with its employees simply because of the status as an employee.

The court also made a public policy argument in noting that if an employer was to be held as an ensurer of the safety of every person coming into contact with his or her employee, an employer would never want to hire a person with a prior conviction for a violent crime regardless of how extensively the convicted person had been rehabilitated.

Duties to Third Parties

A common defense for security companies sued in actions by victims of assault or other crimes is that the company had no duty to the victim as it was obligated only to its principal, usually the landowner. Unfortunately for security companies, this defense is not always valid as a matter of law but, rather, is left to the finder of fact: a jury.

In *Woolridge v. Echelon Security*, 416 S.E.2d 441 (Sup. Ct. Virginia 1992), a trial court's entry of judgment in favor of a murder victim's estate was affirmed where a security guard's inaction was found to be the proximate cause of the murder. In that case, Echelon was retained to provide security services in an office building, which included controlling building access.

On the night of the murder, a security guard noticed a "flash" near the elevators leading from the building's garage, at which point he called out to the individual. The individual boarded another elevator and the guard did not pursue him. Approximately fifteen minutes later, a call came to the security desk noting that a woman was screaming on one of the building's upper floors. When the guards arrived to investigate, they found the assailant, who fled and was later apprehended, and the decedent, who was bleeding heavily.

Echelon tried to argue that there was no nexus between the "flash" and the murder since there was no proof that the person who created the "flash" was the assailant. The court held that since the guard did nothing to investigate the "flash" and there was no proof that the "flash" was a person legally upon the premises, it was reasonable to infer that the "flash" was the assailant since the attack occurred only minutes after the "flash" was seen.

In *Berg v. Allied Security*, 697 N.E.2d 769 (App. Ct. of Illinois 1998), summary judgment in favor of a security company was denied where an issue of fact was found regarding whether the security company assumed control of the premises and with it, a duty to prevent the assault upon the plaintiff. This is contrary to *Cassell v. Collins*, 344 N.C. 160, 472 S.E.2d 770 (N.C. 1996), where it was held that a security company was hired to deter criminal activity by its presence and, therefore, had no duty to the plaintiff who was assaulted. The security company argued that its duty was only to the landowner through the security contract, of which plaintiff was not an intended third-party beneficiary.

Limitation of Liability

It is not uncommon for security companies to try to limit their liability for crimes occurring upon premises that they are hired to protect. In most cases, this is done in the security contract wherein monetary limits of liability are included and usually refer to the cost of the security contract or some other set amount. The enforceability of such provisions have come under scrutiny of late.

In *Schrier v. Beltway Alarm Company*, 533 A.2d 281 (Court of Special Appeals Maryland 1987), a contract's limit of liability clause was upheld. There, a shopkeeper was shot and wounded in a robbery. During the robbery, but before he was shot, the shopkeeper engaged an alarm to the security company to indicate trouble at the store. Unfortunately, no one responded to the alarm.

The shopkeeper sued the security company for his personal injuries sustained as a result of the shooting. In defense of the action, the security company referred to the limit of liability clause in the security contract, which capped any recovery at $250. The court upheld the clause despite arguments that the clause was intended for property damage, not personal injuries, and that it was in contravention of public policy.

A different result was reached in *Wyer v. Sonitrol Systems*, 738 A.2d 1179 (Superior Court of Connecticut 1999). There, a security company was sued for theft of jewelry valued at $6,800, from a premises where the company installed and monitored an alarm system. Apparently, portions of the alarm system failed, which delayed the police's arrival at the scene. The premises owner sued the company for recovery of the cost of the jewelry.

The security company argued that its limitation of liability clause was controlling so as to limit plaintiff's recovery to a set amount of $196. The court struck the contract provision, stating that it was created in part to cover situations where the amount of loss was not quantifiable. Here, the jewelry was clearly of a set cost. In addition, it was apparent that the security company persuaded the homeowner not to take an additional contract for a higher limit of liability to cover such a loss. Lastly, the court held that the clause amounted to nothing more than a liquidated damages clause, which was not enforceable.

♠ CHAPTER 11

Bank Liability for Assaults and Robberies Occurring at Automatic Teller Machines

Due to their rather precious contents, banks have always been the targets of crime. Since the 1980s, the crimes taking place in banks are not those romanticized through Hollywood films in their depiction of infamous bank robbers such as Billy the Kid, Jessie James, or Bonnie and Clyde. Today, robberies and assaults of bank patrons using automatic teller machines have become an unfortunate problem.

The automatic teller machine (ATM) has changed the manner in which most people conduct banking transactions. Now, patrons can visit banks to make withdrawals or deposits during any time of day or night, regardless of a bank's normal hours of operation. Unfortunately, because these transactions often take place during late-night hours, the bank patrons making them are often the targets of crime.

Bank patrons who become the victims of assaults and/or robberies usually do not have a civil recourse against their assailants because these assailants either are not apprehended or are "judgment proof." Thus, patrons turn to the bank in an attempt to secure money damages. In most cases, the ensuing lawsuits are based on a bank's common law negligence. With the advent of legislation regarding ATM safety, victims of ATM crimes are, in some cases, provided with a cause of action based on the bank's breach of a regulatory duty. *See* New York City Administrative Code § 10-160. *Cf.*, Official Code of Georgia §§ 7-8-1 to 7-8-8 which, although providing for ATM security measures, specifically states that a bank's failure to adhere to the guidelines cannot be construed as negligence per se.

When initiating a civil cause of action sounding in common law negligence against a bank, victims of ATM crimes must demonstrate the essential elements of negligence: the bank owed a duty to the victim; the bank breached its duty; and the breach was a proximate cause of the victim's injury.

A review of recent case law reveals that a bank's duty to its ATM patrons, which is a product of the foreseeability of criminal activity at ATMs, has become the most highly debated facet of negligence law involving crimes committed at automatic teller machines.

Duty

Statutory

In keeping with long-standing legal principals, the victim of an ATM crime must demonstrate the existence of a duty of care on the part of the bank. Under the Restatement (Second) of Torts Section 332(3), an ATM user is classified as an invitee and is therefore entitled to a duty of protection from physical harm caused by accidental negligence or intentionally harmful acts of third persons that are foreseeable. *See* Restatement (Second) of Torts § 344. Aside from a common-law duty, in some instances, statutory and regulatory enactments have shaped a bank's duty to the users of ATMs.

For example, in 1992, the City of New York enacted regulations that outlined security measures to be implemented at automatic teller machine facilities. *See* New York City Administrative Code § 10-160. These regulations mandate that all ATM facilities be equipped with surveillance cameras capable of viewing and recording all activity within the facility. The provision also called for camera coverage for all activity within three feet in front of an outdoor automatic teller machine. In order to assist in the apprehension of criminals, banks are required to maintain the ATM surveillance tapes for at least thirty days.

These regulations also require that all entry doors be equipped with locking devices that can only be opened by the user of a bank card or access code.

In order to increase visibility and thereby deter crime within ATM facilities, the regulations mandate specific lighting requirements, reflective mirrors throughout the facility, and require that at least one exterior wall or door be made of glass or other untinted material thereby providing an unobstructed view of the automatic teller machines.

The regulations also call for the placement of a sign containing the following warnings: that the activity within the facility is recorded by surveillance cameras; advising patrons to close the entry door completely upon entering; advising patrons not to permit the entrance of unknown persons at any time; advising customers to secure their cash before leaving; and informing patrons to make complaints to the bank's security department or call the police at the nearest available telephone.

Lastly, these regulatory provisions also contain a strict fine structure for banks not in compliance with the safety/security measures.

New York City is not alone in its effort to promote safety at automatic teller machines. In fact, Georgia has statewide regulations similar to those found in New York City. *See* O.C.G.A. § 7-8-1 *et seq.* (1998). This statutory enactment directs that the operators of automatic teller machines adopt procedures for evaluating the safety of such facilities with regard to lighting, landscaping, and incidents of crime. However, and quite significantly, the statutes specifically indicate that it was not the legislative intent to impose a duty to relocate or modify any ATM facilities in light of criminal activity. Rather, the statutes were enacted "to establish a standard of good faith for the evaluation of all remote service terminals." O.C.G.A. § 7-8-2(b). Moreover, it was clearly noted that "a violation of the provisions of this chapter or any regulation made pursuant thereto will not constitute negligence per se." *Id.*

The statutory enactment also includes specific provisions for the installation and maintenance of lighting within the vicinity of ATM facilities and parking areas, and also directs that warnings regarding basic safety precautions at automatic teller machines be mailed directly to each customer.

Lastly, in what appears to be a great triumph for the banking industry in the state of Georgia, these statutes specifically do not "create any duty, responsibility, or obligation for any person or entity . . . and such person or entity shall have no liability of any nature to any customer or user of a remote service terminal [ATM] and shall not be named in any action by a customer or user of a remote service terminal for any claim concerning any provision of this chapter or relating to the use or attempted use of a remote service terminal." O.C.G.A. § 7-8-7. The statute also pre-empts any other rules, regulations, or codes of any cities, counties, or towns within the state of Georgia. O.C.G.A. § 7-8-8.

New York City's regulations regarding ATM safety and security are not quite as helpful to banks. In fact, a bank's failure to heed the New York City regulations was asserted in a recent action, *Williams v. Citibank, N.A.*, 247 A.D.2d 49, 677 N.Y.S.2d 318 (1st Dept. 1998). In this action, plaintiff alleged that Citibank failed to provide adequate security at one of its ATM facilities. Specifically, plaintiff alleged that after entering a vestibule, but before entering the area where the ATMs were located, he was assaulted by an unidentified assailant. Plaintiff alleged that one of the bank's four surveillance cameras was not operating at the time of the assault in violation of Administrative Code Section 10-160.

However, in dismissing plaintiff's action, the court held that although one camera was broken, only three were necessary to visualize the entire ATM facility. The court also took great efforts to note that Citibank was in full compliance with all of the other administrative code provisions with respect to ATM safety. Plaintiff also made a blanket assertion that ATMs attract criminal activity, which would have required a greater duty on the part of Citibank. In response, the court noted that at the particular ATM facility in question, there were no prior similar incidents of crime thereby putting Citibank on notice that a crime such as that perpetrated upon the plaintiff would be foreseeable.

In addition to the city of New York and the state of Georgia, the District of Columbia has passed legislation that touches upon security in the vicinity of automatic teller machines. D.C. Code Section 22-3312 (1998), entitled "Panhandling Control," states that "no person may ask, beg, or solicit alms within ten feet of any automatic teller machine (ATM)." Obviously, this statute is meant to increase the security provided by personal space at automatic teller machines, thereby decreasing the likelihood of frustrated attacks upon ATM users by panhandlers. This code provision does not direct banks to take any action with regard to increasing safety at ATMs.

Common Law

In other parts of the country where statutory or administrative provisions are absent, courts have held that banks owe a reasonable duty of care to users of their automatic teller machines. See *Fuga v. Comerica Bank-Detroit*, 509 N.W.2d 778, 202 Mich. App. 380 (Mich. App. 1993). Of course, what determines reasonableness will be heavily effected by the foreseeability of criminal acts at the particular ATM in question. In fact, courts have often held that the absence of prior crimes at the ATM will establish the bank's lack of notice of such criminal activity. See, e.g., *Williams v. Citibank, N.A., supra,* and *Williams v. First Alabama Bank,* 545 So. 2d 26 (Supreme Court of Alabama 1989).

The *Williams* decision held that prior crimes in the vicinity of the ATM in question that were remote in time and few in number will not serve to provide the bank with notice that criminal assaults at its ATM are foreseeable. In addition, the court reiterated a prior holding that banks do not owe a "special duty" to their customers by the very nature of their business. See *Berdeaux v. City National Bank of Birming-ham*, 424 So.2d 594 (ALS. Ct. 1982).

In *Haralson v. Banc One Corp.*, 1998 Ohio App. LEXIS 1631 (Ohio Ct. of Appeals, 10th Dist. 1998), the court upheld an award of summary judgment in favor of the defendant bank because before plaintiff's incident, there was no evidence of prior crimes in the vicinity of defendant bank's ATM. In addition, the court held that the bank did not violate any industry standards or building code regulations at the time of the incident.

Aside from demonstrating the existence of prior criminal acts at an ATM, some jurisdictions throughout the United States have adopted a "totally of the circumstances" standard to demonstrate whether or not a defendant bank can be charged with having notice of the foreseeability of a criminal assault at an ATM. Such was noted in *Haralson v. Bank One Corp., supra*, and a nonbank-related case, *Isaacs v. Huntington Memorial Hospital*, 38 Cal. 3d 112, 695 P.2d 653 (Cal. 1985).

The totality of the circumstances analysis takes the following into account: the defective nature of the premises; easy access to the premises; prior criminal acts, whether related to the act in question or not; and the nature of the business. See *Isaacs v. Huntington Memorial, supra*.

In considering matters similar to those under the totality of the circumstances analysis, in a concurring opinion, the Supreme Court of Georgia noted that the foreseeability of a particular type of crime should not dictate a proprietor's duty to protect. Rather, foreseeability of the general risk of criminal activity is what should determine duty. See *Sun Trust Banks, Inc. v. Killebrew*, 464 S.E.2d 207 (1995). In the *Killebrew* case, a trial court granted summary judgment to defendant bank citing that the bank did not have knowledge of prior criminal acts and thereby lacked notice. Summary judgment was reversed on appeal (453 S.E.2d 752 (Ct. of App. of GA. 1995)). The Supreme Court of Georgia reversed the court of appeals, holding that although there were prior criminal incidents at the ATM facility, they were only noted in police records and were never reported to the bank. Thus, the bank lacked notice. The court also noted that the bank did not have a duty to check police records for criminal activity on its premises, as in essence, such would create foreseeability of criminal acts.

In the concurring opinion however, the court noted that despite the absence of prior criminal activity, the defendant bank could have reasonably anticipated criminal activity at its ATM facilities due to the "unique opportunity for criminal activity" presented by ATMs, coupled with the evidence of several dangerous aspects of the ATM involved in the case in question. This, in essence, supports contention that ATMs are hotbeds for criminal activity as a matter of law, regardless of the absence of criminal activity at a particular ATM facility. The concurring opinion worried that by looking solely to prior criminal acts to determine foreseeability would be permitting banks to benefit from a one-bite rule in ATM security cases.

Interestingly, the concurring opinion cited to defendant bank's testimony that the bank took multiple safety measures to protect customers from being robbed such as installation of surveillance cameras, lighting, and altering landscaping and fencing in the vicinity of the ATM. The court seemed to indicate that undertaking such precautions confirms the foreseeability of criminal activity. The concurring opinion went on to create a public policy argument saying that "efficiency and equity dictate that banks be allocated some of the risk in ATM cases. After all, banks have aggressively marketed and promoted the use of ATMs and therefore, imposing the burden on the banks to provide protection to its customers would be fair and equitable." 464 S.E.2d at 210. The opinion cautioned, however, that once creating a bank's special duty, it would be an injured customer's burden to demonstrate that the bank breached this duty.

On remand to the court of appeals, the trial court's granting of summary judgment was again reversed. In doing so, the appellate level adopted the concurring opinion's "one free bite" analysis. The court also cited to the concurring opinion stating "it would be difficult to say that a criminal occurrence at a ATM is unforeseeable as a matter of law." 472 S.E.2d at 506.

Similar to the concurring opinion in the *Killebrew* case, in *Gillen v. Delaware Trust Co.*, 1993 Del. Super. LEXIS 332, the Superior Court of Delaware held that because the defendant bank had knowledge concerning crimes occurring at ATMs across the country, as well as its own ATMs, despite the fact that there was no evidence of criminal activity at the particular ATM facility in question, the court refused to dismiss plaintiff's cause of action.

Based on the varying holdings and mechanisms for determining the foreseeability of criminal activity at ATMs, it would appear to be in each bank's best interest to err on the side of caution and implement security and crime prevention measures such as those set forth in New York City Administrative Codes Section 10-160. Although these measures cannot stop criminal activity from occurring at automatic teller machines, they will certainly be a deterrent to criminals; which, in and of itself, should decrease the number and severity of lawsuits stemming from the operation of ATM facilities.

♣ CHAPTER 12

The Role of
the Assailant at Trial

Often, the most significant tactical decision to be made at trial is whether or not to call the assailant as a witness. Where the assailant's identity has been established, a defendant may be inclined to place the assailant on the stand, in an attempt to influence the jury to apportion liability against him or her. Conversely, a plaintiff's initial reaction may be to keep the assailant out of the civil trial, so as not to detract from its claim against the landowner or security provider. In all instances, the uncertainty of an assailant's potential testimony is of pressing concern to all parties.

There are several important legal issues to consider before a party can make a calculated decision as to the assailant's potential role at trial. First, what are the laws in the particular jurisdiction regarding apportionment? Is a negligent tortfeasor (that is, the building owner or the security provider) allowed to seek an apportionment of liability over and against an intentional tortfeasor (that is, a rapist or an assailant)? Not surprisingly, there is a tremendous disparity of law on this topic. Some jurisdictions will allow a negligent tortfeasor to limit his or her liability by holding an assailant financially responsible for his or her percentage of fault. Other jurisdictions, however, will not permit any reduction in a negligent tortfeasor's responsibility for damages, irrespective of a finding of fault against an intentional tortfeasor. Certain jurisdictions take a middle ground, in that a negligent party may apportion its liability by the percentage of fault attributable to the intentional party, provided the net finding of fault against the negligent defendant is less than 50 percent. In yet other jurisdictions, only certain types of damages may be apportioned, so that a negligent landowner may be responsible only for his or her proportionate share of a crime victim's pain and suffering, but may be responsible for a full award to a crime victim for loss of earnings. Recent examples of how courts have addressed the issue of apportionment between negligent and intentional tortfeasors are referenced in Part Three of this book. Counsel should be aware, however, that the overwhelming majority of jurisdictions have not squarely addressed this issue.

Once there is a clear understanding of the applicable law on apportionment, a party must then decide if it is in his or her best interest to bring the assailant into the lawsuit, either as a party, a third party, or as a nonparty witness at trial.

Naming the Assailant as a Party

This is a decision that initially falls to the plaintiff's lawyers. In my experience, the overwhelming majority of plaintiffs' lawyers I have litigated against have chosen not to name their clients' assailants as parties to any civil litigation. Apparently, their belief is that a jury's focus should be on the theories of liability they are presenting against the landowner, without being distracted by the presence of a rapist or a murderer at trial. Of course, the assailant's inability to satisfy any judgment rendered against him or her is also of practical concern. This strategy, however, places plaintiffs in a difficult position at trial, in that they must argue to a jury that a building owner, and not the actual assailant, is responsible for their clients' injuries. Juries often recognize that the plaintiffs' selection of defendants is affected by the respective defendants' ability or inability to satisfy a judgment. However, not naming the assailant as a party to the lawsuit may show insincerity on the plaintiff's part. Arguably, a plaintiff may appear to a jury to be less concerned with holding the actual assailant responsible for his or her action than with obtaining a collectible judgment if they consciously decide to sue a building owner or a security provider and not the assailant.

Choosing to name the assailant as a defendant, however, is also a risky decision for a plaintiff. With the assailant as a party to the lawsuit, a jury may be more inclined to find the assailant solely responsible for the incident than if the assailant were not named as a direct defendant. Of course, if the plaintiff were to name the assailant as a defendant, he or she must then try to argue that the landowner or security provider must nevertheless share in the fault for the underlying occurrence.

Either way, it is a difficult decision for a plaintiff's lawyer that will be affected primarily by controlling case law, and upon the expected nature of the assailant's testimony.

Third-Party Pleadings

Assuming the plaintiff foregoes naming the assailant as a defendant, the next tactical decision must then be made by the landowner or security provider, in determining whether or not to implead the assailant into the case as a third-party defendant. Again, this decision may be influenced by controlling case law, in that there may be greater arguments in favor of impleading the assailant in jurisdictions where a defendant can apportion his or her liability, than for impleading the assailant in jurisdictions that would only permit a landowner the right to seek indemnification from the assailant. Just as a plaintiff may not be desirous of securing an uncollectible judgment against an assailant, a landowner may be equally undesirous of pursuing a claim for indemnification against the assailant.

Generally, as a defense lawyer, I elect to implead the assailant into the case wherever possible. Having the assailant named in the case, regardless of whether he or she participates at trial or not, allows the jury a better opportunity to assess the respective actions of all parties and, perhaps, reach a fairer verdict in apportioning percentages of fault. The assailant's presence in the case, at least as a named defendant, is also important from the perspective of a jury. If the assailant is not named, the jury may erroneously conclude reasons as to why he or she is not participating in the trial. The jury may conclude that the assailant had reached a settlement, or that there is another reason why he or she is not in the lawsuit.

Calling the Assailant as a Witness at Trial

With certain exceptions, known assailants will have already been apprehended, prosecuted, and imprisoned by the time the civil case reaches trial. Producing a prisoner to court for a civil trial requires specific adherence to local court rules.

There are specific regulations in each jurisdiction for compelling the production of prisoners to court to give testimony in civil cases. These requirements must be strictly adhered to or the prisoner will not be transported from the correctional facility to court. In my experience, however, if these requirements are properly followed, assailants will be directed to court for the purposes of giving testimony at trial, even if it requires their being transported hundreds of miles.

Lawyers should be cognizant of any criminal appeals or other procedures that may still be in effect before deciding whether to try to produce a prisoner as a witness during trial.

Assuming there are no procedural details to prevent the production of the prisoner as a witness, counsel must give careful consideration in deciding whether or not to then call the assailant as a witness.

Clearly, there are risks involved for all parties. For a plaintiff, a jury might see the assailant as the sole cause of the crime, and might hold him or her solely responsible. For a defendant, a jury might experience a greater sense of the assault, and might be inclined to increase an award for damages. Defense counsel should also be careful to seek to excuse the plaintiff from the courtroom whenever an assailant is expected to be present.

Beyond those concerns, however, are issues that pertain to a particular case. Would the assailant's testimony support a party's contention that security at a location was or was not a factor leading to the incident? Would such testimony support a party's contention that the assailant did or did not lawfully gain entrance to the location? Did the assailant know the plaintiff or know anyone who lived at the building? Did the assailant specifically target the plaintiff for crime? What is the assailant's criminal history? These are all questions that must be considered before determining whether or not to call an assailant as a witness. Similarly, how a jury perceives a plaintiff or defendant calling the assailant as a witness at all is something that must be decided on a case-by-case basis.

The testimony of the assailant is very dramatic and must be conducted in a manner by counsel so as not to offend the sensibilities of the jury. In recent cases wherein I have called rapists and other assailants as witnesses during trial, the juries clearly paid careful attention to their testimony and recognized why I called them to testify. Although the jurors seemed uncomfortable, they nevertheless recognized the importance of this testimony. In each case wherein I have opted to call an assailant as a witness, their testimony was a major factor in the ultimate outcome of the trial. Understandably, lawyers often go to great lengths to avoid the assailant's participation at the trial. Yet in many cases, the assailant is the only witness who possesses specific information that is often critical to the liability issues in the case. The assailant's testimony, however unpleasant, and however believable, is important information for a jury to consider.

I have won and lost several trials, I believe, based upon my decision to call or not call specific assailants as witnesses. It is a decision to which lawyers must place utmost importance in their respective cases.

♠ CHAPTER 13

Security
Surveys

It is very common for security experts to be retained by both plaintiffs and defendants in premises security lawsuits. While a plaintiff's and defendant's security expert can be expected to render opposite opinions about whether or not a particular location had an appropriate level of security, the opinion of a security expert retained outside of the scope of litigation usually proves to be the most instrumental.

Security surveys are conducted for a variety of reasons. Potential purchasers of property may want to evaluate a property based upon security concerns. Landowners may wish to receive an independent assessment of a property's security need or boards of directors may need guidance about the budgetary concerns pertaining to security.

In the event a security survey was conducted, a landowner may wish to present evidence at trial of survey findings and recommendations as an indication of his or her attention to security concerns at the property. Of course, a landowner must be able to document why he or she accepted and/or rejected any specific recommendation given by the security expert who conducted the original survey.

Since a security survey is conducted outside the context of any litigation, the opinion of such a security expert can have great impact upon a jury. Landowners must give significant consideration toward retaining any expert to perform a security survey of the property.

A proper security survey must be thorough, taking into consideration all relevant factors pertaining to the property location, physical structure, past history of criminal occurrences, and overall use of the property.

The balance of this chapter provides helpful suggestions for performing a security survey and for evaluating the efficiency of an already completed survey.

Nature and Use of the Property

A security survey must consider the intended use of the property in question as well as relevant factors about surrounding locations. Careful consideration must be given to parking facilities, as a large percentage of crimes perpetuated upon properties occur in parking areas. Traffic patterns and volume, both vehicular and pedestrian, are often overlooked in security surveys, but may be significant in designing an overall security plan. Similarly, the stability of tenancy, both residential and commercial, must be considered in conducting a thorough site plan. Questions to ask include the following:

- Is the property solely residential?
- If the property is apartments, are they high rise or low rise?
- What is the property acreage?
- What is the population density?
- Does the property have commercial tenants?
- What is the nature of the business(es) conducted on the property?
- How will commercial tenants affect activity/behavior of the property?
- Does the property house a bank, credit union, doctor's office, or similar public-access office?
- Does the property have a community center, child care facility, or similar function?
- What is the age of the buildings?
- How stable is the tenancy and on-site management personnel? [conduct interviews]
- Does the property have open parking, decks, or underground parking?
- Do access controls exist at entrances?
- What is the composition of daily people and vehicle traffic on the property?
- What is the structural composition of the building(s)?
- Do you have a current site plan?

Location of the Property

To be effective, a proper security survey must consider more than just the areas immediately surrounding a particular location. In many instances, courts have allowed plaintiffs to attempt to establish the foreseeability of an underlying crime by demonstrating a building's proximity to either a shopping center or a business district where crime is more common. Advanced security surveys will include a careful assessment of relevant factors pertaining to an expanded area of the property beyond the immediate neighborhood. Some questions to pose include the following:

- What is the property's location relative to major highways and thoroughfares?
- Are there high-impact facilities nearby such as schools, shopping malls, stadiums, parks, movie theaters, and taverns?
- What is the property's location relative to public transportation routes and/or stations and terminals?
- Is the property located in or near a flood plain or weather-related danger area (tornado or hurricane)? What is the likelihood of a natural disaster?
- What is the makeup of the neighborhood and all contiguous properties?
- Is it likely that people and activities from nearby properties will spill over onto the property?
- Will the complex be affected or influenced by outside forces? If so, identify them and estimate the likelihood.
- What is the location of the property relative to the nearest police station, fire station, or emergency rescue station?

Demographics

Demographics are another major component of proper security surveys. Employment data, stability of tenancy, and social changes to the surrounding community must be considered. Questions to pose include the following:

- What demographic elements effect the subject property and how? (Consider economic data, area housing data, population mobility/stability, education data, and social changes in the community and on the property.)

- What is the level of unemployment in the area and among the tenancy?
- Who are the major employers in the area or community?

History of Crime on the Property

A good security survey will include an analysis of all prior crimes known to have been committed upon the property and adjacent properties for a significant period of time prior to the incident. Management may maintain incident reports of certain occurrences, but the security survey should also include an analysis of police reports and other governmental statistical information, including the following:

- Obtain incident reports of all incidents that have occurred on the property for the past (minimum) three years or (preferred) five years. *Consideration should be given to a comparison of local reports with police data.*
- Examine the FBI's Uniform Crime Reports for the community in which the property is located.
- Consider obtaining a Cap Index report.
- Interview local police regarding activity on the property and in the neighborhood.
- If the property is adjacent to or nearby vacant property, determine the possibility of an impact property being developed on the vacant land.
- Obtain crime statistics from the local police department.
- Obtain underlying police reports in coordinating further analysis of crime statistics.

Reviewing Existing Security Measures

At trial, lawyers often focus on obvious security features, such as door locks, intercoms, and surveillance cameras, in stressing the adequacy or inadequacy of existing security features. A good security survey, however, will consider many other often overlooked, but nonetheless important, components of an overall security plan. The effectiveness of these other security components may prove to be of great significance during a premises security lawsuit. Examine the following for effectiveness and functionality:

- Perimeter barriers (walls, fences, sidewalks, shrubbery, building exterior)

- Locks and locking systems (front entry, lobby doors, emergency exits, apartment doors and windows)
- Lighting (exterior, building entry, hallways, stairways, perimeter)
- Communication systems (entry intercom, stairwell intercom, telephones, emergency assistance stations, two-way radios to fire department and police)
- Access controls—intrusion alarms (public space, maintenance, offices, storage, property perimeter)
- CCTV system
- Public address system
- Fire safety system/alarm(s)
- Sprinkler system
- Smoke detectors, heat detectors, gas detectors
- Pull stations
- Portable fire extinguishers
- Emergency backup systems
- Air handling system controls and status indicators
- Elevator status panel and operations
- Annunciator and status control panels (all systems)
- Standpipe and hose systems
- Emergency management and evacuations plans
- Security guard operations and management (hiring, training, staffing, deployment patrols, contract requirements, and so forth)
- Site-specific controls

Premises Security Considerations for the Property

A proper security survey must go beyond information provided by building personnel. Interviews of various outside persons, such as police officers and other governmental personnel from appropriate agencies, should be conducted. The nature of any prior lawsuit brought against the property management must also be considered. The following actions should also be considered:

- Describe the physical layout of the building, including the number of entrances, access control, intercoms, and lighting exterior protection (fences, bushes, walkways).
- Review the insurance contract and coverage provided.
- Meet with the community patrol officer and/or the crime analysis officer or the local precinct of the police department to discuss crime activity in and around the building, patrols, and any problems in the building.

- Conduct a search for all inspecting agencies (examples include Housing Preservation and Development, Department of Buildings, Department of Housing and Community Development, Environmental Control Board, Fire Department, and Department of Health).
- Conduct a deed, mortgage, and tax search.
- Identify all owners/managing agents and perform a civil court search for actions brought against the landlord to determine frequency and type of complaints.
- Conduct a landlord-tenant search for actions brought by and against the landlord, and review stipulations of settlement for indications of maintenance problems.
- Contact the local environmental health organization and identify any violations/abatement orders.

Finally, you may want to ask the following questions:

- Does the building have a security guard? If so, who directs, controls, and supervises the guard?
- Does the building have video monitoring? If so, who maintains the equipment and who reviews videotapes and monitors screens?
- Does the building have a tenant patrol and/or tenant association? If so, review all association correspondence for advice on maintenance and/or security problems.

Conclusion

Landowners should give careful consideration to conducting a security survey, either on an annual or other basis, to demonstrate their commitment to security. The testimony of a security expert who was retained prior to any litigation can be very effective and is often of great significance in a premises security trial.

However, if a security survey is going to be performed, the landowner must be certain to choose a well-qualified consultant to perform the survey, and must be prepared to accept various recommendations presented by the consultant or properly explain why certain suggestions for security were not implemented. Issues of possible confidentiality must also be considered, as security surveys may or may not be deemed discoverable.

Finally, the following list of standards organizations may be a useful resource for locating security experts:

STANDARDS ORGANIZATIONS

AA   The Aluminum Association
            818 Connecticut Avenue, NW
            Washington, DC 20006

AAMA   Architectural Aluminum Manufacturers Association
            35 E. Wacker Drive
            Chicago, IL 60601

AATC   American Association of Textile Chemists & Colorists
            P.O. Box 12215
            Research Triangle Park, NC 27709

ACI   American Concrete Institute
            P.O. Box 19150
            Detroit, MI 48219

ACPA   American Concrete Paving Association
            2625 Clearbrook Drive
            Arlington Heights, IL 60005

AHAM   Association of Home Appliance Manufacturers
            20 N. Wacker Drive
            Chicago, IL 60606

AI   The Asphalt Institute
            Asphalt Institute Building
            College Park, MD 20740

AICE   American Institute of Chemical Engineers
            345 E. 47th Street
            New York, NY 10017

AIHA   American Industrial Hygiene Association
            475 Wolf Ledges Parkway
            Akron, OH 44311

AISC   American Institute of Steel Construction
            400 N. Michigan Avenue
            Chicago, IL 60611

AISE   Association of Iron & Steel Engineers
            3 Gateway Center
            Suite 2350
            Pittsburgh, PA 15222

AITC   American Institute of Timber Construction
            333 W. Hampdern Avenue
            Englewood, CO 80110

AMCA   Air Movement & Control Association
            30 W. University Drive
            Arlington Heights, IL 60004

ANSI   American National Standards Institute
            1430 Broadway
            New York, NY 10018

APA   American Plywood Association
            P.O. Box 11700
            Tacoma, WA 98411

ARI   Air-Conditioning & Refrigeration Institute
            1815 N. Fort Myer Drive
            Arlington, VA 22209

ASA   Acoustical Society of America
            335 E. 45th Street
            New York, NY 10017

ASHRAE   American Society of Heating, Refrigerating &
            Air-Conditioning Engineers
            1791 Tullie Circle, NE
            Atlanta, GA 30329

ASME   American Society of Mechanical Engineers
            345 E. 47th Street
            New York, NY 10017

ASTM   American Society for Testing & Materials
            1916 Race Street
            Philadelphia, PA 19103

AWCI	Association of the Wall & Ceiling Industries 25 K Street, NE Suite 300 Washington, DC 20002
AWI	Architectural Woodwork Institute 2310 S. Walter Reed Drive Arlington, VA 22206
AWPA	American Wood Preservers Association 7735 Old Georgetown Road Bethesda, MD 20184
AWS	American Welding Society P.O. Box 351040 Miami, FL 33135
BHMA	Builders Hardware Manufacturers Association 60 E. 42nd Street New York, NY 10165
BIA	Brick Institute of America 1750 Old Meadow Road McLean, VA 22102
BOCA	Building Officials & Code Administration 17926 S. Halsted Street Homewood, IL 60430
CI	Cordage Institute 444 N. Capitol Street, Suite 711 Washington, DC 20001
CIMA	Construction Industry Manufacturers Association 111 E. Wisconsin Avenue Marine Plaza 1700 Milwaukee, WI 53202
CLFMI	Chain Link Fence Manufacturers Institute 1101 Connecticut Avenue, NW Suite 700 Washington, DC 20036

CPSC   Consumer Product Safety Commission
            (Commercial Practices)
            Superintendent of Documents
            U.S. Government Printing Office
            Washington, DC 20402

CRSI   Concrete Reinforcing Steel Institute
            933 N. Plum Grove Road
            Schaumburg, IL 60195

CSI   Construction Specifications Institute
            601 Madison Street
            Alexandria, VA 22314

EIA   Electronic Industries Association
            2001 Eye Street, NW
            Washington, DC 20006

EJMA   Expansion Joint Manufacturers Association
            25 N. Broadway
            Tarrytown, NY 10591

FCC   Federal Communications Commission
            1919 M Street, NW
            Washington, DC 20554

FM   Factory Mutual System
            Factory Mutual Engineering Corp.
            Training Resource Center—Order Processing Dept.
            1151 Boston-Providence Highway
            Norwood, MA 02062

GA   Gypsum Association
            1603 Orrington Avenue
            Suite 1210
            Evanston, IL 60201

GTA   Glass Tempering Association
            White Lakes Professional Building
            3310 Harrison Street
            Topeka, KS 66611

HEI   Heat Exchange Institute
             1230 Keith Building
             Cleveland, OH 44115

HPMA   Hardwood Plywood Manufacturers Association
             1825 Michael Faraday Drive, P.O. Box 2789
             Reston, VA 22090

HVI   Home Ventilating Institute
             4300-L Lincoln Avenue
             Rolling Meadows, IL 60008

IAPMO   International Association of Plumbing &
             Mechanical Officials
             5032 Alhambra Avenue
             Los Angeles, CA 90032

IEEE   Institute of Electrical & Electronics Engineers
             345 E. 47th Street
             New York, NY 10017

IES   Illuminating Engineering Society
             345 E. 47th Street
             New York, NY 10017

ISA   Instrument Society of America
             67 Alexander Drive
             P.O. Box 12277
             Research Triangle Park, NC 27709

ISDSI   Insulated Steel Door Systems Institute
             712 Lakewood Center North
             14600 Detroit Avenue
             Cleveland, OH 44107

JIC   Joint Industrial Council
             7901 Westpark Drive
             McLean, VA 22101

MHI   Material Handling Institute
             1326 Freeport Road
             Pittsburgh, PA 15238

MSSVFI   Manufacturers Standardization Society of the
           Valve & Fittings Industry
           5203 Leesbury Pike
           Suite 502
           Falls Church, VA 22041

MTI   Metal Treating Institute
           1311 Executive Center Drive
           Suite 200
           Tallahassee, FL 32301

NAAMM   National Association of Architectural
           Metals Manufacturers
           221 N. LaSalle Street
           Suite 2026
           Chicago, IL 60601

NACM   National Association of Chain Manufacturers
           111 W. Washington Street
           Chicago, IL 60602

NAPCA   National Association of Pipe Coating Applicators
           717 Commercial National Bank Building
           Shreveport, LA 71101

NBS   National Bureau of Standards
           Office of Product Standards Policy
           Washington, DC 20234

NCMA   National Concrete Masonry Association
           P.O. Box 781
           2302 Horse Pen Road
           Herndon, VA 22070

NCSA   National Crushed Stone Association
           1415 Elliott Place, NW
           Washington, DC 20007

NEI   National Elevator Industry
           600 Third Avenue
           New York, NY 10016

NEMA   National Electrical Manufacturers Association
            2101 L Street, NW
            Suite 300
            Washington, DC 20037

NFPA   National Fire Protection Association
            Batterymarch Park
            Quincy, MA 02269

NOFMA   National Oak Flooring Manufacturers Association
            804 Sterick Building
            Memphis, TN 38103

NPA   National Particleboard Association
            2306 Perkins Place
            Silver Spring, MD 20910

NWMA   National Woodwork Manufacturers Association
            205 W. Touhy Avenue
            Park Ridge, IL 60068

OSHA   Occupational Safety & Health Administration
            U.S. Department of Labor
            Room N-3637
            Washington, DC 20210

PCI   Prestressed Concrete Institute
            201 N. Wells Street
            Suite 1410
            Chicago, IL 60606

PDI   Plumbing & Drainage Institute
            5342 Boulevard Place
            Indianapolis, IN 46208

PFI   Pipe Fabrication Institute
            1326 Freeport Road
            Pittsburgh, PA 15238

RMA   Rubber Manufacturers Association
            1901 Pennsylvania Avenue, NW
            Washington, DC 20006

SDI

Steel Deck Institute
P.O. Box 3812
St. Louis, MO 63122

SIGMA

Sealed Insulating Glass Manufacturers Association
111 E. Wacker Drive
Suite 600
Chicago, IL 60601

SJI

Steel Joist Institute
1703 Parham Road
Suite 204
Richmond, VA 23229

SMACN

Sheet Metal & Air Conditioning Contractors'
National Association
P.O. Box 70
Merrifield, VA 22116

SPI

Society of the Plastics Industry
355 Lexington Avenue
New York, NY 10017

SSFI

Scaffolding, Shoring & Forming Institute
1230 Keith Building
Cleveland, OH 44115

SWI

Steel Window Institute
1230 Keith Building
Cleveland, OH 44115

TCA

Tile Council of America
P.O. Box 326
Princeton, NJ 08540

TIMA

Thermal Insulation Manufacturers Association
7 Kirby Plaza
Mount Kisco, NY 10549

UL   Underwriters' Laboratory
            333 Pfingsten Road
            Northbrook, IL 60062

            2602 Tampa E. Boulevard
            Tampa, FL 33619

            1285 Walt Whitman Road
            Melville, NY 11747

            1655 Scott Boulevard
            Santa Clara, CA 95050

WHA   Wood Heating Alliance
            1101 Connecticut Avenue, NW
            Suite 700
            Washington, DC 20036

WMMP   Wood Moulding & Millwork Producers Association
            P.O. Box 25278
            1730 Southwest Skyline
            Portland, OR 97225

WWPA   Western Wood Products Association
            1500 Yeon Building
            Portland, OR 97204

♠ CHAPTER 14

Preparing for an Appeal in a Premises Security Case

While most of this book discusses the preparation required for a premises security case as well as the various issues that arise during the litigation phase, it is important to keep in mind the appellate process while preparing a case for trial. In fact, appellate review can be a useful tool at various stages of the litigation process. Therefore, anticipate an appeal from the outset—not only from the perspective of an appellant but also from the perspective of an appellee. This chapter discusses some of the major considerations for a lawyer who chooses to take and perfect an appeal, as well as the considerations for a lawyer who must oppose an appeal. The chapter ends by briefly summarizing a few premises security cases decided by intermediate appellate courts, which demonstrate the value of assuring a successful appeal, as well as cases where the failure of a trial attorney to anticipate appellate issues has proved fatal to his or her appellate argument.

Taking and Perfecting an Appeal

As every practitioner knows, each state has its own rules and time limits for taking and perfecting an appeal. Be careful not to let these time limits pass, as most states statutory requirements are jurisdictional in nature and must be strictly adhered to. For example, in New York an appeal as of right must be taken within thirty days after service by a party upon the appellant of a copy of the judgment or order appealed from and written notice of its entry (*see* CPLR 5513). A party who fails to take an appeal within the time limits will forfeit his or her right to an appeal. Additionally, the failure to perfect an appeal within the time limit will have severe consequences. One of the best appellate resources for a lawyer preparing for an appeal or opposing an appeal are appellate printing companies. Appellate printers can offer guidance and insight into the appellate process. Remember, it is an appellate printer's job to know the court's rules and the court's requirements. If an appellate printer is not available in your state, call the clerk's office at the court. The clerk's office usually has a copy of its rules or, at the very least, should be able to answer your question or provide you with some guidance.

The most important word for a trial lawyer to remember if anticipating an appeal, and the most significant word to a seasoned appellate practitioner, is *preservation*. Simply stated, if an issue is not preserved for appellate review it is quite likely that it will not be addressed by an appellate court. Although preservation will be addressed in more detail below, it is imperative that all defenses are asserted; that objections to pleadings, evidentiary matters, and charges are timely made; and that objections are made with specificity, rather than as general objections. Not only does this provide the trial court a timely opportunity to correct any error, but it maximizes the likelihood that the record will provide a sufficient basis for an appellate court's review. Even though an issue might not be fully preserved, because of its possible interrelationship with other issues, it might be worthwhile briefing and arguing the point in the interest of justice. Additionally, the appellate court might address the issue if it is reversing on other grounds.

Pretrial Motions

Pretrial motions, including summary judgment motions, are often utilized in premises security cases to dismiss an action prior to trial. In seeking dismissal, a defendant landowner may argue, among other things, that it cannot be liable because (1) adequate, reasonable, and/or minimal security was provided as a matter of law; (2) the crime was initiated outside of or off of the defendant's premises or was committed by a co-tenant inside the building; (3) it was not on notice, either actual or constructive, of a defective or dangerous condition or of criminal activity; and (4) its actions were not the proximate cause of the incident. Often it seems as though one argument might be quite strong and that, therefore, dismissal is quite likely. Nevertheless, to assure a successful appeal, careful attention to detail is crucial in the motion process. A summary judgment motion should include every possible legal ground for dismissal, the facts that support that ground, and any exhibit that may possibly be relied upon. Additionally, all necessary aspects of motions and cross-motions should be addressed. As previously explained, most appellate courts will not address an issue if it was not raised in the lower court and new exhibits/documentation generally cannot be added to a record at a later date. Notably, even on appeal, if all issues mentioned in the notice of appeal are not briefed, they may be found to be abandoned.

Trial

The scope of review for most appellate courts following a trial is generally limited to issues or theories made at the nisi prius court. While an intermediate appellate court can take judicial notice of the common law, constitutions, and public statutes of the United States and of every state, territory, and jurisdiction of the United States, and so forth, or can review issues in the interests of justice, you should strive to make all your objections clearly on the record. It would be a shame if an error made by the trial judge constitutes reversible error but an appellate court will not review the error because a proper objection was not made. Therefore, the key to protecting the record is to anticipate the issues, as well as the critical evidentiary rulings, and prepare for them.

In many jurisdictions, the failure to move for a directed verdict waives any subsequent claim for judgment, notwithstanding the verdict. For that matter, in failing to move for judgment as a matter of law at the conclusion of the evidence, a party effectively concedes the existence of a fact issue. If either party is granted a directed verdict or judgment as a matter of law, the opposing lawyer should not only object but should articulate all the grounds for the objection. During summations, improper remarks should be objected to and a motion for a mistrial should be made before the jury is charged so that the court can take corrective action. If a case is going to be given to a jury, each side should request the specific charges and take an exception if the court refuses or fails to give the charge as requested. All written requests to charge should be marked as court exhibits.

Compiling a Record on Appeal and Drafting an Appellate Brief

When perfecting an appeal and/or filing a brief with the court, the record and the brief must be in conformity with the court's rules. As previously stated, each appellate court has its own rules—even within the same state. For example, some intermediate appellate courts require an appeal to be submitted on the original papers, others require an appendix (excerpts of the record) and others require a full reproduced record on appeal. In New York, a record on appeal that is submitted following a motion must include the notice of appeal, the order/judgment appealed from, and all the papers that the lower court reviewed in deciding the motion. For an appeal following a trial, the record on appeal must include the notice of appeal, the judgment appealed from, the judgment roll (including the pleadings), the trial transcript, the exhibits, and any reviewable orders and opinions of the court. In most jurisdictions an appeal from a final judgment generally brings up for review any nonfinal judgment or order that necessarily affects final judgment. A fundamental rule in preparing a record or an appendix is that nothing de hors the record shall be included.

The contents of an appellate brief may also vary. It is recommended, however, that the brief include a table of contents and table of authorities. The brief should begin with a preliminary statement that provides a summary of the appeal. Following the preliminary statement is the statement of the facts. The goal of the statement of facts is to present a concise, coherent, compelling, and persuasive narrative, but it should not be argumentative. Ideally, the statement of facts should allow the appellate court to discern the principal issues presented. Therefore, do not include facts that are not relevant to the appeal or that do not provide necessary background for the case.

The brief should then include a section entitled "Questions Presented," where the issues before the court are provided along with short answers explaining to the court why it should either reverse (or if a respondent, affirm) the lower court. Following the questions presented section comes the argument portion of the brief. Your main goal as an advocate is to persuade the court of the merits of your client's case. Once again, it is imperative that you present the argument with concision, candor, and clarity. The conclusion of the brief should indicate the relief sought on the appeal.

Arguing an Appeal

The primary purpose of oral argument is to allow appellate counsel to answer any questions the justices may have about the appeal. In most situations, the record and the briefs have been thoroughly reviewed and a decision made even before oral argument. Thus, appellate counsel should be well prepared for argument. An unprepared lawyer will lose credibility with the court as will a lawyer who is not honest with the court. Most importantly, you should know the facts of your case, the law, and the procedures of the court. Be careful not to mislead the justices: It is better to concede an issue than try to mislead. Also, be sure to answer the questions posed to you by the bench. Lastly, if the appeal has numerous issues, do not address all of them during your argument—focus on the main issues and the issues that have the most merit.

Keep in mind that after a notice of appeal is filed circumstances may change that impact upon the ability of the appeal to proceed including, but not limited to, the settlement of the case in whole or in part or the death of a party. This can happen before or after the appeal is perfected. When such an event happens, you should notify the court immediately.

Case Law

In *Estate of Barrear v. Rosamond Village Limited Partnership*, 983 S.W.2d 795 (Ct. App. of Texas, 1998), a premises liability case brought against an apartment owner for the wrongful death of a guest at a party in the owner's building, the "take nothing verdict" was entered in favor of the building owner because the jury found that the guest was 70 percent negligent. On appeal, the plaintiffs argued that the trial court erred in entering a take nothing judgment as to exemplary damages because exemplary damages are not subject to the proportionate responsibility statute. Although the plaintiffs' point of error was a correct statement of law, the appellate court held that the issue was unpreserved for appellate review because exemplary damages require a finding of gross negligence before properly being awarded. The jury in this case, however, failed to answer the gross negligence question and proceeded to answer the next question regarding the specific dollar amount of exemplary damages. Because the plaintiffs failed to object to the jury's incomplete verdict sheet before the jury was discharged, the appellate court held that the plaintiffs had waived the trial court's error of entering the judgment on an incomplete verdict sheet.

In *Smith v. Hooligan's Pub & Oyster Bar, Ltd.*, 2000 WL 159019 (Fla. Dist. Ct. App., Feb. 16, 2000), the parents of a bar patron, who was shot and killed by another bar patron, brought a wrongful death action against Hooligan's bar for negligent failure to provide adequate security. The jury found in favor of the parents but also found that their son was 60 percent responsible for his own death. On appeal, the parents argued, inter alia, that the trial court wrongly reduced the $500,000 verdict by the comparative negligence attributed to their son because principles of comparative fault are not applicable to negligence action bottomed on an intention tort. The court held that the comparative fault apportionment issue was unpreserved for appellate review because the parents failed to move for a directed verdict or a motion for judgment, notwithstanding the verdict on this specific issue. Significantly, however, the appellate court did reverse the judgment because the parents had preserved for review a different point—that the trial court wrongly allowed Hooligan's to offer evidence regarding the decedent's purported bad character as circumstantial evidence of his conduct on the night of his death.

In *LaGestee v. Days Inn Management Co.*, 303 Ill. App. 3d 935 (1999), an employee of a waste hauling firm brought a premises liability action against the defendant hotel for injuries allegedly sustained in a fall. Following a jury verdict in favor of the defendant, the plaintiff argued on appeal that the trial court had improperly excluded him from calling a rebuttal witness. Significantly, although the defendant argued that the plaintiff had failed to preserve the issue for appellate review, the appellate court held that plaintiff's counsel, by making an appropriate offer of proof regarding the excluded evidence, had in fact preserved the issue. Therefore, the appellate court reversed and remanded for a new trial. On the contrary, in *Decker v. Domino's Pizza, Inc.*, 268 Ill. App. 3d 521 (1994), the appellate court held that the defendant's failure to timely object when a witness provided hearsay testimony- resulted in a waiver of the issue.

Lastly, in *Rodriguez v. New York City Hous. Auth.*, 215 A.D.2d 362 (2nd Dept. 1995), a personal injury action wherein the plaintiff claimed to have been injured as she descended broken steps, defense counsel timely objected to various evidentiary rulings made by the trial court. For example, defense counsel objected when the trial court improperly excluded the admission of the plaintiff's notice of claim wherein she stated that the accident occurred at a location other than the location testified to at trial. He also objected when the trial court precluded testimony given by the plaintiff at her examination before trial, which seemed to indicate that her accident was due to factors other than the defendant's negligence. Furthermore, at the damages portion of the trial, the plaintiff was permitted to introduce evidence that she suffered from incontinence, an injury not claimed in her bill of particulars. In that vein, defense counsel's request for a one-day adjournment to have the plaintiff examined by a urologist was also denied. As a result of all of these errors, which were timely objected to, the appellate division was left with no other option but to order a new trial.

These cases are only a few examples of the significance of preserving issues for appellate review. Thus, when working on a premises security case, always keep in mind that the trial court is not a court of last resort.

♠ CHAPTER 15

The Future of
Premises Security Litigation

Clearly, litigation on behalf of crime victims against building owners will continue, arguably in record numbers, over the course of the next few years.

The liberalization of important concepts such as "foreseeability" and "causation" by a majority of courts across the country has made it easier for plaintiffs to present prima facie allegations of negligence in many instances. Since costs associated with premises security litigation are often significant, plaintiffs may be more inclined to pursue litigation, possibly recognizing that their burden of proof in establishing liability may be somewhat easier today than it was several years ago.

However, there are still difficult cases for plaintiffs to win, and well they should be, since, in almost all cases, it is not the named defendant who committed the crime that caused the underlying injuries. It seems appropriate, then, that even with a somewhat relaxed standard of proof on certain important issues, premises security cases present considerable challenges at trial for plaintiffs. This is particularly the case concerning issues of causation. Interestingly, while courts have made it somewhat easier for plaintiffs to establish negligence, they seem to have made it more difficult for the plaintiffs to show that such negligence was a legal "cause" of the damages incurred by the plaintiffs. Instead of focusing on issues of foreseeability, premises security trials today are more likely to be concerned with causation issues, such as an assailant's means of ingress to a building or the nature of any connection of an assailant to a specific location.

As these bodies of cases continue to expand, we have also seen a dramatic increase in the number of individuals called as experts during trials. The quality of experts in the field of security (as is the case, I imagine, in all other fields), varies greatly. Former law enforcement personnel, in my opinion, often present themselves as the best expert witnesses. I have seen seriously injured crime victims lose at trial because their security expert was simply unqualified and could not help the plaintiff make out the necessary elements of negligence. Additionally, many other qualified experts have testified so often—usually for the same lawyers—that their credibility comes under attack.

Verdicts will likely continue to edge higher. Once liability is established, jurors remain unhesitant to award substantial damages to injured crime victims. Unlike other types of personal actions such as automobile accidents and trip-and-fall cases, where a plaintiff's injuries are often subject to review, it is difficult for a defendant to raise serious questions about the physical and emotional status of either a rape victim or a victim of another type of serious crime. Before jurors even consider awards for pain and suffering, there may already be evidence of considerable damages due to loss of earnings or medical care.

Many landowners, however, are becoming more proactive in their implementation of security features upon their properties. Advancements in technology have presented opportunities for landlords to improve all aspects of security, from door locks to surveillance cameras, and juries have been receptive to arguments presented by landlords when these security enhancements have been implemented.

The expansion of premises security litigation has also led to extraordinary increases in resources available to the premises security practitioner. Security seminars designed for lawyers—once unheard of—are now commonplace. Trade groups are also devoting considerable efforts toward meeting the litigation concerns of their members. The Internet is replete with information and resources available to lawyers in this area of practice.

Importantly, as the law in many states develops, we can get a better understanding of the rights of crime victims and the obligations of landowners to protect persons lawfully upon their property from criminal attack. We can also expect more of these cases to be taken to trial, as plaintiffs and defendants become more certain in their respective positions.

CHAPTER 16

Lessons Learned
from Trials

I'd like to say that I have won each premises security case I have
defended. But what I can say is that I have learned very important
lessons from each of the dozens of cases I have taken to trial. Not surprisingly, the most important lessons were learned from the cases I
have lost.

This chapter presents a summary of various premises security
cases I have defended at trial and, in hindsight, why I believe the cases
were won or lost.

Case #1 (N.Y. State Court)

The plaintiff had been assaulted by an unknown assailant who she
claimed entered her residential building through an unlocked side
door. She contended that her assailant grabbed her purse from behind
as she was walking up a flight of stairs. There had been a history of
crime in the building. As a result of this attack, the plaintiff, during the
course of being robbed, fell backwards and fractured her ankle.

Result: jury verdict for the defendant.

Lesson Learned: The jury found the defendant negligent, but determined that my client's negligence was not a cause of the plaintiff's
injuries. We argued to the jury that the willful acts of the assailant
caused the plaintiff's injuries. After jury selection was completed, we
felt comfortable that this particular jury would be able to dismiss this
case on causation issues, and we tried the case accordingly. The lesson

learned from this case was that one needs to make significant modifications to one's trial strategies depending upon the selection of jurors. Going into jury selection, we were inclined to argue that we simply were not negligent. After assessing our jury, we changed our defense to argue that any negligence on the defendant's behalf was not a legal cause of the plaintiff's injuries.

Fortunately, the jury agreed.

Case #2 (Federal Court)

The plaintiff in this action was shot several times as she was on her way to court to provide testimony against a suspected drug dealer. The plaintiff claimed that the defendant police force owed her a duty of protection because she had notified them about the likelihood of violence being perpetrated against her. The plaintiff had obtained an order of protection prior to the shooting and presented the order to the police precinct.

Result: jury verdict for the defendant.

Lesson Learned: The jury dismissed the case very reluctantly, and only because the plaintiff failed to demonstrate that she actually relied on any promised police protection. Although the plaintiff did prove to the jury's satisfaction a "special relationship" had been established that entitled her to protection, the court's instructions to the jury were that she could not recover unless she actually relied on that protection. The lesson learned in this case was the importance of impressing upon a jury a plaintiff's burden of proof. Here, the plaintiff was able to fully prove all aspects of her case except one relatively small component. Nevertheless, the case was dismissed.

Case #3 (State Court)

The plaintiff in this case was a young man who was shot while he and his friend were confronted by an assailant in the lobby of his building. Apparently, the plaintiff did not respond quickly enough to the assailant's demand that he hand over his wallet. The building had a history of crime, and the contention at trial was that the assailant had been observed entering the building through an unlocked door. The bullet struck the plaintiff in the neck and left him a virtual quadriplegic. The assailant's identity was suspected, but never established. The trial was extremely emotional, and included testimony from some prominent medical and liability experts, vocational experts, and economists. In addition to the inherent sympathy the case generated, the plaintiff was represented by an extremely capable lawyer and the case was presided over by a judge who was extremely sympathetic to the plaintiff's plight and, in my opinion, was unable to conceal her pro-plaintiff bearings from the jury.

Despite this, the prevailing law appeared to be favorable for the defendant on issues of causation.

Result: Jury verdict for the plaintiff in the amount of $5.3 million; set-aside as insufficient by the trial court and increased to $8.1 million; reduced back to the original verdict by the appellate court.

Lesson Learned: The issue of sympathy is present in every premises security case. Usually, this element of the case can be sufficiently addressed and neutralized during jury selection and at trial. In this case, however, it was not to be. The trial court set the tone, and the combination of a tragically injured plaintiff, a characteristic plaintiff's lawyer, and a judge whom I regarded as highly sympathetic for the plaintiff was too much to overcome. Issues of causation were lost on the jury.

Lawyers go to great lengths to try to select fair—if not favorable—jurors for their case. This case taught that the judge who presides over the case is probably of much greater significance, and can have a much greater impact on a jury's ultimate verdict, than the jurors selected to preside over the case.

Case #4 (State Court)

In this case, an elderly gentleman was shot in the abdomen as he was entering the elevator of his building after going out to buy a newspaper. He claimed that the assailant entered the building due to faulty front-door locks, and further claimed that the locks had been broken for three days before the occurrence. We contended that the locks were actually working satisfactorily. The building was a high-rise development, and there had been numerous crimes in the premises before the incident.

Result: jury verdict for the defendant.

Lesson Learned: My client employed several maintenance persons who worked at this location. Often, the temptation is to call one witness and refrain from calling other witnesses to avoid possible inconsistencies in their testimony. Here, however, we felt it was important to call each maintenance worker to support or position and reinforce their testimony. In speaking with the jurors after their verdict, it was clear that we made the right decision. One witness alone would not have been persuasive. But the consistent testimony of several witnesses convinced the jury that my client was not negligent.

Case #5 (State Court)

The plaintiff, a 16-year-old student at the time, did not feel well, and left school early to go home. Numerous witnesses testified that the door locks and intercom at the building were she lived had been broken for a period of time before this incident. She claimed that as she opened the door, a man entered the building behind her, went into the elevator with her, and got off on her floor. She claimed that he forced her at knifepoint to open her apartment door and then to perform sexual acts on her uncle, who was in the apartment when they arrived. The assailant then tied up the plaintiff's uncle and her seven-year-old brother, and raped and sodomized her before fleeing the premises. He was later apprehended and arrested. We impleaded the assailant into the case as a third-party defendant, and he defaulted.

The plaintiff claimed that the defendant failed to properly maintain the locks, and that it had notice of the defective condition, which was long-standing. The defendant argued that although it was aware that the locks were repeatedly broken, its personnel continually fixed them on an ongoing basis. The defendant contended that the locks were working on the date of this incident, and produced two detectives (one who interviewed the plaintiff in her apartment, and one who interviewed her at the hospital) who testified that the plaintiff told them that she used a key to open the lobby door, and that the assailant entered the lobby behind her before the lobby door closed. The plaintiff testified at trial, however, that she only meant that he entered the building after she did. She testified that she had been waiting by the elevator for about 20 seconds before seeing the intruder. The judge ruled that even if the locks were broken, if the jury found that the assailant entered the building behind the plaintiff after she opened the door and before the door closed, the broken door locks could not be a cause of the occurrence. *Note:* The same intruder had accosted another woman in the building one week prior to this incident.

Result: The jury deliberated for three days, at which point they notified the court of their inability to reach a verdict, resulting in a mistrial.

Lesson Learned: The testimony read into evidence of the prior crime victim was pervasive. However, we relied on the testimony of the police officers to challenge the plaintiff's claim that the locks were broken at the time she came home that morning. A thorough investigation into this case uncovered important testimony from the police officer and medical personnel. Hence, the lesson learned here is quite basic, but critically important: Interview all witnesses and secure all documents in preparing your case for trial. Further, the temptation at trial is to refrain from vigorously cross-examining a crime victim, for fear of alienating the jury. However, a lesson learned here is that even sympathetic crime victims must be cross-examined thoroughly on their version of events.

Case #6 (Federal Court)

The plaintiff was a middle-aged woman who was allegedly raped by an assailant who followed her to her building and allegedly gained entry to the building due to faulty security. We contended that this particular assailant was so violent that he would not have been deterred by increased security and, therefore, any negligence in maintaining the building could not be considered a legal cause of the attack. The evidence confirmed that this building had a high occurrence of criminal activity.

During the trial, we called the rapist as a witness. He was produced to the court by state corrections officers, and answered all questions posed to him.

Result: The jury returned a verdict in favor of the plaintiff for $3 million, and apportioned liability among my client and the assailant.

Lesson Learned: Calling the assailant as a witness was very risky. However, the trial had taken on a certain "atmosphere" that left us with no choice but to take a chance that putting the assailant on the stand would afford the jury the opportunity to conclude that the assailant, and not my client, was responsible for the occurrence. The jury did not agree.

Case #7 (State Court)

The plaintiff, a 17-year-old student, claimed that she was robbed by third-party defendant in the elevator as she returned to her apartment building. The plaintiff testified that the assailant then forced her to the roof where he raped and attempted to strangle her. The plaintiff claimed that the defendant was negligent because the front-door locks were broken, and argued that there was considerable documentation that the locks had been broken for a long period of time before this incident. The plaintiff testified that she was certain that the door lock was broken when she came home on the date of this incident. The plaintiff's expert testified that the security measures in the building were grossly inadequate. He claimed that the defendant was not operating at an acceptable standard of security, particularly in light of prior known crimes in the area. The assailant was found guilty and was incarcerated.

We did not dispute that the door locks had been broken in the past, but argued that on the date of this incident they were working properly. We introduced testimony that the locks were inspected on the morning of this incident and were shown to have been working. We contended that the door locks were checked daily, and argued that adequate security measures were in force, as there were five or six police officers on the premises on the date of the incident.

Result: The jury returned a verdict in favor of the defendant.

Lesson Learned: The jury ultimately concluded that the door lock was working on the date of the occurrence. We produced certain documents during trial that seemed to support that conclusion. The significance of maintaining, securing, producing, and placing such documentation into evidence cannot be overstated. Several cases I have tried have been won or lost primarily on the basis of various record-keeping documents.

Case #8 (State Court)

The plaintiff was 16 years old on the date of the incident. He brought this action against the building owner when the "superintendent" of the defendant's building shot him after an argument. The plaintiff claimed that the man shot him because he was loitering in front of the building. We contended that the man who shot the plaintiff was a tenant of the building, not the superintendent. We also contended that the shooting did not arise out of any employer/employee relationship. The plaintiff suffered gunshot wounds to the shoulder causing damage to his arm and shoulder.

Result: At the end of the case, the judge granted our motion for a directed verdict due to the plaintiff's failure to produce evidence of an employer/employee relationship between the defendant and the assailant.

Lesson Learned: Courts are reluctant to dismiss cases during a trial. However, when the allegations in a case are completely unsupported by the evidence, courts will remove cases from the province of a jury. Here, there was simply no evidence of an employer/employee relationship, and the case was dismissed as a matter of law.

♟ CHAPTER 17

Terrorism and Civil Lawsuits

From assaults to rapes, shootings and murders, landowners have been sued by thousands upon thousands of crime victims for crimes committed upon their premises.

Many of the scores of cases I have defended at trial involved comparable allegations of negligence on behalf of my clients, namely that my client did not have proper security on the premises to protect the crime victims from criminal assault.

Often, the specific allegations will include claims of broken door locks, faulty intercom systems, inadequate lighting, or insufficient security personnel. Occasionally, there might be a novel claim involving issues of surveillance cameras, signage, or even landscaping and visibility.

Yet none of the cases I had previously defended, and none of the theories of liability brought against my clients could prepare for the inevitable—that one day, one of my clients would be sued for an act of horrific violence, committed by an individual possibly linked to an organized terrorist group in the Middle East.

On October 23, 1993, a lone gunman opened fire on several diners in the Intercontinental Hotel in Cairo, Egypt, killing four and wounding two.

A lawsuit was filed in the District Court for the Southern District of New York on behalf of the families of two of the defendants, and also on behalf of one of the survivors, against Intercontinental Hotels, alleging that the hotel failed to provide adequate security to protect persons against foreseeable criminal occurrences.

For several years, the case worked its way through the district court and the Court of Appeals for the Second Circuit, and addressed such issues as the applicability of Egyptian or American law and forum non conveniens. Ultimately, the case was tried in federal court in New York.

The facts presented at trial showed that the Egyptian government had been aware of scores of terrorist attacks aimed at tourists in the months preceding this attack and actually issued warnings to all four-star hotels to be on heightened alert for any such possible attacks. Terrorists had been specifically targeting the tourism industry in an attempt to bring down the Egyptian government, and the Egyptian Ministry of Tourism issued direct orders to hotels visited by tourists on matters of security. Acting under orders of the government, the Intercontinental Hotel placed guards at all of its entrances and equipped the guards with handheld scanners to search for possible metal objects.

Apparently, the assailant was able to walk into the hotel with a gun hidden in his jacket, as it was the hotel's policy to use metal scanners only to check packages and briefcases for possible bombs. Security personnel did not use the scanners to search persons entering the hotel.

Once in the hotel, the assailant walked upstairs to the restaurant where he sought out persons who were speaking English. Once he found his targets, he began screaming Islamic phrases and opened fire. Hotel security ultimately approached him and turned him over to Egyptian authorities.

During trial, the plaintiffs sought to establish foreseeability by introducing into evidence reports of scores of terrorist bombings throughout Egypt, including numerous bombings in the relative vicinity of the hotel. Experts produced on behalf of the plaintiff opined that given the dramatic amount of terrorist activity throughout Egypt, the hotel should have had metal detectors at all entrances, to scan persons and not just briefcases and packages. The plaintiffs' experts testified that walk-through metal detectors, similar to those used at airports, should have been in place at all hotel entrances. The plaintiffs also contended that the hotel's policy of scanning only packages and not persons was a negligent policy that allowed the gunman to enter the hotel unchecked.

The claims brought on behalf of the plaintiffs were for tens of millions of dollars. The defendants vigorously challenged both the issue of foreseeability and the contention that the security provided at the hotel was inadequate.

During the trial, the defendants called experts formerly affiliated with the FBI, the CIA, and the State Department to provide the jury with an overall view of terrorist activity throughout the Middle East in general and specifically in Egypt. The testimony showed that the U.S. government monitored all such reports of terrorist activity, analyzed each such act, and noted that virtually each and every act of terrorism inside Egypt aimed at tourists involved the setting off of a bomb. The experts were of the opinion that the hotel's policy of using handheld detectors to check packages for possible bombs was reasonable, because there was no basis, based upon prior occurrences, to suspect that a terrorist attack would be committed with a gun. The shooting at the Intercontinental Hotel was the first time a terrorist had used a gun to commit such an act of violence.

Further testimony at trial included hotel security experts from the Middle East who decided that the security measures utilized by the Intercontinental Hotel were comparable, if not better, than security measures in place at other four-star hotels along the Nile River, where the hotel was located. In fact, testimony showed that the U.S. government often hosted events at the hotel because U.S. government officials believed the hotel provided a proper level of security.

Testimony elicited from Egyptian officials supported the defense contention that the hotel abided by all security directives issued by the Egyptian authorities. Over the course of the multiweek trial, which is believed to have been the first civil lawsuit in the country wherein the plaintiffs sought to hold a landowner liable for an act of terrorism committed upon its premises, hundreds of prior terrorist acts throughout the Middle East were analyzed by various experts in attempts by both parties to either establish or challenge the allegation that the incident was foreseeable. Similarly, there was an abundance of evidence presented by both sides as they attempted to establish or refute allegations that the level of security provided by the hotel was or was not reasonable.

Clearly, the case presented very sympathetic testimony on behalf of the plaintiffs. The decedent had been traveling to Egypt as part of a proposed joint business venture between an American company and the governments of Egypt and Israel.

At the conclusion of the trial, the jury concluded that the hotel was not negligent, resulting in a dismissal of the case. The verdict was upheld by the district court and the Court of Appeals for the Second Circuit.*

---

*The author of the book served as lead trial counsel for the defendant. The verdict was cited as one of the "Top Ten Defense Verdicts of the Year" by the *National Law Journal*.

Smith v. Halliburton Company, ____ *F.Supp.2d* ____, 2006 WL 2521326 (S.D. Tex., August 30, 2006)

Plaintiffs Savanah Ilise Smith, Brandy Leigh Wilkison, and Pamela Gene Karm, individually and as representatives of the Estate of Allen Keith Smith, deceased, filed this action against defendants, Halliburton Company, Kellogg, Brown & Root Services, Inc., and Kellogg, Brown & Root, Inc., alleging negligence stemming from a suicide bomb attack on a base in Iraq. On or about December 21, 2004, a suicide bomber walked into the dining facility (DFAC) at Forward Operating Base (FOB) Marez in Mosul, Iraq, and detonated explosives packed with ball bearings and other shrapnel. Allen Keith Smith was killed, along with twenty-one other people. A division of defendant Kellogg Brown & Root, Inc. was operating in Iraq pursuant to Contract No. DAAA09-02-D-0007 (the LOGCAP Contract), under which the defendants provided numerous services to the U.S. military throughout the world.

The plaintiffs alleged that the defendants were negligent in (1) failing to properly secure the DFAC, (2) failing to properly monitor the DFAC, (3) allowing a large number of people to gather at the mess tent at the same time, (4) not providing a search of the people who entered the DFAC, (5) failing to have a secure perimeter around the DFAC, (6) failing to warn people who came into the DFAC that defendants had provided no security, and (7) failing to take reasonable precautions to make the DFAC safe from attacks and explosions of the type that killed Smith. As a result of this negligence, the plaintiffs alleged that the suicide bomber was able to enter and detonate explosives, killing Smith. The defendants filed a motion to dismiss the case for lack of subject matter jurisdiction, arguing that the case should be dismissed as non-justiciable under the political question doctrine.

This court had previously concluded that the central inquiry in the political question determination was who had responsibility for security at the DFAC: the defendants or the U.S. military? The defendants argued that the evidence produced demonstrated that the U.S. military was solely responsible for force protection at FOB Marez. The court, in turn, used the applicable contract to provide a factual framework with which the court then analyzed this legal question.

The LOGCAP Contract and Task Order 59 serve as the principal legal bases for the relationship between the Department of Defense and the contractor. No provisions of the LOGCAP Contract or Task Order 59 give the defendants responsibility for providing force protection in the FOB Marez DFAC. Force protection is defined as "[s]ecurity programs designed to protect Service members, civilian employees, family members, facilities, information, and equipment in all locations and situations, *accomplished through the planned and integrated application of combating terrorism*, physical security, operations security, personal protective services, and supported by intelligence, counterintelligence, and security programs" (emphasis added).

The defendants submitted a sworn declaration from the administrative contracting officer responsible for oversight of the relevant contract stating that "[t]he Army retained the authority and responsibility for the 'security' and 'force protection' functions at FOB Marez and the Marez DFAC at all times under this contract; KBR was never entrusted with such 'security' or 'force protection' functions." Instead, the defendants' responsibility was to provide food services at the FOB Marez DFAC. Not only are the defendants without force protection responsibilities, but the contract provides that the service theater commander will provide force protection to defendants and their employees.

In the absence of any contractual directive to provide security, the Army assigns responsibility for force protection, including security, to the military, not to civilian contractors. As contractors, the defendants are required to adhere to military guidance, instructions, and general orders issued by the theater commander, including "any and all guidance and instructions issued based upon the need to ensure mission accomplishment, force protection, and safety." In addition, as contractors, the defendants cannot "command, supervise, administer or control Army or Department of the Army Civilian (DAC) personnel." Although contractors may be armed, they may only be armed for the purpose of individual self-defense. The LOGCAP contract provides that the theater commander has discretion to allow contractors to carry government-issue firearms. The defendants stated that no such authorization was given to defendants at FOB Marez.

The defendants' evidence also demonstrated that as a practical matter, the military, not the defendants, actually provided security at the DFAC. This security took the form of periodically stationing soldiers to check identification of personnel entering the DFAC and ensuring that loaded weapons were not brought into the DFAC. There were apparently no soldiers performing these functions on December 21, 2004, when the DFAC was bombed, or for the several days preceding the bombing. Nor did the military provide the defendants with any warning that the DFAC might be targeted for attack by a suicide bomber, or targeted for any attack at all on December 21, 2004.

The evidence submitted established that the defendants had no responsibility for force protection, notwithstanding the plaintiffs' arguments to the contrary. The linchpin of the plaintiffs' argument that the defendants have force protection responsibilities as contractors is paragraph 6-4 of Field Manual 100-21, Contractors on the Battlefield, which states that "[t]he responsibility for assuring that contractors receive adequate force protection starts with the combatant commander, extends downward, and includes the contractor." The plaintiffs attempted to characterize this as establishing a chain of command for force protection, starting with the combatant commander and extending downward to the contractors. But the court found that the full text of the cited paragraph did not support the plaintiffs' argument. The entire paragraph states as follows:

> Protecting contractors and their employees on the battlefield is the commander's responsibility. When contractors perform in potentially hostile or hazardous areas, the supported military forces must assure the protection of their operations and employees. The responsibility for assuring that contractors receive adequate force protection starts with the combatant commander, extends downward, and includes the contractor.

The first sentence of this document makes it clear that the intent is not to delegate force protection responsibilities to the contractor. Furthermore, the cited paragraph deals with protecting the contractors by military force, not with requiring contractors to provide force protection to other parties. The last sentence ensures that contractors comply with force protection measures ordered by the commanders for their own benefit, such as using personal protective equipment, and does not, as the plaintiffs argue, demonstrate that the military delegated some of its force protection responsibility to the defendants.

The plaintiffs also cited a provision of Task Order 59 relating to firefighting services. Task Order 59 of the LOGCAP contract requires that the defendants provide firefighting protection services for U.S. government–owned or –leased property, personnel, and equipment on all Enduring Base Camps. . . . The contractor shall provide fire department and fire protection functions according to DoD, local, state, federal, and industry standards. These functions include fire protection support, emergency response, equipment and vehicle management, fire prevention and education, and training. The plaintiffs argued that firefighting and prevention services include preventing a fire caused by a bomb explosion. But reading fire prevention as broadly as the plaintiffs suggest would bring this portion of Task Order 59 in unnecessary conflict with the contractual provisions requiring the U.S. government to provide force protection to contractor personnel. In addition, the plain language of the contract belies the plaintiffs' argument. The term "fire prevention" cannot reasonably be read to encompass prevention of infiltration or explosions caused by suicide bombers. Preventing suicide bomb attacks is more appropriately characterized as a force protection measure, contractually entrusted to the U.S. government and the military. The plaintiffs' arguments regarding the contractual provision that the defendants shall be "responsible for the safety of employees and base camp residents during all operations in accordance with the Army and OSHA safety regulations and guidance" is similarly unavailing. The reference to OSHA safety regulations indicates that "safety" in this provision is safety in the workplace, not security measures related to hostile forces.

The court stated that while the plaintiffs couched this lawsuit in terms of simple premises liability by arguing that the court need only determine what duties defendants, as possessor, occupier, and operator of the DFAC, owed to Allen Keith Smith as the invitee, this formulation failed to recognize that were the case to proceed, this court would have to second-guess the decisions of the U.S. military, even though the suit is ostensibly against only military contractors. Although the military contracted out the logistical aspects of FOB Marez's DFAC operations to the defendants, it did not delegate the force protection responsibilities to the defendants.

The court also discussed another district court case recently addressing the issue of how government contractors affect the political question doctrine. In *Whitaker v. Kellogg Brown & Root, Inc.,* ____ F.Supp.2d ____, 2006 WL 1876922 (M.D. Ga., July 6, 2006), the surviving parents of a soldier serving in Iraq sued the government contractor after their son was killed while escorting a military supply convoy operated by the government contractor. *Id.* at *1. The plaintiffs alleged that the defendant's drivers were negligent and that the defendant was negligent in hiring, training, and supervising those drivers. *Id.* The court dismissed the case on political question grounds despite the fact that the plaintiffs' allegations were against the civilian contractor. *Id.* at *3. "When the military seeks to accomplish its mission by partnering with government contractors who are subject to the military's orders . . . the use of those civilian contractors to accomplish the military objective does not lessen the deference due to the political branches in this area." *Id.*

In this case, the court found that the negligence allegations in the plaintiffs' complaint directly addressed the security of the DFAC. The plaintiffs repeatedly argued that their complaint questions only the conduct of the defendants in failing to provide security, not the military's force protection policies. But this argument fails because the evidence shows that the defendants had no security responsibilities for the DFAC. By alleging that the defendants were negligent in providing security for the DFAC at FOB Marez, the plaintiffs are, in effect, alleging that the military was negligent in providing security for the DFAC at FOB Marez.

Even assuming, for the sake of argument, that the military and the defendants had concomitant responsibility for security, the defendants were still operating pursuant to the military's orders, instructions, and regulations. The *Whitaker* court held that an injury "at the hands of a contractor which is performing military functions subject to the military's orders and regulations also raises . . . political questions." *Whitaker*, 2006 WL 1876922 at *3. This court agreed. Even if the defendants had some responsibility for implementing force protection measures promulgated by the military, the court would still be called upon to examine the military's decision-making in many respects, including determining whether the military gathered adequate intelligence regarding the threat of terror attacks, whether it conveyed this threat to the defendants, how the military planned for and implemented base access measures, and whether the implementation of force protection measures was reasonable when measured against the risk assessment level.

Allowing this action to proceed, therefore, would have required the court to substitute its judgment on military decision-making for that of the branches of government entrusted with this task. To determine whether the force protection in place was adequate, the intelligence-gathering, risk assessment, and security measures implemented by the military at FOB Marez would have to be examined. Because the suicide bomber managed to enter the base, the court would also have to examine base perimeter security. "The control of access to a military base is clearly within the constitutional powers granted to both Congress and the President." *Cafeteria and Restaurant Workers Union, Local 473 v. McElroy*, 81 S.Ct. 1743, 1746 (1961). Thus, judicial review of such decisions would intrude on critical areas reserved for the legislative and executive branches of government by the Constitution.

Moreover, there exists a lack of judicially discoverable and manageable standards to resolve this case. In order to determine if the defendants acted reasonably as possessor, occupier, and operator of the DFAC, the court would have to decide what constitutes reasonable security measures at a military base located in an area of Iraq subject to threats from hostile forces. The court would have to assess what intelligence had been gathered regarding potential threats and evaluate whether the security measures implemented were reasonable in light of the potential threats. Security measures on military bases balance the need for functionality and access with the need for force protection. In striking this balance the military must also allocate limited personnel and resources, with the need for security on base competing with mission requirements off base in Iraq as well as throughout the world. The court would have to determine if the military was reasonable in striking this balance. Courts lack the facts, expertise, and standards necessary to evaluate whether reasonable care was taken in these circumstances.

Finally, the issues in this case could not be resolved without an initial policy determination of a kind clearly for nonjudicial discretion. The court would substitute its judgment for that of the military on the issue of whether adequate force protection measures were in place. The court would also have to examine the military's policy of feeding soldiers by gathering them in one centralized location. Since the suicide bomber was apparently wearing an Iraqi uniform, the decision to allow Iraqi troops to dine in the DFAC would also be at issue. These are just a few examples of the many policy determinations that were involved in implementing force protection measures at the FOB Marez DFAC. "The complex subtle, and professional decisions as to the composition, training, equipping, and control of a military force are essentially professional military judgments, subject always to civilian control of the Legislative and Executive Branches." *Gilligan v. Morgan*, 93 S.Ct. 2440, 2446 (1973). Policy determinations involving force protection measures in a hostile area of Iraq are clearly not appropriate for judicial determination. As such, the court concluded that it lacked jurisdiction to hear this case because it constituted a nonjusticiable political question.

In the Matter of World Trade Center Bombing Litigation, 3 Misc.3d 440, 776 N.Y.S.2d 713, 2004 N.Y. Slip Op. 24030 (New York County 2004)

In consolidated actions against the Port Authority of New York and New Jersey, in its capacity as owner of World Trade Center (WTC), alleging that negligent security resulted in injuries due to 1993 terrorist bombing in the parking garage of the WTC, the Port Authority moved for summary judgment. The court held that (1) the Port Authority was not entitled to sovereign immunity, and (2) triable issues of fact existed as to whether bombing was foreseeable.

This action primarily involved the negligence claims of individuals and businesses that asserted various injuries resulting from the bombing of the World Trade Center in 1993. It joins more than 175 cases, which have been consolidated for trial, discovery, and motions. On February 26, 1993, a bomb exploded in the public parking garage located beneath the concourse of the buildings, killing six people, injuring many others, and disrupting businesses. The explosives were placed in a van that was driven in and parked in the public parking area of the garage; the perpetrators left the garage and then detonated the bomb. In March 1994, four individuals were convicted of placing and detonating the explosive device. The plaintiffs basically contend that the Port Authority failed to implement security measures, by, inter alia, keeping the parking garage open to public transient parking, which would have kept the bomb out of the garage, and failed to mitigate the resulting injuries and destruction. The Port Authority moved for summary judgment dismissing the plaintiffs' negligence claims.

First, the Port Authority argued that it could not be held liable in negligence as a matter of law for failing to protect the plaintiffs from the criminal acts of third parties, because providing such protection is a governmental function. The Port Authority contends that the plaintiffs' claims are based on the failure to provide security, which it urges is a governmental function. It points to the legislation establishing the Port Authority, McKinney's Uncons. Law § 6610, as proof that it was performing an essential governmental function in undertaking to provide safety and security to the patrons at the WTC. It asserted that the activities for which the plaintiffs want to hold the Port Authority liable essentially involve, or grow directly out of, the failure to allocate police resources. The court, however, found that although the Port Authority serves a governmental function in many of its undertakings, it was not immune from suit. In short, because this court held that the negligent acts that the plaintiffs were pursuing involve the Port Authority's proprietary functions, there was no basis as to those acts to grant the Port Authority summary judgment on its governmental immunity defense.

Second, the Port Authority contended that, even if it were determined that it was not performing a governmental function, it still would not be liable, because the bombing was not foreseeable as a matter of law. It points to the lack of evidence of similar criminal acts at the WTC. The Port Authority claims that the prerequisite for liability is the likelihood of crime, not the mere possibility. It urges that the courts have repeatedly held that the existence of ambient crime in the neighborhood is not a sufficient basis for holding a building owner liable for the criminal acts of third parties on the premises. It contends that the alleged basis for the predictability of the bombing, a security report, is not the equivalent of crime on the premises or actual crime in the neighborhood. The Port Authority maintains that the plaintiffs have failed to present any evidence that an explosive-laden vehicle had been placed in the WTC prior to February 26, 1993, and that, therefore, the plaintiffs have failed to establish a predicate for holding the Port Authority liable.

The court ultimately found that there were triable issues of fact as to the foreseeability of this catastrophic event, warranting denial of the Port Authority's motion. Contrary to the Port Authority's apparent argument, the court found that a landlord does not need to have had a past experience with the exact criminal activity, in the same place, and of the same type, before liability can be imposed for failing to take reasonable precautions to discover, warn, or protect. The inquiry focuses on what risks were reasonably to be perceived. Whether knowledge of prior activities is sufficient to make injuries foreseeable "must depend on the location, nature and extent of those previous criminal activities and their similarity, proximity or other relationship to the crime in question." *Jacqueline S. by Ludovina S. v. City of New York*, 81 N.Y.S.2d at 295, 598 N.Y.S.2d 160, 614 N.E.2d 723 (citations omitted). Where ambient crime has infiltrated a landlord's premises, or where the landlord is otherwise on notice of a serious risk of such infiltration, the landlord's duty to protect arises. *See Todorovich v. Columbia Univ.*, 245 A.D.2d at 46, 665 N.Y.S.2d 77.

In particular, the court found that the Port Authority's claim that this bombing was unforeseeable as a matter of law strained credulity. The Port Authority's duty is defined by what risks or dangers were and should reasonably have been anticipated by the Port Authority from having a high-profile building, with a public parking garage under it, which permitted "unvetted" vehicles to enter and exit without encountering any barriers or surveillance. The Port Authority clearly perceived a risk since it sought a report from its security experts and other outside consultants regarding the risk of a terrorist attack on the WTC, and seeking recommendations for security measures to protect against the risk.

The Port Authority's argument that ambient crime in the neighborhood is not enough, as a matter of law, to establish foreseeability amounts to a contention that landlords can close their eyes to plainly perceived risks, and ignores the plaintiffs' proof, which goes beyond simply ambient crime. The plaintiffs have presented proof, including the Port Authority's own report, the reports from its outside security consultants, reports of bomb threats in the WTC itself and in and around buildings in the downtown area several years earlier, and a bomb threat communicated by the FBI only a month before the bombing; such proof tends to establish, or at the least creates a triable issue, that the Port Authority had foreseen the risk, or that the risk was foreseeable. This evidence, at the least, put the Port Authority on notice of the risk of the infiltration of criminal activity in the WTC.

The predicted scenario, eerily accurate, in the Port Authority's security reports, of a vehicle bomb in the garage, and the evidence of bomb threats in the complex, are sufficiently similar in nature to the bombing to raise a triable issue as to foreseeability. The fact that an explosive-laden vehicle had not previously been placed in the WTC garage does not, as the Port Authority appears to be arguing, make this event unforeseeable as a matter of law. The court is aware, as the defendant strenuously argues, that there are no cases in which a landlord was subjected to liability for an unprecedented terrorist bombing in its building, particularly where the ambient crime was not necessarily in the immediate vicinity; however, the evidence of the Port Authority's actual notice of the risk of infiltration of this kind of terrorist activity cannot be ignored. Besides, the court reasoned, landlords have been denied summary judgment in other cases on the issue of foreseeability, even where there was no evidence of similar crimes in the building.

In Re September 11 Litigation,
280 F.Supp.2d 279 (S.D.N.Y. 2003)

Victims who were injured, and survivors of victims who were killed, in terrorist-related aircraft crashes of September 11, 2001, brought action against airlines, airport security companies, owners and operators of the buildings destroyed in the crash, and the aircraft manufacturer. On the defendants' motion to dismiss, the district court, Hellerstein http://web2.westlaw.com/Find/Default.wl?DB=WLD%2DPEOPLECITE&DocName=0116863401&FindType=h&AP=&mlac=FY&fn=_top&utid=%7b75DF786E-BBDD-4F6F-B875-ABD16EFD7B21%7d&rs=WLW7.04&mt=NewYork&vr=2.0&sv=Split, J., held that: (1) under New York law, the duty of airlines and airport security companies to secure aircraft against potential terrorists and weapons smuggled aboard extended to ground victims of crashes; (2) the crash of the planes hijacked by terrorists was within the class of foreseeable hazards resulting from negligently performed security screening by airlines; (3) federal statutes and regulations providing for protection of passengers and property on aircraft in the event of air piracy did not preempt the plaintiffs' negligence claim under New York law; (4) the owners and operators of the office building owed duty under New York law to the building's occupants to create and implement adequate fire safety measures; (5)

the plaintiffs pleaded sufficient facts to the alleged legal proximate cause against the owners and operators; (6) the plaintiffs' allegations were sufficient to establish the manufacturer's duty under Virginia and Pennsylvania law; and (7) the failure of the manufacturer to design an impenetrable cockpit door was the proximate cause of the crashes.

The plaintiffs' individual pleadings were consolidated into five master complaints, one for the victims of each crash and one for the property damage plaintiffs. The plaintiffs allege that the airlines, airport security companies, and airport operators negligently failed to fulfill their security responsibilities, and in consequence, the terrorists were able to hijack the airplanes and crash them into the World Trade Center, the Pentagon, and the field in Shanksville, Pennsylvania, killing passengers, crew, and thousands in the World Trade Center and the Pentagon and causing extensive property damage. The complaints allege that the owners and operators of the World Trade Center, World Trade Center Properties LLC and the Port Authority of New York and New Jersey negligently designed, constructed, maintained, and operated the buildings, failing to provide adequate and effective evacuation routes and plans. The plaintiffs who died in the crashes of American Flight 77 and United Flight 93 also sued Boeing, the manufacturer of the two 757 airplanes, for strict tort liability, negligent product design, and breach of warranty.

The Aviation Defendants conceded that they owed a duty to the crew and passengers on the planes, but contended that they did not owe any duty to "ground victims." The Port Authority and WTC Properties argued that they did not owe a duty to protect occupants in the towers against injury from hijacked airplanes and, even if they did, the terrorists' actions broke the chain of proximate causation, excusing any negligence by the WTC Defendants. And Boeing argued that it did not owe a duty to ground victims or passengers, and that any negligence on its part was not the proximate cause for the harms suffered by the plaintiffs.

Aviation Defendants' Motion to Dismiss

The Aviation Defendants argued that they did not owe a duty to the ground victims; that the injuries suffered by the plaintiffs were beyond the scope of any foreseeable duty that may have been owed; and that the federal laws that regulate aviation preempt any state law to the contrary.

The plaintiffs alleged that the Aviation Defendants negligently failed to carry out their duty to secure passenger aircraft against potential terrorists and weapons smuggled aboard, enabling the terrorists to hijack and crash four airplanes. The plaintiffs argued that the Aviation Defendants employed their security measures specifically to guard against hijackings, and knew or should have known that the hijacking of a jumbo jet would create substantial risks of damage to persons and property, not only to passengers and crew, but also to people and property on the ground. The plaintiffs asserted also that terrorism was a substantial international concern, and that suicidal acts by terrorists seeking to cause death, injury, and havoc to as many innocent people as possible had become a frequently used strategy.

Airplane crashes in residential areas are not unknown. In January 1952, an American Airlines Convair crashed into a residential area of Elizabeth, New Jersey, on its approach to Newark airport, killing passengers and crew, as well as seven residents of houses it struck. *Elizabeth Recalls First of 3 Crashes*, N.Y. Times, Dec. 17, 1952, at 27. A month later, another plane out of Newark, a National Airlines DC-6, struck an apartment house in New Jersey, killing twenty-nine passengers and four tenants of the apartment house. *Id.* Military airplanes have had to make emergency landings on highways and have collided with automobiles. *See Rehm v. United States*, 196 F.Supp. 428 (E.D.N.Y.1961). On July 9, 1982, a Pan American World Airways jet crashed shortly after takeoff, killing all on board and eight individuals on the ground. The airline and the government acknowledged liability for the crash, which was caused by windy conditions. *Pan Am and U.S. Accept Responsibility for Crash*, N.Y. Times, May 13, 1983, at 6. In January 1990, a Columbian passenger airplane exhausted its fuel supply while circling La Guardia Airport waiting for clearance to land, and crashed into a residential backyard in Long Island's populated North Shore. *See In re Air Crash Disaster at Cove Neck*, 885 F.Supp. 434 (E.D.N.Y.1995). On November 12, 2001, two months after the aircraft crashes of September 11, 2001, a jumbo-jet passenger airplane lost its stability in takeoff from JFK Airport and crashed into a populated area of the Rockaways, causing the deaths of over two hundred passengers and crew members and five people on the ground. Dan Barry and Elissa Gootman, *5 Neighbors Gone*, N.Y. Times, Nov. 14, 2001, at D11. Such incidents are inevitable in the context of the sheer number of miles flown daily in the United States. None matches the quantity or quality of tragedy arising from the terrorist-related aircraft crashes of September 11.

Airlines typically recognize responsibility to victims on the ground. *See, e.g., Rehm*, 196 F.Supp. at 428; *Cove Neck*, 885 F.Supp. at 439–40. As counsel for the Aviation Defendants stated in argument, "Assuming negligence and assuming there is damage to houses on the ground that is the type of traditional ground damage negligent maintenance cases in which the courts have imposed duty. . . . [W]e would concede in those circumstances assuming the facts of liability are proven there is a legal duty." (Tr. of May 1, 2003 at 8.) However, counsel did not concede duty in relation to those killed and injured on the ground in the September 11, 2001, aircraft crashes. The "potential for a limitless liability to an indeterminate class of plaintiffs," he argued, made the instant cases distinguishable. *Id.* The distinction, in his opinion, is "no[t] [a] difference in kind," but "the law of extraordinary consequences [which] can sometimes draw a distinction based on degree." Id. at 9–10. He explained: "We are in an area of policy and there are lines to be drawn that may occasionally seem arbitrary. But what really distinguishes our case from [the hypothetical example of an airplane crash into Shea Stadium while taking off from, or landing at, La Guardia Airport] is the intentional intervening acts of the third party terrorists." Counsel suggested, without legal citation, that the extraordinary nature of the attacks, involving intervening acts by the terrorists, should negate the duty air carriers owed to ground victims. *Id.* As defense counsel commented, "we are in an area of policy" where "the existence and scope of a tortfeasor's duty is . . . a legal question for the courts." *532 Madison Ave. Gourmet Foods, Inc. v. Finlandia Center, Inc.*, 96 N.Y.2d 280, 72*7* N.Y.S.2d 49, 750 N.E.2d 1097, 1101 (2001) (Kaye, Ch. J.).

Here, the judge held that the Aviation Defendants owed a duty of care, not only to their passengers to whom they conceded they owed this duty, but also to victims on the ground. The plaintiffs and society generally could have reasonably expected that the screening performed at airports by the Aviation Defendants would be for the protection of people on the ground as well as for those in airplanes. The Aviation Defendants perform their screening duties not only for those boarding airplanes, but also for society generally. It is both their expectation, and ours, that the duty of screening was performed for the benefit of passengers and those on the ground, including those present in the Twin Towers on the morning of September 11, 2001. Thus the Aviation Defendants, and the plaintiffs and society generally, could reasonably have expected that the screening methods at Logan, Newark, and Dulles Airports were for the protection of people on the ground as well as for those on board the airplanes that the terrorists hijacked.

The plaintiffs, the ground victims in the cases before me, complain of directly caused physical injuries to their persons or property. Their number may be large, tragically large, and the potential liability may be substantial if negligence and cause is proven, but the class is not indefinite and claims at this point cannot proliferate. Furthermore, the defendants will be liable only if the plaintiffs sustain their burden of proof, with the aggregate liability of the air carriers, aircraft manufacturers, airport sponsors, and persons with a property interest in the World Trade Center capped by federal statute to the limits of their liability insurance coverage. Act § 408(a)(1). Thus, "the likelihood of unlimited or insurer-like liability" did not weigh heavily against a finding of duty.

Further, in determining who was best able to protect against the risks at issue and weighing the costs and efficacy of imposing such a duty, the court found that the airlines and the airport security companies could best screen those boarding and bringing objects onto airplanes. The same activities reasonably necessary to safeguard passengers and crew are those that would protect the public as well. Hijacking presents a substantial elevation of risks, not only to those aboard the hijacked airplane, but also to those on the ground. This case is thus distinguishable from other cases where courts did not find a duty to protect against third-party conduct.

Lastly, recognition of a duty on the part of the Aviation Defendants would not substantially expand or create "new channels of liability." New York courts have found on other occasions that aircraft owners and operators owe a duty to those on the ground who may be harmed or sustain property damage resulting from improper or negligent operation of an aircraft. *See, e.g., Hassanein v. Avianca Airlines,* 872 F.Supp. 1183, 1188–90 (E.D.N.Y.1995) (denying defendant's motion for summary judgment where a plane crash could have caused a handrail in the plaintiff's house to loosen, causing her fall down the stairs). The same general principle governs here, that air carriers owe a duty to people on the ground as well as to passengers and crew. Clearly, the duty of care extends to cover those embraced by the risk of the terrorists' conduct.

Having found that the Aviation Defendants owed a duty of care to the ground victims, the court next turned to the issue of foreseeability. The defendants argued that the ground victims lost their lives and suffered injuries from an event that was not reasonably foreseeable, for terrorists had not previously used a hijacked airplane as a suicidal weapon to destroy buildings and murder thousands. The defendants contended that because the events of September 11 were not within the reasonably foreseeable risks, any duty of care that they would owe to ground victims generally should not extend to the victims of September 11. Construing the factual allegations in the light most favorable to the plaintiffs, the judge concluded that the crash of the airplanes was within the class of foreseeable hazards resulting from negligently performed security screening. While it may be true that terrorists had not before deliberately flown airplanes into buildings, the airlines reasonably could foresee that crashes causing death and destruction on the ground were a hazard that would arise should hijackers take control of a plane. The intrusion by terrorists into the cockpit, coupled with the volatility of a hijacking situation, creates a foreseeable risk that hijacked airplanes might crash, jeopardizing innocent lives on the ground as well as in the airplane. While the crashes into the particular locations of the World Trade Center, Pentagon, and Shanksville field may not have been foreseen, the duty to screen passengers and items brought on board existed to prevent harms not only to passengers and crew, but also to the ground victims resulting from the crashes of hijacked planes, including the four planes hijacked on September 11.

Therefore, based on the grounds outlined above, the court denied the Aviation Defendants' motion to dismiss the claims of the ground victims.

World Trade Center Defendants' Motions to Dismiss

The Port Authority of New York and New Jersey and WTC Properties LLC moved to dismiss all claims brought against them as owners and operators of the World Trade Center for loss of life, personal injury, and damage to nearby property and businesses resulting from the collapse of the Twin Towers. The plaintiffs alleged that the WTC Defendants: (1) failed to design and construct the World Trade Center buildings according to safe engineering practices and to provide for safe escape routes and adequate sprinkler systems and fireproofing; (2) failed to inspect, discover, and repair unsafe and dangerous conditions, and to maintain fireproofing materials; (3) failed to develop adequate and safe evacuation and emergency management plans; (4) failed to apply, interpret, and/or enforce applicable building and fire safety codes, regulations, and practices; and (5) instructed Tower Two occupants to return to their offices and remain in the building even while the upper floors of Tower One were being consumed by uncontrolled fires following the airplane crash into Tower One.

The WTC Defendants argued that the complaints against them should be dismissed because they had no duty to anticipate and guard against deliberate and suicidal aircraft crashes into the Towers, and because any alleged negligence on their part was not a proximate cause of the plaintiffs' injuries. The Port Authority argued also that it is entitled to immunity because the complained-of conduct essentially consisted of governmental functions. The WTC Defendants contended that they owed no duty to "anticipate and guard against crimes unprecedented in human history." The plaintiffs, on the other hand, argued that the defendants owed a duty, not to foresee the crimes, but to have designed, constructed, repaired, and maintained the World Trade Center structures to withstand the effects and spread of fire, to avoid building collapses caused by fire, and, in designing and effectuating fire safety and evacuation procedures, to provide for the escape of more people.

First, the court found that the parties and society would reasonably expect that the WTC Defendants would have a duty to the occupants of the Twin Towers in designing, constructing, repairing, and maintaining the structures; in conforming to appropriate building and fire safety codes; and in creating appropriate evacuation routes and procedures should an emergency occur. Second, although a large number of claims have been filed against the WTC Defendants, there is no danger that the number will proliferate beyond those who died in the collapse of the structures or were injured while trying to escape. Similarly, the WTC Defendants are not subject to unlimited or insurer-like liability, for they can be held liable only after a showing of fault and only to those who suffered death, personal injury, or property damage resulting from their alleged negligence. Furthermore, by specific provision of the Air Transportation Safety and System Stabilization Act, their liability is limited to their insurance coverage. Act § 408(a)(1). Fourth, the defendants' relationship with the plaintiffs, as their landlord or the landlord of their employer, placed the WTC Defendants in the best position to protect against the risk of harm. And fifth, imposing a duty on the WTC Defendants in the situation at hand would not create new channels of liability, for the New York courts have held traditionally that landlords owe duties of safety and care to the occupants of leased premises and their invitees.

A finding of duty also requires a consideration of the nature of the plaintiffs' injuries and the likelihood of their occurrence from a particular condition. "Defining the nature and scope of the duty and to whom the duty is owed requires consideration of the likelihood of injury to another from a dangerous condition or instrumentality on the property; the severity of potential injuries; the burden on the landowner to avoid the risk; and the foreseeability of a potential plaintiff's presence on the property." *Kush*, 462 N.Y.S.2d 831, 449 N.E.2d at 727. The criteria are clearly satisfied, for the severity and likelihood of potential injuries of people unable to escape from a heavily occupied building before fires envelop evacuation routes is high. The more difficult question is whether the injuries arose from a reasonably foreseeable risk.

The plaintiffs argued that the WTC Defendants had a duty to exercise reasonable care in order to mitigate the effects of fires in the Twin Towers. They alleged that the defendants knew about the fire safety defects in the Twin Towers, as evident by the Allied litigation concerning inadequate fireproofing in the construction of the buildings; that the defendants could have reasonably foreseen crashes of airplanes into the Towers, given the near miss in 1981 of an Aerolineas Argentinas Boeing 707 and the studies conducted during the Towers' construction reporting that the Towers would be able to withstand an aircraft crash; that the defendants were aware of numerous fires and evacuations that had occurred at the World Trade Center since its creation, including arson fires in 1975 and the 1993 terrorist-caused explosion in the garage under Tower One; and that the World Trade Center continued to be a prime target of terrorists. A finding of duty does not require a defendant to have been aware of a specific hazard. *See Sanchez v. State of New York*, 99 N.Y.2d 247, 754 N.Y.S.2d 621, 784 N.E.2d 675, 679–81 (2002). It is enough to have foreseen the risk of serious fires within the buildings and the goal of terrorists to attack the building.

Because this motion was made at a very early point in the litigation, with no discovery having taken place, and the defendants' motions to dismiss accept, as they must, all allegations of the complaints, the judge held that the WTC Defendants owed a duty to the plaintiffs, and that the plaintiffs should not be foreclosed from being able to prove that the defendants failed to exercise reasonable care to provide a safe environment for their occupants and invitees with respect to reasonably foreseeable risks.

The WTC Defendants also argued that even if they were held to have owed a duty to the plaintiffs, and even if a jury ultimately found that they acted negligently, their negligence was not the proximate cause of the plaintiffs' damages. This is because, they claim, the terrorist-related aircraft crashes into the Twin Towers were so extraordinary and unforeseeable as to constitute intervening and superseding causes, severing any link of causation to the WTC Defendants.

Again, at this early stage of the case and in the absence of a factual record, the judge found that the plaintiffs had pleaded sufficient facts to allege legal proximate cause. The plaintiffs alleged that the WTC Defendants' negligence was a substantial cause of their injuries, because adequate fireproofing and evacuation would have enabled many more escapes. According to the plaintiffs, the terrorist acts did not merely "operate upon" the defendants' negligence. *Derdiarian v. Felix Contracting Corp.*, 51 N.Y.2d 308, 434 N.Y.S.2d 166, 414 N.E.2d 666, 670 (1980); rather, the failure to provide certain safeguards caused the entrapment of many more people and the loss of many more lives. Large-scale fire was precisely the risk against which the WTC Defendants had a duty to guard and which they should have reasonably foreseen. The judge also declined at this stage to find that the acts of the terrorists qualified as "extraordinary" intervening cause. *Kush*, 462 N.Y.S.2d 831, 449 N.E.2d at 729. While the specific acts of the terrorists were certainly horrific, the judge could not find that the WTC Defendants should be excused of all liability as a matter of policy and law on the record before him, especially given the plaintiffs' allegations regarding the defendants' knowledge of the possibility of terrorist acts, large-scale fires, and even airplane crashes at the World Trade Center. The defendants may well be able to show at a later stage in this litigation that the conduct of the terrorists "so attenuates defendants' negligence from the ultimate injury that responsibility for the injury may not be reasonably attributed to the defendant." *Kush*, 462 N.Y.S.2d 831, 449 N.E.2d at 729. Discovery will either supply evidence to substantiate or eviscerate the parties' divergent claims about foreseeability. *See Mason v. U.E.S.S. Leasing Corp.*, 96 N.Y.2d 875, 730 N.Y.S.2d 770, 756 N.E.2d 58, 60 (2001) (discovery necessary to determine foreseeability of an intruder's assault within an apartment complex). At this point, however, the court found that both the plaintiffs and the defendants should be allowed to proceed to discovery on these issues of causation.

Boeing's Motions to Dismiss

Some of those who were injured and the successors of those who died in the Pentagon, in American Airlines Flight 77 which crashed into the Pentagon, and in United Air Lines Flight 93 which crashed into the Shanksville, Pennsylvania field, claimed the right to recover against Boeing, the manufacturer of the two 757 jets flown by United and American. The plaintiffs alleged that Boeing manufactured inadequate and defective cockpit doors, and thus made it possible for the hijackers to invade the cockpits and take over the aircraft. Boeing moved to dismiss the lawsuits. The court held that the plaintiffs alleged legally sufficient claims for relief under the laws applicable to the claims, Virginia and Pennsylvania, respectively.

Thus far, three individual complaints have been filed with respect to the Flight 77 crash. They charge Boeing with strict tort liability and negligent design based on an unreasonably dangerous design of the cockpit doors. *See Edwards v. American Airlines, Inc.*, No. 02 Civ. 9234 (brought on behalf of a decedent who was a passenger on Flight 77); *Powell v. Argenbright Security, Inc.*, No. 02 Civ. 10160 (brought on behalf of a decedent who died while working at the Pentagon; *Gallop v. Argenbright Security, Inc.*, No. 03 Civ. 1016 (plaintiffs injured at the Pentagon site). The court dismissed the claims relating to strict liability because

Virginia does not permit recovery on a strict liability theory in product liability cases. *See Sensenbrenner v. Rust, Orling & Neale, Architects, Inc.,* 236 Va. 419, 374 S.E.2d 55, 57 n. 4 (1988).

In regard to the plaintiffs' negligence claim, the court found that the record at that point of litigation did not support Boeing's argument that the invasion and takeover of the cockpit by the terrorists must, as a matter of law, be held to constitute an "efficient intervening act" that breaks the "natural and continuous sequence" flowing from Boeing's allegedly inadequate design. The plaintiffs alleged that Boeing should have designed its cockpit door to prevent hijackers from invading the cockpit, that acts of terrorism, including hijackings of airplanes, were reasonably foreseeable, and that the lives of passengers, crew, and ground victims would be imminently in danger from such hijackings. Virginia law does not require Boeing to have foreseen precisely how the injuries suffered on September 11, 2001, would be caused, as long as Boeing could reasonably have foreseen that "some injury" from its negligence "might probably result." *See Blondel v. Hays,* 241 Va. 467, 403 S.E.2d 340, 344 (1991). Given the critical nature of the cockpit area and the inherent danger of crash when a plane is in flight, one cannot say that Boeing could not reasonably have foreseen the risk flowing from an inadequately constructed cockpit door.

Moreover, the danger that a plane could crash if unauthorized individuals invaded and took over the cockpit was the very risk that Boeing should reasonably have foreseen. "Privacy" within a cockpit means very little if the door intended to provide security is not designed to keep out potential intruders. Further, the plaintiffs alleged that Boeing could reasonably have foreseen that terrorists would try to invade the cockpits of airplanes, and that easy success on their part, because cockpit doors were not designed to prevent easy opening, would be imminently dangerous to passengers, crew, and ground victims. As such, the judge ruled that the plaintiffs' allegations that duty and proximate cause existed could not be dismissed as a matter of law on the basis of the record now before the court.

*Motion to Dismiss Claims Arising out of the Crash of
United Air Lines Flight 93*

The successors of the passengers who died in the crash of United Air Lines Flight 93 in Shanksville alleged claims against Boeing based on strict tort liability, for an unreasonably dangerous design of the cockpit doors; negligence, for failure to design cockpit doors and accompanying locks in a manner that would prevent hijackers and/or passengers from accessing the cockpit; and express or implied warranty, for creating a product that was unfit for the purposes for which it was designed, intended, and used.

Boeing asked the court to hold that since the terrorists who hijacked the airplanes were not the intended users of the cockpit doors, one cannot say that the doors were unreasonably dangerous or unsafe in relation to the use that terrorists would be expected to make of the doors. Clearly, however, the intended users of the cockpit doors were not the terrorists who broke through them, but the pilots who had the right to protection from unwanted intrusion, and the passengers who had the right to believe that the pilots could continue to guide the plane, free from intrusion, to ensure their safe arrival at their intended destination. If, as Boeing argues, a person who breaks through a door is considered to be an unintended user, no manufacturer of a door and lock system could ever be liable. The intended user of a door is the person who wishes it to be closed and stay closed, not the person who can easily force it open. The pilots and passengers are not mere "casual bystanders," but people with a vital stake in the door's performing its intended purpose. *See* Restatement (Second) Torts § 402A, Comments (l) and (o) (intended users include "those who are passively enjoying the benefit of the product, as in the case of passengers in automobiles or airplanes . . . casual bystanders, and others who may come in contact with the product, as in the case of employees of the retailer, or a passer-by injured by an exploding bottle, or a pedestrian hit by an automobile have been denied recovery").

Boeing may be able to show that the cockpit doors were not unreasonably dangerous, and that it was not unreasonable to design them to provide privacy without making them impenetrable. At this point, however, the judge found that it was inappropriate for him to make such a determination. The record would have to be developed to show if the cockpit doors, incapable of keeping out unwanted intruders, were unreasonably dangerous, taking into consideration: 1) the gravity of the danger posed by the design; 2) the likelihood that the danger would occur; 3) the feasibility of a safer design; 4) the adverse consequences to the product and to the consumer that would result from a safer design; 5) the usefulness and desirability of the product; 6) the likelihood that the product would cause injury and the probable seriousness of the injury; 7) the availability of a substitute product that meets the same needs and is not unsafe; 8) the manufacturer's ability to eliminate the unsafe character of the product without impairing usefulness or making the product too expensive; 9) the user's ability to avoid danger by the exercise of care in the use of the product; 10) the user's anticipated awareness of the dangers inherent in the product and their avoidability; and 11) the ability of the manufacturer to spread loss through price-setting or insurance coverage.

Boeing argued that the plaintiffs' negligent design claims must be dismissed because it did not owe a duty of care to the plaintiffs, and because its alleged negligence was not the proximate cause of the plaintiffs' damages. The plaintiffs alleged that without the defendant's negligence, the hijackers would not have been able to intrude into the cockpit and take over the airplane. Again, for the reasons previously discussed, the court found that the terrorists' unauthorized entry into the cockpit was not unforeseeable and did not constitute an "intervening" or "superseding" cause that could, as a matter of law, break the chain of causation. Accordingly, Boeing's motion to dismiss the complaints against it arising from the crash of Flight 93 into Shanksville was denied.

Update to In re September 11 Litigation,
280 F. Supp 2d 729 (S.D.N.Y. 2003)

Judge Alvin K. Hellerstein thereafter set a trial date of September 24, 2007—2,205 days since the September 11 attacks. Of the original ninety-five suits on behalf of ninety-six victims, fifty-three cases have been settled, one has been dismissed, and forty-one cases remain to be resolved. In an unusual legal procedure, Judge Hellerstein ordered six trials for damages to take place before any trial on the issue of liability, in the hope that both sides would use those figures as an impetus toward settlement. After Judge Hellerstein ruled that the jury would be allowed to hear a few minutes of a cockpit recording that captured the sounds of passengers trying to take control of United Airlines Flight 93 before it crashed into a field in Pennsylvania, fourteen cases settled. Six other cases settled prior this ruling, and as such, only twenty-one cases remained to be tried. Of these remaining cases, one concerns a passenger on United Flight 93; fifteen concern American Flight 77; three involve American Flight 11; and two concern United Flight 175. The settlements were a direct result of Judge Hellerstein's decision to have the damages be tried before any liability was determined. Judge Hellerstein expressed his decision in that he did not want anyone to reduce the issue to money, and he expressed dissatisfaction with the government's resistance in releasing "sensitive security information" that had delayed the preparation for a liability trial. On October 17, 2007, however, Judge Hellerstein ruled that he would exclude some of the plaintiffs' more sensational and speculative evidence in the trial, which will probably hasten the pace of settlements. As of October 17,

2007, only twelve wrongful death cases and four active personal injury cases remained. Specifically, Judge Hellerstein ruled that the jury would not be allowed to see photographs of at least one of the hijackers and one of the passengers killed on September 11 taken when they passed through a security checkpoint at Dulles International Airport, where American Airlines Flight 77 originated. Judge Hellerstein also excluded testimony from C. Everett Koop, a former United States surgeon general, "to the effect that" a passenger killed on American Airlines Flight 77 would have gone on to be surgeon general, a cabinet member, a senior delegate to the World Health Organization, and "dean of a major school of public health" as speculative, and that the passenger had been living "paycheck to paycheck" as a doctor before he died.

PART II

The Multimillion-Dollar Claim of a Twenty-One-Year-Old Rape Victim against Her Landlord for Inadequate Security

Summit v. Forest Town National Housing Association

The Facts of the Case

The following case study is based on a compilation of several premises liability actions the author has defended at trial. All names are fictitious. The comments following each section are based on interviews with actual jurors who served on the trials.

Ladies and gentlemen, have you reached your verdict?
We have, your Honor.
Madam foreman, in the matter entitled Summit v. Forest Town National Housing Association, *what say you?*

And so, after a seven-week trial that followed three years of pretrial litigation and six months of exhaustive and unrelenting trial preparations, the jury, in a matter of seconds, would tell the parties to this long-anticipated trial their respective fates.

For the plaintiff, the stakes were high. Previously a vibrant twenty-one-year-old college student with a lifetime of promise ahead of her, she now faced decades of therapy and medical care, and a very uncertain future, all as a result of a gruesome incident that occurred years earlier while she was returning to her apartment after having gone to the movies with her friend. That night, as she entered the lobby of her building and proceeded to walk into the elevator, so did a young male. He followed her off the elevator on the eighth floor, dragged her up the stairs and onto the roof of the building, raped her over the course of nearly twenty minutes, and slashed her chest and shoulders with a knife, leaving her with permanent physical, mental, and emotional injuries.

This lawsuit, and the potential for a large monetary recovery, was the plaintiff's only legitimate hope for financial security. Although she had been performing well in college, this incident necessitated her withdrawing from school in her junior year. Her inability to overcome the trauma associated with this occurrence rendered it a virtual certainty that her academic career would never be resumed.

The defendant similarly faced enormous risk. Although its $1 million in general liability coverage normally afforded more than ample protection, a verdict well in excess of that amount was a distinct possibility. With assets exceeding $20 million, the principals of Forest Town National Housing Association were capable of satisfying such a judgment, and a restraining order obtained by the plaintiff's lawyer two years before the trial began prevented them from transferring a significant portion of their corporate assets. Punitive damages, for which the principals were uninsured, were also being sought by the plaintiff.

When the stakes are so high, it is not only the parties whose futures the juries decide. Oftentimes the futures of the respective lawyers are also decided. A multimillion-dollar verdict would mean more money through future case referrals to the plaintiff's lawyer than the one-third fee the lawyer would receive for handling the case before the court. An unsuccessful verdict for the defense lawyer could mean not only the loss of a client for the firm, but also a permanent derailment of the lawyer's career as a trial lawyer, whereas a victory could produce an avalanche of assignments from insurance carriers nationwide.

So before presenting the jury's verdict in the case of *Summit v. Forest Town National Housing Association*, this part of the book will review the strategies developed by both lawyers, and assess the respective strengths and weaknesses of their cases.

The Parties' Contentions

Plaintiff

The plaintiff had the burden of establishing negligence on behalf of the defendants and providing sufficient evidence to show that such negligence was a cause of the attack. To establish negligence, the plaintiff would have to focus on the building itself, to demonstrate that the building, on the date of the occurrence, did not have reasonable security features.

The landlord was under a statutory duty only to provide working front-door locks. Because the building was so equipped, the plaintiff would have to proceed under a common law theory of negligence—that regardless of their compliance with the statute, the defendants were nevertheless negligent for failing to take greater safety precautions.

The plaintiff also would argue that the attack was caused by the building's security lapses. Therefore, Ms. Summit needed to show that she was attacked by someone who would not have had access to the premises if additional security features had been in place on the day of the crime.

Defendant

The defendant's strategy would be to show that the assailant may have actually known Ms. Summit, and specifically chosen her as his victim. The defense could then argue that because the plaintiff was an intended—rather than a random—victim, the assailant would not have been deterred from entering the premises and the condition of the building was therefore not a cause of the attack. The defendant would also contend that the security features provided by the landlord were reasonable under the circumstances, and hence the building owners were not negligent. The defendant would argue that the mere fact that a crime was committed in the building does not equate to negligence, as no building is immune from criminal activity by third persons.

Lastly, the defendants would seek to have 100 percent of the responsibility for the attack apportioned upon the assailant.

The Plaintiff's Case

Preliminary Matters

The plaintiff's lawyer was retained by her family five weeks after the incident occurred. Immediately, the lawyer faced his first dilemma: Should he contact his friends in the media and advise them of his proposed $28 million lawsuit against one of the region's top real estate conglomerates, or should he forego the self-aggrandizing publicity and use the intervening months to gain a head start in preparing his case? The lawyer made a tactical decision to trade the benefits of any such publicity for the advantage of commencing his investigation of the incident without formally starting the litigation, which might put the defendant or its insurance company on notice of his intent to bring such a lawsuit.

Because the applicable statute of limitation was two years, the lawyer reasoned that if he began his investigation surreptitiously, the defendant and its insurance company would be content to allow months to go by without undertaking any preparatory actions.

As it turned out, even though the defendant notified its broker of the occurrence, the carrier made no effort to conduct any investigation of the incident until it formally received lawsuit papers from the plaintiff's lawyer. Brilliantly, and against the temptation to seek a prompt, pre-lawsuit settlement of the claim, the plaintiff's lawyer waited to file the lawsuit papers until fourteen months after the date of the crime. So, after fourteen months, the defendant had nothing. Following is what the plaintiff had.

Plaintiff's Investigation

During the two-year period before Ms. Summit's rape, eight other violent crimes were reported to have occurred in the building. Four elderly women were mugged (three at gunpoint, one at knifepoint), two people were slashed (reportedly drug-related occurrences), one teenager was assaulted, and another person was sexually assaulted. Four of the crime victims still lived in the building and, with little effort, the plaintiff's investigator obtained sworn statements from them describing their respective ordeals and more important, documenting their complaints about the security lapses within the building.

The plaintiff also located and obtained a statement from the building's former superintendent, who had been employed at the building for over six years. Without hesitation, this former employee gave a vivid account of problems that regularly occurred within the premises. Loitering, drug transactions, and the presence of unauthorized persons in the building were described as "routine" by someone who was not only present in the building seven days a week, but who was also employed by building management and partly responsible for the tenants' safety.

Clearly the plaintiff's lawyer had made great progress in supporting the plaintiff's case, long before the claim had ever been presented.

There was more. A simple "freedom of information request" enabled the plaintiff to secure records from the police precinct office, setting forth—by category—the total number of crimes reported for the particular building over the last six years, as well as the total number of crimes reported for the same period throughout the entire precinct that included the building. These reports gave not only detailed accounts of prior criminal activity throughout the entire community, they were also replete with the names of nearly one hundred potential witnesses, who could ultimately provide valuable testimony about the unsafe nature of the overall vicinity, including the building in the case.

The plaintiff also obtained photographs of the rear entrance door in an open position (the former superintendent explained that his staff would often prop open the door whenever they mopped the floor, or whenever deliveries were made to the building).

The plaintiff also learned much about the building itself. The dwelling was erected in 1958. It was twelve stories high with six apartments on each floor. On the night of Ms. Summit's attack, slightly more than two hundred residents lived in the building, including sixty-five families. There were two passenger elevators and one freight elevator, as well as two internal staircases that went from the basement to the roof.

The building had two entrances, including the previously mentioned rear door. The main entrance consisted of a set of double doors that opened to the vestibule, and another set of doors that opened into the lobby. The outside doors were unlocked. The inner doors were equipped with locks. Entry could be gained only by using a key, or by someone "buzzing" a visitor into the building. The intercom system included a panel in the vestibule area, and closed-circuit cameras in each apartment enabled the tenants to see a person in the vestibule before "buzzing" them into the building. The building did not have a doorman, although management did provide a lobby guard from 9:00 A.M. to 5:00 P.M., Monday through Friday.

The Complaint

So now, fourteen months after Ms. Summit was brutally raped, and possessing all the above information and ammunition, the plaintiff was ready to bring forth her claim. Instead of sending a letter of representation or attempting to make any contact with the landlord's insurance company, the plaintiff's lawyer chose to file the lawsuit. The complaint alleged negligence on behalf of the building owners for failing to provide reasonable security features at their premises, and for failing to protect the tenants from foreseeable criminal activity. The complaint further alleged that the lack of reasonable security features caused the plaintiff's injuries. A claim for punitive damages was also set forth, asserting that the defendant's total disregard for tenants' safety constituted reckless behavior. The complaint sought $28 million in damages.

The complaint was forwarded to the landlord's insurance carrier, providing the carrier (as the plaintiff hoped) with its first notice of a lawsuit that had been planned for over one year. A prominent local insurance defense firm was retained, and the case was assigned to a young trial lawyer who, despite considerable successes early in his career, had never before handled a case of this magnitude.

Because the plaintiff had conducted its own discovery before filing the lawsuit, its strategy was to prosecute the case quickly and be ready for trial in less than one year. Conversely, the defendant—who required three months just to set up a meeting with the building owners and go through their various records—wanted to stretch out the pretrial litigation process over two years.

Plaintiff's Retention of Experts

The plaintiff retained numerous experts to bolster the case and to testify at trial. The first expert retained was Mr. Mo Mayce, a retired chief of police from New York City, who recently formed his own security consulting firm for companies and landowners. His testimony would focus on the prevalence of criminal activity in the general neighborhood and the inadequacy of the defendant's security features in place at the building. Mr. Mayce surveyed the building less than two months after the occurrence and made a list of nine security lapses. These security deficiencies included inadequate illumination in the staircases and rear entrance doors that were not self-locking. Mr. Mayce also opined that the building was prone to criminal activity because it was located less than one hundred feet from a major thoroughfare, affording easy avenues of escape for a criminal.

A leading psychiatrist, Dr. Emma Brent, was retained to address issues about her ongoing treatment of Ms. Summit, and to testify about the trauma suffered by rape victims and the counseling the plaintiff would continue to require in future years. Dr. Brent authored two books on the subject of rape trauma, and was a noted speaker on post-traumatic stress disorder. As the plaintiff's treating psychiatrist, Dr. Brent had been working closely with her since she first sought counseling, approximately four months after the attack.

To support the contention that Ms. Summit's earning capacity had been diminished by the occurrence, the plaintiff retained a "work placement" specialist, who would review the plaintiff's scholastic and employment history and render projections about her lost earnings resulting from the incident. The plaintiff also retained a professor of economics, who would take those figures and, using appropriate statistics, would project the future value of those losses properly adjusted for inflation.

The plaintiff's team of experts was also complemented by Ms. Summit's treating orthopedic and neurological surgeons, as well as a nurse who prepared a "life-care plan" for the plaintiff's future medical needs. The plan ranged from simple supplies and prescription medicines to projected therapy and nursing costs the plaintiff would be expected to incur when she reached middle and old age. Based upon these figures, the plaintiff presented a firm settlement demand of $6.5 million.

Plaintiff's Strategy

Hence, the plaintiff's strategy had taken the following form:

- Crime was prevalent throughout the neighborhood that encompassed the defendant's building.
- The security features at the premises were grossly insufficient.
- The building owners knew of numerous prior crimes within the premises and were indifferent to their tenants' safety.
- The assailant gained entry into the building and raped and assaulted Ms. Summit specifically due to the lack of appropriate safety features.
- Ms. Summit, who had been studying to become a teacher, would never be able to achieve her career goals.
- The plaintiff's loss of enjoyment of life, lost earnings, and medical expenses were projected to be nearly $28 million.

The Defendant's Case

No firm evidence suggested there was merit to the defendant's primary defense argument—that the assailant knew Ms. Summit and may have stalked her before the incident and, conceivably, simply followed her into the building as she unlocked the front door with her key. No arrests were ever made, although the detective who led the investigation into the crime expressed his belief about the identity of a potential suspect. The plaintiff vehemently denied knowing the assailant's identity, although she told the police she recognized a necklace her assailant had been wearing as "looking slightly familiar," similar to a necklace she had given to an old boyfriend a year earlier.

Given the absence of direct evidence to support its contentions, the defendant retained a criminologist, Dr. Joseph Nathaniel, to re-create the crime. The defendant hoped Dr. Nathaniel would conclude, from selective circumstantial evidence, that the assailant deliberately chose Ms. Summit as his victim in advance of the attack and, in all likelihood, knew of her whereabouts earlier that evening, stalked her as she went to the movies with her friend, and followed her through the front door as she returned home that evening. The defense would use Dr. Nathaniel to try to convince the jury that the assault would have occurred regardless of the security at the building, and that the security features of the building were therefore not the proximate cause of the occurrence.

The defendant also retained its own building security expert, Mr. Ed Lerner, who, like Mr. Mayce, was a retired police chief. Unlike Mr. Mayce, Mr. Lerner believed the building was satisfactorily secured on the night of the rape, and that the landlord therefore fulfilled its duty to provide reasonable security measures.

The defense lawyer was so focused on challenging the claims of liability, that not until the eve of trial did the defense retain appropriate medical experts to rebut expected claims concerning Ms. Summit's damages.

The defendant's lead expert on damages was Dr. Mel Dauber, whose opinion about a rape victim's potential to overcome the trauma related to the event was often thought to be influenced by his $4,000 daily fee for providing expert testimony. There were better witnesses, to be sure, but two noted psychiatrists turned down the assignment, and Dr. Dauber was the best psychiatric expert the defense could retain with the trial less than three weeks away.

Pretrial Matters and Jury Selection

Finally, the parties were ready for jury selection. One last try at a settlement was ordered by Judge Bernard, who, while enjoying a reputation as being among the fairest judges in the country, was nevertheless anxious to see this case settle. It was obvious, however, that a settlement was not forthcoming. The plaintiff's settlement demand never wavered from the original figure of $6.5 million. For the first time, the defendant proposed a counteroffer, representing to the plaintiff that it would agree to settle the case for $1 million provided the plaintiff accepted a structure of the settlement that, in effect, reduced the present value of the $1 million to $600,000. That offer was rejected, and no further settlement discussions were held until the plaintiff formally represented to the court that the defendant was acting in bad faith for not settling the lawsuit. Finally, after the building owner's personal lawyer exerted tremendous pressure, the landlord's insurance carrier offered the full limits of the $1 million policy. Again, the offer was rejected. The respective lawyers reaffirmed that the case would be tried to a verdict, and Judge Bernard ordered the prompt commencement of jury selection.

The parties' strategies for selecting a jury were simple. The plaintiff wanted to select young, working-class men or women, preferably apartment dwellers, who seemed sympathetic to the plaintiff's plight. School teachers, nurses, or artists would be strong candidates. Conversely, the defendant was hoping that middle-aged homeowners, perhaps bankers or businesspersons who were somewhat immune to the concerns of suburban apartment dwellers, would end up in the jury box.

After three days of jury selection, during which eight potential jurors asked to be excused because they felt their sympathy for the plaintiff might influence their verdict, four women and two men were chosen to serve as the jurors for this trial. Five of the jurors were over forty years of age, and four were homeowners. The defendant was pleased with the composition of the jury. The plaintiff was concerned.

The Trial

The Plaintiff's Witnesses

From the moment the plaintiff's lawyer began formulating his trial strategy, he planned that Ms. Summit would be the first witness called to the stand during the plaintiff's presentation of evidence. However, when the sixth and final juror was sworn in, the plaintiff's lawyer drastically altered his trial strategy. He believed the individuals selected as jurors were not sympathetic enough to Ms. Summit's plight and that they needed to be "conditioned" to the trauma that she experienced, and would continue to experience, as a result of the rape. Therefore, the plaintiff opted to call Dr. Brent, the psychiatric expert, as the first witness. Having worked with Dr. Brent in the past, the plaintiff's lawyer was confident that Dr. Brent would impressively convey the horrific ordeal Ms. Summit experienced, so that by the time Ms. Summit testified the jurors would be receptive—and sympathetic—to Ms. Summit's situation.

This tactic also surprised the defendant, who spent the preceding weeks preparing primarily for the cross-examination of Ms. Summit. Dr. Brent had not been expected to testify until later in the trial.

DR. BRENT. Dr. Brent portrayed a picture of a young woman whose life was shattered as a result of the encounter with her assailant. Dr. Brent testified that she had provided therapy for over sixty rape victims in the past three years and, over the defendant's objections, described Ms. Summit as among the most dire of all her patients. The plaintiff's lawyer successfully elicited testimony from Dr. Brent about the harrowing nature of the incident itself, which is then magnified by a sense of isolation from the victim's family and friends. Dr. Brent noted that an overwhelming number of rape victims are unable to resume their normal day-to-day activities, including, but not limited to, returning to their career paths, resuming relationships with close friends, and continuing their education. Dr. Brent diagnosed the plaintiff as suffering from post-traumatic rape disorder, and discussed in detail the manifestations of that condition being shown by Ms. Summit.

On cross-examination, the defendant challenged Dr. Brent's impartiality by questioning her fee for testifying in court, but she told the jury that as Ms. Summit's treating psychiatrist, she was waiving her fee for testifying at trial and instead was concerned about the plaintiff's well-being.

Comment:

The plaintiff's calculated decision to call Dr. Brent as the lead witness was well received by the jury. Dr. Brent eloquently impressed upon the jury the trauma all rape victims experience and, in particular, the tremendous difficulty and lack of progress Ms. Summit has had with her therapy in attempting to overcome the occurrence. Importantly, the fact that Dr. Brent was a treating therapist rather than an expert retained solely for the purposes of testifying at trial, was not lost upon the jurors. In short, the plaintiff was clearly on the offensive as the trial began.

MS. LOPEZ AND MS. STEINBERG. The plaintiff's second and third witnesses were residents of the building who had been victims of crime during the twelve months before the assault on Ms. Summit. Ms. Lopez, a soft-spoken woman of approximately sixty-five years of age, testified that she was mugged at gunpoint as she was walking from the incinerator room to her apartment. She testified that the assailant pulled the gun out of the inside pocket of his sport coat, ordered her to freeze, pointed the gun at her head, and demanded that she hand over her necklace and her rings. She explained that as she nervously handed over her jewelry, the assailant struck her on the right side of her body with the gun, causing her to fall to the ground. The assailant fled down a flight of stairs and was not apprehended.

The witness then stated that she reported the incident to building management, and for several weeks following the attack, she noted that the lobby guard was somewhat more careful in his patrol of the building. She explained that soon after that time, however, the nominal increase in building security was gone.

On cross-examination, the defendant's lawyer was careful to avoid agitating the jury by challenging Ms. Lopez's testimony. Rather, the lawyer pointed out that Ms. Lopez had lived in the building for twenty-one years and, with the exception of this particular incident, felt relatively safe within the premises. Through Ms. Lopez, the defendant was also able to show that during the entire twenty-one-year period she lived in the building, the building was always equipped with front-door locks that, with minor exception, were always working satisfactorily.

Ms. Steinberg was permitted to testify about the criminal act perpetrated upon her six months before Ms. Summit's assault. The defendant had contested, outside the jury's presence, that Ms. Steinberg's testimony was cumulative and that she should be precluded from testifying. Over that objection, the plaintiff was permitted to call Ms. Steinberg to the stand.

As did the prior witness, Ms. Steinberg described the mugging that occurred as she and her husband, both in their sixties, were waiting in the lobby for the elevator. Although they were not physically injured, Ms. Steinberg stated that she is still afraid to leave her apartment for fear of being mugged once again.

Ms. Steinberg, a twelve-year resident of the building, was permitted to respond to questions about whether she had ever observed individuals loitering in her building. The witness stated that she occasionally saw unknown individuals congregating in the lobby of the building, and that she complained to building management about several instances, insisting that they do something about this problem.

On cross-examination, the witness acknowledged that the building is equipped with an intercom and buzzer system, and she conceded that, on occasion, she herself has "buzzed" people into the building without properly checking their identification on the video monitor. In addition, the defense lawyer emphasized the total dissimilarity between the occurrences concerning the witness and the crime committed on the plaintiff.

Comment:

Although these two witnesses served to document that prior crimes had been committed in the building, the jury noted that neither woman was seriously physically injured, and almost seemed to dismiss their experiences as events that could be expected when living in a large metropolitan city.

While the witnesses undeniably had been prior victims of crime within the defendant's premises, their crimes were quite dissimilar from the crime perpetrated on Ms. Summit, and their testimony was not very effective.

The jurors noted that both women were longtime residents of the building and, except for these isolated incidents, lived in relative safety for long periods of time.

The plaintiff's lawyer sensed that the prior crime victims' testimony was not enthusiastically received by the jury, and for that reason, called Sergeant Kirschner as his next witness. (Sergeant Kirschner had been subpoenaed to appear in court pursuant to a "so ordered" subpoena issued by Judge Bernard.)

SERGEANT KIRSCHNER. After establishing the sergeant's credentials, which included overseeing hundreds of investigations into crimes reported in his precinct, the plaintiff's lawyer submitted as evidence eight incident reports prepared by the city police department. The reports described the eight prior crimes committed in the building during the two-year period before the attack on the plaintiff. The court permitted the witness to read the sections of the reports concerning the nature of the crimes, as reported by the victims to the responding police officer. Sergeant Kirschner read about the four muggings, including those of Ms. Lopez and Ms. Steinberg, the two slashings, the assault on a teenage resident of the building, and the sexual assault.

On cross-examination, the sergeant stated that the crime statistics for this particular building were "no better and no worse" than for other high-rise buildings within the precinct. The court permitted the officer to render an opinion, based upon his expertise as a police officer, that most sexually related crimes are committed by assailants who are familiar with their victims. According to Sergeant Kirschner, rapes in particular were oftentimes perpetrated by assailants who had previous encounters with their victims.

Comment:
The plaintiff's lawyer had the sergeant read the police reports in chronological order to highlight to the jury that five of the eight previously reported crimes were committed less than seven months before Ms. Summit was raped. The reports were admitted into evidence, and it could safely be assumed that the plaintiff's lawyer would refer to them in his closing argument. The jurors noted a pattern to the reported crimes, including the fact that the crimes were becoming more serious and were occurring with greater frequency in recent months.

The defendant scored its first real points during the trial when the court permitted Sergeant Kirschner to provide opinion testimony that most sex crimes are committed by assailants who know their victims, rather than choosing them at random.

CHIEF MO MAYCE. After highlighting his experience as a chief of police, as well as his more recent experience as a security consultant to numerous companies, Chief Mayce was qualified as an expert in security, without a defense objection.

Chief Mayce stressed the need for building owners to respond to the dramatic rise in crime by enhancing their building's safety features. He described various safety measures, ranging from simple magnetic locks, to state-of-the-art computerized systems that were being implemented by numerous landowners.

The plaintiff's lawyer took Chief Mayce through his inspection of the premises, and had him explain the litany of security lapses at the building:

- The front-door locks appeared not to have been changed in four years, and the defendant's own records showed that forty five families requested replacement keys during that time period because their allotted keys were lost.
- The lobby guard was merely decorative, as he neither checked the identification of anyone entering the building nor monitored the activities of anyone who entered or left the premises.
- The intercom system was faulty, as records showed it was repaired four times during the month of the plaintiff's attack.
- The emergency exit "fire door" did not comply with building code ordinances, as it did not automatically close shut after opening.
- The lighting in the staircases and elevators was insufficient.
- The landlords failed to rid the building of loiterers.
- The landlords failed to evict a known drug dealer who lived in the building.
- The building was not a participant in a neighborhood crime prevention program.

Chief Mayce testified that, in his expert opinion, the security features of the building were grossly insufficient. According to Chief Mayce, the lack of appropriate security was the primary cause of the attack on Ms. Summit. He described the rape as a crime of opportunity, stating that if the building had more efficient security, the assailant would have been either deterred or prevented from entering the location.

On cross-examination, Chief Mayce conceded that he was only speculating about whether improved lighting, a more efficient self-locking fire exit door, or any other such enhanced safety feature would have prevented the crime. Regarding his opinion that the attack on Ms. Summit was a random crime of opportunity, Chief Mayce was somewhat taken aback when the lawyer inquired about whether he had looked into Ms. Summit's prior relationships, and the fact that her assailant was wearing a necklace that "looked familiar" and similar to a necklace Ms. Summit said she gave to an old boyfriend. The chief also placed no significance on the assailant having been described as roughly the same age as the plaintiff.

Comment:

Chief Mayce's testimony was well received by the jurors. From the plaintiff's perspective, it was essential to document, one by one, the various deficiencies in the building's security. The jurors noted that there were virtually no improvements in the building's security for the last two years, despite a dramatic increase in crimes reported in the neighborhood. The jurors found Chief Mayce to be a very credible witness, and were not at all concerned about his $2,500 witness fee, or the $150,000 he earned as a consultant.

Importantly, however, the jurors noted Chief Mayce's surprise at being questioned about Ms. Summit's past relationships.

MR. BARRY HAGAT. The plaintiff subpoenaed its next witness, Mr. Barry Hagat, the principal owner of Forest Town National Housing Association. Mr. Hagat was questioned at length about his proprietary interests in several real estate developments, including Forest Town units.

The plaintiff's lawyer established that with over sixty families living in the building, the rent roll for the relevant year exceeded $750,000.

The plaintiff attempted to portray Mr. Hagat as being aloof about the security concerns of his tenants and, despite his lawyer's best preparations, Mr. Hagat seemed to fall into that carefully laid trap. Several times, Mr. Hagat stated that issues such as security concerns were the responsibility of his building manager. He indicated that not until the commencement of this lawsuit did he become aware of the eight prior crimes reported in his building.

On cross-examination, the defendant brought out the fact that, despite generating over $750,000 in rental income, the building did not produce a profit, due to a soft real estate market that contributed to the existence of empty units in the building.

Mr. Hagat emphasized the security features that were present in the building, and documented the $45,000 spent for a lobby attendant each year; the $150,000 allotted per year for a superintendent, maintenance personnel, and building upkeep; and the enormous costs associated with installing and maintaining the intercom system.

The defendant was permitted to present the exorbitant costs associated with hiring doormen and security/patrol officers as justification for the lack of such personnel at the building. Mr. Hagat testified that his research concerning such expenditures suggested that hiring a full-time doorman would have necessitated a 15 percent increase in monthly rental charges. An informal poll of the building residents indicated that the large majority of tenants opposed such a rent increase.

Comment:
Through discovery, the plaintiff's lawyer knew that Mr. Hagat was not involved in the day-to-day operations of the building, and he successfully portrayed him as such during the trial. The jurors expressed surprise at the costs associated with hiring building personnel, and several jurors seemed receptive to the cost-benefit argument raised by the defendant.

However, despite the fact that the real estate market had turned "soft," none of the jurors seemed overly concerned about Mr. Hagat's financial security.

MRS. SHIRLEY SUE SUMMIT. Interrupting the parade of liability witnesses was Mrs. Shirley Sue Summit, the plaintiff's mother.

Having become well acquainted with Mrs. Summit over the past two years, the lawyers knew that she would be a formidable witness, detailing the horror that has been endured not only by the plaintiff, but by the plaintiff's entire family.

On direct examination, Mrs. Summit began by describing the phone call she received from the police, informing her that her daughter had been raped and was receiving care in the West-Side Hospital emergency room.

She described the nightmares her daughter still has, and how she has cared for her daughter since she withdrew from college to live at home. Mrs. Summit also provided a comparison of her daughter—how she was before the rape, and how she has been ever since.

The defendant chose not to cross-examine Mrs. Summit.

Comment:
By now, the jury was anxious to hear the plaintiff testify. Calling Mrs. Summit served as a natural prelude to the plaintiff's testimony, and seemed to heighten the jury's desire to hear from the plaintiff herself.

Importantly, the plaintiff's lawyer was careful to limit the testimony of Mrs. Summit, thus avoiding the possibility of having the victim's mother detract from the plaintiff's own testimony.

THE PLAINTIFF. As the trial entered its eighth day of testimony, it was time for the plaintiff to take the stand. Renee Summit, now twenty-three years old, was called as the day's first witness.

In a soft-spoken voice, Ms. Summit provided some details about her high school and college careers, her hobbies, her friends, and her dreams. She elected to attend a local college so she could live on her own yet still be close to her family. She was an "A" student in high school, held a part-time job as a cashier, and spent her free time reading and going out with friends.

She said she enjoyed college, although she admitted that, at times, it was a difficult adjustment period in her life.

She moved into the defendant's building shortly after she started her freshman year in college. The rent was affordable, her parents lived less than an hour away, and she had a ten-minute bus ride to the campus. She described the two years or so she had lived in the building—up to the night of the attack—as having been uneventful.

On the day of the attack, Ms. Summit called a girlfriend and suggested they see a movie, as they had often done before. She left her apartment, took a cab to her girlfriend's apartment, and then together she and her friend went to the movie theater. Because it was a weeknight, they decided they would not go out after the movie. Instead, each went home in separate cabs. Ms. Summit's cab dropped her off in front of her building. She opened the lobby door with her key, and waited for the elevator. She stated she did not recall whether anyone else entered the building at or around the same time, or whether other people were waiting for the elevator in the lobby.

When the elevator door opened, she entered and pressed the button for the eighth floor. As the door began to close, a young man she did not recognize hurried into the elevator but did not press a button for a particular floor. The elevator went directly to the eighth floor and the plaintiff got out of the car, as did the individual who was in the elevator with her. She walked down the hall toward her apartment, and as she reached the door leading to the internal staircase, the person following her put his hands over her mouth and dragged her onto the staircase, up four flights of stairs, and onto the roof landing. Once there, he pulled out a knife, threatened to kill her, and used the knife to rip off her clothes. He proceeded to rape her over the course of nearly twenty minutes. She testified that she was hysterical during the entire time. She said the assailant kept asking her questions she did not understand, and when she apparently failed to give a satisfactory answer, he stabbed her in the chest and shoulders. When the assailant fled, she was able to get to her apartment and call the police.

For the remainder of the morning, Ms. Summit described her physical and emotional injuries, recounting her counseling and therapy sessions and the flashbacks she continued to experience. Photographs of the scarring to her shoulders and chest were admitted into evidence.

Ms. Summit gave a detailed description of the assailant to the police, but he was never apprehended. She denied having any knowledge about why anyone would do this to her. She also stated that for two years, she lived with the fear that she possibly contracted the AIDS virus, until she finally had a test that came back negative.

The defense lawyer was very careful to be noncombative during his cross-examination of Ms. Summit. Instead, he elaborated on her "failure to recall" whether anyone followed her into the building, and her failure to recall whether anyone else was in the lobby while she was waiting for the elevator.

Ms. Summit admitted telling a detective that the assailant was wearing a religious necklace that looked very similar to a necklace she gave to a former boyfriend two years earlier. She was adamant that, although her ex-boyfriend had been abusive to her, the assailant was neither her ex-boyfriend nor anyone she ever associated with him.

The defense lawyer also had the plaintiff acknowledge that at no time during the year preceding the occurrence did she ever complain to building management about a security-related problem. She agreed with the defense lawyer that she knew the building did not have a doorman when she signed the lease, and conceded that she never had any problems in the building until the date of her attack. The plaintiff acknowledged she originally considered moving into a building that had a doorman, but that the rents in such buildings were prohibitive.

Comment:
Both parties accomplished their respective intentions concerning Ms. Summit's testimony. The plaintiff's lawyer portrayed his client as a true victim, in no way causing or contributing to her attack. The jurors were visibly moved during her account of the incident, and shared her frustration that her assailant was never apprehended. Ms. Summit's testimony was very emotional, and there was no doubt the jurors took an immediate liking to the plaintiff.

Appropriately, the defense lawyer did not take a confrontational approach to the plaintiff. Rather, by emphasizing her own testimony regarding her failure to recall whether the assailant followed her into the building, the defense lawyer successfully raised legitimate doubt about whether the security features—or lack thereof—at the building were a causative factor in her attack.

REHABILITATION NURSE, ECONOMICS PROFESSOR, AND WORK-PLACEMENT EXPERT. The plaintiff's final three witnesses were a rehabilitation nurse, a work-placement specialist, and a professor of economics.

Together, they projected the plaintiff's lost earnings to be in excess of $19 million once present-value figures were adjusted upward for current rates of inflation. Similarly, the $800,000 necessary for a lifetime of proper medical care was also adjusted upward to roughly $8.5 million.

With those figures before the jury, the plaintiff rested.

The Defendant's Witnesses

MR. JEROLD DANN. The defendant's first witness was Jerold Dann, managing agent for the building. Mr. Dann explained that nearly 15 percent of the rental income generated by the building is allocated to expenditures for security, including the lobby guard's salary, the superintendent's salary, intercom system upkeep, and regular maintenance costs, such as intercom and lock repairs. Mr. Dann also stated that building management is deeply concerned about residents' safety, and he emphasized that twice a year, representatives from the police department give presentations about ways residents can protect themselves from crime.

The witness acknowledged receiving complaints about loiterers in the lobby. He also acknowledged receiving anonymous phone calls reporting that a third-floor tenant was using his apartment to conduct drug transactions. However, Mr. Dann expressed frustration with the difficulty of trying to evict a tenant without proper evidence of crimes being committed.

Although the witness did not know Ms. Summit personally, he said she had been a very good tenant and he expressed regret about the crime.

On cross-examination, the plaintiff's lawyer reminded Mr. Dann that eight prior crimes had been reported in his building, and challenged him to tell the jury about any specific actions he undertook to improve security following each criminal act. "What security measures were implemented after the first mugging?" asked the lawyer. "What features were installed after the second robbery? How about the third, or the fourth?" The witness responded that it would be impossible to eliminate all crime from the premises, and stated that the building owners continually monitor the situation whenever a crime is reported. The plaintiff's lawyer obtained a concession from the witness that the amount allocated to security (15 percent of the rental income) included the superintendent's salary, but that the superintendent provided only limited security services. Mr. Dann also conceded that one of the lobby guard's main functions was to assist with rent collections and make bank deposits.

Comment:
The jury was impressed with the witness's direct testimony, and seemed surprised that 15 percent of the rental income was expended on security. Hence, the plaintiff accomplished a major feat when Mr. Dann acknowledged that the superintendent's functions were mostly unrelated to security, though his entire salary was included in the 15 percent figure.

The choice of Mr. Dann as the defendant's first witness was important, because to the extent he could, he helped personalize Forest Town Housing. Up until now, the defendant was merely a real estate development company, and it was a proper strategic decision for the defense lawyer to personalize his client as quickly as possible.

MS. NAOMI HANNAH. Ms. Hannah was the self-appointed head of the loosely knit tenants group in the building. According to Ms. Hannah, the tenants' primary concerns with the building have always been related to maintenance. Letters sent by the tenants group to building management routinely stressed the desire for improved maintenance (such as faster response times for apartment repairs) but did not raise any security concerns.

Ms. Hannah's records also showed that the tenants had considered a rent strike two years before the attack on the plaintiff, but again, the threatened rent strike pertained to maintenance issues only.

Comment:
The defendant had hoped that by presenting evidence that the tenants were primarily concerned with maintenance issues, the jury would infer that the tenants were satisfied with the building's security. The jurors, however, were unconvinced of that inference. The jurors believed that if building management was not respon-

sive to maintenance issues, they could deduce that management was similarly unresponsive to security matters.

CHIEF EDWARD LERNER. The defendant's security expert began by immediately acknowledging that the building's security was not state-of-the-art. Chief Lerner was, however, adamant that the existing security features were satisfactory and afforded tenants a comfortable level of safety.

Chief Lerner stated that even with working front-door locks and an intercom system, preventing all unauthorized persons from entering the building was impossible. Significantly, tenants often used the buzzer system to allow individuals into the building without properly checking their identification. Further, because so many persons entered and exited the building daily, an unauthorized person would have little difficulty simply following someone into the building when that person opened the front door.

Chief Lerner summarized his assessment of front-door locks by stating, "Locks are for honest people."

On cross-examination, the plaintiff's lawyer agreed that the costs associated with state-of-the-art security features were prohibitive, and instead questioned Chief Lerner about less expensive security measures. That part of the cross-examination occurred in the following way, with the plaintiff's lawyer asking the questions and Chief Lerner answering them:

"Is a tenant patrol effective in reducing crime?"

"Yes."

"Is a volunteer tenant patrol cost-prohibitive?"

"No."

"Did the building have a tenant patrol?"

"No."

"Is a neighborhood crime watch effective in deterring crime?"

"Yes."

"Is a neighborhood crime watch cost-prohibitive?"

"No."

"Did the building participate in a neighborhood crime watch?"

"Not that I know of."

"Is it important to regularly change front door locks and issue new keys to the tenants?"

"Yes."

"How often would you recommend that be done—every few years?"

"Yes."

"When was the last time it was done prior to my client being raped?"

"I believe about three years before."

"Do you know how many keys were lost and replaced during that time?"

"No."

"Would you imagine it to be more than fifty?"

"Probably."

Comment:
The defendant's cost-benefit argument was challenged successfully when the plaintiff's lawyer noted that the building lacked certain basic security features that were inexpensive, if not completely cost-free. Although the defense lawyer noted that it is up to the tenants to organize tenant patrols and other such tenant-based initiatives, the jurors believed that the landlord was in the best position to foster such programs.

The defendant did, however, use Chief Lerner to confirm just how easily an unauthorized person could gain entry into a building with heavy traffic, regardless of any front-door locks.

DR. MEL DAUBER. Dr. Dauber's testimony centered on his diagnosis that the plaintiff had recovered from post-traumatic rape disorder, which was based on his review of her medical records and his three-hour examination of Ms. Summit earlier in the year. While acknowledging that post-traumatic rape disorder is a legitimate diagnosis for many rape victims, Dr. Dauber stated that, in his opinion, Ms. Summit was not suffering from such a disorder. Stressing the support she had received from her family, Dr. Dauber testified that Ms. Summit, in time, would be able to return to college and ultimately pursue a career in the teaching profession. Dr. Dauber noted that being tested for the AIDS virus two years after the incident was a good indication that the plaintiff was slowly trying to confront the event and take steps to overcome the trauma.

Aside from challenging his credentials and impartiality, the plaintiff's lawyer had Dr. Dauber recap the extensive nature of the counseling and therapy the plaintiff had received since the rape.

Comment:

Because the defendant did not want to shift the focus of the trial from liability to damages, it did not keep Dr. Dauber on the stand any longer than necessary. As expected, Dr. Dauber did not have as much an impact on the jury as Dr. Brent. The jurors gave much more credence to the testimony of Dr. Brent as a treating physician than to Dr. Dauber as an expert paid for his testimony.

DETECTIVE ROBBIE DONHAH. Detective Donhah headed the investigation of the crime. He interviewed Ms. Summit within hours after the incident, while she was receiving emergency room care. There were very few leads and, after three months, the investigation became inactive. No suspects were ever apprehended.

The officer was allowed to testify about studies showing that a large percentage of rapes are committed by persons who know their victims. For that reason, Detective Donhah questioned Ms. Summit at length about her prior relationships. He was particularly intrigued by the plaintiff's statements about the assailant's necklace, but no leads ever evolved from those remarks.

Over vehement objection, the court permitted the witness to state that, in his opinion, Ms. Summit was not being entirely candid with the police about her past relationships. The detective discussed the crime investigation in detail, noting that none of the computer searches for any similar crimes committed in the precinct resulted in useful information.

On cross-examination, the plaintiff's lawyer suggested that the detective's current opinion that his client was being less than candid about her past may be a way for the detective to justify his inability to solve the crime.

Comment:

Because it came from an impartial witness, the detective's testimony supported the defendant's theory that the assailant may have deliberately targeted Ms. Summit as his victim. Also, by eliciting testimony that the plaintiff may not have been entirely cooperative with the investigation, the defendant was able to attack the plaintiff's credibility without needing to directly confront Ms. Summit about her truthfulness.

The jury's focus returned to issues of liability, and Detective Donhah was the perfect prelude to the defendant's star witness, criminologist Anthony Barnell.

DR. BARNELL. Dr. Barnell elaborated on his many credentials, which included a doctoral degree in behavioral science and various awards from police departments across the country for his assistance in designing and implementing strategies for combating crime in inner cities. Dr. Barnell's area of expertise was the study of criminals' minds—the reasons why criminals behave in certain ways, and the measures that would be successful in deterring criminals from committing particular types of crimes.

The court gave Dr. Barnell sufficient latitude to render wide-ranging opinions about the rape of Ms. Summit. According to Dr. Barnell, the plaintiff's hesitancy to supply the detectives with complete information about her social life indicated the she possibly believed someone from her past was somehow involved with the crime. Having studied hundreds of violent crimes, Dr. Barnell concluded that over 70 percent of such crimes are perpetrated by assailants who target specific victims, and that Ms. Summit was, indeed, such a targeted victim.

A key exchange went as follows, with the defendant's lawyer asking the questions and Dr. Barnell answering them:

"Would enhanced security features at a building be more likely to deter a criminal from a random crime or a nonrandomcrime?"

"Random."

"Please explain why."

"Front-door locks and the like help deter only crimes of opportunity. A criminal intending to assault a specific target would not be the type of person deterred from entering a building due to the building's security features."

"In your opinion, would the rape of the plaintiff still have occurred if the building had a tenant patrol?"

"Yes."

"Similarly, would the rape still have occurred even if new door locks had been installed the week before the attack?"

"Yes. The front-door locks were not a factor. Very possibly, the assailant had been following Ms. Summit earlier that evening and simply followed her into the building."

The plaintiff's strategy for cross-examination was not to challenge Dr. Barnell's opinions, but to challenge his credentials for rendering those opinions. The lawyer emphasized that criminology is far from being an exact science, that other jurisdictions have refused to recognize criminology as a legitimate science, and that Dr. Barnell had never even met or spoken with the plaintiff before he testified.

Comment:
The jury's reaction to Dr. Barnell was split. While several jurors were fascinated with the witness's credentials and studies, others were actually insulted by his conclusions about building safety, and his assertions that because Ms. Summit did not want to tell everything about her past, she must therefore somehow be partly responsible for her rape.

REHABILITATION AND ECONOMIC EXPERTS. The defendant called two expert witnesses to counter the cost projections and other testimony of the plaintiff's experts.

The defendant's rehabilitation expert testified that after Ms. Summit received therapy for two more years, he would have no difficulty placing her in a program that would virtually ensure her ability to obtain gainful employment as a teacher.

The defendant's economist projected lifetime figures for lost earnings and future medical care that were less than one-fourth of the figures calculated by his counterpart.

After four weeks of testimony, the parties rested.

Jury Deliberations

The jurors spent two days sorting through the evidence. They focused mainly on the definitions of "reasonable security" and "negligence" and, on two occasions, they asked the judge to read back the definitions of those terms.

They also requested a review of the plaintiff's testimony where she said she "did not recall" if anyone followed her into the building or if anyone was present in the lobby as she waited for the elevator.

The jurors virtually disregarded Mr. Hagat's testimony, considering it to be self-serving. Similarly, they were not overly influenced by the testimony of either security expert, as they believed the building's security features did not require expert explanations.

The eight reported prior crimes in the building had a tremendous impact on the jury. Given the large number of residents who lived in the building, the likelihood of becoming a crime victim in that building was far less than becoming a victim in other buildings in the neighborhood. Nevertheless, the jurors believed that the eight prior crimes were substantial, and warranted specific responses by the landlord. The jurors noted that no improvements were made to the building's security following each previous crime.

On the issue of proximate cause, the jurors suspected that the assailant deliberately targeted the plaintiff, and very possibly knew her and simply followed her into the building. The jurors struggled with this issue before rendering a final verdict.

The Verdict

By a unanimous vote, the jury found the defendant negligent, but found that the defendant's negligence was neither a cause nor a substantial factor contributing to the plaintiff's damages. As a result, the court entered a verdict in favor of the defendant.

The jury expressed sympathy for the plaintiff, but was determined not to have their verdict affected by personal concern for Ms. Summit's future.

The court denied the plaintiff's motion to set aside the verdict.

PART III

State-by-State Overview of Premises Security Cases and Court Decisions

An Analysis of Landlords' and Building Owners' Obligations to Protect Persons from Criminal Activity within Their Premises as Set Forth by the Appellate Courts of All Fifty States

Research contributed by
Richard Lerner, Esq.

Introductory Comments from the Author

My trial preparations for a premises security case in New York, in which a young girl was shot in my client's building and was rendered paralyzed, required travel up and down the east coast as I interviewed witnesses and conducted discovery. One of the out-of-state officials I deposed was represented by a personal lawyer who expressed disbelief that a crime victim in New York could actually bring a negligence action for millions of dollars against a building owner. "We do not have any cases like that here," he proclaimed, somewhat proudly, as I expressed my mutual disbelief that his state would not entertain such a lawsuit.

Even with that background, I was amazed at what our research uncovered as we compiled the following analysis of premises liability cases across the country. If there is a nationwide trend, it is that courts, although reluctantly, appear to be expanding landowners' obligations to protect persons from criminal actions committed on the landowners' premises.

Many states have replaced the "prior similar acts" rule for determining a crime's foreseeability with the much more liberal "totality of the circumstances" approach. The latter method may allow for recovery even when there were no reported prior crimes, let alone prior similar crimes, committed on the premises.

Perhaps judges are expressing their frustration with the national crime epidemic in the same way juries are doing so—by making someone pay.

However, the news for landlords is far from all bad. Many jurisdictions continue to place substantial limitations on a plaintiff's ability to bring negligence actions against landowners for criminal acts committed by third persons. Further, for the first time, courts in numerous states will allow a plaintiff to recover only in proportion to the landowner's share of fault. These same courts also imply that more than 50 percent of liability for the crime must rest with the assailant.

Not surprisingly, states with the highest crime rates tend to have the largest number of decisions delineating landowners' obligations to provide security. Many states are only now beginning to develop a body of law in this area, and their courts continue to look to decisions from other states as nonbinding, yet influential, precedent.

Additionally, courts in many states readily look to the Restatement (Second) of Torts (1965) for guidance. Section 344 is worth noting:

> A possessor of land who holds it open to the public for entry for his business purposes is subject to liability to members of the public while they are upon the land for such a purpose, for physical harm

caused by the accidental, negligent, or intentionally harmful acts of third-persons or animals, and by the failure of the possessor to exercise reasonable care to (a) discover that such acts are being done or are likely to be done, or (b) give a warning adequate to enable the visitors to avoid the harm, or otherwise to protect them against it.

Comment (f) to section 344 further provides:

Since the possessor is not an insurer of the visitor's safety, he is ordinarily under no duty to exercise any care until he knows or has reason to know that the acts of the third person are occurring, or are about to occur. He may, however, know or have reason to know, from past experience, that there is a likelihood of conduct on the part of third persons in general which is likely to endanger the safety of the [*640] visitor even though he has [**39] no reason to expect it on the part of any particular individual. If the place or character of his business, or his past experience, is such that he should reasonably anticipate careless or criminal conduct on the part of the third persons, either generally or at some particular time, he may be under a duty to take precautions against it, and to provide a reasonably sufficient number of servants to afford a reasonable protection.

Our state-by-state analysis is intended only to provide a cursory review of some of the leading premises cases in each state. It is not intended to be a definitive reference, and readers are urged to supplement the cited cases with thoroughly documented research.

UPDATE

Since the publication of the first "state-by-state" overview a few years ago, there have been hundreds of important "premises security" decisions rendered by courts across the country. In populous states such as New York, California, and Texas, appellate decisions are often rendered that continually modify the still evolving area of premises security litigation. Even less populous jurisdictions have addressed important premises security issues, as courts in those states—and every state in between—have struggled to balance the rights of crime victims to seek redress for their injuries, and the rights of property owners, who, it must be recognized, are not ensurers of public safety.

Reviewing the hundreds of decisions cited in this book reveals some interesting trends. The majority of jurisdictions seem to suggest that a landowner may only be held responsible for criminal acts perpetuated upon his or her property by third persons over whom he or she has no control where the landowner had reason to know of the likelihood of criminal activity being committed on his or her property, failed to provide a reasonable level of security under the existing circumstance, and the failure to provide a reasonable level of security despite having knowledge that criminal occurrences were foreseeable was a prominent factor in causing the underlying crime.

The issue of causation has also been the subject of considerable judicial analysis. Assuming a landowner is negligent, under what circumstances should that landowner's negligence be considered a "cause" of the plaintiff's underlying injuries? What if the landlord was negligent, but the plaintiff was assaulted by a co-tenant? What if the landlord was negligent, but the plaintiff was assaulted by someone who was lawfully upon the premises? What if the plaintiff could not establish the assailant's identity or the assailant's means of ingress into the premises? Perhaps the leading decision in this area is the New York case of *Gomez v. New York City Housing Authority*, 249 A.D.2d 175, 672 N.Y.S.2d 676 (N.Y. App. Div. 1998). A few words on this case are in order, as the author had the pleasure of representing the defendant in this case, both at trial and on the ensuing appeal.

Marisella Gomez was a young lady who claimed to have been raped by an unknown individual who she alleged she observed enter her apartment building through an unlocked rear door. The door in question was acknowledged to have been broken for a period of time, and the building concededly had been the scene of prior violent crimes. It was our contention, however, that while the rear door admittedly was broken, the condition of the door was irrelevant- since we presented evidence to suggest that the assailant had actually been afforded voluntarily entrance to the building through the front door. The trial ended in a verdict for the defendant, but the plaintiffs appealed on various issues, and the intermediate appellate court ordered a new trial on evidentiary grounds.

The second trial held no surprises as virtually all of the original witnesses testified and were consistent with their original trial testimony. This time, however, the jury found for the plaintiff, and awarded a total of $500,000 in damages. (Amazing how two different juries can preside over virtually the same trial, and render two different verdicts). The trial court, however, granted our motion to set aside the verdict on the ground that the evidence presented at trial could not support a finding in favor of the plaintiff and entered judgment for the defendant. The trial judge agreed with our contention that there was insufficient evidence to conclude that the assailant was an intruder into the premises, as opposed to either a resident or guest of a resident of the high-rise building who would have had access to the premises, regardless of security. Again, the plaintiffs appealed, and the intermediate appellate court upheld the trial court's decision, agreeing that a verdict for the plaintiff was not supported by the evidence. As a final measure, the plaintiffs appealed the ruling of the intermediate appellate court to the New York State Court of Appeals, the highest court in New York. The decision rendered by that court ultimately reinstated the jury's verdict in favor of the plaintiff. The decision, which has already been cited by scores of other courts, contains language favorable to plaintiffs and defendants in premises security cases. *Gomez* is illustrative of the many issues courts must address in attempting to balance the interests of crime victims and property owners.

Over the past ten years, I have had the pleasure of defending landowners against hundreds of claims brought on behalf of crime victims. Premises security litigation is an exciting area of law. I acknowledge the plaintiffs' lawyers who fight hard to protect the interests of the clients, and I acknowledge my colleagues who work equally hard to protect the interests of landowners.

I look forward to the next edition of this book.

Alabama

Alabama courts strictly limit the situations in which landlords or business owners face liability for criminal acts committed on their premises by third persons.

In the leading case of *Thetford v. City of Clanton*, 605 So. 2d 835 (Ala. 1992), the court held that the duty to protect a person from criminal acts arises only when one's negligence creates a situation in which it is foreseeable that a third person will commit a crime.

Applying the court's holding in *Thetford*, the court in *E.H. v. Overlook Mountain Lodge*, 638 So. 2d 781 (Ala. 1994), dismissed claims of negligence asserted on behalf of six minors who had been assaulted by a third person on a hotel's premises. The court found no evidence to suggest that the hotel should have foreseen the assailant's assault on the plaintiffs.

A similar rationale was applied by the court in *O.H. v. Ballard Realty Co.*, 516 So. 2d 519 (Ala. 1987). The court stated that a duty to take reasonable precautions to protect persons from criminal occurrences may be imposed upon a landowner only in the exceptional cases where the store owner possessed actual or constructive knowledge that the criminal activity was a probability

The issue of foreseeability was addressed by an Alabama court in the case of *Moye v. Gaston Hotels*, 499 So. 2d 1368 (Ala. 1980). In *Moye*, an action for negligent security was brought against a motel on behalf of a decedent who had been shot and killed outside the motel's premises following a dance. The court dismissed the complaint, holding that no evidence of prior similar instances at the premises existed.

In *Dailey v. Housing Authority for Birmingham District*, 639 So. 2d 1343 (Ala. 1994), the court found the defendants had no duty to provide protection to the plaintiff, resulting in a dismissal of the case. The decedent had been killed as the result of cross fire during a gunfight between alleged drug dealers near the defendants' premises. The plaintiffs contended that the defendants assumed a duty to provide security by hiring patrols at the location, and then performed the duty negligently. The court, however, rejected the plaintiffs' argument that the defendants' employment of a security guard gave rise to a duty to protect the decedent from the crime. The court emphasized that the defendants had no reason to suspect that anyone would commit the criminal act upon the victim.

UPDATE

The general rule in Alabama remains that "absent special relationships or circumstances, a person has no duty to protect another from the criminal acts of third persons." *Tenn Tom Bldg. v. Olen, Nicholas and Copeland, P.C.*, 908 So.2d 230, 232(2005).

However, there have been some notable developments in this area. For example, in *Tenn Tom Bldg.*, a landowner sued the defendant after an arsonist had started a fire that damaged the plaintiff's adjoining property. Though the defendant admitted that it was aware of trespassers prior to the arsonist, the court found that this only raised the "possibility" of a trespasser setting a fire, and the plaintiff had to show a "probability" of a trespasser setting a fire.

In *Alabama Dept. of Corrections v. Thompson*, 855 So.2d 1016, 1025 (2003), the court found no duty to protect the plaintiff on the part of a prison that allowed a prisoner to escape and injure the plaintiff. The court held that the prison had to know of a specific threat by the prisoner against the plaintiff before a special circumstance or special relationship existed that would create a duty.

In *Carroll v. Shoney's, Inc.*, 775 So. 2d 753, 756 (2000), the Supreme Court listed the elements necessary to create a duty on behalf of the landowner. The three elements are: (1) the particular criminal conduct must have been foreseeable; (2) the defendant must have possessed "specialized knowledge" of the criminal activity; and (3) the criminal conduct must have been a probability.

Next, the Alabama Supreme Court decided that a special relationship is not created by the fact that the plaintiffs were the defendant's business invitees. *Ex parte McRae's of Alabama*, 703 So.2d 351 (1997).

Not all of the decisions have been defense-oriented. For example, in *Whataburger, Inc. v. Rockwell*, 706 So.2d 1220, 1223 (1997), the Alabama Supreme Court permitted a case to go to a jury where the plaintiff was injured by third parties in a fight in the defendant's parking lot. The court noted that there were factual issues regarding whether the defendant's manager knew that a fight was about to break out but failed to call the police despite this knowledge.

Similarly, in *Rayburn v. Wal-Mart Stores, Inc.*, 776 So.2d 137, 139 (1999), an Alabama court of appeals permitted a plaintiff to take a case to a jury to determine whether the defendant should be liable to the plaintiff injured during a shoplifting incident at the defendant's store. The issue of fact was whether an employee negligently performed an "assumed duty of care" in apprehending and detaining the shoplifter.

According to the court of appeals, while there may not be an initial duty for a business owner to prevent injuries to invitees arising from criminal acts, Alabama law still recognizes that liability could result from the negligent performance of a "voluntary undertaking." The court found that a person who initially has no duty to act but then voluntarily undertakes action will have a duty of due care once he voluntarily acts.

Alaska

Alaska had no cases reported.

UPDATE

In *Anderson v. PPCT Management Systems, Inc.*, 145 P.3d 503, 511 (2006), the defendant had developed a use-of-force training program. A state employee injured the plaintiff while training her to work for the state department of corrections. The plaintiff sued the defendant who developed the program.

The Alaska Supreme Court held that the general rule is that a person is not required to act to protect another. However, an exception to this rule may arise "when an actor undertakes to render services to another." The court adopted the Restatement's position that "undertakings can create a duty of care" and that "one who voluntarily assumes a duty must then perform that duty with reasonable care."

Arizona

In Arizona, courts adhere to common law classifications in these cases. The case law holds that business owners have a duty to exercise reasonable care to protect their invitees from injury. *McFarlin v. Hall*, 127 Ariz. 220, 619 P.2d 729 (1980); *Jesik v. Mariocopa County Community College District*, 125 Ariz. 543, 611 P.2d 547 (1980).

In *McFarlin*, the plaintiff was shot in the parking lot of a tavern. The plaintiff and the assailant had been patrons. The assailant had previously participated in bar fights and had caused other trouble at the bar. The defendant argued that it did not know the assailant would shoot another customer. The Arizona high court held that for the plaintiff to prevail against the tavern, he need not show that the defendant knew the assailant would use a gun to injure the plaintiff. Rather, the court held that as long as the defendant was aware that the assailant's presence on the premises posed a risk of some physical harm, the defendant would be liable for the full extent of the injury inflicted. The court explained that "when the evidence shows . . . that the owners are aware that a patron has a propensity for violence . . . there is a duty while that person remains intoxicated on the premises to take the necessary precautions to prevent violence to other invitees."

A dissenting opinion noted that the assailant had actually left the bar before the shooting and was lurking in the parking lot, waiting for the plaintiff. The dissenter asserted that liability should not be imposed, because there was no reason to believe the assailant had not left the premises entirely.

Relying on case law holding that a student is an invitee and is thus owed reasonable protection, the high court held in *Jesik* that the defendant could be held liable for failing to provide reasonable security. The plaintiff in *Jesik* told a security guard that another student had threatened to shoot him. Immediately after the guard questioned the other student, the student pulled his gun and shot the plaintiff. The court held that liability could be imposed on the school district because it realized or should have realized there was a likelihood of harm to the plaintiff.

Other Arizona cases of note follow.

In *Pierce v. Lopez*, 16 Ariz. App. 54, 490 P.2d 1182 (2d Div. 1971), the court held that although a bartender observed a verbal altercation between two patrons, the bartender did not have reason to believe the dispute would erupt in violence. After the verbal altercation ended, all witnesses, including the plaintiff, believed the matter had ended. No one anticipated that the assailant would grab a pool cue and swing it at the plaintiff. The court offered the following analysis: "Before liability may be imposed for failing to act, the prevision of a reasonable person to recognize danger or harm to one in plaintiff's position is necessary. We cannot conclude that a brief exchange of words will erupt into violence. . . . [A] tavern keeper [need not] possess extraordinary powers of foreseeability greater than those of a reasonable person in similar circumstances." See also, *Sucanick v. Clayton*, 152 Ariz. 158, 730 P.2d 867 (2d Div. 1986); *Hebert v. Club 37 Bar*, 145 Ariz. 351, 701 P.2d 847 (2d Div. 1984).

Sufficient evidence to hold a tavern liable was proffered in the case of *Cotterhill v. Bafile*, 177 Ariz. 76, 865 P.2d 120 (1st Div. 1993), which involved a dispute between two groups. The fight persisted for ten to fifteen minutes and included loud and hostile verbal exchanges. The court found that a "reasonable jury could have inferred that the probability of a fight was evident for several minutes before it occurred, and that the bartender neglected to take reasonable action to avert violence." See also, *Delozier v. Evans*, 158 Ariz. 490, 763 P.2d 986 (1st Div. 1988) (assailant's threat to return with friends and inflict damage sufficiently specific to put reasonable persons on notice that all patrons in the tavern might be in danger).

Defense lawyers are advised to take note of the case *Chavez v. Tolleson Elementary School District*, 122 Ariz. 472, 595 P.2d 1017 (1st Div. 1979), which involved an abduction and murder of a student after the student left school grounds. The court stated: "To say that murder is a foreseeable potential creating an unreasonable risk of harm to each child leaving school grounds each day in the state of Arizona is untenable. The heinous criminal conduct involved here, while shocking, is clearly in the category of the unforeseeable. If it were otherwise, prevision would become paranoia and the routines of daily life would be burdened by intolerable fear and inaction."

UPDATE
The general rule in Arizona is still derived from the holding in *Hill v. Safford Unified School District*, 191 Ariz. 110, 952 P.2d 745 (Ariz. Ct. App. 1997) that before liability may be imposed for an act (or failure to act), the prevision of a reasonable person must be able to recognize the danger of harm to the plaintiff or one in the plaintiff's situation.

Recently, in the case of *White v. United States*, 422 F.Supp.2d 1089 (D. Ariz. 2006), the U.S. District Court took the opportunity to visit the state court's holding in the *Hill* case. Therein, the court noted, in citing *Hill* and Arizona law, the general test as to whether a defendant's conduct breached the standard of care is whether a foreseeable risk of injury resulted from the defendant's conduct.

Additionally, a review of *Thomas v. First Interstate Bank of Arizona*, 930 P.2d 1002 (Ariz.Ct. App. 1997) shows that the law in Arizona still allows a defendant to reduce his or her liability by seeking apportionment of fault between the defendant and an intentional tortfeasor.

Arkansas

The appellate courts in Arkansas have yet to squarely address landowners' obligations to provide protection from criminal occurrences on their premises.

In *MIC v. Barrett*, 313 Ark. 527, 855 S.W.2d 326 (1993), the plaintiff was assaulted in the defendant's parking lot. The court, on a motion to set aside a verdict for the plaintiff, held that under Arkansas law a landowner owes a duty of reasonable care to an invitee for his safety and, if the landowner knows or reasonably should know that the invitee is in danger, he or she owes a duty to use reasonable care to prevent injury to the invitee. However, because the verdict was reversed due to erroneous jury charges, further guidance on premises security law in Arkansas was not provided by the court.

UPDATE

The *Boren v. Worthen National Bank of Arkansas*, 921 S.W.2d 934 (1996) case was cited approvingly in *Coca-Cola Bottling Co. of Memphis, Tennessee v. Gill*, 100 S.W.3d 715, 724 (2003). As such, in Arkansas, a business owner's duty to provide reasonable protection to patrons arises only where the owner is aware of the danger presented by a particular individual or has failed to exercise proper care after an assault has commenced.

An Arkansas court of appeals also cited *Boren* in *Tackett v. Merchant's Security Patrol*, 44 S.W.3d 349 (2001). In so doing, the court found that a security company that contracted with a tavern did not owe a duty to protect the driver of a vehicle injured by a drunk driver who got drunk at the tavern.

California

California has abandoned the common law distinctions among the roles of those who enter upon premises, whether as a trespasser, licensee, or invitee. *Rowland v. Christian*, 69 Cal. 2d 108, 443 P.2d 561, 70 Cal. Rptr. 97 (1968). Before the elimination of the common law distinctions, applicable case law held that an owner of land had a duty "to take affirmative action to control the wrongful acts of third persons which threaten invitees where the [occupant] has reasonable cause to anticipate such acts and the probability of injury resulting therefrom." *Taylor v. Centennial Bowl, Inc.*, 65 Cal. 2d 114, 416 P.2d 793, 52 Cal. Rptr. 561 (1966).

Now, California imposes a uniform standard on all landowners regarding those who come upon their premises. The standard is whether the landowner has acted as a reasonable person in view of the probability of injury to others. Thus, in cases involving an alleged failure to provide adequate security, a landlord has a duty to take reasonable steps to protect tenants and other persons who come upon the premises from the criminal acts of third parties, and may be held liable for failing to do so. *Ann M. v. Pacific Plaza Shopping Center*, 6 Cal. 4th 666, 863 P.2d 207, 25 Cal. Rptr. 2d 137 (1993) (lack of high degree of foreseeability results in finding no duty); *Frances T. v. Village Green Owners Association*, 42 Cal. 3d 490, 723 P.2d 573, 229 Cal. Rptr. 456 (1986) (owner of condominium unit could maintain action against condominium association); *Isaacs v. Huntington Memorial Hospital*, 38 Cal. 3d 112, 695 P.2d 653 (Cal. 1985) (doctor shot in outdoor hospital parking lot could maintain action against hospital); *Peterson v. San Francisco Community College Dist.*, 36 Cal. 3d 799, 685 P.2d 1193, 205 Cal. Rptr. 842 (1984) (student could maintain action against community college, but claims limited by sovereign immunity doctrine).

As noted in these cases, foreseeability is the most important factor in determining a landlord's liability. However, as discussed in the next section, the legal standard for establishing foreseeability has been in a state of flux in California. The cases are discussed in chronological order, and not in order of significance. For example, in the most recent case, *Ann M.*, the court greatly limited a plaintiff's ability to establish a claim against a defendant landlord.

Foreseeability and Duty Cases Decided by the California Supreme Court

The elements necessary to establish foreseeability are the most hotly contested issues in California premises security cases. In 1985, the high court held that "evidence of prior similar incidents is not the sine qua non of a finding of foreseeability." *Isaacs v. Huntington Memorial Hospital*, 38 Cal. 3d 112, 695 P.2d 653 (Cal. 1985). Rather, foreseeability depends on the facts in each case, and the nature, condition, use, and location of the premises could also be considered in determining foreseeability.

To hold otherwise, reasoned the *Isaacs* court, would discourage landowners from providing security to protect premises they know to be dangerous. The first crime victim would always lose, while subsequent victims could establish foreseeability. Moreover, requiring strict similarity between the prior and present crimes was considered unworkable, because then the courts would be required to enunciate arbitrary distinctions between and among various crimes. Thus, in *Isaacs*, the court ruled that a jury should determine whether the prior and present crimes are sufficiently similar to establish foreseeability, unless, under the undisputed facts, there is no room for a reasonable difference of opinion on the matter. Therefore, to raise an issue of fact, and to establish that an attack upon the plaintiff was foreseeable, the plaintiff must demonstrate only that the general character of the event was foreseeable.

The *Isaacs* court held that evidence of prior crimes should be admitted "if plaintiffs can satisfactorily demonstrate the probative value of [the] incident to the foreseeability of criminal activity on the [defendant's] premises. The trial court may [exclude such evidence] if it believes that the link between the two occurrences is too tenuous or if it finds that the defendant did not know and could not reasonably have known of the incident." Presumably, a plaintiff could accomplish this by proffering expert testimony that the prior crimes showed that criminal activity existed in the area and, therefore, the defendant should have guarded against such activity.

The court also rejected the trial court's exclusion of evidence of crimes that occurred more than three years before the assault on the plaintiff. According to the court, there should be no arbitrary cutoff; instead, each crime should be considered independently. The more similar the crime to the assault on the plaintiff, the more likely it may be used as evidence, regardless of how long ago it occurred.

The *Isaacs* court held that the nature and scope of a landlord's duty is related to the degree of foreseeability of criminal attack by third persons. The greater the likelihood of crime, the greater the duty. In determining the extent of the duty, the *Isaacs* court (citing *Rowland v. Christian*) explained that several factors must be weighed, such as, "(1) the degree of certainty that the plaintiff suffered injury, (2) the closeness of the connection between the defendant's conduct and the injury suffered, (3) the moral blame attached to the defendant's conduct, (4) the policy of preventing future harm, (5) the extent of the burden to the defendant and the consequences to the community of imposing a duty to exercise care with resulting liability for breach, and (6) the availability, cost and prevalence of insurance for the risk involved."

The *Isaacs* court held that, as a matter of law, the defendant owed a general duty to the plaintiff. The court did not explain how it reached this result, for if duty is partly a function of foreseeability, and if foreseeability is a jury question, it appears the court usurped the fact-finding role of the jury regarding foreseeability. The court circumvents the analytical problem, however, by stating that the jury decides whether the security measures were reasonable under the circumstances.

In a footnote, the *Isaacs* court suggested that an affirmative finding of duty would establish the element of causation, because the finding of duty would include a finding of foreseeability. In criticizing the court's reasoning, a lower court called the footnote "a simple slip of the pen." *Nola M. v. University of Southern California*, 16 Cal. App. 4th 421, 20 Cal. Rptr. 2d 97 (2d Dist. 1993). Other courts were also critical of the decision. *See, e.g., Onciano v. Golden Palace Restaurant, Inc.*, 219 Cal. App. 3d 385, 268 Cal. Rptr. 96 (2d Dist. 1990) (concurring opinion).

The next case the California high court decided that involved an alleged failure to provide adequate security was *Peterson v. San Francisco Community College Dist.*, 36 Cal. 3d 799, 685 P.2d 1193, 205 Cal. Rptr. 842 (1984). The case was heard on appeal after the complaint was dismissed for failure to state a claim; it did not involve a motion for summary judgment or a post-trial appeal. Therefore, as the lowest standard of review was applied, the case's precedential value is somewhat circumscribed.

In *Peterson*, the plaintiff was accosted and raped in a stairwell of a parking lot at the defendant's college. The assailant had raped before and, in fact, had previously raped another woman at the same location. As the foreseeability issue was virtually uncontestable, the case focused on the nature of the duty the college owed to the student. The *Peterson* court held that the plaintiff stated a cause of action regarding the defendant's breach of duty to warn of the serial rapist. The court noted that the defendant failed to trim the foliage the assailant used as a cover. However, the court upheld the dismissal of a claim regarding the failure to provide adequate and sufficient security personnel, on the ground that a statute granted immunity to public entities for failure to provide police protection.

In *Frances T. v. Village Green Owners Association*, 42 Cal. 3d 490, 723 P.2d 573, 229 Cal. Rptr. 456 (1986), the court held that because the defendant was aware of a crime problem and knew that adequate lighting would deter crime, the plaintiff could maintain a cause of action against the landowner. Moreover, the court stated that the "[d]efendant need not have foreseen the precise injury to plaintiff so long as the possibility of this type of harm was foreseeable." (The use of the word "possibility" by the court is unfortunate: all crime is possible.) *See also,* *O'Hara v. Western Seven Trees Corp.*, 75 Cal. App. 3d 798, 142 Cal. Rptr. 487 (1st Dist. 1977) (apparently the first California case holding that a residential landowner could be liable for an attack by a third person; a serial rapist raped several tenants, the landlord was aware of conditions that rendered further rapes on the premises likely, and the landlord misrepresented to a prospective tenant that the premises were safe. The court held such allegations by a plaintiff who was raped in her own apartment, rather than in a common area, sufficient to allow a claim against a defendant landlord.)

In the case of *Ann M. v. Pacific Plaza Shopping Center*, 6 Cal. 4th 666, 863 P.2d 207, 25 Cal. Rptr. 137 (1993), California's high court reconsidered the foreseeability doctrine and the scope of a landowner's duty, recognizing the iniquities of the "totality of the circumstances test" enunciated in the *Isaacs* case, and the abandonment in *Isaacs* of the "prior similar incidents" rule.

Ann M. involved a claim brought by a store employee against the owner of the shopping center where the store was located. After the plaintiff opened the store one morning, an unidentified assailant entered and raped her at knifepoint. The court held that, as a matter of law, the attack was unforeseeable notwithstanding the existence of prior crimes at the shopping center. Those incidents included bank robberies, purse snatchings, assaults by unruly minors, and one instance of a man pulling down a woman's pants. Similar incidents allegedly occurred at a neighboring apartment building, and transients loitered in the common areas.

In the absence of evidence that the plaintiff was raped by one of the transients, or that the presence of transients contributed to the rape of the plaintiff, the court found the evidence insufficient to establish that the plaintiff's rape was reasonably foreseeable. Additionally, the tenants association had rejected the use of security guard foot patrols because the cost, which would have been passed along to them, was prohibitive.

The court noted that the *Isaacs* decision had been criticized by lower courts. The court further recognized that "random, violent crime is endemic in today's society" and that there is probably no public place that is free of the probability of violence. Therefore, the court held that the question of foreseeability ("when to determine the existence or scope of a duty") must be resolved as a matter of law by the trial court, and not as a question of fact for the jury. The court analyzed the matter as follows:

> While there may be circumstances where the hiring of security guards will be required to satisfy a landowner's duty of care, such action will rarely, if ever, be found to be a "minimal burden." The monetary costs of security guards is not insignificant. Moreover, the obligation to provide patrols adequate to deter criminal conduct is not well defined. "No one really knows why people commit crime, hence no one really knows what is `adequate' deterrence in any given situation." (Citation omitted). For these reasons, we conclude that a high degree of foreseeability is required in order to find that the scope of a landlord's duty of care includes the hiring of security guards. We further conclude that the requisite degree of foreseeability rarely, if ever, can be proven in the absence of prior similar incidents of violent crime on the landowner's premises. To hold otherwise would be to impose an unfair burden upon landlords and, in effect, would force landlords to become the insurers of the public safety, contrary to well established policy in this state.

Because of the foregoing public policy issues and the dissimilarity between the prior crimes at the shopping center and the attack on the plaintiff, the *Ann M.* court held that the defendant landlord was under no duty to provide security guards. In an important footnote, however, the court suggested that if a defendant's commercial premises posed a temptation for criminal conduct, as would a parking garage or twen-ty-four-hour convenience store, a duty to provide security guards may arise even absent prior similar incidents.

Other cases of note are discussed below.

Lower Court Decisions Regarding Foreseeability and Duty

In *Pamela W. v. Millsom*, 25 Cal. App. 4th 950, 30 Cal. Rptr. 2d 690 (4th Dist. 1994), the "high foreseeability" test of the *Ann M.* case was relied upon in dismissing the plaintiff's claim. The plaintiff in *Pamela W.* sub-leased a condominium in a two-building project. The parties all believed the neighborhood was safe, yet the plaintiff was raped in her condominium. She was aware of only one prior criminal act in the area, a burglary that occurred in a neighboring apartment during the month before the rape. Apparently, the assailant entered the plaintiff's resi-dence through a window and raped her. During the assault, the assailant called the plaintiff by her name and told her that he had been watching her.

The plaintiff claimed that the defendants (the sublessor and the condominium association) should have improved the physical securi-ty of the premises. She also argued that the condominium was in a high-crime area and, considering the totality of the circumstances, that crime was reasonably foreseeable.

The court rejected the plaintiff's contentions and held that in the absence of prior assault-like conduct on the premises, the defendants had no duty to provide security against attack. Because the security measures that might have prevented the attack would have imposed a substantial burden on the landlord, the plaintiff was required to demonstrate that the attack was highly foreseeable. In the absence of similar prior crimes on the premises, the plaintiff could not meet this requirement.

The court then added another hurdle to the plaintiff's case when it ruled that "[t]he scope of a landlord's duty to provide protection from foreseeable third-party crime is determined in part by balancing the foreseeability of the harm against the burden of the duty to be imposed (citation omitted). But what may be a minimal burden for the owner of a large apartment building or shopping center may also be, in the case of the owner of a single unit in a four-unit project, a significant burden indeed."

In holding that the attack upon the plaintiff was not highly fore-seeable, the court explained that "there is little utility in evidence that, for example, the Pacific Beach area of San Diego is a high crime area.

Unfortunately, random, violent crime is endemic in today's society. It is difficult, if not impossible, to envision any locale open to the public where the occurrence of violent crime seems improbable."

Similarly, in *Noble v. Los Angeles Dodgers, Inc.*, 168 Cal. App. 3d 912, 214 Cal. Rptr. 395 (2d Dist. 1985), the court stated that "it is sad commentary but it can be said that in this day and age anyone can foresee or expect that a crime will be committed at any time and at any place in the more populous areas of the country."

In *Nola M. v. University of Southern California*, 16 Cal. App. 4th 421, 20 Cal. Rptr. 2d 97 (2d Dist. 1993), which involved the rape of a student on a college campus, the court stated:

> We think it comes down to this: When an injury can be prevented by a lock or a fence or a chain across a driveway or some other physical device, a landowner's failure to erect an appropriate barrier can be the legal cause of an injury inflicted by the negligent or criminal act of a third person. (Citations omitted). But where, as here, we are presented with an open area which could be fully protected, if at all, only by a Berlin Wall, we do not believe a landowner is the cause of a physical assault it could not reasonably have prevented.

In a rhetorical flourish, the court then added:

> Otherwise, where do we draw the line? How many guards are enough? Ten? Twenty? Two hundred? How much light is sufficient? . . . Are plants of any kind permissible or is USC to chop down every tree and pull out each bush? Does it matter if the campus looks like a prison? . . . Who is going to pay for all this security? It is no answer to say that insurance is available. . . . [T]he cost just gets passed on to the consuming public, either by the insurer, the insured, or both. So who pays? Are USC's employees willing to take a cut in pay to cover the cost of additional security? What about USC's students? How much more tuition can they afford? What happens when enrollment drops because fewer students can afford the luxury of a perfectly safe education? We could go on, but we think this makes the point.

In *Totten v. More Oakland Residential Housing, Inc.*, 63 Cal. App. 3d 538, 134 Cal. Rptr. 29 (1st Dist. 1976), the court considered the factors relevant to a determination of whether a landowner owes a duty to one who comes upon the premises, and held that a tenant's guest who was shot in cross fire in the laundry room of the defendant's apartment building was not owed a duty of care.

Residential Premises

The "special relationship" doctrine was held to apply to the relationship between a residential landlord and a tenant in *Kwaitkowski v. Superior Trading Co.*, 123 Cal. App. 3d 324, 176 Cal. Rptr. 494 (1st Dist. 1981). In *Kwaitkowski*, the tenant was raped and robbed in the lobby of her apartment building. She claimed the landlord knew that the lobby entrance door had a broken lock, that the building was in a high-crime area, and that there had been a prior assault and robbery in a common area of the building. The court held that the attack was foreseeable, and that the plaintiff could therefore maintain a claim against the landlord. Further, the court held that knowledge of the particular assailant was not required; rather, knowledge that the entrance lock was defective and notice of a prior crime sufficed. The court also held that liability could be predicated upon a breach of an implied warranty of habitability.

See also, *Penner v. Falk*, 153 Cal. App. 3d 858, 200 Cal. Rptr. 661 (2d Dist. 1984), which held that a negligence cause of action was properly stated against an apartment building owner who knew about prior assaults by third persons on the premises. Notably, the court also held that a cause of action for breach of a duty to provide security could not be predicated upon an implied warranty of habitability of the premises.

In *Anaya v. Turk*, 151 Cal. App. 3d 1092, 199 Cal. Rptr. 187 (2d Dist. 1984), the court held that the lessee of a residential apartment could not be held liable for mere "nonfeasance" when his social guest was shot by another social guest. But regarding the claim that the defendant lessee also created a dangerous condition by selling drugs on the premises, the court held that such "misfeasance" could state a cause of action.

Condominium Association and Directors

In *Frances T. v. Village Green Owners Association*, 42 Cal. 3d 490, 723 P.2d 573, 229 Cal. Rptr. 456 (1986), it was held that a condominium association and its individual directors could be held liable for the rape of an owner of a unit. A crime wave swept through the plaintiff's condominium development and newsletters had urged residents to leave their exterior lights on as a means of deterring crime. Plaintiff then installed additional exterior lighting that did not comply with the rules of the development. The condominium board directed her to remove the additional lighting, and pending the removal she could not use it. The court deemed this directive by the association as evidence that the association exercised control over the common areas of the development.

The additional lighting had been connected to the same electrical circuits as the old lighting; so by shutting off the new lighting, the plaintiff also shut off the old lighting. Her assailant then gained entry under cover of darkness, and raped her.

The court held the condominium association to the same duty of care as a landlord, notwithstanding that it was a nonprofit association of homeowners. Because the directors had personally directed the alleged tortious conduct, they could be held liable. Were the rule otherwise, the court reasoned, a director could inflict injuries on others and then escape liability behind the corporate shield. The directors were subject to liability not because of their *status* as board members, but because of their *actions* as board members—they allegedly caused injury to the plaintiff and failed to take reasonable measures to prevent the harm. The court further reasoned that because the only persons in a position to remedy a hazardous condition were the directors, their unreasonable failure to avoid the harm could result in their personal liability.

Lighting

In *Constance B. v. State*, 178 Cal. App. 3d 200, 223 Cal. Rptr. 645 (3d Dist. 1986), the allegations included a claim of inadequate lighting in the bathroom area of a highway rest stop. However, considering that the assailant had been standing out in the open, not hidden in the darkness, the court rejected the claim, and offered the following comments: "Nor are we persuaded that the matter should go to the jury on the vague supposition that . . . even brighter lights might have deterred the assault. This theory has nothing to do with the creation of an opportunity to commit crime by providing a place of concealment. It is premised on the notion that the assailant's psychological propensity for crime is affected by the quantity of light. It is a theory of mood lighting. . . . If we are unwilling as a matter of policy to insure against losses occasioned by crimes, we ought not foist that burden haphazardly on persons not at fault for criminal misbehavior." *See also, Wiedenfeller v. Star & Garter*, 1 Cal. App. 4th 1, 2 Cal. Rptr. 2d 14 (4th Dist. 1991).

Security Guards

In *Marois v. Royal Investigation & Patrol*, 162 Cal. App. 3d 193, 208 Cal. Rptr. 384 (4th Dist. 1984), the court held that security guards owe a direct duty to customers to protect them against attack by third persons upon the premises being guarded. According to the court, by "contracting with the business to provide security services, the security guard creates a special relationship between himself and the business's customers."

In the previously cited case of *Totten v. More Oakland Residential Housing, Inc.*, an owner was held not liable for a sudden attack on a stranger to the premises by another stranger. In view of the sudden nature of the attack, the court noted that the presence of security guards would not have made a difference. *See also, Rogers v. Jones*, 56 Cal. App. 3d 346, 128 Cal. Rptr. 404 (4th Dist. 1976).

Failure to Warn

In *Koepke v. Loo*, 18 Cal. App. 4th 1444, 23 Cal. Rptr. 2d 34 (4th Dist. 1993), the court held that an assailant's employer had no duty to warn the plaintiff that it returned the assailant's gun to him. The employer had previously taken the gun from the assailant when he threatened the plaintiff. The court held that the assailant's actions did not arise out of his employment and, moreover, that the employer was obligated to return the gun because it was the assailant's property. In analyzing the applicable case law, the court reasoned that although professionals, such as psychiatrists and other physicians, may have a duty to warn, nonprofessionals have no such duty.

In *Hayes v. State of California*, 11 Cal. 3d 469, 521 P.2d 855, 113 Cal. Rptr. 599 (1974), which involved an attack upon the beach of a state university, the court stated that the prevalence of crime is so well known that there would be little or no use in providing further warning, and that such warning may also result in reduced use of the premises, thus causing other problems.

However, in the previously cited case of *Peterson v. San Francisco Community College Dist.*, the California high court, after discussing the *Hayes* case favorably, held that plaintiff stated a viable claim against the defendant, a local college, for failing to warn of a specific unknown danger—that a serial rapist was afoot. *See also, Tarasoff v. Regents of University of California*, 17 Cal. 3d 425, 131 Cal. Rptr. 14, 551 P.2d 334 (1976) (duty of psychiatrist to warn intended victim of psychiatrist's patient); *Johnson v. State*, 69 Cal. 2d 782, 73 Cal. Rptr. 240, 447 P.2d 352 (1968) (state required to warn foster parents of child's violent propensities because, by failing to warn, state created a foreseeable peril, not readily discoverable by a foster parent); *Carpenter v. City of Los Angeles*, 230 Cal. App. 3d 923, 281 Cal. Rptr. 500 (2d Dist. 1991) (prosecutor who learned a criminal defendant had arranged a "hit" owed a duty to warn plaintiff, a witness for the prosecution who had been assured by the prosecutor that the criminal defendant was not dangerous); *Wallace v. City of Los Angeles*, 12 Cal. App. 4th 1385, 16 Cal. Rptr. 2d 113 (2d Dist. 1993) (same holding as *Carpenter* case).

These cases were decided on the ground that the plaintiff and the defendant had a special relationship; where there is no special relationship, the courts have found no duty. *See, e.g., Davidson v. City of*

Westminster, 32 Cal. 3d 197, 649 P.2d 894, 185 Cal. Rptr. 252 (1982) (no duty to warn lawful user of premises that the premises had been staked out by police); *Denton v. City of Fullerton*, 233 Cal. App. 3d 1636, 285 Cal. Rptr. 297 (4th Dist. 1991) (no duty to warn building occupant of possible presence of criminal on premises); *Thompson v. County of Alameda*, 27 Cal. 3d 741, 614 P.2d 728, 167 Cal. Rptr. 70 (1980) (no duty to warn neighbors that juvenile delinquent had been released to the custody of child's mother).

In an opinion worth noting, the court in *Taylor v. Centennial Bowl, Inc.*, 65 Cal. 2d 114, 416 P.2d 793, 52 Cal. Rptr. 561 (1966), held that a landowner does not discharge its obligation to one who comes upon its premises by merely warning of a danger.

Sovereign Immunity

In the *Peterson* case, a claim regarding the failure of a public college to provide adequate and sufficient security personnel was dismissed on the ground of sovereign immunity, pursuant to a statute enacted to protect the budgetary and political decisions involved in hiring and deploying a police force. But in *Leger v. Stockton Unified School Dist.*, 202 Cal. App. 3d 1448, 249 Cal. Rptr. 688 (3d Dist. 1988), which involved an attack on a high school student by a nonstudent, the court held that the school employees could be held liable in their individual capacities. However, as *Peterson* makes clear, a plaintiff can circumvent the sovereign immunity defense by pleading negligent hiring, supervision, or maintenance of premises, or by pleading negligent lighting. *Slapin v. Los Angeles International Airport*, 65 Cal. App. 3d 484, 135 Cal. Rptr. 296 (2d Dist. 1976); *see also, Virginia G. v. ABC Unified School Dist.*, 15 Cal. App. 4th 1848, 19 Cal. Rptr. 2d 671 (2d Dist. 1993) (high school's special relationship with its students may affect its duty).

Apportionment of Liability

In *Weidenfeller v. Star & Garter*, 1 Cal. App. 4th 1, 2 Cal. Rptr. 2d 14 (4th Dist. 1991), the court held that under California's apportionment statute, the liability of the owner of the premises upon which the plaintiff is assaulted may be apportioned among the owner, plaintiff, and assailant, and any award to the plaintiff may be limited accordingly. In that case, the court limited the award against the landowner to 20 percent of the total damages. The issue is still alive, however: *See Pamela B. v. Hayden*, 31 Cal. Rptr. 2d 147 (Cal. Ct. App. 1994) (trial court apportioned 90 percent of damages to apartment owner and 10 percent to a rapist, and the appeals court reversed).

In *Weidenfeller*, the assailant had been impleaded as a third-party defendant. Courts have not yet resolved whether there may be apportionment against an unknown assailant.

Experts

In *Nola M. v. University of Southern California*, 16 Cal. App. 4th 421, 20 Cal. Rptr. 2d 97 (2d Dist. 1993), an expert testified that the defendant's security measures were insufficient to prevent the plaintiff's rape. Because the expert "did not, and on the facts of this case could not, say that 2 or 10 or 20 more guards or other security measures could have prevented Nola's injuries," the court held that the testimony was insufficient. Evidence of more than sixty violent crimes on the college campus, and of a far greater crime rate in the vicinity of the campus during the previous two to three years, was also insufficient to establish that further security measures were necessary. "Absolute safety," the court recognized, "is not an achievable goal."

In *Noble v. Los Angeles Dodgers, Inc.*, 168 Cal. App. 3d 912, 214 Cal. Rptr. 395 (2d Dist. 1985), plaintiff's expert posited that seven more security guards should have been deployed. The court noted that abstract negligence unconnected to an injury will not support liability, and stated that "it appears that a growth industry is developing consisting of experts who will advise and testify as to what, in their opinion, constitutes `adequate security.' The $64 question, of course, is `adequate for what?' As noted, in each case where such testimony would be relevant, the security in existence has already proven to be inadequate to prevent the injury which did occur."

The court rejected the expert's testimony because the expert could not state that the additional guards would have prevented the crime. "It seems anomalous," stated the court in a footnote, "that a public entity which has the primary role in providing police protection is . . . immunized while persons not generally considered to have that general responsibility are not so immunized. It also appears anomalous that at a time when the trend in the law is to control the conduct of police and render them less effective in deterring crime, the law should at the same time encourage the expansion of private police forces."

Lastly, the *Noble* court rejected the expert's testimony on the ground that it failed to establish a causal connection between the alleged breach of duty and the alleged negligence: "It is one thing for an expert to testify concerning the mechanical devices such as locks, safes, fences, etc., which are designed to protect property by `hardening the target,' [but] it is quite another for such expert to discuss deterring conduct such as rape, robbery or physical assaults." One cannot know, reasoned the court, what measures will protect against rapists, thugs, drug addicts, and psychopaths.

Other opinions worth noting are *Onciano v. Golden Palace Restaurant, Inc.*, 219 Cal. App. 3d 385, 268 Cal. Rptr. 96 (2d Dist. 1990) (testimony that crime rate in area is minimal must be based upon expert testimony) and *Thai v. Stang*, 214 Cal. App. 3d 1264, 263 Cal. Rptr. 202 (4th Dist. 1989).

In *7735 Hollywood Blvd. Venture v. Superior Court*, 116 Cal. App. 3d 901, 172 Cal. Rptr. 528 (2d Dist. 1981), the court held that the plaintiff failed to state a viable claim predicated upon an alleged failure to provide adequate lighting. The court offered the following analysis:

> Plaintiff's position here, if accepted, would impose an affirmative duty, on any owner of rental property, to install security devices "adequate" to deter crime, because under plaintiff's theory it was the lack of "adequate" lighting which formed the basis for liability. That lack could include failure to install outside lighting in the first place as well as failure to maintain existing lighting. The question is thus "Does an apartment owner have a duty to install and maintain lighting for security purposes?" If such a duty could be said to exist, the questions that would logically follow are of what candle power? and in what areas? To ask the questions is to demonstrate the futility of attempting to impose and define such a duty.

Further, plaintiff's theory proceeds from the premise that "lighting" in and of itself can deter crime. In this day of an inordinate volume of criminal activity, there are myriad "security devices" available to the public, including the hiring of security guards. No one really knows why people commit crime, hence no one really knows what is "adequate" deterrence in any given situation.

As these cases suggest, expert testimony relative to security-related issues is not necessarily enthusiastically received by the California appellate courts.

Crime Statistics

In *Isaacs*, it was noted that although citywide crime statistics were not themselves admissible, statistics could be admitted through an expert witness if they formed a basis for the expert's opinion. A proper foundation for the use of the statistics must be laid, however. The expert must obtain the statistics from a proper source. In the previously cited case of *Pamela W. v. Millsom*, the court stated that the citywide crime statistics offered were of little utility in establishing foreseeability.

Parking Lots

In California, it seems that much crime takes place in parking lots. Two of the leading high court cases involve crimes that took place in parking lots. Those previous cases are *Isaacs v. Huntington Memorial Hospital*, and *Peterson v. San Francisco Community College District*. Other significant cases involving parking lots follow.

In *Gomez v. Ticor*, 145 Cal. App. 3d 622, 193 Cal. Rptr. 600 (2d Dist. 1983), the court held that the plaintiff could maintain an action based on a killing that took place in the parking structure of defendant's office building located in a high-crime area. The court explained that in "its very operation of a parking structure, defendant may be said to have created 'an especial temptation and opportunity for criminal misconduct,' thus increasing the foreseeability of the attack." The court also noted that the deserted nature of the structure made it a likely place for robbers and rapists to lie in wait. The court held that due to the foreseeability of the attack, the defendant was under a minimal duty to provide security: the greater the foreseeability, the greater the duty.

In *Campodonico v. State Auto Parks, Inc.*, 10 Cal. App. 3d 803, 98 Cal. Rptr. 270 (2d Dist. 1970), the plaintiff alleged that the defendant's parking lot was constructed and maintained in a manner that encouraged loitering by disreputable persons. The court held that the plaintiff could maintain a cause of action based on such allegations. *See also, Onciano v. Golden Palace Restaurant, Inc.*, 219 Cal. App. 3d 385, 268 Cal. Rptr. 96 (2d Dist. 1990) (triable issue of fact regarding whether lighting in parking lot was adequate, whether fence provided adequate security, and whether parking-lot attendant should have been on duty); *Sykes v. County of Marin*, 43 Cal. App. 3d 158, 117 Cal. Rptr. 466 (1st Dist. 1974); *Rogers v. Jones*, 56 Cal. App. 3d 346, 128 Cal. Rptr. 404 (4th Dist. 1976) (attack in parking lot after football game was unforeseeable, and to have prevented the attack defendant "would have been required to assign an attendant or guard to each of the 53,000 fans in attendance"); *Slapin v. Los Angeles International Airport*, 65 Cal. App. 3d 484, 135 Cal. Rptr. 296 (2d Dist. 1976) ("That a mugger thrives in dark places is a matter of common knowledge").

Armed Robberies

In *Cohen v. Southland Corp.*, 157 Cal. App. 3d 130, 203 Cal. Rptr. 572 (4th Dist. 1984), a customer at a 7-Eleven store was shot while attempting to thwart an armed robbery. A store open twenty-four hours a day creates a temptation and opportunity for criminal misconduct, the court noted. Because there had been prior robberies on the premises and at other 7-

Eleven stores, and because nighttime robberies were frequent, the court held that a triable issue of fact existed concerning whether the shooting was foreseeable.

In *Young v. Desert View Management Corp.*, 275 Cal. App. 2d 294, 79 Cal. Rptr. 848 (2d Dist. 1969), a waitress, who heard that a coworker had just been robbed, asked a customer to get the license plate number of the robber's car. When the customer went outside, he was shot. Holding that the defendant did not breach a duty to warn the customer that the robber had a gun, the court noted that in "the excitement and confusion of an armed robbery, neither the victim nor spectators can be expected to react as calmly as observers in a chess match." According to the court, asking for help "is not a springboard . . . for a successful dive into litigation." *See also, Vandermost v. Alpha Beta Co.*, 164 Cal. App. 3d 771, 210 Cal. Rptr. 613 (2d Dist. 1985); *Forrand v. Foodmaker, Inc.*, 182 Cal. App. 3d 196, 227 Cal. Rptr. 74 (2d Dist. 1986) (court held it would not impose a duty to warn of a gun, "which presupposes rational thought during a time which normally produces the antithesis").

Stalkers/Family Disputes

Considering that the plaintiff had been stalked, the court in the previously cited case of *Pamela W. v. Millsom* stated that "no one really knows why people commit crime, hence no one really knows what is adequate deterrence in any given situation." The court added, "Some persons cannot be deterred by anything short of impenetrable walls and armed guards." Similarly, the court in the previously cited case of *Koepke v. Loo* stated that while the plaintiff and the assailant "were not married, their dispute was essentially a domestic dispute. Not only in law enforcement circles, but indeed to all people today, it is well known that domestic disputes are common, they are often vexatious and distressful not only to those parties to the dispute, but also to their friends and associates, and it is not uncommon that they lead to violence."

Mass Murderers/Bombers

California courts are unlikely to impose liability upon a landowner when the underlying crime is extraordinarily horrific. In *Lopez v. McDonald's Corp.*, 193 Cal. App. 3d 495, 238 Cal. Rptr. 436 (4th Dist. 1987), which involved the killing of twenty-one persons and wounding of eleven others at the San Ysidro McDonald's restaurant, the court held that the attack was so extraordinary that, as a matter of law, there was no causal connection between the alleged breach of security and the injuries.

In *Moncur v. City of Los Angeles*, 68 Cal. App. 3d 118, 137 Cal. Rptr. 239 (2d Dist. 1977), the court held that liability could not be imposed on the defendant for allegedly placing lockers inside the "security screen" area, where a locker was later used for the placement of a bomb. The court held that the bombing was not reasonably foreseeable, and that the defendant's actions did not cause the bombing.

Drive-by Shootings/Youth Gangs

In *Thai v. Stang*, 214 Cal. App. 3d 1264, 263 Cal. Rptr. 202 (4th Dist. 1989), the court held that the presence of a security guard on the defendant's premises would not have deterred the shooting of the plaintiff. In rejecting the expert's testimony as speculative, the court noted the words of the trial court: "Cloaking a man with the aura of ostensible expertise and saying he feels that, had there been a security guard out there, this crazy wouldn't have taken a pot shot at your client, to me, has absolutely no force and effect." The court noted that the random nature of drive-by shootings makes them impossible to guard against.

In *Gregorian v. National Convenience Stores*, 174 Cal. App. 3d 944, 220 Cal. Rptr. 302 (2d Dist. 1985), the court held the defendants had no duty to protect the plaintiff who was attacked by a youth gang in defendants' store. No such attacks previously occurred in the defendants' store or in the area. The court stated that nothing in the record supported "the claim that defendants possessed knowledge of criminal activities any more precise than the knowledge of any citizen residing and working in the County of Los Angeles."

Punitive Damages

The court in *Penner v. Falk*, 153 Cal. App. 3d 858, 200 Cal. Rptr. 661 (2d Dist. 1984) held that punitive damages may be awarded when the long-standing physical condition of the premises portends danger to the tenants. Under the applicable California punitive damages statute, the defendant must be guilty of oppression, fraud, or malice before such damages may be imposed.

Volunteer Principle

In *Riley v. Marcus*, 125 Cal. App. 3d 103, 177 Cal. Rptr. 827 (2d Dist. 1981), the plaintiff argued that the owner of the residential premises had undertaken a duty to provide security, yet failed to do so. Holding that the security devices provided (doors, door locks, windows, and outside lighting) were commonplace, the court stated that "a landlord's efforts to make his premises more secure against criminal activity should not be greeted by a pronouncement that if such efforts are later found to be inadequate he will incur a liability which would have been nonexistent had he done nothing. Absent a duty to take reasonable precautions to prevent the reoccurrence of criminal acts which are known to be likely to reoccur, a landlord incurs no liability by attempting, albeit unsuccessfully or inadequately, to make his premises less vulnerable to criminal intrusions."

UPDATE

In *Pamela W. v. Millsom*, 25 Cal.App.4th 950, 30 Cal.Rptr.2d 690 (Cal.App. 4 Dist.,1994), the court of appeals declined to extend *Ann M. v. Pacific Plaza Shopping Center*, 6 Cal.4th 666, 25 Cal. Rptr.2d 137, 863 P.2d 207 (1993). *In Pamela W.*, a home owner was raped by an assailant who gained entrance to the plaintiff's apartment. The plaintiff brought a premises liability action against the landlord, the condominium association, and others, alleging negligence, breach of the implied warranty of habitability, and nuisance. In the proceedings, the trial court determined that the first element, duty owed the plaintiff, was not present in the particular facts of the case. The court asserted that *Ann M. v. Pacific Plaza Shopping Center*, like the *Pamela W.* case, concerns whether a landowner has a duty to a tenant to take measures to prevent a criminal assault. However, the major distinction between *Ann M.* and this case is the nature of the corrective measures that, it is urged, the various defendants ought to have employed. In *Ann M.* the question was "whether the scope of the duty owed by the owner of the shopping center to maintain common areas within its possession and control in a reasonably safe condition includes providing security guards in those areas." Here, in contrast, the urged corrective measures only extended to a suggested need for improving the physical security of the premises that the plaintiff rented from the defendants. The plaintiff here argues that the minimal nature of the proposed burden justifies ready imposition of the duty. It is of course true that "the scope of a landlord's duty to provide protection from foreseeable third-party crime . . . is determined in part by balancing the foreseeability of the harm against the burden of the duty to be imposed." *Ann M. v. Pacific Plaza Shopping Center*, 6 Cal.4th 666, 25 Cal. Rptr.2d 137, 863 P.2d 207 (1993). But what may be a minimal burden for the owner of a large apartment building or a shopping center may also be, in the case of the owner of a single unit in a four-unit project, a significant burden indeed. That is, the burden of providing security guards for a shopping center is likely no more onerous than the burden of providing greatly increased physical security for the defendants' condominium unit. Thus, when this case is compared with *Ann M.*, the foreseeability in each instance of any third-party criminal activity should be approximately comparable in order to impose a burden of additional security, whether human or physical.

In *Robison v. Six Flags Theme Parks Inc.*, 25 64 Cal.App.4th 1294, 75 Cal.Rptr.2d 838 (Cal.App. 2 Dist., 1998), the court of appeals declined to extend *Ann M. v. Pacific Plaza Shopping Center*, 6 Cal.4th 666, 25 Cal. Rptr.2d 137, 863 P.2d 207 (1993). In *Robison*, amusement park patrons brought a negligence action against the amusement park, seeking recovery for injuries received when an out-of-control automobile left the parking lot and collided with a table in an adjacent picnic area. The court of appeals held that *Ann M. v. Pacific Plaza Shopping Center*, which was heavily relied upon by the defendants and apparently formed the basis for the trial court's ruling, provided no support for the defendants in the instant case. The court of appeals further held that

> as the Supreme Court noted in *Ann M.* a criminal can commit a crime anywhere. The burden of requiring a landlord to protect against crime everywhere has been considered too great in comparison with the foreseeability of crime occurring at a particular location to justify imposing an omnibus duty on landowners to control crime. Hence, the common law has imposed limitations on the duty of a landowner to protect against crime, specifically because crime can occur anywhere. Rather than imposing a duty to take precautions (such as security guards) generally in all instances, the common law instead looks for a higher level of foreseeability of crime in a particular location, such as might be provided by prior similar incidents at that location.

The court of appeals held that the instant case is fundamentally different. "Crime can happen anywhere, but cars cannot crash into picnic tables just anywhere. In order for a car to crash into a picnic table, the picnic table must first be placed in harm's way." There is no legal requirement in such circumstances for the type of heightened notice that might be provided by a prior similar incident, as *Ann M.* found may be necessary in instances of third-party crimes. Thereafter, the court of appeals determined that the extent of the defendant's duty (i.e., what reasonable protective measures should have been employed) would require a balancing of the probability of an accident, the severity of the expectable harm, and the burden of providing specific protective measures.

Additionally, in *Lopez v. Baca*, 98 Cal.App.4th 1008, 120 Cal.Rptr.2d 281 (Cal.App. 2 Dist., 2002), the court of appeals declined to extend *Ann M. v. Pacific Plaza Shopping Center*, 6 Cal.4th 666, 25 Cal. Rptr.2d 137, 863 P.2d 207 (1993). In *Lopez*, a nightclub patron, who was shot in the head by another customer, brought a premises liability action against the nightclub owner. The court of appeals contended that the *Lopez* case was dissimilar from *Ann M.* because the nightclub itself affirmatively created a dangerous condition conducive to violence by operating an illegal *Fichera* bar and that "this is not the typical premises liability case where the defendant may claim it was surprised by some random unexpected criminal act." In *Ann M.* the Supreme Court left open the question whether some commercial property is, by its very nature, so "inherently dangerous that, even in the absence of prior similar incidents, providing security guards will fall within the scope of a landowner's duty of care." *Ann M. v. Pacific Plaza Shopping Center,* 6 Cal.4th 666, 25 Cal. Rptr.2d 137, 863 P.2d 207 (1993). In conclusion, the court of appeals held that Baca owed no duty to provide security guards to protect Lopez.

The Supreme Court of California in *Sharon P. v. Arman, Ltd.* 21 Cal.4th 1181, 989 P.2d 121 (Cal., 1999) dealt with a tenant who was attacked and sexually assaulted in an underground commercial parking garage. The tenant sued the owner and operator of the garage for negligence. The Superior Court of Los Angeles County entered summary judgment for the defendants. The tenant appealed. The court of appeals reversed and remanded. The supreme court granted review, superseding the opinion of the court of appeals, stating that: (1) underground parking structures are not so inherently dangerous that providing security guards would fall within the scope of a landowner's duty of care, even in the absence of prior similar incidents; (2) sexual attack was not sufficiently foreseeable to give rise to a duty of care to provide security guards in the parking garage; and (3) the defendants were not under a duty to provide better lighting or better security monitoring. In the instant case, an unknown assailant sexually assaulted the plaintiff at gunpoint in a commercial parking garage owned and operated by the defendants. The court was presented with the question of whether and to what extent the defendants' duty of care to their tenants required that they provide security in the garage, when no assaults had occurred on the premises during the ten years preceding the attack upon the plaintiff. The court concluded that the occurrence of a violent third-party sexual assault in the subject garage was not sufficiently foreseeable to support such a requirement; it therefore reversed the contrary judgment of the court of appeals and remanded the matter to that court with directions to enter judgment in favor of the defendants.

On Thursday, April 8, 1993, the plaintiff parked in her assigned space, and as she was preparing to leave her car, a masked assailant came up from behind and sexually assaulted her. The plaintiff sued defendant Arman, Ltd. (Arman), the owner of the premises, and defendant Apcoa, Inc., doing business as Parking Services, Inc. (Apcoa), which provided parking services for Arman. The complaint alleged, among other things, that the defendants' failure to provide adequate security for users of the parking garage resulted in the attack upon the plaintiff. Arman purchased the office building and parking garage in 1982. There is a bank on the ground floor of the building, with its entrance facing southwest. The bank's internal records show that it had been robbed seven times between February 1991 and January 1993, with one report of physical injury. Records of the Los Angeles Police Department reflect that a total of 363 crimes, including two rapes, occurred in the fifty square blocks surrounding the office building in 1992. During the first quarter of 1993, just prior to the plaintiff's assault, seventy-two crimes, but no rapes, were recorded. The trial court granted the motions based upon the foreseeability analysis articulated in *Ann M. v. Pacific Plaza Shopping Center*, 6 Cal.4th 666, 25 Cal. Rptr.2d 137, 863 P.2d 207 (1993). Although noting the plaintiff's evidence of other crimes occurring in the surrounding area, the court found it significant that there was no evidence of crimes occurring within the parking garage. Judgment was entered in favor of the defendants. The court of appeals reversed by a divided vote. The majority determined that *Ann M.* was not controlling because commercial parking structures such as the one in the *Sharon P.* case are "inherently dangerous" and, by their very nature, facilitate the commission of crime and increase its likelihood. The majority concluded that, notwithstanding the absence of prior incidents of sexual assault in the tenant garage, criminal assaults on patrons of the garage were highly foreseeable as a matter of law given the inherently dangerous nature of commercial underground garages, the increasing number of criminal assaults occurring in such structures generally, the physical conditions existing at this particular garage, and the seven serious felonies (robberies) occurring at the ground floor bank during the two-year period preceding the plaintiff's assault. After determining that the assault was foreseeable, the majority analyzed the policy considerations set forth in *Rowland v. Christian*, 69 Cal. 2d 108, 70 Cal. Rptr. 97, 443 P.2d 561 (1968) and concluded that the defendants owed a duty of care to the plaintiff to provide "reasonable" security in the tenant garage, which "might or might not include security guards." The matter was remanded to allow a jury to determine the issues of breach and causation based on the totality of the circumstances presented in the case. Thereafter, the Supreme Court of California granted the defendant's petition for review.

To resolve whether the sexual attack upon the plaintiff was sufficiently foreseeable to require the hiring of security guards, the court considered *Ann M. v. Pacific Plaza Shopping Center*, 6 Cal.4th 666, 25 Cal. Rptr.2d 137, 863 P.2d 207 (1993). The court in *Ann M.* determined that the plaintiff failed to establish the high degree of foreseeability necessary to require the posting of security guards in the common areas of the shopping center. The court held that there was no evidence the defendants had notice of the assaults, purse snatchings, and bank robberies allegedly occurring on the premises. Furthermore, even assuming there had been notice, the plaintiff had conceded that the prior crimes were not similar in nature to the violent assault she suffered. Finally, neither the evidence regarding the presence of transients, nor the evidence of the statistical crime rate of the surrounding area, was of a type sufficient to establish the requisite foreseeability. *Id*. In applying the foregoing analysis to the *Sharon P.* case, the court also held that the defendants were not required to provide security guards in their garage. Significantly, the prior robberies, which all specifically targeted a bank elsewhere on the premises and did not involve violent attacks against anyone, were not sufficiently similar to the sexual assault inflicted upon the plaintiff to establish a high degree of foreseeability that would justify the imposition of such an obligation. *Id*. at 680.

Upon deliberation, the court rejected the view that underground parking structures are "so inherently dangerous that, even in the absence of prior similar incidents, providing security guards will fall within the scope of a landowner's duty of care." *Ann M. v. Pacific Plaza Shopping Center*, 6 Cal.4th 666, 25 Cal. Rptr.2d 137, 863 P.2d 207 (1993). Several considerations factored into the court's decision. First, the court was not directed to any evidence or authorities from which they might confidently conclude that all underground parking structures, regardless of their individual physical characteristics and locations, are prone to violence and therefore are inherently dangerous in nature. In the absence of solid support for the categorical conclusion that all parking garages are inherently dangerous, and are distinctly so in comparison to other types of premises, the court was reluctant to single out garage owners for imposition of the substantial monetary and social costs associated with the hiring of security guards.

Finally, the court held that "adoption of the view that violent crime in underground parking structures is highly foreseeable as a matter of law would lead to incongruous results." In addition, it is questionable whether the plaintiff's proposed measures would have been effective to protect against the type of violent assault that occurred there. The court concluded that "it is difficult to quarrel with the abstract proposition that the provision of improved lighting and maintenance, operational surveillance cameras and periodic walk-throughs of the tenant garage owned and operated by defendants might have diminished the risk of criminal attacks occurring in the garage. But absent any prior similar incidents or other indications of a reasonably foreseeable risk of violent criminal assaults in that location, we cannot conclude defendants were required to secure the area against such crime."

The Supreme Court of California in *Zelig v. County of Los Angeles*, 27 Cal.4th 1112, 45 P.3d 1171 Cal., 2002, dealt with the children of a woman who was fatally shot by her ex-husband in a courthouse. The plaintiffs sued the county and the sheriff's department for negligence. The Superior Court of Los Angeles County sustained a demurrer without leave to amend. Appeal was taken. The court of appeals reversed.

On September 1, 1995, Eileen was murdered by her former husband inside what was then the Central Civil Courthouse in Los Angeles. Lisa Zelig, then six years of age, witnessed her father shoot her mother. The plaintiff was in the courthouse for the purpose of attending a family court hearing regarding spousal and child support. Eileen had secured restraining orders that prohibited her husband from possessing or carrying any firearms, that ordered him to turn over his firearms to his lawyer, and that prohibited him from being "within 100 yards of any firearm" while in the presence of Eileen and the children. The plaintiffs alleged that the defendants had a general duty to protect litigants from "such dangerous conditions, as well as a specific duty to protect [Eileen] because of the special relationship" she had with the county and the sheriff's department.

The plaintiffs alleged that the defendants violated their duty to protect Eileen, because they countenanced the dangerous condition of the courthouse "to the extent they allowed weapons into the courthouse, knowing that litigants, especially in the Family Courts, could be hostile and prone to violence, and once knowing the likelihood of danger to persons in the Courthouse, failed to take steps to prevent the danger."

The supreme court began its analysis of the plaintiffs' claims with some observations about the obligation of public entities to protect the public against crime. Contrary to the suggestion of the court of appeals, the supreme court stated that the general rule is that although the government may assume responsibility for providing adequate police protection against third-party violence, this does not create a legal duty that normally will give rise to civil liability. Thereafter, the court asserted that it is well established that public entities generally are not liable for failing to protect individuals against crime.

The court asserted that they recognized that private landowners have a duty to "maintain their premises in a reasonably safe condition, and that in the case of a landlord, the general duty of maintenance includes 'the duty to take reasonable steps to secure common areas against foreseeable criminal acts of third parties that are likely to occur in the absence of such precautionary measures.'" *Sharon P. v. Arman, Ltd.*, 21 Cal.4th 1181, 1189, 91 Cal.Rptr. 2d 35, 989 P.2d 121 (1999). As such, the court held that "in appropriate circumstances, a public entity may owe members of the public a similar duty not to maintain public premises in a dangerous condition and, specifically, not to maintain its premises in a condition that will increase the reasonably foreseeable risk that criminal activity will injure such individuals." The court emphasized that public entity liability in this regard is statutory. As noted, *Government Code Section 835* imposes a duty on public entities not to maintain property in a "dangerous condition." The plaintiffs' decedent was killed by the criminal act of a third party, and the court had previously pointed out that "third party conduct by itself, unrelated to the condition of the property, does not constitute a 'dangerous condition' for which a public entity may be held liable." *Peterson v. San Francisco Community College Dist.*, 205 Cal.Rptr. 842, 685 P.2d 1193. The court had indicated, however, that a public entity may be liable if it "maintained the property in such a way so as to increase the risk of criminal activity" or in such a way as to "create a reasonably foreseeable risk of . . . criminal conduct." *Id.* The supreme court stated that in the *Zelig* case, the risk of injury was not increased or intensified by the condition of the property, and the necessary causal connection between the condition of the property and the husband's crime was not present. "Indeed, the risk of injury to Eileen at the hands of her ex-husband was at least as great outside the courthouse." The court concluded that the allegations of the complaint, even if proved, failed to demonstrate that the injury was "caused by a dangerous condition of [the] property," as required by *Government Code Section 835. Id.*

The supreme court believed that the plaintiffs' claim simply constituted a complaint that the county failed to protect Eileen against a danger presented by a third party. The public entities and their employees did not create the danger she faced, nor did they make it appreciably greater. The danger faced by Eileen that her husband would shoot her was the same inside the courthouse as outside. For the foregoing reasons, the court reversed the judgment of the court of appeals and remanded the matter to that court with directions to affirm the judgment rendered by the trial court in favor of the defendants.

In *Barnes v. Black*, 71 Cal.App.4th 1473, 84 Cal.Rptr.2d 634 (Cal.App. 4 Dist., 1999), the court of appeals declined to extend *Rosen-*

baum v. Security Pacific Corp., 43 Cal. App. 4th 1084, 1091, 50 Cal.Rptr.29 917 (1996). In *Barnes*, tenants, as survivors of a child, brought claims of negligence and premises liability against their landlord. The claims related to the child's death from being struck by an automobile on a public street after a steeply sloped on-premises driveway allegedly carried the child and his tricycle onto the street. The defendant cited several cases involving the failure to take affirmative action to protect persons from dangerous conditions on an adjacent property. *Rosenbaum v. Security Pacific Corp.*, 43 Cal. App. 4th 1084, 1091, 50 Cal.Rptr.29 917 (1996). The court held that *Rosenbaum* was distinguishable, as the plaintiff alleged that the injury was a result of his child being ejected from the defendant's premises by its dangerous configuration at a point where resident young children were known to ride wheeled toys.

In *Saelzler v. Advanced Group 400*, 25 Cal.4th 763, 107 Cal.Rptr.2d 617 (2001) the court of appeals declined to extend *Rosh v. Cave Imaging Systems, Inc.*, 26 Cal. App. 4th 1225, 32 Cal.Rptr. 2d 136. In *Saelzler*, a delivery person brought general negligence, premises liability, and intentional negligence claims against an apartment complex owner after she was attacked by unknown assailants at the apartment complex. The court held that this case differed substantially from *Rosh v. Cave Imaging Systems, Inc.*, 26 Cal. App. 4th 1225, 32 Cal.Rptr.2d 136, on which the plaintiff relied. In *Rosh*, the plaintiff was shot and severely injured by a disgruntled former employee who had recently been terminated from employment. The plaintiff sued the security firm that was hired specifically to protect the plaintiff and other employees from such incidents. The evidence showed that the defendant had repeatedly ignored the plaintiff's directions to bar the former employee from entering the premises. As such, the court held that under such circumstances, the *Rosh* court properly found that the defendant's negligence was a "substantial factor" in facilitating the former employee's attack on the plaintiff. *Id.* Unlike the situation in *Rosh*, defendants in the *Saelzler* case had no advance notice that a particular assailant was on the premises, and therefore *Rosh* was dissimilar to the *Saelzler* case.

Colorado

Under Colorado decisions, landlords and business owners owe a duty of providing reasonable measures to protect patrons and residents from criminal occurrences when ample evidence of prior crimes on the premises exists, even if the prior crimes differ in nature from the crime in the particular case.

In *Taco Bell, Inc. v. Lannon*, 744 P.2d 43 (Colo. 1987), the plaintiff had been injured during an armed robbery at the defendant's fast-food premises. In this case of first impression for the Colorado courts, the court specifically rejected the notion that prior crimes must be similar to the crime in the case before a landowner can be found liable. In further expanding situations in which a landowner may be found to have breached its duty of protection to an invitee, the court stated that "as the gravity of the harm increases, the apparent likelihood of its occurrence need be correspondingly less to generate a duty of protection."

In *Allen v. Ramada Inn, Inc.*, 778 P.2d 291 (Colo. Ct. App. 1989), the plaintiff had been raped in the defendant's hotel by an intruder who apparently entered the room through a window from which bars had been earlier removed. The court stated that a duty of protection existed, given the special relationship of an innkeeper and a guest. The court ordered a new trial, noting that for these cases, Colorado follows the Restatement (Second) of Torts, Section 344, which provides that a landowner may be liable in such cases, given the nature of the relationship between the parties.

UPDATE

In *Molosz v. Hohertz*, 957 P.2d 1049 (Colo. Ct. App. 1998), the Colorado Court of Appeals held that defendant landlords did not have a duty to protect their tenant's neighbors from the tenant's harmful behavior. The claim for negligent retention of a violent tenant arose after the tenant fired several shots through the neighbors' windows. The court directed a verdict in favor of the defendants, concluding that the law imposed no duty upon them with respect to their tenant's conduct. The shooter remained a party to the suit and the plaintiffs won a jury verdict against him.

Interestingly, the tenant in this case was the defendants' son! However, the shooter was an adult and the parents were sued in their capacity as landlords; thus, when the court of appeals stated that "defendants could not reasonably predict when the tenant might be violent, nor did they have the power to place or keep him in a lock-up situation to prevent harm to others," 957 P.2d at 1051, it is irrelevant that they are in fact his parents. Accordingly, the court found that defendants, as lessees, did not have a "special relationship with the tenant such as to be able to control his conduct concerning third parties." *Id.* Even when the plaintiffs demonstrated the defendants' awareness of the shooter's criminal record, such evidence was insufficient to establish that a duty should have been imposed on the landlords to protect third parties from the harm that occurred. Because the trial court correctly ruled that no duty existed, no issue remained for the jury, and thus the directed verdict for defendant landowners was proper.

In the case of *Grizzell v. Hartman Enter., Inc.*, 68 P.3d 551 (Colo. Ct. App. 2003), the mother of a minor who was shot by an unknown individual after business hours in a locked Subway shop sued the shop's owner. In relevant part, this action was brought pursuant to a Colorado state statute, the Premises Act, § 13-21-115, C.R.S. 2002. Under the Premises Act, a landowner's duty of care depends on the injured person's purpose for entering the property. The court focused on the deceased's classification, ruling that the victim was a licensee, not an invitee, and therefore the plaintiff could recover only for damages caused:

I) By the landowner's unreasonable failure to exercise reasonable care with respect to dangers created by the landowner of which the landowner actually knew; or

II) By the landowner's unreasonable failure to warn of dangers not created by the landowner which are not ordinarily present on property of the type involved and of which the landowner actually knew. § 13-21-115(3)(b).

The plaintiff's assertion that the victim was invited by the owner's employee into the premises sufficiently alleged that the victim was a licensee. Additionally, the complaint alleged that the owner negligently operated the premises by allowing drugs to be sold out the back door, which sufficiently alleged that the owner had knowledge of a dangerous condition. The language of the complaint provided sufficient notice of the claim, specifically that the owner breached its duty. The court of appeals thus held that the plaintiff had stated a claim under the Premises Act.

The Supreme Court of Colorado in *Keller v. Koca*, 111 P.3d 445 (Colo. 2005) held that an employer, owner of a dry cleaning business, did not owe a twelve-year-old sexual assault victim a duty to prevent an employee from assaulting her on a Sunday morning, when the establishment was closed for business. Regarding the plaintiff's claim of negligent supervision against the employer, the court held that while the employer knew the employee/assailant had engaged in sexual misconduct toward female workers, the sexual assault of a daughter of the employee's friends when he was supposed to be alone in the store was "not a foreseeable result of the known risk of harm." 111 P.3d at 446. It was significant that the victim was neither an employee nor a customer and that the employer had no knowledge of her presence in the store. The court remanded the case for consideration of the plaintiff's alternate theory of premises liability.

Connecticut

Connecticut courts have held that a landowner or occupier of land has a duty to exercise reasonable and ordinary care to make its premises safe for those who enter upon them. The exercise of reasonable care includes protecting customers from injuries caused by third persons, when such acts are generally foreseeable. *Antrum v. Church's Fried Chicken*, 40 Conn. Supp. 343; 499 A.2d 807 (1985).

In *Antrum*, the plaintiff was assaulted by an unknown assailant while waiting in the drive-through lane of defendant's restaurant. In denying the defendant's motion for dismissal, the court held that, given the prevailing facts of the case, the assault could be deemed by a trier of fact to have been foreseeable, even without evidence of prior crimes on the premises. Hence, Connecticut seems to have adopted the "totality of circumstances" standard for determining foreseeability.

The court in a one decision concluded that a defense of governmental immunity may also be a question of fact in certain security cases.

In *Foley v. Hartford Civic Center*, 1994 WL 133428 (Conn. Super. Ct. 1994), the plaintiff was injured during a concert at the defendants' premises, and alleged that the defendants failed to provide adequate security measures. The defendants contended they were acting in a governmental capacity, and moved for the case to be dismissed. The court held that a question of fact existed concerning whether the defendants were acting in a governmental or ministerial capacity. *See also, Foley v. Hartford Civic Center*, 1995 WL 107319 (Conn. Super. Ct. 1995) (same case: denying defendants' motion for summary judgment on issues of duty and negligence).

UPDATE

In *Suarez v. Sordo*, 43 Conn. App. 756, 685 A.2d 1144 (1996), cert. denied, 240 Conn. 906, 688 A.2d 334 (1997), the Appellate Court of Connecticut declined to extend *Stewart, supra*. *Suarez* involved a police officer who sued the owners of an apartment building for negligence based on injuries he sustained when he was shot by a suspect he was pursuing. The suspect entered the defendants' building through the back door, which had no lock, and proceeded to a vacant third-floor apartment, which had no lock or doorknob, from which he emerged shooting, wounding the officer. After a jury trial, judgment was entered for the plaintiff. On appeal, the court noted that in analyzing proximate cause, an intervening intentional or criminal act generally relieves a negligent defendant of liability. The court held that the negligent conduct of the landlords in failing to install locks and doorknobs did not create a risk of the type of harm suffered by the plaintiff and thus was not the proximate cause of the officer's injuries. Accordingly, the defendants were not liable to the officer.

Several years later, the Appellate Court of Connecticut heard *Medcalf v. Washington Heights Condo. Ass'n, Inc.*, 57 Conn. App. 12, 747 A.2d 532 (2000), in which it held that, as a matter of law, the jury could not have reasonably found that the assault on the plaintiff was foreseeable. The plaintiff, a visitor to the condominium, was attacked and injured by a third party while she was waiting for a resident to come downstairs to let her in after the electronic buzzer failed to work. The dispositive issue on appeal was whether there was a causal connection between the assault and the failure of the security system.

As to whether the defendants' negligence created the risk of the type of harm suffered by the plaintiff, the plaintiff offered no evidence that the malfunctioning intercom system was designed to provide security to someone *outside* the building. The court called the defendants' failure to maintain the intercom security system "inconsequential" and concluded that such failure could not reasonably have been found to be the proximate cause of the assault. Specifically, as a matter of law, the assault and injury were not "within the foreseeable scope of risk created by the defendants' failure to maintain the intercom system." 57 Conn. App. at 18. Therefore, the plaintiff failed to establish the necessary causal relationship.

The case of *Monk v. Temple George Assoc., LLC*, 273 Conn. 108, 869 A.2d 179 (2005) arose when a nightclub patron who was assaulted by another nightclub customer in a nearby parking lot brought a negligence action against the owner and operator of the parking lot. At the time of the attack, there was no attendant supervising the lot. The appellate court did not consider the issue of proximate cause, but affirmed the trial court's judgment on public policy grounds, explaining that:

> To impose a legal duty on the defendants under the circumstances of this case would (1) be tantamount to imposing strict liability on a parking lot owner or operator for any injury occurring on its property no matter what the circumstances, (2) not act as a deterrent, given the unique circumstances of the attack at issue, where a known attacker attacked the plaintiff because of a personal dispute that arose two years earlier and (3) shift the cost of the plaintiff's harm to parties who were not directly, if at all, responsible for the injuries. *Monk v. Temple George Assoc., LLC*, 82 Conn. App. 660, 664–65 (2004).

The Supreme Court of Connecticut disagreed, holding that: (1) imposing a duty of care on the parking lot owner and operator was not inconsistent with public policy, and thus, the owner and operator owed a reasonable duty of care to the nightclub patron; and (2) material issues of fact existed as to whether the attack was foreseeable and whether the alleged negligence of the parking lot owner and operator in failing to properly supervise the lot was a substantial factor in causing the patron's injuries. Thus, summary judgment for the owner and operator was precluded.

In *Sullivan v. Metro-North Commuter R.R. Co.*, 96 Conn. App. 741, 901 A.2d 1258 (2006), a railroad passenger's estate brought a wrongful death action against the railroad to recover for the fatal shooting that occurred at a train station. The plaintiff alleged that the defendant was negligent in failing to maintain adequate security at its station. Among the defendant's defenses was that the decedent's death was a result of the intentional and/or criminal actions of a third person that superseded any possible negligence on the part of defendant. The jury found that the decedent was an invitee of the defendant and that his death was not foreseeable to the defendant.

On appeal, the Appellate Court of Connecticut held that: (1) it was proper to preclude testimony by the plaintiff's premises security expert, because he had neither railroad nor railroad security experience; (2) it was proper to exclude as evidence (a) a third-party report regarding railroad crime in Connecticut, because it was too remote in time, and (b) a surveillance video from a nearby building, because it was irrelevant and prejudicial; and (3) it was proper to give a jury instruction on superseding and intervening cause, because, contrary to the plaintiff's claim, the doctrine was still valid in Connecticut. Therefore, the judgment was affirmed in favor of the railroad.

Regarding apportionment of liability in premises security cases, the Supreme Court of Connecticut in *Bhinder v. Sun Co.*, 263 Conn. 358, 819 A.2d 822 (2003) held that the prior decision issued in this case was superseded by statute. The court previously held that while the comparative negligence statute did not allow apportionment of liability between negligent and intentional tortfeasors, apportionment would be allowed as a matter of common law. *Bhinder v. Sun Co.*, 246 Conn. 223, 717 A.2d 202 (1998) ("*Bhinder I*"). Briefly, this case arose when a convenience store employee was killed during a robbery. His estate brought a wrongful death action against the owner of the store for failure to provide adequate security, and the owner filed an apportionment complaint against the assailant.

The issue on appeal was whether the trial court properly granted the plaintiff's motion to strike the defendant's apportionment complaint when they applied General Statutes § 52-572h(o), which precludes the apportionment of damages between parties on any basis other than negligence. (The legislature passed this statute in response to the court's decision in *Bhinder I*, and it now entirely precludes apportionment on any basis other than negligence.) The Supreme Court of Connecticut examined the language and history of the statute and found that "the legislature made clear its intent to overrule the common-law portion of *Bhinder I.*" 263 Conn. at 371.

Delaware

Delaware courts require landlords and business owners to provide reasonable protection against criminal occurrences in situations where the defendant has reason to know that criminal acts may occur on his or her premises. Decisions over the past decade seem to expand the nature of evidence that will be considered in determining the foreseeability of a particular crime.

In *Koutoufaris v. Dick*, 604 A.2d 390 (Del. 1992), the plaintiff was assaulted in the parking lot of the defendant's restaurant premises. Among the plaintiff's allegations of negligence were claims of inadequate lighting and negligent security. The defendant denied owing any duty to the plaintiff, but the appellate court held otherwise, concluding that the defendant owed the plaintiff a duty to provide reasonable protection.

In *Hughes v. Jardel, Inc.*, 523 A.2d 518 (Del. 1987), the court held that the nature of the defendant's business, as well as evidence of prior crimes, may result in the imposition of a duty of protection on the landowner. In *Hughes*, the plaintiff was abducted as she was about to leave the defendant's shopping mall, and subsequently was sexually assaulted. At trial, the jury found the defendant negligent for not providing reasonable security. The appellate court noted that possessors of land are not ensurers of public safety, and are under no duty to exercise any care until they know or have reason to know that criminal acts of third persons are occurring or are about to occur.

Hence, while Delaware courts clearly require that a crime be deemed foreseeable before they will impose a duty on a landowner, it appears that foreseeability can be established through a wide array of factors, and not only through evidence of prior reported crimes.

UPDATE

In *Harvey v. Super Fresh Food Markets, Inc.*, 782 A.2d 264 (Del. 2001), the Supreme Court of Delaware affirmed the jury's determination that the defendant was negligent but that such negligence was not a proximate cause of the plaintiff's injury. This case arose out of a robbery of a Super Fresh Supermarket, during which the plaintiff, a customer, was shot and seriously injured by a robber. The plaintiff claimed that the defendant was negligent in the plan and operation of its security. The defendant admitted that some of its security devices (the panic button, alarm system, and surveillance cameras) were not operational at the time of the robbery, but contended that, "under the circumstances of a violent takeover robbery, those devices, even if functioning, would not have prevented the injury to (plaintiff)." *Id.*

While the evidence provided a basis for establishing negligence against the grocery store, the victim also had to prove that "but for" the defendant's conduct, the injury would not have occurred. On appeal, the plaintiff relied on this court's decision in *Jardel Co., Inc. v. Hughes*, 523 A.2d 518 (Del. 1987), claiming that the standard for premises liability set forth therein dispenses with the need to establish proximate cause where the owner's negligence is established. This claim was without merit, because *Jardel* "focused on defining the store owner's duty of foreseeability with respect to criminal activity that might pose harm to customers" and "no issue of proximate cause was posed"; thus, *Jardel* "did not eliminate the standard requirement for recovery in a tort action: that the violation of a duty proximately caused the claimed harm." *Id.* Accordingly, the verdict was affirmed.

Two years later, the Supreme Court of Delaware heard *Rhudy v. Bottlecaps, Inc.*, 830 A.2d 402 (Del. 2003), in which a bar patron's estate brought a wrongful death action against the bar's owner, claiming the owner was liable for the patron's death, which occurred in a public parking lot behind the bar when the patron was shot during a robbery. The trial court reasoned that because the defendant did not possess or control the lot, it did not owe a duty to the decedent. On appeal, the court reviewed de novo the grant of summary judgment to the defendant, taking into account all of the relevant factors and not just the degree of control the defendant had over the lot.

The evidence against the defendant was considerable. The bar management was aware of crime in the area, including robberies in the lot, yet still encouraged patrons to take advantage of the free parking directly behind the bar. In fact, the plaintiffs' decedent parked in the lot based on a radio advertisement on the day of the attack, which mentioned that parking was available there. Further, though the defendant did not have possessory rights to the lot, it did assume some minor responsibilities for the lot, including trash collection. In response to increased crime in the area, the bar hired off-duty police officers for security during events when large crowds were expected (but did not take any special precautions for ordinary nights). Perhaps most striking, a bar patron was robbed in the lot on the night before the shooting at issue, and the management was aware of this crime.

Still, this evidence was not sufficient to hold the landowner liable. Though "control" of the lot was not outcome-determinative, it was significant. The court found that the bar "could neither anticipate nor be expected to protect its patrons from the crime that occurred on the lot to any greater extent than it could protect patrons who parked on any nearby public street." *Id.* at 406. The plaintiffs' argument that the defendant should be liable because the defendant obtained an economic benefit from the parking lot was also unavailing. Holding that the bar owner did not owe a duty either to warn patrons of, or to protect patrons from, criminal acts that occurred in the public parking lot, the court found that "plaintiffs failed to produce facts sufficient to create an inference that the bar owner controlled the parking lot or was otherwise responsible for its patrons' exposure to criminal conduct in the area." *Id.* at 403.

District of Columbia

Several cases, including an impassioned decision authored by then-Appellate Court Judge Ruth Ginsberg in *Doe v. Dominion Bank of Washington*, 963 F.2d 1552, 295 U.S. App. D.C. 385 (1992), have dramatically altered the criteria for assessing when a landowner has a duty to provide reasonable security to guard against criminal occurrences.

In *Doe v. Dominion*, the plaintiff was raped in an office building owned by the defendants, and later alleged that the landlord owed a duty to protect persons from foreseeable criminal occurrences. The defendants contended they owed no duty to protect the plaintiff because, among other reasons, the building was used only for commercial purposes. Although the lower court found that the crime was not foreseeable and therefore dismissed the action, the appellate court rejected that finding and held that considerable evidence supported a conclusion that the landlord could have foreseen the crime.

In addressing the issue of a crime's foreseeability, the court stated that a crime could be deemed foreseeable even without evidence of prior similar crimes on the premises. Instead, according to the court, foreseeability is determined by considering all relevant circumstances, including the overall condition of the building and prior crimes of a dissimilar and even less serious nature.

In support of its decision, the court cited the following leading cases:

- **Duty of Landlord:** *Kline v. 1500 Massachusetts Ave. Apt. Corp.*, 439 F.2d 477, 141 U.S. App. D.C. 370 (1970) (residential landlords owe a duty to exercise reasonable care to protect tenants from foreseeable criminal acts in common areas of leased premises)
- **Foreseeability:** *District of Columbia v. Doe*, 524 A.2d 30 (D.C. 1987) (the condition of premises is a factor to be considered in assessing foreseeability of a criminal occurrence)
- **Standard of Care:** *District of Columbia v. Carmichael*, 577 A.2d 312 (D.C. 1990) (standard of care a landlord must use in providing security to tenants is reasonable care under the circumstances)
- **Residential vs. Commercial Cases:** *Sinai v. Polinger Co.*, 498 A.2d 520 (D.C. 1985) (no apparent distinction between residential and commercial property when determining a landlord's duty to provide security)

In *Clement v. Peoples Drug Store*, 634 A.2d 425 (D.C. 1993), an unknown assailant shot and killed a drug store manager after the manager left the store. The claim of negligence against the decedent's employer alleged that the shooting was a foreseeable act, and cited prior criminal activity in the area to support that contention.

Interestingly, the *Clement* court said that to establish foreseeability and possible liability, the defendant must have a "heightened awareness" of criminal activity. The mere showing of criminal activity, the court concluded, was insufficient to establish this "heightened awareness."

UPDATE

The District of Columbia, in both its federal and "state" courts of appeals, has decided premises security cases that go both ways in recent years. The case of *Varner v. District of Columbia*, 891 A.2d 260 (D.C. 2006) involved the murder of a college student, killed by a fellow student who had several months prior killed another student but who had not yet been apprehended. The decedent's parents brought a wrongful death action, alleging that the university was negligent in its security procedures following the death of the first student, thereby proximately causing the plaintiffs' decedent's death. The plaintiffs claimed that the university should have altered the students' key cards to permit students to enter only their own dormitories.

This claim failed, however, because on the night of the murder, the assailant was in the process of moving out of the decedent's residence hall, where he had been properly admitted and signed in by a resident assistant. Further, the decedent voluntarily admitted his attacker into his bedroom, which was equipped with a bolt lock. The plaintiffs' expert testimony failed to articulate a standard of care owed to students against which the university's security could be measured. Clearly the plaintiffs would not be able to prove at trial that the defendants' negligence proximately caused the decedent's death. The District of Columbia Court of Appeals held that the evidence presented by the plaintiffs was insufficient to raise a genuine issue of material fact.

In *Novak v. Capital Mgmt. & Dev. Corp.*, 452 F.3d 902, 371 U.S. App. D.C. 526 (2006), two patrons leaving a dance club were assaulted and seriously injured in an alley immediately outside the only exit from the club. The plaintiffs alleged that the owners knew that there had been numerous attacks and fights in and around the club, including some witnessed by the club's security guards, and that the defendants failed to take reasonable steps to protect their customers. The court addressed the question of whether the club's operators had a duty, under District of Columbia law, to use reasonable care to protect the plaintiffs from the danger of an attack in the alley.

The lower court held that there was no duty because the club did not exercise "exclusive control" over the alley. The lower court also concluded that the evidence of prior, similar assaults witnessed by the club's security guards was insufficient to make the attack on the plaintiffs foreseeable.

Applying District of Columbia case law, the U.S. Court of Appeals, District of Columbia Circuit determined that the proper inquiry was whether the club put the alley to a "substantial special use." The court ruled that a reasonable jury could find that the club put the alley to a substantial special use. Further, it was foreseeable that a criminal attack would occur in the alley in light of significant evidence of fights that had repeatedly occurred in the alley. Accordingly, the case was reversed and remanded.

Florida

Florida is one of the states leading the way in the liberalization of the law of negligent security; nearly every case gets to the jury. Quite a number of cases hold that owners of residential buildings and complexes owe a duty to provide security. Thus Florida diverges from the common law rules providing that only innkeepers, businesses and business invitees, and common carriers have a duty of care. No special relationship is required to impose a duty of care; rather, the foreseeability of crime within the vicinity imposes a duty on a landowner to take reasonable measures to prevent a crime.

The law has developed step-by-step, however. In *Paterson v. Deeb*, 472 So. 2d 1210 (Fla. Dist. Ct. App. 1985), a scholarly decision containing abundant references to cases arising in Florida and in other states, the court held that, due to a statute imposing an affirmative duty to install entrance door locks and maintain the premises in a safe condition, the defendant could be held liable for failing to repair broken door locks. The tenant was abducted and raped in a common bathroom in the hallway adjacent to her apartment. The court held that she was within the class of persons intended to be protected by the statute. Additionally, due to the breach of the statutory duty, the court held that the trial court erred in dismissing the plaintiff's claim for punitive damages.

The *Paterson* case is cited most often, however, for the principle that evidence of crime in the vicinity of the premises where the particular crime occurred can be offered to demonstrate that the particular crime was foreseeable. What constitutes the borders of the vicinity remains subject to dispute. Offering a broad definition, the *Paterson* court stated that evidence of crime in the same geographic area would be admissible. *See also, Harrison v. Housing Resources Administration*, 588 So. 2d 64 (Fla. Dist. Ct. App. 1991); but *see Admiral's Port Condominium Association v. Feldman*, 426 So. 2d 1054 (Fla. Dist. Ct. App. 1983) (crimes "substantial distances" away not probative of foreseeability); *Highlands Insurance Company v. Gilday*, 398 So. 2d 834 (Fla. Dist. Ct. App. 1981) (evidence of crime in same geographic area not sufficiently close to establish foreseeability of violent attack on premises; evidence of minor larcenies in vicinity also not sufficient).

In another leading case, *Ten Associates v. McCutchen*, 398 So. 2d 860 (Fla. Dist. Ct. App. 1981), which cites case law far and wide, a tenant was raped in her apartment building. The court held that liability could be imposed on the landlord because it assumed a duty by providing twenty-four-hour security guards. Apparently believing that security guards should be perfect professionals, the court noted there had been complaints of poor performance. The guard on duty at the time of the rape had been reprimanded twice, and did not respond to a scream for help by one of the plaintiff's neighbors. The court also noted that substantial criminal activity had occurred in the apartment complex. The court held that the defendant "recognized and assumed the duty to protect the tenants from foreseeable criminal conduct." The hiring of the security guards was deemed further evidence of knowledge of a danger. The court held that the evidence was, therefore, sufficient to allow a jury to determine whether the landlord had breached a duty of care to the plaintiff.

Finally, in the case of *Czerwinski v. Sunrise Point Condominium*, 540 So. 2d 199 (Fla. Dist. Ct. App. 1989), the court held that, apart from statute or a voluntary duty to provide security, a duty to provide security arises when there is a reasonable foreseeability that crime will occur. Foreseeability creates the duty and a five-year history of crime, including one rape, one armed robbery, and numerous burglaries, was sufficient to establish that the attack on the tenant was foreseeable.

Other Florida cases worthy of note follow.

Crime Statistics

In *Newell v. Best Security Systems, Inc.*, 560 So. 2d 395 (Fla. Dist. Ct. App. 1990), the court held that the trial court properly excluded the security expert's testimony regarding crime statistics because the testimony was based solely on a police grid breakdown. As the expert had not consulted the actual records of the incidents, he could not state whether the crimes were residential burglaries, thus creating a duty for the landowner to provide security. Additionally, the court held that evidence of crime against property could suffice to establish the foreseeability of a crime against persons.

Co-Tenants and Nonviolent Crime

In *Larochelle v. Water & Way Limited*, 589 So. 2d 976 (Fla. Dist. Ct. App. 1991), an assailant gained entry to a building through the plaintiff's window, which she had left open. The court held that evidence of crime in another apartment (occupied by—as the dissent described—"a snake-tattooed, nude dancer") where numerous fights had broken out, plus evidence of crime in the neighborhood (including twenty-five incidents in the same apartment complex, only two of which were actually crimes—a burglary and an automobile theft) was sufficient evidence to put the landlord on notice of the possibility the particular crime would occur.

In *Ameirjeiras v. Metropolitan Dade County*, 534 So. 2d 812 (Fla. Dist. Ct. App. 1988), the court deemed evidence of homosexual activity, illicit drug dealing, and arson attempts as insufficient to establish foreseeability of violent crime.

In *Holley v. Mt. Zion Terrace Apartments, Inc.*, 382 So. 2d 98 (Fla. Dist. Ct. App. 1980), the assailant gained entry to the building through a window adjacent to a common walkway, and the defendant argued that the perpetrator was most likely another tenant. The appellate court held that a triable issue of fact existed because the defendant failed to affirmatively show that security would not have prevented the crime.

Knowledge of Propensities of Specific Assailant

The court in *Allen v. Babrab, Inc.*, 438 So. 2d 356 (Fla. 1983) held that there is no requirement that a tavern owner know of the violent propensities of a particular individual. Rather, knowledge of the propensity patrons in general have for disorderly conduct suffices to create a tavern owner's duty to protect other patrons from misconduct.

Trailer Park

In *Salerno v. Hart Finance Corp.*, 521 So. 2d 234 (Fla. Dist. Ct. App. 1988), a tenant of a mobile home park was murdered inside a trailer. The court held that a triable issue of fact existed concerning whether the trailer park owner provided reasonable security.

Outdoors

In a case where the plaintiff was stabbed in the parking lot of the defendant's restaurant, the court held that triable issues of fact existed concerning whether the crime was foreseeable and whether reasonable security was provided. *Odice v. Pearson*, 549 So. 2d 705 (Fla. Dist. Ct. App. 1989).

A kidnapping from a bank's parking lot occurred in *Drake v. Sun Bank and Trust Company of St. Petersburg*, 400 So. 2d 569 (Fla. Dist. Ct. App. 1981). The court held that triable issues of fact existed regarding whether the bank's security guards were negligent in allowing a dangerous condition to develop, and whether the crime was foreseeable.

In *Winn-Dixie Stores, Inc. v. Johnstoneaux*, 395 So. 2d 599 (Fla. Dist. Ct. App. 1981), a robbery occurred at 11:00 A.M. in the parking lot. No security guards were present at that time, although the store had guards during the evening. The court held that a triable issue of fact existed concerning whether reasonable security was provided.

The case of *Holiday Inns, Inc. v. Shelburne*, 576 So. 2d 322 (Fla. Dist. Ct. App. 1991) involved the shooting of a patron in a parking lot next to the defendant's premises. Although the defendant did not own the lot, it had directed patrons to use it. The court held that triable issues of fact existed about whether the crime was foreseeable and whether reasonable security was provided.

Sovereign Immunity/State University

Relyea v. State, 385 So. 2d 1378 (Fla. Dist. Ct. App. 1980) involved the murder of students on the premises of a state university. The court held that allegations regarding the failure of the state university to provide adequate security fell within the definition of a discretionary function, thus limiting the extent of the university's liability. The court explained that whether "to provide security guards, parking attendants, security gates, and the numbers thereof, are clearly discretionary decisions, partially based upon budgetary limitations controlled by the Legislature (citation omitted). In many ways, a state campus resembles a small municipality. In addition to performing its educational function, it provides various other services to its students and the general public. Further, the campuses uniformly encompass rather large areas, and the facilities are open to the public as well as the students. Consequently, the campus security force is in many ways analogous to a municipal police force."

UPDATE

The Florida courts have made distinctions in the area of premises security on the following issues: (1) foreseeability, (2) when to apply certain legal tests, and (3) whether there are different standards for landowners and security companies.

In *Burns Int'l Sec. Servs., Inc. of Fla. v. Philadelphia Indem. Ins. Co.*, 899 So.2d 361 (Fla. App. 4th Dist. 2005), the court held that the mere fact that there was no evidence of prior similar acts such as the one that gave rise to the loss in this case would not relieve a security company of its obligations under a security agreement. The court reasoned that "[t]he very purpose of what Burns agreed to do was to exercise reasonable care to prevent any criminal incident from occurring and it cannot matter that the incident in question was the first one." *Id*. at 365.[1]

The court noted that the duty undertaken by a security provider is different from that of a landowner in that the duty to guard against crime is the precise undertaking that a security provider has agreed to perform. *See also Vazquez v. Lago Grande Homeowner's Ass'n.*, 900 So.2d 587 (Fla. App. 3rd Dist. 2004) (holding that "[i]t simply makes no sense that liability arising from what is essentially a breach of contract or voluntary undertaking would require a prior breach of the agreement to establish responsibility. . . . [S]ince the very purpose of what [the security company] agreed to do was to exercise reasonable care to prevent

---

[1]This is a departure from the holding in *Highlands Ins. Co. v. Gilday*, 398 So.2d 834 (Fla. Dist. Ct. App. 1981), where the court held that there was no liability imposed on the landowner because the plaintiff failed to provide the landowner with evidence of prior similar assaults upon persons in that geographical area. The courts tend to hold security companies at a different standard than landowners.

any criminal incident from occurring, it cannot matter that the deadly incident in question was the first one." *Id*. at 593.

In a departure from the holding in *Ameijeiras v. Metropolitan Dade County*, 534 So.2d 812 (Fla. Dist. Ct. App. 1998), where the plaintiff's submission of evidence of past crimes not similar to the one committed against him was insufficient to establish foreseeability, the district court in *Mulhearn v. K-Mart Corp.*, No. 6:01 CV5230RL31KR, 2006 WL 2460664 (M.D. Fla. August 23, 2006) held that the plaintiff was not required to list evidence of similar past crimes. The plaintiff's submission of evidence of any crimes committed in the last two years was sufficient to satisfy the issue of foreseeability.

Georgia

A prominent decision by a Georgia appellate court has clearly expanded landowners' potential for liability for crimes committed on their premises.

In *Matt v. Days Inns of America, Inc.*, 212 Ga. App. 792, 443 S.E.2d 290 (1994), the plaintiff had been shot during a robbery of the defendant's hotel and alleged that the defendant was negligent for failing to provide adequate protection from the crime. Although evidence of prior crimes in the hotel existed, the lower court dismissed the case. On appeal, the court reversed the lower court's decision, holding that evidence of prior crimes, although dissimilar from the crime in the case, could nevertheless be sufficient to establish foreseeability. The *Matt* court held that the determination of foreseeability should be made by considering whether the prior crimes would have put an ordinary, prudent person on notice that the guests faced increased risks of danger.

Importantly, the *Matt* court expanded on earlier Georgia decisions that required evidence of at least one "substantially similar act" committed upon the defendant's premises before liability could be found. In so doing, the court specifically rejected the notion that a landlord be allowed "one free crime" before liability can attach.

However, in *Knudson v. Lenny's Inc.*, 202 Ga. App. 85, 413 S.E.2d 258 (1991), the court held there was insufficient evidence that an attack on the plaintiff in the defendant's restaurant could have been foreseen by the defendant, and therefore dismissed the case. The court further noted that the defendant appeared to have acted reasonably in providing adequate security measures.

Georgia, accordingly, is among the various jurisdictions that have rejected the "prior similar acts" test for determining foreseeability.

UPDATE

In *Hillcrest Foods, Inc. v. Kiritsy*, 227 Ga. App. 554, 489 S.E.2d 547 (1997), the court of appeals declined to extend *Doe v. Prudential-Bache/A.G. Spanos Realty*, 222 Ga.App. 169, 474 S.E.2d 31 (1996). In *Hillcrest*, a restaurant customer was struck by two bullets and paralyzed from the waist down in a drive-by shooting committed by the husband of a waitress. The customer brought a premises liability action against the owner. The trial court denied the owner's summary judgment motion, relying on *Doe* and *Wallace v. Boys Club of Albany*, 211 Ga.App. 534, 439 S.E.2d 746 (1993) to hold that prior similar criminal acts are not the only way of proving foreseeability, and as such, a question of fact regarding foreseeability remained as to the premises liability claim. The court of appeals, noting that the Georgia courts had not dealt previously with a proprietor's duty in a drive-by shooting case, reversed and held that the drive-by shooting was *not* foreseeable to the owner so as to impose a duty to protect the customer from the harm that occurred.

In evaluating the evidence, the court of appeals explained that while several crimes against persons had occurred on Hillcrest's property in the three years before the drive-by shooting, none of the prior crimes involved a drive-by shooting, and there was nothing in the record to put Hillcrest on notice of the likelihood of a future drive-by shooting. The court of appeals also found that a drive-by shooting is a totally different crime from that in which all actions constituting a crime occur on the defendant's property, because, as in this drive-by shooting, the perpetrator was not even on the defendant's property, but rather was traveling on a busy public thoroughfare; as such, it was difficult to imagine what effective action Hillcrest could reasonably have taken that could have prevented a drive-by shooting, even had there been a prior event of this nature.

The court of appeals found that the trial court's reliance on *Wilks v. Piggly Wiggly Southern*, 207 Ga.App. 842, 429 S.E.2d 322 (1993) as authority for the proposition that the law does not require that the criminal act occur on the premises or approaches of the proprietor's premise in order to establish foreseeability was misplaced. In *Wilks*, the victim was mugged around the corner from the defendant's property. *Id.* The court of appeals reversed the trial court's grant of the property owner's motion for summary judgment, however, because the property owner had allowed the attackers to loiter on his premises waiting for victims. *Id.* at 844. Thus, *Wilks* was factually distinguishable from the *Hillcrest* case. The trial court's reliance on *Doe* (a case involving a rape that occurred in a parking garage where the court acknowledged that if the defendant admitted the existence of a dangerous condition, foreseeability may be established even in the absence of a prior substantially similar criminal act) and on *Wallace* (a case involving the failure to properly supervise a child who was injured after wandering from the defendant's premises) was also found to be misplaced as the cases are factually distinguishable. Here, there was no admission by Hillcrest, and the criminal conduct was not initiated on its property. Therefore, *Doe* was inapplicable to the *Hillcrest* analysis. And *Wallace* was not a true premises liability case, as it involved failure to supervise a child and had no application to the *Hillcrest* case.

In conclusion, the court held that under the facts of this case, the plaintiff had failed to establish that the drive-by shooting was foreseeable by the defendant, and that while there may be situations in which off-premises criminal conduct would not preclude a proprietor's liability, any such case would necessarily involve *a higher degree of foreseeability*, not here present, than would those cases involving on-premises conduct.

Hawaii

The law on premises security cases in Hawaii is only starting to develop.

In *Myers v. South Seas Corp.*, 76 Haw. 161, 871 P.2d 1231 (1994), a person ultimately died from injuries sustained in an altercation that occurred in a lounge area located in the lobby of the defendants' premises. Among other contentions, the plaintiffs alleged that the defendants failed to provide adequate security and failed to reasonably protect their patrons from harm.

A jury trial resulted in a finding of negligence, but also a finding that such negligence was not a legal cause of the injury to the plaintiff. The appellate court found the verdict to be irreconcilably inconsistent, and ordered a new trial. The Hawaii Supreme Court affirmed the appellate court's rulings on different grounds and remanded the case.

UPDATE

In *Doe v. Grosvenor Center Associates*, 104 Hawaii 500, 92 P.3d 1010 (Intermediate Court of Appeals of Hawaii 2004), a commercial sublessee brought a cause of action against the lessors and the security service for negligence and breach of warranty after she was robbed and raped in rented premises. The lessors and the security service filed motion for summary judgment. The intermediate court of appeals held, among other things, that (1) the sublessee was not a business visitor entitled to a special relationship; (2) the theory of implied warranty of habitability did not apply; and (3) any duty by the security service to the sublessee was limited to voluntary undertaking.

In this case, Jane Doe, a sublessee of one office within a lessee's suite of seven offices in an owner-lessor's office building, was in her office one Saturday afternoon when she was robbed and raped by an unidentified man. The court summarized the precedent created by the Hawaii Supreme Court's opinions in *Doe v. Grosvenor*, 73 Haw. 158, 162, 829 P.2d 512 (1992); *Maguire v. Hilton Hotels Corp.*, 79 Hawai'i 110, 113, 899 P.2d 393 (1995); and *Moody v. Cawdrey & Associates, Inc.*, 68 Haw. 527, 721 P.2d 707 (1986), rev'd 6 Haw.App. 355, 721 P.2d 708, as follows: (1) a landlord that owns and operates an office building and leases and rents offices to tenants (a) never owes the "business visitor" "special relationship" duties to its tenants, but (b) owes the "business visitor" "special relationship" duties to its tenant's employee (i) while the tenant's employee is in the landlord's office building's common areas that are open to the public so as to provide and facilitate public access to the tenant's office, and (ii) while, upon consideration of the totality of the relevant circumstances, it is reasonably foreseeable that the act of one or more third persons will harm the tenant's employee, and (2) a hotel owes the "business visitor" "special relationship" duties to an employee of the company hired by the hotel to provide cleaning services to the restrooms in the hotel (i) while the employee is in one of the public restrooms in the hotel, and (ii) while, upon consideration of the totality of the relevant circumstances, it is reasonably foreseeable that the act of one or more third persons will harm the employee.

In applying the totality of circumstances test, the court explained that prior criminal acts would still be helpful, but the inquiry was broad enough to examine other factors as well. The court also explained that applying the totality of the circumstances test did not mean that it was imposing strict liability on landowners to protect invitees against all actions by third parties. To the contrary, use of the totality of circumstances rule simply meant that the court's inquiry would not be unfairly limited and that foreseeability must still be determined reasonably. In applying these factors to the facts in this case, the court disagreed with Jane Doe's contention that she was a "business visitor" of Grosvenor to whom a "special relationship" duty existed.

Jane Doe further argued that in *Trentacost v. Brussel*, 82 N.J. 214, 412 A.2d 436 (N.J.1980), the New Jersey Supreme Court noted that the majority of jurisdictions have found an implied warranty of habitability in the landlord-tenant context, including Hawaii, in *Lemle v. Breeden*, 51 Haw. 426, 462 P.2d 470 (1969). The New Jersey Supreme Court therefore held that "the landlord's implied warranty of habitability obliges him to furnish reasonable safeguards to protect tenants from foreseeable criminal activity on the premises." *Trentacost* at 443. Jane Doe also argued that an important distinction in her case is that she need not assert that the mere failure to provide security was a breach of the implied warranty; rather, she argued that because the landowner provided security services, it and the security company implied warranted protection for its tenants against the criminal acts of third parties. On this point, the court explained that, while Hawaii was one of the first jurisdictions to extend the theory of implied warranty of habitability and fitness for intended use to residential leases, this court had never extended the theory to commercial leases, and few jurisdictions had done so. In the few cases in which the courts in Hawaii had extended such an implied warranty to a commercial lease, the subject lease had expressly provided that the lessor would furnish the disputed service. Thus, the court held that Hawaii generally does not apply the theory of an implied warranty of habitability to commercial leases, and Jane Doe's sublease being a commercial sublease without any special clause, her claim on this point was groundless.

Finally, the court held that in Jane Doe's case, the "business visitor" "special relationship" question pertained to the lessors, not the security service. Thus, the lower court had properly instructed the jury that "[t]o establish that defendant [security service] owed a duty to plaintiff [Jane Doe], plaintiff [Jane Doe] must prove by a preponderance of the evidence that defendant [security service] voluntarily undertook a duty of reasonable care to protect [Jane Doe] against criminal harm," and Jane Doe's argument that the trial court had "erroneously limited the existence of a duty to a 'voluntary undertaking' by [the security services]" was denied.

Idaho

Idaho has long applied the "totality of circumstances" test for determining whether a landowner is under a duty to provide protection from criminal occurrences.

In *Sharp v. W.H. Moore, Inc.*, 118 Idaho 297, 796 P.2d 506 (1990), the court reversed the lower court's grant of summary judgment for the defendants, holding that a question of fact may exist concerning whether the landlord owed a duty to provide protection to the plaintiff, who had been raped by an unknown person while working in her office.

UPDATE

In 2002, the Supreme Court of Idaho issued their decision in *Hunter v. State*, 138 Idaho 44, 57 P.2d 755 (2002), abrogating *Doe v. Garcia*, 131 Idaho 578, 961 P.2d 1181 (1998). *Hunter* was a wrongful death action brought by the parents of a teenager who was raped and murdered by a probationer with whom she had worked at a car wash. She quit the job six weeks before her rape and murder, which occurred in the probationer's home. At trial, the liability was apportioned among the victim, her father, the car wash/employer, the State of Idaho, and the probationer. The court explained that while submitting the case to the jury was consistent with *Doe*, both cases "extend the duty of an employer too far for consequences outside employment over which the employer has no realistic control." The court in *Hunter* held, among other things, that the probationer's employer owed no duty to the probationer's former coworker to foresee that the probationer would murder her, abrogating *Doe v. Garcia*.

Illinois

Several Illinois decisions suggest it will be difficult for a plaintiff to prevail against a landowner in a premises security lawsuit. Although Illinois courts recognize situations in which a landlord may be under a duty to provide protection against criminal acts committed by third persons, such situations appear to be infrequent.

In *Costa v. Gleason*, 628 N.E.2d 199, 256 Ill. App. 3d 150 (1993), the plaintiff was assaulted by an assailant who entered the premises through a door that had been opened by patrons leaving a lounge shortly after it had closed. The plaintiff alleged negligence by the defendant lounge owner for failing to provide adequate security against the assault. The court held that the dismissal of the case was warranted because the assault was an isolated occurrence that, as a matter of law, was not foreseeable by the defendant. The *Costa* court reaffirmed prior Illinois decisions standing for the proposition that landowners, under most circumstances, do not owe a duty to protect persons from criminal acts of third persons.

Similarly, in *Badillo v. DeVino*, 515 N.E.2d 681, 161 Ill. App. 3d 596 (1987), the court dismissed a claim of negligence brought against a bar by a patron who had been ejected from the bar, and who was later assaulted outside by a third person with whom he had an earlier argument inside the bar. The court held that, under the facts presented, the defendant did not owe a duty to protect the plaintiff.

In *Taylor v. Hooker*, 428 N.E.2d 662, 101 Ill. App. 3d 639 (1981), the court rejected a claim of negligence brought by the injured plaintiff, on the ground that there was not sufficient evidence presented to establish foreseeability. The court stated that evidence of prior property crimes alone is not necessarily sufficient to establish foreseeability of violent crimes.

In *N.W. v. Amalgamated Trust & Savings Bank*, 554 N.E.2d 629, 196 Ill. App. 3d 1066 (1990), an Illinois appellate court affirmed the dismissal of the complaint brought by a tenant against her landlord. The plaintiff had been sexually assaulted in her apartment by an unknown assailant. Importantly, in dismissing the case, the court noted an absence of prior criminal activity at the premises, as well as an absence of any evidence about how the assailant entered the premises.

A 1994 decision also dismissed a wrongful death action brought against a decedent's employer under applicable provisions of the Illinois Workers' Compensation Act. In *Bercaw v. Domino's Pizza, Inc.*, 630 N.E.2d 166, 258 Ill. App. 3d 211 (1994), the decedent was killed during the course of making a delivery for his employer. In finding an absence of any evidence to suggest that the defendant intended to harm the decedent, the court held that the complaint must be dismissed as being barred by the Illinois Workers' Compensation Act.

UPDATE

Illinois courts, observing that the attack in *Badillo* occurred a block away from the defendant's establishment, have refused to hold that an innkeeper's duty ends at the doorway. *Osborne v. Stages Music Hall, Inc.*, 312 Ill.App.3d 141, 726 N.E.2d 728 (Ill. App. Ct. 2000). Instead, courts have held that the owner's duty may be extended to disturbances arising in the parking lot if it was reasonably foreseeable that an assault might occur there. *Shortall v. Hawkeye's Bar and Grill*, 283 Ill.App.3d 439, 670 N.E.2d 768 (Ill. App. Ct. 1996).

Nevertheless, a tavern owner has only a duty to take reasonable steps to protect his invitees. That duty is not breached where, upon receiving notice of a fight, the owner prevented anyone from entering or exiting the tavern and called the police. *Getson v. Edifice Lounge, Inc.*, 117 Ill.App.3d 707, 453 N.E.2d 131 (Ill. App. Ct. 1983).

Finally, it is well established that the landlord-tenant relationship is not a special relationship imposing a general duty on a landlord to protect his tenants against third-party criminal acts. Regardless, the voluntary undertaking exception to the general rule provides that a landlord may be held liable for the criminal acts of third parties when it voluntarily undertakes to provide security measures but performs the undertaking negligently, if the negligence is the proximate cause of injury to the tenant. However, this exception is not boundless. For example, where a landlord provided door buzzers and an intercom system for an apartment building, such provision did not constitute a voluntary undertaking to provide security for tenants, absent evidence showing that the door buzzers and intercom system were provided for security, and, in particular, as a security device for alerting people inside the apartment building that a person outside needed help. Thus, there could be no imposition of liability upon the landlord on this basis for damages that resulted when a tenant was raped by a third party on the premises of her apartment building. *Bourgonje v. Machev*, 362 Ill.App.3d 984, 841 N.E.2d 96 (Ill. App. Ct. 2005).

Indiana

Indiana courts have liberally expanded landowners' obligations to provide security against criminal occurrences, applying the "duty to control" and "voluntary assumption of duty" standards for determining when a duty to provide protection will exist. Indiana courts have found a duty to exist when a landlord provided security features at its building, when crimes were committed on premises not owned by the defendant, and even when a plaintiff's former husband failed to protect her against an assault by his girlfriend.

In *Ember v. BFD Inc.*, 490 N.E.2d 764 (Ind. Ct. App. 1986), a bar patron was assaulted and injured while in a parking lot across from the defendants' bar. The evidence showed that the bar patrons regularly used the parking lot, and that there had been prior criminal occurrences at the location.

The court noted that the bar owners were aware that their patrons regularly used the parking lot, and considered evidence that suggested the defendants were aware of prior crimes occurring there. The court held that a question of fact existed concerning whether the defendants had gratuitously assumed a duty to provide protection to their patrons in the area surrounding their establishment. Importantly, the *Ember* court expressly stated that while a landowner's duty to provide protection normally extends only to its premises, the definition of "premises" is not necessarily limited to the area actually owned or leased by the party. A subsequent Indiana decision in another appellate district emphasizes that *Ember* is a "gratuitous assumption of duty" case and its use should be limited to its facts. *State v. Flanigan*, 489 N.E.2d 1216 (Ind. Ct. App. 1986).

In *Kinsey v. Bray*, 596 N.E.2d 938 (Ind. 1992), the court reversed the dismissal of an action brought by the plaintiff against her former husband. The plaintiff contended she had been assaulted by her ex-husband's girlfriend, and that her ex-husband owed her a duty to protect her from the assault. Under the specific circumstances presented by the case, the court of appeals agreed. The court held that, given the relationship between the parties, the defendant may be found to have owed a duty to control his girlfriend's conduct.

In *Nalls v. Blank*, 571 N.E.2d 1321 (Ind. Ct. App. 1991), an Indiana court of appeals held that a landlord, under certain circumstances, may owe a duty to protect tenants against criminal acts of third persons. In *Nalls*, the plaintiff was assaulted by an assailant who entered his apartment by using a key obtained by vandalizing a key box affixed to the outside of the building. The box was intended for use by the postal service. The court rejected Indiana's general rule that a landlord does not owe a duty to protect a tenant from criminal actions of a third person. The court held that a question of fact existed regarding whether the defendant had voluntarily undertaken an obligation to provide security by furnishing self-locking doors and other security measures at the building.

UPDATE

In 2003, when a bar patron was beaten in the bar parking lot by another patron, the Indiana Supreme Court addressed whether the trial court properly denied the plaintiff's motion for judgment on the evidence because the defendant failed to prove the elements of duty and proximate cause. *Paragon Family Restaurant v. Bartolini*, 799 N.E.2d 1048 (Ind. 2003).

In *Bartolini*, the court held that landowners have a duty to take reasonable precautions to protect their invitees from foreseeable criminal attacks. In addition, the court repeated that the duty of a business to exercise reasonable care extends to keeping its parking lot safe and providing a safe and suitable means of entrance and exit. The *Bartolini* court established the rule that there is usually no need to redetermine what duty a business owner owes to its invitees because the law clearly recognizes that "proprietors owe a duty to their business invitees to use reasonable care to protect them from injury caused by other patrons and guests on their premises, including providing adequate staff to police and control disorderly conduct." *Id.* at 1052–53. This duty only extends to harm from the conduct of third parties that, under the facts of a particular case, is reasonably foreseeable to the proprietor. Finally, the court acknowledged that whether the criminal act of a third party was reasonably foreseeable was determined by the totality of the circumstances surrounding the event, including the nature, condition, and location of the land and prior similar incidents. *Id.* at 1052–53.

Importantly, the court recognized that whether an individualized redetermination of duty was necessary where the general duty was otherwise well-settled had been the subject of procedural inconsistency. *Id.* at 1053. The court stated, "There is no doubt, however, that reasonable foreseeability is an element of a landowner or business proprietor's duty of reasonable care. The issue is merely at what point and in what manner to evaluate the evidence regarding foreseeability." *Id.* at 1053.

Since the Indiana Supreme Court decided *Bartolini*, Indiana courts have attempted to apply its holding to a range of cases. In *Lane v. St. Joseph's Reg'l Med. Ctr.*, 817 N.E.2d 266, 268 (Ind. Ct. App. 2004), a teenage boy in an emergency room waiting area walked up to another patient in the waiting area and began hitting her on the arm and shoulder. In determining whether summary judgment was proper, the *Lane* court considered two possible readings of *Bartolini*. In the first, the court observed that *Bartolini* could be read to mean that reasonable foreseeability exists because the criminal attack occurred. *Id.* It went on to discount this reading because the result would hardly seem logical in that it would suggest that every criminal act that occurs would be foreseeable, and all landowners and proprietors would automatically be subject to liability.

Alternatively, the *Lane* court also suggested that *Bartolini* meant that the facts did not actually establish the duty but allowed for its application. In other words,

> the duty to protect business invitees from criminal acts of third parties has always existed and business proprietors owe that duty to invitees regardless of whether a criminal act has ever occurred. However, that conclusion should not be read so broadly to encompass all business proprietors. Rather, any conclusion that a duty is owed to protect patrons from criminal acts of third parties must include the consideration of whether the acts were foreseeable. Effectively, while one may expect that a criminal act would occur at a bar and that some precautions should be taken to protect patrons, one would not reasonably expect that a criminal attack would occur in a doctor's office. Thus, a doctor's office would not generally have the duty to maintain security measures to protect its patients. *Id.* at 272.

Thus, the *Lane* court concluded, "the existence of a duty is well-settled when one would expect that a criminal act of third party is likely to occur on the premises." *Id.* at 273.

In attempting to interpret these opinions, the appellate court in *Winchell v. Guy*, 857 N.E.2d 1024 (Ind. App. 2006) (plaintiff shot by another customer while waiting in the drive-thru line at Taco Bell) acknowledged the ambiguity in *Bartolini* and *Lane*, concluding that the *Lane* court's second reading of *Bartolini* requires a court to perform an individualized determination of whether a duty exists where one is already well settled. The *Winchell* court asserted that the *Lane* approach had been clearly rejected in *Northern Indiana Public Service Co. v. Sharp*, 790 N.E.2d 462 (Ind. 2003), where the court specifically explained that it is well settled: proprietors owe a duty to their invitees to use reasonable care to protect them from injury caused by other patrons and guests on their premises.

Using this analysis, the *Winchell* court restated and exercised the *Bartolini/Sharp* approach by concluding that Taco Bell did owe a duty to its customers, including Winchell, to use reasonable care to protect them from injuries caused by other patrons and guests on their premises without conducting an individualized analysis. The court held that the question was whether Taco Bell satisfied this duty by exercising reasonable care to protect Winchell from the reasonably foreseeable acts of other people on its premises. Consequently, the appellate court overturned the trial court's ruling in favor of Taco Bell's motion for summary judgment "because Taco Bell owed Winchell a duty as a matter of law and there are questions of fact regarding the elements of breach and causation." *Id.* at 1031.

Iowa

Not surprisingly, there are few premises security cases reported in Iowa. The Iowa courts had an opportunity to address important security issues in the case of *Eley v. Pizza Hut of America, Inc.*, 500 N.W.2d 61 (Iowa 1993), in which several questions were presented to the supreme court for certification. Among those was whether an occupier of a business premises open to the public has a duty to exercise reasonable care to prevent injury or harm to a person who is not on the property, but is injured by the criminal acts of a person who is on the property.

In *Eley*, the plaintiff was standing near the defendant's property and was struck by a rock allegedly thrown by someone who was among a group of people on the defendant's parking premises. However, because the facts were deemed in dispute, the court refused to certify the question.

UPDATE

In *Freeman v. Busch*, 150 F. Supp. 2d 995 (S.D. Iowa 2001), the victim was a guest of a college student and was on campus at a party when sexually assaulted. Noting that this was an educational setting and the victim was a guest of a college student (distinguishable from *Tenney v. Atlantic Associates*, 594 N.W.2d 11 [Iowa 1999], where landlords owed a duty to take reasonable steps to protect tenants from foreseeable criminal acts), the district court held that "a college is an educational institution, not a custodian of the lives of each adult, both student and non-student, who happens to enter the boundaries of its campus." *Id.* at 1002. The court further held that to hold the university responsible "would directly contravene the competing social policy of fostering an educational environment of student autonomy and independence." *University of Denver v. Whitlock*, 744 P.2d 54, 62 (Colo. 1987). Also, the harm alleged was not foreseeable because there were intervening acts by third parties who fondled the plaintiff at the party. The court found that their acts relieved the university of any liability resulting from its negligence.

Roycroft v. Hammons, 203 F. Supp. 2d 1053 (S.D. Iowa 2002) involves a plaintiff who was the sole survivor of a victim who was murdered while staying at a hotel. In this case, there were no indications of forced entry into the hotel room, and investigators initially concluded that the victim knew her attacker. Applying the reasonableness test in this context, the court did not find it unreasonable for the plaintiff to rely upon the investigative report and opined that the defendant's suggestion that the plaintiff would have found out that the killer was a stranger through due diligence would place an "extraordinarily high standard upon plaintiff." *Id.* at 1057. Summary judgment was precluded.

Kansas

Surprisingly, Kansas courts have decided a fair number of premises security cases. These decisions, which address primarily issues of foreseeability, appear to follow a moderate approach in assessing landowners' liability for crimes committed on their premises.

Under Kansas law, a landowner owes a duty to provide protection only when the crime is deemed reasonably foreseeable. In *Nero v. Kansas State University*, 253 Kan. 567, 861 P.2d 768 (1993), the plaintiff had been sexually assaulted by a fellow residential hall student, and alleged that the university owed her a duty to provide protection from the occurrence. The supreme court reversed the lower court's dismissal of the case, holding that the defendant, as a landlord, owed a duty to use reasonable care to protect students from foreseeable criminal conduct, and that a question of fact existed concerning whether the attack on the plaintiff was foreseeable. The court further held that landowners owe no duty to protect persons from criminal acts unless the occurrences are foreseeable, and stated that prior occurrences of crime can be considered in evaluating the foreseeability of a particular crime.

Use of the "totality of the circumstances" doctrine to assess foreseeability was adopted by the appellate court in *Siebert v. Vic Regnier Builders, Inc.*, 253 Kan. 540, 856 P.2d 1332 (1993). In *Siebert*, the plaintiff was injured during an armed robbery in the defendant's shopping center parking lot. The court held that, in determining foreseeability, the "totality of the circumstances" should be considered, and not just evidence of prior similar crimes.

The Kansas Supreme Court has had the opportunity to also consider whether an apportionment of liability for a criminal act can be imposed on the assailant. *Kansas State Bank & Trust v. Specialized Transportation Services, Inc.*, 249 Kan. 348, 819 P.2d 587 (1991), involved allegations of sexual abuse and was brought against a bus driver, a bus company, and a school district. The court held that under applicable Kansas statutes, the negligent tortfeasors were precluded from apportioning their liability against the intentional tortfeasor.

An earlier important decision helping to influence Kansas law was the case of *Flood v. Wisconsin Real Estate Investment Trust*, 503 F. Supp. 1157 (D. Kan. 1980). The plaintiff, who had been assaulted and raped in her apartment, alleged that her landlord failed to provide adequate protection from the attack. The evidence suggested that the building, at one time, did have night security guards, but they were not employed on the night of the attack. The court held that a reasonable inference could be made that (1) when she entered her lease the plaintiff relied on the guards being employed and (2) by no longer employing the guards, the defendant breached its warranty of supplying guard protection to the plaintiff.

UPDATE

In *South v. McCarter*, 119 P.3d 1 (Kan. 2005), parents of a minor were injured in a fistfight inside a mobile home park and then brought suit against the mobile home owner. In this case, the court summarized the Kansas Supreme Court's current position on premises liability as follows: "this court has eliminated the common-law distinctions between the duties owed to licensees and invitees and set up reasonableness of action and foreseeability of injury as the foundations of liability." *See Cunningham v. Braum's Ice Cream & Daily Stores*, 80 P.3d 35 (2003).

The court distinguished this case from *Nero v. Kansas State Univ.*, 861 P.2d 768 (Kan. 1993) because even though *Nero* also involved a landlord-tenant relationship, *Nero* was in the context of a student-university relationship in which the university possessed solid information regarding the alleged criminal conduct and the landlord took reasonable steps to keep the alleged perpetrator away from the location of the incident. In the *South* case, no such evidence was presented, and thus the harm experienced was not foreseeable under the totality of circumstances test. Here, there was no duty to control the conduct of third parties and no special relationship existed; furthermore, there was no specific information about past conduct and actual risk involved.

Kentucky

Kentucky had no cases reported.

UPDATE

Businesses

In *Stalbolsky v. Belew*, 205 F.3d 890 (6th Cir.2000), the court found that an employer did not know of its employee's dangerous propensities. While driving a truck for the employer, the employee raped and killed a woman. Before the employee applied for his job, he was convicted of arson, but he did not disclose this on his application. The pre-employment investigation consisted of obtaining his driving record, contacting his previous employer, and submitting him to drug screening. The employee worked for the company for three years without any incident. Three days before the crime, the employee was found guilty of aggravated battery that occurred six weeks prior to the crime. The court followed the *Oakley* decision by finding that the employer was not liable. The employee was a driver and was not a supervisor; thus the court found that this limited the employer's knowledge of the employee's dangerous propensities.

In *Patterson v. Blair*, 172 S.W.3d 361 (2005), the court addressed vicarious liability of an employer for criminal acts of an employee. The employee, while trying to repossess vehicles, shot out the tire of the vehicles. In changing how vicarious liability would be evaluated in Kentucky, the supreme court stated that to determine whether an act matter was within the scope of employment, the focus should be on the purpose of the act or whether the act advanced the employer's purposes. The court found that the employer could be held liable since the repossession efforts served the employer's interests.

In *Murphy v. Second Street Corporation*, 48 S.W.3d 571 (Ct.App. 2001), the court ruled in favor of a tavern in a suit brought by a patron for failure to protect against an assault by another patron. The court stated that for a tavern to be liable, the plaintiff must show that the proprietor had knowledge that the plaintiff was about to be injured, or that the conduct of the patron present in the tavern would lead a prudent person to believe that the patron would injure other guests or patrons. Since the plaintiff testified that the events transpired quickly, the court found for the defendant.

Louisiana

Louisiana decisions have reinforced the doctrine set forth in *Banks v. Hyatt Corp.*, 722 F.2d 214 (5th Cir. 1984), that a business owner, in most cases, does not owe a duty to protect persons from crime, unless the owner has knowledge of the criminal's intent to commit such crime.

In *Douchette v. Bellsouth Tele. Commun., Inc.*, Civil Action No. 94-216 (E.D. La. 1994), the plaintiff was shot by an unknown assailant while using the defendant's night depository to pay his phone bill. The court concluded that the shooting was unforeseeable and, accordingly, that the defendant did not owe a duty to protect the plaintiff.

An absence of a duty to provide protection was also found in the case of *Dye v. Schweggman Brothers Giant Supermarkets, Inc.*, 627 So. 2d 688 (La. 1993), where an action was brought on behalf of the decedent who was murdered in the defendant's parking lot during an armed robbery. The court held that the defendant did not owe a duty to protect persons against "unarticulated criminal conduct."

In *Schneider v. Brown & Root, Inc.* (E.D. La. 1994), an action alleging negligent security was commenced against the defendants and on behalf of a decedent who had been abducted in a refinery parking lot and later murdered. In dismissing the complaint, the court held that defendant Brown & Root had no ownership interest in the property and therefore no duty to secure the premises. The court also dismissed the complaint against another defendant, citing an absence of any evidence that the defendant had acted negligently.

Although Louisiana courts have found only limited situations in which a landlord owes a duty to protect, that duty has been imposed in cases where it is voluntarily assumed, and then negligently performed. In *Harris v. Pizza Hut of Louisiana, Inc.*, 455 So. 2d 1364 (La. 1984), a patron was shot and killed during a robbery. The restaurant had stationed a guard on the premises, but the guard was not conspicuously posted at the time of the occurrence. The Louisiana Supreme

Court noted that the restaurant was located in a high-crime area, and that the incident might have been deterred had the guard been more visible. Accordingly, the court concluded that the restaurant could be found liable for negligently assuming a duty to provide security.

UPDATE

The state of Louisiana has been busy in this arena since 1999. In *Peterson v. Gibraltar Savings & Loan*, 733 So.2d 1198 (La. 5/18/99), the court addressed liability of a mall owner, a parking garage, and a security company for the attack, sexual assault, and abduction of the plaintiff in a 600,000-square-foot garage at approximately 1:00 A.M. The parking garage adjoined a mall and the nightclub the plaintiff visited the night of the attack. The garage had security service personnel to patrol the garage on foot and by vehicle. There were also security personnel inside the mall. The *Peterson* court noted that Louisiana followed a duty-risk analysis that required the plaintiff to prove the following: (1) the conduct in question was the cause-in-fact of the resulting harm; (2) the defendant owed a duty of care to the plaintiff; (3) the duty was breached by the defendant; and (4) the risk of harm was within the scope of the protection afforded by the duty breached. The court noted that a business establishment has a duty to take reasonable care for the safety of its patrons, but this duty did not extend to unforeseeable or unanticipated criminal acts by third parties. However, the court noted that if a duty to protect others against criminal misconduct had been assumed, liability may be created by a negligent breach of that duty. The court held for the owners, finding that there were no significant prior criminal acts to place them on notice that the garage posed an unreasonable risk of harm to its user or that an attack and abduction by gunpoint were foreseeable. The court also found for the security company because there was no evidence that the guard's patrol would have deterred the attackers, there were quite a number of people in and out of the garage all night, and the guards were randomly patrolling.

The supreme court addressed this issue later that year in its seminal case of *Posecai v. Wal-Mart Stores, Inc.*, 752 So.2d 762 (La. 11/30/99). Louisiana adopted the balancing test that previously was adopted in California and Tennessee. In *Posecai*, at 7:20 P.M., the plaintiff was placing her purchases in a trunk when she was robbed at gunpoint. At the time, a security guard was stationed inside the store to protect the cash office from 5:00 P.M. until the store closed at 8:00 P.M. The plaintiff presented police officers' testimony that the store was in a high crime area and expert testimony evidence that there had been three robberies on the defendant's premises. The expert testified that security for the parking lot was required. After reviewing the law and other jurisdictions, the court adopted the balance test approach to determine what duty, if any, was owed by the defendant to the patron. The court wrote, "The greater the foreseeability and gravity of the harm, the greater the duty of care that will be imposed on the business. A very high degree of foreseeability is required to give rise to a duty to post security guards, but a lower degree of foreseeability may support a duty to implement lesser security measures such as using surveillance cameras, installing improved lighting or fencing, or trimming shrubbery." 752 So.2d 768. The court noted that the foreseeability and the gravity of the harm is to be determined by the facts and circumstances of each case. The court also noted that the most important factors to be considered are the existence, frequency, and similarity of prior incidents of crime on the premises, but the location, nature, and condition of property should also be taken into account. *Id.* The court stated that if there was no previous crime, it was unlikely that security guards were required. After reviewing the evidence, which revealed only three prior criminal incidents on the property over six years, and only one involving a patron during business hours, the court found that the defendant did not possess the requisite degree of foreseeability for the imposition of a duty to provide security patrols in its parking lot, or even lesser security standards. 752 So.2d 769.

The supreme court again addressed this issue in *Goins v. Wal-Mart Stores, Inc.*, 800 So.2d 783 (La. 11/28/01). The store employed two security guards with one in the store while the other patrolled the parking lot. Upon starting their shift, the security guards noticed three individuals around a car in the parking lot. They approached the individuals, who told them that they were fixing a broken-down car. The individuals were quite cooperative. The officers ran a background check on them that came up empty. Following this encounter, the female plaintiff was walking through the parking lot when she was harassed by the three individuals. She went into the store but did not mention this to anyone. When leaving the store, the individuals pulled up in a car, confronted the plaintiff with a gun, and advised her to get in the car. She was subsequently attacked and raped. The plaintiff brought suit against the defendant for the failure of the security guards to search the car or the individuals to find the gun. In ruling for the defendant, the court found the deputies' actions reasonable and that to do a pat-down of the individuals or a search of the car would not have been appropriate under the circumstances.

The Supreme Court of Louisiana again addressed the issue of criminal acts of third parties in *Pinsonneault v. Merchants & Farmers Bank & Trust Company*, 816 So.2d 270 (La. 4/3/02). In *Pinsonneault*, the plaintiff was shot and killed by two escapees from a jail while making a night-time deposit at a branch bank. The bank had a program of updating security measures for its branches. The appellate court found that the bank was negligent because it did not install video cameras, did not trim its shrubbery, did not extend its fence to enclose the property, and did not improve its lighting. The supreme court specifically held in a footnote that a business does not assume a duty to protect its customers from criminal acts merely by undertaking some security measures. 816 So.2d 278. The court followed the *Posecai* decision and overruled the appellate court, which had reversed the trial court's finding that the bank was not liable. The evidence showed that a security camera would not have been a deterrence, a change of shrubbery would not have changed the circumstances, a change in the fencing would not have helped, and the lighting was more than adequate.

Business Properties/Owners

The plaintiff in *Bonds v. Abbeville General Hospital*, 782 So.2d 1188 (La.App.3 Cir. 4/4/01) sued her employer for failure to prevent her abduction and rape. The hospital had security personnel. The court followed *Posecai* by finding that a property owner has a duty to protect its patrons from foreseeable criminal acts. The hospital was in a high crime area, but the defendant was not liable since there was no evidence of any type of prior crime and the defendant already had security guards.

In *Marmer v. Queen of New Orleans at the Hilton*, 787 So.2d 1115 (La.App. 4 Cir. 5/16/01), the plaintiff sued a casino after he was attacked in the bathroom. The court ruled in favor of the defendant, citing the lack of prior incidents of violent crime. The court also noted that there were no reports of any altercations involving the assailant, and the defendant had a security guard on each floor as well as rovers.

The defendant batted fifty-fifty in *Junot v. Morgan*, 818 So.2d 152 (La.App. 1 Cir. 2/20/02). The first plaintiff sued a fast-food restaurant after improper physical contact was initiated by another patron. The court followed the *Posecai* analysis and found that there was no evidence to show that this first contact was foreseeable. After the first contact, the patron who made contact with the first plaintiff then struck the second plaintiff. The court found that the defendant could have anticipated the subsequent fight.

In *Smith v. AAA Travel Agency*, 859 So.2d 286 (La.App.2 Cir. 10/29/03), the court ruled that since there was minimal crime in the area and the property was located in a nice neighborhood, there was no reason to place a duty on the defendant.

In *Brown v. Ascension Parish*, 887 So.2d 39 (La.App. 1 Cir. 8/18/04), the plaintiff brought a wrongful death action contending that the owner of the premises should have provided security due to prior acts. In finding for the defendant, the court held that the most important factor to determine the defendant's liability was the frequency and similarity of prior criminal acts. Since there were no prior shootings or violent crime, the court found that the defendant did not have a duty to provide security.

In *Patton v. Strogen*, 809 So.2d 1282 (La.App. 2 Cir. 8/17/05), the court held that the landowner could have foreseen that there could be attacks requiring security. This was a wrongful death action arising out of a shooting in a strip mall. One of the defendants owned the strip mall. In the strip mall, there were a fast-food restaurant and a nightclub. These establishments owned their lots. The nightclub was known by the police to have had gang activity and a number of shootings prior to the occurrence. The police officer who was at the scene for an unrelated accident testified that the entire strip mall and the nightclub area were packed. The plaintiff's decedent was shot while on the fast-food restaurant's premises. The court found that the strip mall owner could be found liable for failure to employ reasonable security measures. The court cited *Pinsonneault*, which stated that business owners are in a better position to judge risks. Since there were questions of fact regarding prior criminal activities, the court found that a strip mall owner could be held liable by a jury for failure to pass sufficient security forces.

In *Mackey v. Jong's Super Value #2*, 940 So.2d 118 (La.App. 2 Cir. 9/27/06), intervening served the defendant well. The plaintiff (a patron) got into an argument with an acquaintance in the defendant's grocery store. During the argument, the defendant's employees intervened and asked the plaintiff whether she wanted the police called or wanted to press charges. She replied in the negative. A couple of minutes later, the acquaintance came back and shot her. The lack of crime on the property for five years justified finding that the defendant had no duty to provide a security guard.

Taverns

In *Ledet v. Doe*, 762 So.2d 24 (La.App.5 Cir. 5/17/00), the court found that a bar was not liable to a patron who had not yet entered the premises for an attack that had occurred on a parking lot adjacent to the premises. A defendant was liable in *Lamkin v. Kenny's Key West, Inc.*,

791 So.2d 769 (La.App. 4 Cir. 6/27/01) since its employees were active participants in the fight that caused the plaintiff's injuries.

The court found no liability for the tavern owner when its employees interceded in a confrontation in *Albritton v. Woods*, 795 So.2d 1239 (La.App. 2 Cir. 9/28/01). The plaintiff had words with a known troublemaker outside the premises. A bouncer and an off-duty employee intervened. After all seemed quiet, the plaintiff was warned specifically not to approach the troublemaker. However, the plaintiff went across the street to talk with the troublemaker and was beaten. The court ruled for the defendant because it had intervened in the first occurrence and could not be held liable since the plaintiff decided to re-engage the troublemaker.

In *Daniels v. Essex Insurance Company*, 890 So.2d 599 (La.App. 5 Cir. 11/30/04), the plaintiff was involved in the prior fight, but there was only one bartender present. Since there was no security present, the court found that the tavern could be held liable for the second fight since the lack of security was in fact the cause of the injuries.

In *Fredericks v. Daiquiris & Creams of Mandeville*, 906 So.2d 1282 (La.App. 2 Cir. 8/17/05), the plaintiff was beaten in a parking lot by individuals who had been cyeing his girlfriend. There was no evidence that the attackers did anything to place the defendant on notice that they would attack anyone. The court noted that a tavern owner must exercise reasonable care to protect its guests from the harm of an employee, guest, or third party. It can fulfill its duty by calling the police if a disturbance arises.

Landlords/Tenants

In *Terrell v. Wallace*, 747 So.2d 748 (La.App. 1 Cir. 12/28/99), the court addressed whether a landlord had a special duty to control or warn against criminal actions of third parties in a common area. The plaintiff brought a wrongful death action after he was shot following two confrontations with nonresident males. The court held that the plaintiff's lease did not include the provision of security on the premises, and the landlord's duty to maintain the common areas did not encompass a duty to protect tenants from the actions of third parties. The court upheld the Louisiana law that there was no special relationship between landowners and tenants. Thus, it upheld the dismissal of the action.

Maine

Maine had no cases reported.

UPDATE

Kaechele v. Kenyon Oil Company, Inc., 747 A.2d 167 (Me 2000) is the first case that addressed liability of a landowner for the criminal acts of a third party. The plaintiff went to the defendant's convenience store where his wife was working. There was an off-duty employee with the plaintiff. A patron became quite agitated and loud after he was required to present identification to buy cigarettes. One of the parties present suggested that they call the police. After the patron left the store, the plaintiff went out, confronted him in the parking lot, and was attacked. The supreme court noted that a proprietor must guard patrons not only against risk that they have knowledge of, but also against those risks they should anticipate, citing the Restatement (Second) of Tort §344. The court noted that all of the individuals present were concerned about the dangerous behavior of the patron and that his dangerous propensities increased the risk of harm. The court found the store liable.

Maryland

In Maryland, a landowner's duty to persons on the premises depends on the status of those persons while on the landowner's property. A landowner owes a duty to exercise reasonable and ordinary care to keep the premises safe for invitees, and to protect them from injury caused by an unreasonable risk. *McGarr v. Baltimore Area Council Boy Scouts of America, Inc.*, 74 Md. App. 127, 536 A.2d 728 (1988).

The duty to protect invitees from the conduct of third parties is the same as the general duty of care that is imposed on a landowner. *Tucker v. KFC National Management Company*, 689 F. Supp. 560 (D. Md. 1988). A higher standard of care is imposed only where a special relationship is found to exist between the parties.

In *Hailman v. M.J.J. Production, Inc.*, 2 F.3d 1149 (4th Cir. 1993) (unpublished disposition), the court did not find a special relationship between the plaintiff and defendants. The plaintiff was knocked down and injured during a concert when other concertgoers became involved in an argument. The plaintiff alleged that the defendants were negligent for failing to provide adequate crowd control and security measures.

In dismissing the complaint, the court found that a special relationship between the parties did not exist, and further concluded that the security measures provided by the defendants were reasonable.

Interestingly, the court believed the incident would not have been prevented even if extra security guards had been posted, because the underlying argument appeared to be spontaneous. In support of its holding, the *Hailman* court cited the *Tucker* decision for the proposition that landowners are not the ensurers of the safety of business invitees.

Hence, Maryland courts continue to limit the situations in which landowners face liability for criminal acts committed on their premises by third persons.

UPDATE

The Court of Appeals of Maryland addressed the duty of a common carrier to protect an individual against the criminal acts of third parties in *Todd v. Mass Transit Administration*, 373 Md. 149, 816 A.2d 930 (Md. 2003). The plaintiff was on a bus when a number of teenagers boarded the bus. The teenagers immediately began cursing and irritating other passengers. They harassed other passengers for approximately five minutes before striking the plaintiff. After the plaintiff questioned them, they immediately started beating him. While the attack was underway, another passenger told the bus driver to stop the bus since the teenagers were beating the plaintiff in the back of the bus. At that time, the driver was trying to negotiate a bridge that was clogged with cars watching a Fourth of July fireworks presentation. After clearing the bridge, the driver made a left turn, stopped the bus, and then pressed the panic button. The attackers were able to flee the scene. The trial court entered summary judgment. The court was presented with a novel issue of whether the defendant had a duty to take affirmative action to protect the plaintiff. The court found that common carriers owe a duty to take affirmative action to protect their passengers if (1) in the exercise of care, the carrier knew or should have known that an assault was imminent; and (2) its duty to take protective action arose well enough in advance of the assault to have prevented it with the force in its command. 373 Md. 149, 159, 815 A.2d 935. The court noted that Maryland had adopted Section 314A of the Restatement (Second) of Torts 1965, which provides that an employee has a duty to take affirmative action for the aid or protection of an invitee when the employee knows of the danger. The court noted that it had addressed this issue previously. It had reversed a summary judgment for the owner of a convenience store when the store's clerk failed to call the police after the clerk was alerted that a customer was being assaulted by a group of teenagers. 373 Md. 164, 816 A.2d 938–939. In *Todd*, the court found that the defendant had breached its duty to the plaintiff since there was sufficient evidence for a jury that the attack was foreseeable based on the teenagers' conduct. There also was a question of fact as to whether the defendant could have prevented the attack.

The court of appeals addressed protection for criminal acts in the landlord setting in *Hemmings v. Pelham Wood Limited Liability Limited Partnership*, 375 Md. 522, 826 A.2d 443 (Md.2003). In *Hemmings*, an assailant broke into the plaintiff's decedent's apartment through his sliding door and shot the plaintiff's decedent. The landlord had instituted a security program of deadbolt locks, using horizontally mounted bars to secure the sliding doors. The landlord had also provided lighting in the common areas and an alarm system. There was contradictory testimony as to the adequacy of the lighting. Over a two-year period prior to the occurrence, police had filed reports for twenty-nine burglaries and two attempted armed robberies. The court found that the landlord-tenant relationship was not the sort of relationship (such as one finds between a common carrier and a passenger) that gives rise to a special duty in tort. 375 Md. 540, 826 A.2d 453. Much of the court's analysis focused on liability for leased premises since Maryland law typically holds that a landlord cannot be responsible for events that occur within leased premises. The court determined that negligent maintenance or failure to correct known defects in common areas under the control of a landlord may result in liability for injuries that occur within the leased premises. 375 Md. 543, 826 A.2d 455. The court then stated that the landlord had a legal duty to take reasonable security measures within the common areas when the landlord had knowledge or should have had knowledge of criminal activity on the premises. Furthermore, the court stated that based on the nature of past criminal activity, the landlord should have foreseen the harm suffered. The court also found that the landlord had a continuing obligation to maintain the security measures. 375 Md. 546, 826 A.2d 457. The court then found that summary judgment was not proper and remanded the matter back to the trial court since there were questions on the actions taken by the defendant.

The court of appeals also addressed the issue of an attack by a third party in *Rhaney v. University of Maryland Eastern Shore*, 388 Md. 585, 880 A.2d 357 (Md. 2005). This action arose when one dormitory roommate struck another. The attacker had previously been suspended by the university for fighting, but the suspension could be lifted if he received some professional counseling. After attending a program, the defendant readmitted the attacker. The plaintiff brought suit against the university, alleging that he was invitee and the defendant breached its duty to him by failing to disclose the attacker's dangerous tendencies and negligently assigning the attacker to be his roommate. A jury verdict was entered in favor of the plaintiff. The court reversed the finding, indicating that he was a tenant to whom no special duty was owed and that the plaintiff knew the character of the attacker prior to the occurrence, which obviated any liability.

Special Court of Appeals

In *Moore v. Jimel, Inc.*, 147 Md.App. 336, 808 A.2d 10 (Ct.Sp.App. 2002), the plaintiff brought an action after being raped in a bar's bathroom. The bar had a number of bouncers and had security personnel at all of the exits. The court reaffirmed Maryland law that a business has no special duty to protect its invitees from criminal activity. The court also noted that if a business inviter or landlord knows or should know of criminal activity against people on the property, the business owner or landlord has the duty to take reasonable measures to eliminate the conditions contributing to the criminal activity. Since there was no evidence of any type of prior criminal activity or any abnormal behavior from the attacker, the court affirmed the entry of summary judgment on behalf of the bar.

In *Smith v. Dodge Plaza Limited Partnership*, 148 Md.App. 335, 811 A.2d 881 (Ct.Sp.App. 2002), the plaintiff brought an action against a nightclub's landlord or property owner after he was stabbed by a patron at the nightclub. The plaintiff introduced no evidence that the nightclub had any notice of any criminal acts that occurred in the nightclub or in the parking lot. The plaintiff did produce evidence from the police of a number of incidents involving guns, shootings, and the requirement of off-duty police. The plaintiff also produced evidence of a lawsuit for a prior stabbing. The court affirmed the summary judgment entered in favor of the landlord. It followed the prior decision in *Scott v. Watson*. The court noted that there was no special duty to protect against criminal acts and that there is no special duty between a landlord and a tenant's invitee. The court applied the approach found in California of balancing the foreseeability of the harm against the burden of the duty to be imposed. The court found that there was no evidence of any type of knives or guns used in any prior altercation. The court also noted that the property owner or landlord was limited by the lease in sending and entering upon the premises to protect against criminal acts, which would limit its knowledge and ability to provide security.

In *Corinaldi v. Columbia Courtyard, Inc.*, 162 Md.App. 207, 873 A.2d 483 (Ct.Sp.App. 2005), the court confronted the question of whether a hotel was responsible for a shooting that occurred in a room that a customer was using for a party. During the night, the party had been quite noisy. A few minutes before the shooting, the clerk at the front desk was approached by the customer having the party, who advised that the party was getting out of control and that one of the attendees had a gun. Approximately ten minutes later, there was a shooting. The hotel did not call the police. The court reaffirmed the general rule that there was no duty to protect a victim from the criminal acts of a third person in the absence of a special relationship that imposes the duty either to control the third person's conduct or to protect the victim. Based on the party's increasing noise, the employees' concerned calls to the manager, and the fact that someone warned of a gun, the court found that there was a sufficient question of fact as to whether the hotel could be held liable.

The court of special appeals has also addressed these issues in *Veytsman v. New York Palace, Inc.*, 170 Md.App. 104, 906 A.2d 1028 (Ct.Sp.App. 2006), in which the court reaffirmed Maryland's unique law that there is no cause of action for damages against the owner of a tavern by a patron for injuries caused by the tavern's intoxicated patrons. 170 Md.App.104, 123, 906 A.2d 1038. The court found that the defendant had no obligation to protect the plaintiffs from other intoxicated patrons. This matter arose out of a dinner and a wedding. After the plaintiffs had dinner at the defendant's establishment, there was an altercation between the plaintiff and one of the members of the wedding party. Shortly thereafter, attendees of the wedding who were on a chartered bus outside the premises stormed back in and beat the plaintiff. The court reiterated Maryland's law indicating that there is no duty to control a third person's conduct so as to prevent personal harm to another unless a special relationship exists between either the actor and the third person or between the actor and the person injured. 170 Md.App. 114, 906 A.2d 1033. The court noted that a special relationship would have existed if the owner controlled the dangerous condition, had knowledge of the injury-causing condition, or if the harm was a foreseeable result. The court held in favor of the defendant. There was no security necessary because there had been no prior incidents at the location. The court also found that the initial altercation did not place the restaurant on notice that there was going to be a subsequent brawl. Thus the court found that there was insufficient evidence to establish a duty on behalf of the defendant.

Massachusetts

In Massachusetts, courts have partially abandoned the common law distinctions among invitees, licensees, and trespassers. In the case of

Mounsey v. Ellard, 363 Mass. 693, 297 N.E.2d 43 (1973), the Massachusetts high court held that the distinctions between licensees and invitees were no longer to be observed. Regarding trespassers, however, the common law rules remain in effect. Nevertheless, in analyzing the duties of defendant landowners, Massachusetts courts still consider the nature and purpose of the defendants' premises.

Thus, a private residential landowner or a public housing authority may not be liable for an attack occurring on its premises, but businesses such as hotels, restaurants, taverns, hospitals, colleges, and common carriers may be liable for a similar attack. As a general rule, however, it must still be shown in each case that the criminal attack was reasonably foreseeable. As was noted in the case of *Whittaker v. Saraceno*, 418 Mass. 196, 635 N.E.2d 1185 (1994), prior similar occurrences on or near the defendant's premises should be considered, "but the foreseeability question is not conclusively answered in favor of a defendant landlord if there has been no prior similar criminal act." In balancing the considerations, the court then stated, "society should not place the burden of all harm caused by random violent criminal conduct on the owner of the property where the harmful act occurred, without proof that the landowner knew or had reason to know of a threat to the safety of persons lawfully on the premises against which the landowner could have taken reasonable preventive steps."

Public Housing Projects

In *Wheeler v. Boston Housing Authority*, 34 Mass. App. Ct. 36, 606 N.E.2d 916 (1992), the court held that the defendant, a public housing authority, could not be held liable for failing to provide adequate security because the decision about the types of security to provide, and how much to provide, is entirely discretionary. The court stated that

> the determination of what security measures to take to protect persons on its premises from criminal activity is an integral part of defendant's policy making and planning process. In this case, the defendant had established a department of public safety, to whom was entrusted the responsibility for the design and implementation of all security measures for the premises. Given the wide range of choices the director could make to provide security to the premises and the necessary constraints imposed on those choices by budgetary considerations, the particular conduct which the plaintiff claims caused the injury is characterized by a "high degree of discretion and judgment involved in weighing [security] alternatives and making choices with respect to public policy and planning."

There is also no question that the imposition of liability on the defendant for inadequate security leading to the criminal acts of third persons would undoubtedly affect the ability of the defendant to provide the quantity and quality of low cost housing now provided by requiring diversion of significant resources to combat criminal activity. . . . Finally, an alternate available remedy to a plaintiff suffering a criminal assault is civil action against the perpetrator or, alternatively, recompense under the Victims of Violent Crimes Act.

Private Residential Premises

In *Husband v. Dubose*, 26 Mass. App. Ct. 667, 531 N.E.2d 600 (1988), the court held that a private residential homeowner has no duty to prevent an attack by one guest on another: "We are . . . not prepared to say that prevailing values and expectations required the defendant to be more vigilant of security, to intervene directly, or to summon assistance at the risk of serious personal injury to herself or of causing greater danger to the plaintiff."

Taking into consideration the "damned-if-you-do, damned-if-you-don't" predicament in negligent security cases, the *Husband* court stated that it found great merit in the defendant's argument that "if the defendant had immediately run to a neighbor's house to `get help' or had gone to another room to use a telephone, and the plaintiff had been stabbed during that time, the plaintiff would, instead, be alleging that the defendant negligently left her and [the assailant] alone. And if the defendant had attempted to physically intervene in the physical confrontation and the plaintiff had been injured during this involvement, the plaintiff would, instead, be alleging that the defendant was guilty of negligence in actively participating in the altercation."

In *Choy v. First Columbia Management, Inc.*, 676 F. Supp. 28 (D. Mass. 1987), the plaintiff was attacked in her apartment by a person she had allowed inside because he claimed he was a maintenance man. The court held that considering the lack of evidence about how the assailant entered the apartment building, liability could not be imposed on the defendant. Without such evidence, reasoned the court, it would be purely conjecture to say that providing security guards would have prevented the attack: "The assailant may have entered the building in the company of another tenant in which case a security guard would not have had authority to stop his entry. Alternatively, the assailant may have been buzzed in by a tenant who did not first identify him." Additionally, the court noted the lack of evidence that twenty-four-hour security guards are typically provided in apartment buildings such as the one in which the attack occurred.

Colleges

In *Mullins v. Pine Manor College*, 389 Mass. 47, 449 N.E.2d 331 (1983), the plaintiff was accosted during the early morning hours while in her dormitory room at a small, all-women's college. With a pillowcase over her head she was then led outside and raped in the dining hall, which was unlocked. Although there was no evidence about how the assailant gained entry to the college premises, the court noted (1) that certain parts of the fence surrounding the college were only four feet high; (2) that there were only two guards on duty, one of whom was stationed at the observation post at the main entrance gate to the campus, and the other of whom made rounds, each lasting about fifteen minutes; and (3) that one could gain entry through one of the other entrance gates by crawling beneath it. Thus, the court held that the jury could have reasonably concluded that it was more probable than not that the assailant was a trespasser, rather than someone who had been brought onto the premises by another student.

Although the college area had little crime, the court held that the rape was foreseeable considering the fact that the college was all-female. That the defendant took measures to protect students was considered by the court to be evidence that it had notice of a potential risk.

Additionally, the court held that the security provided by the defendant was not gratuitous, as the students were charged for this service through their tuition or dormitory fees. According to the court, adequate security "is an indispensable part of the bundle of services which colleges, and Pine Manor, afford their students." But the court also reasoned that even if the security provided was purely voluntary, the plaintiff nevertheless relied on the security (to her eventual detriment) when she selected the college she would attend. Therefore, liability could be imposed even if the defendant did not have a legal duty to provide security.

Common Carriers/Innkeepers

In *Fund v. Hotel Lenox of Boston, Inc.*, 418 Mass. 191, 635 N.E.2d 1189 (1994), a hotel guest was stabbed to death in her room. Although there was no evidence establishing how the assailant entered the premises or whether the assailant was another hotel guest, the court held that a jury could find it was more probable than not that the stabbing was a reasonably foreseeable consequence of the failure to provide adequate security. The court further noted, among other items, that (1) the hotel was in a moderately high-crime area, (2) the hotel had a problem with transients and other trespassers, (3) there had been larcenies in the hotel and robberies in the vicinity, (4) the fire escape afforded a means of access, (5) one entrance did not have a doorman, and (6) the single security guard was also assigned to patrol another hotel five blocks away. Considering these facts, it is certainly fair to say that the assailant probably gained entry due to a breach in security. Nevertheless, it is rare to see a court candidly state that probabilities may be a substitute for hard proof.

In *Sharpe v. Peter Pan Bus Lines, Inc.*, 401 Mass. 788, 519 N.E.2d 1341 (1988), the victim was stabbed and killed in the waiting area of a bus terminal. Holding that common carriers owe a high degree of care to their patrons, and noting that the terminal was in a run-down, high-crime area and was frequented by drunks and homeless persons, the court stated that "the jury could reasonably have concluded that as a deterrent to crime the defendants had a duty to provide uniformed security personnel in the terminal at the time of the attack." Thus, although the attack on the plaintiff was unprovoked, and although the court conceded that the attack could not likely have been prevented, the court imposed liability on the ground that the attack could have been deterred. But even though the court recognized that deterrence, not prevention, was the key, it nevertheless paid homage to the plaintiff's expert's testimony that a uniformed security guard would probably have been able to prevent the attack.

A scathing dissent included the following remarks:

> For some, the bus is the only affordable method of travel. There exists a current tendency by some to find liability in every case, even in the absence of fault or where, as here, the fault of the defendant is unconnected to the acts which caused the plaintiff's decedent's injuries. This trend is justified on the theory of society's interest in diffusing the costs of a plaintiff's injuries. But, as we should all know by now, there is no free lunch. Here, the increased cost of insuring against such unforeseeable incidents will be borne by those who can least afford it—the bus-riding public. And when these costs are added to the price of a ticket, the result will be that a greater segment of working class Americans can no longer afford the most economical means of long distance travel and that fewer bus companies will offer service to fewer locations. In the name of egalitarianism, disenfranchisement is created.

In *McFadden v. Bancroft Hotel Corp.*, 313 Mass. 56, 46 N.E.2d 573 (1943), a hotel guest was punched by another guest who had been causing trouble for more than an hour before the attack. The defendant argued that the plaintiff assumed the risk of harm by attending what he should have known would be a raucous party. The argument was rejected, and liability was imposed on the hotel.

In *Quigley v. Wilson Line of Massachusetts, Inc.*, 338 Mass. 125, 154 N.E.2d 77 (1958), the court held a shipowner liable for failing to protect the plaintiff from an attack by two drunks who were previously escorted out of the ship's bar because they were fighting. The defendant argued that the drunks were not properly guarded by the off-duty police officers who had been hired, as independent contractors, to provide security. The court held that the shipowner was responsible for the breach of duty by the police officers because the owner had a right to control the officers' conduct, and that, ultimately, the shipowner has the duty to keep the ship safe.

Taverns/Restaurants

In *Greco v. Sumner Tavern, Inc.*, 333 Mass. 144, 128 N.E.2d 788 (1955), the court held a bar owner liable for failing to prevent an assault on one patron by another who had been drinking and was rowdy for a long time before the assault. *See also, Carey v. New Yorker of Worcester*, 355 Mass. 450, 245 N.E.2d 420 (1969) (attack by known troublemaker); *Kane v. Fields Corner Grille, Inc.*, 341 Mass. 640, 171 N.E.2d 287 (1961).

Movie Theaters

In *Rawson v. Massachusetts Operating Co., Inc.*, 328 Mass. 558, 105 N.E.2d 220 (1952), the plaintiff, a theater patron, was punched by another patron who was among a group that had been disruptive for over an hour. The plaintiff offended the assailant by asking him to leave. The court upheld the jury's finding that the theater owner was negligent for not stopping the disturbance, and stated that if theater personnel did not try to control the group, then the owner could reasonably anticipate that another patron would.

Subways

In *Magaw v. Massachusetts Bay Transportation Authority*, 21 Mass. App. Ct. 129, 485 N.E.2d 695 (1985), the court held the defendant liable for a robbery and assault in a subway passageway. The court rejected the asserted defense that to impose liability would be to impose an impossible burden of ensuring the safety of all subway riders. The court seized on the defendant's concession that it owed a duty to protect its passengers from being attacked by others. Perhaps the decision would have been different had the defendant not made that concession and instead argued that as a public authority, it has no duty to any specific passenger absent a special duty. *See, e.g., Weiner v. Metropolitan Transit Authority,* 55 N.Y.2d 175, 448 N.Y.S.2d 141, 433 N.E.2d 124 (1982) (holding that New York City subway system has no duty to provide adequate police protection); *Crosland v. New York City Transit Authority,* 68 N.Y.2d 165, 506 N.Y.S.2d 670, 498 N.E.2d 143 (1986) (holding no duty to provide police protection, but duty to summon aid if transit employee witnesses attack from position of safety).

The court then held that the defendant had sufficient notice of prior criminal attacks to impose a duty to provide security. Within the two months before the attack, there were numerous incidents of rowdiness at the station, and one report of a lost or stolen purse; none of the incidents, however, occurred in the specific passageway where the plaintiff was attacked. Some of the lights in the passageway were out, and the plaintiff testified that a few days before the incident she complained about the lighting. The attack occurred about ninety feet from the toll booth, and although the plaintiff screamed for help for two to five minutes, no one came to her aid. The lack of adequate lighting was the principal basis upon which the court imposed liability.

The court considered the fact that security personnel had been deployed at the station as evidence that the defendant had notice of a risk of attack. The court also believed it significant that the defendant's security officer testified that all the prior incidents were serious.

Convenience Stores

In *Flood v. Southland Corp.,* 416 Mass. 62, 616 N.E.2d 1068 (1993), the court imposed liability on the defendant for an attack that occurred outside a 7-Eleven store. The evidence against the defendant was thin and, considering the more restrictive language in the previously cited *Whittaker* case, the *Flood* case probably represents the outer limits of when liability may be imposed on a defendant in Massachusetts.

In *Flood,* the assailant and the plaintiff, both seventeen years old, had smoked marijuana and drunk beer together before going to a 7-Eleven store with a group of other boys. The boys entered the store and "fanned out," and the store clerk thought they were planning to shoplift. They made some purchases, then went outside. The assailant returned to complain about a sandwich he bought, and the clerk told him to leave the store. Then the plaintiff entered the store, warned the clerk to be careful of the assailant, and then left. A few minutes later, another boy came inside and told the clerk that the plaintiff had been stabbed.

The court held that the plaintiff submitted sufficient evidence to establish a triable issue of fact concerning whether the defendant breached a duty of care to the plaintiff. A security expert testified that the design of the premises was inadequate because the area where the boys gathered outside was not visible from inside the store. Additionally, before the stabbing, police received numerous complaints that youths had caused disturbances at the 7-Eleven store. The court did, however, allow the jury to consider whether the plaintiff's own culpable conduct contributed to the occurrence.

Hospitals

In *Copithorne v. Framingham Union Hospital*, 401 Mass. 860, 520 N.E.2d 139 (1988), the court held that a material issue of fact existed about whether a hospital negligently allowed a doctor to remain on staff after it received actual notice that he previously committed sexual assaults.

UPDATE

In *Doe v. Walker*, 193 F.3d 42 (1st Cir. 1999), the First Circuit Court of Appeals considered the earlier decision of the Massachusetts Court of Appeals in *Husband v. Dubose*, 26 Mass. App. Ct. 667, 531 N.E. 2d 600 (1988) and reversed the district court's dismissal of a claim from a woman who said she had been raped. Plaintiff Doe had occasionally dated Antonie Walker, a professional basketball player. After a night out with Walker and some of his friends, Doe returned to Walker's home where she claims she was raped by Walker's friends. During the alleged attack, Walker entered the room but took no action to stop the assault, instead leaving the room. The district court dismissed the claim, holding that Walker was under no obligation to act. The First Circuit Court of Appeals reversed, holding that additional research needed to be conducted. It acknowledged that under *Husband*, if Walker was in some danger himself, he did not need to act to protect Doe. But the court reasoned that the *Husband* decision did not foreclose liability on Walker if he could have taken action to protect Doe without exposing himself to any danger.

In *Westerback v. Harold F. LeClair, Co., Inc.*, 50 Mass. App. Ct. 144, 735 N.E.2d 1256 (2000), the plaintiff was raped after leaving the defendant's tavern while intoxicated. As she was walking home, two men stopped and offered her a ride, but instead of taking her home, they took her to a trailer where they beat and raped her, leaving her in the woods. The next day she was taken to a hospital where her blood-alcohol content was measured at .248. The court held that the rape was not foreseeable merely because she had become intoxicated at the tavern.

The appeals court again considered the foreseeability of a criminal attack in *Luisi v. Foodmaster Supermarkets, Inc.*, 50 Mass. App. Ct. 575, 739

N.E.2d 703 (2000). In *Luisi*, the plaintiff was stabbed by a mentally ill patron who grabbed a knife from a display case that had no protective covering. The court held that even if the supermarket or mall in which the incident took place had a security guard on site, it would not have deterred the criminal attack. The court noted that the perpetrator did not drop the knife when initially told to do so by the police. The court did find, however, that there was a factual question about the danger of Foodmaster displaying uncovered knives, which precluded summary judgment.

In *Brum v. Town of Dartmouth*, 428 Mass. 684, 704 N.E.2d 1147 (1999), the Supreme Judicial Court of Massachusetts overturned the decision of the court of appeals and upheld the dismissal of the plaintiff's claim for the wrongful death of her son. The supreme court focused on the technical language of the Massachusetts Tort Claim Act in reaching its decision.

Michigan

Michigan courts have repeatedly rejected various arguments presented by plaintiffs for the imposition of a duty on landowners to protect persons from criminal occurrences. Accordingly, the current status of Michigan law makes difficult attempts to establish negligence in premises security cases.

In *Williams v. Cunningham Drug Store*, 429 Mich. 495, 418 N.W.2d 381 (1988), the plaintiff was shot by a robber fleeing the defendant's premises, and later claimed the defendant failed to protect him from the crime. The court rejected that contention, holding that the defendant did not owe a duty to protect the plaintiff or other invitees from criminal acts committed by third persons.

In other cases, Michigan courts concluded that no duty would be imposed on a bank when a patron was assaulted while using an automatic teller machine, or on a business owner when a patron was injured by another patron after both had been ejected from the premises. *Fuga v. Comerica Bank-Detroit*, 202 Mich. App. 380, 509 N.W.2d 778 (Mich. App. 1993) (liability may not be imposed on landowner absent any evidence that landowner created or maintained criminal activity, or failed to act reasonably to end criminal activity that occurred on premises); *DeMare v. Woodbridge 1985, Inc.*, 182 Mich. App. 356, 451 N.W.2d 871 (1980).

In *Gouch v. Grand Trunk Western R.R. Co.*, 187 Mich. App. 413, 468 N.W.2d 68 (1991), the plaintiff was rendered paraplegic after being struck by a bullet while walking alongside elevated railroad tracks. The plaintiff alleged that the railroad tracks created an "attractive nuisance" and, therefore, the court should find that the defendants owed a duty to provide protection from criminal acts. Not surprisingly, the court rejected that novel contention.

What was somewhat surprising, however, was the court's decision in *Scott v. Harper Recreation*, 444 Mich. 441, 506 N.W.2d 857 (1993). In *Scott*, an unidentified assailant shot the plaintiff in the parking lot of the defendant's premises. The evidence suggested the defendant specifically advertised that the parking lot area was guarded and illuminated. The plaintiff contended that by making those representations, the defendant assumed a duty to protect its patrons and then performed the assumed duty in a negligent manner. In holding that it was not reasonable to expect merchants to assure patrons their property is free of crime, the court refused to impose greater liability on landlords who undertake efforts to prevent criminal activity than on those who undertake no such efforts. The court therefore rejected the argument that the defendant assumed a duty to provide a greater level of security than would otherwise be required because there was no evidence that the defendant negligently assumed that duty.

As indicated in the previously cited *Williams* case, Michigan courts adhere to the proposition that a party does not owe a duty to protect a person from criminal acts, absent a special relationship between the parties. Although courts have found special relationships to include those involving owners and occupiers of land, *Holland v. Liedel*, 197 Mich. App. 60, 494 N.W.2d 772 (1992), courts seem generally reluctant to impose affirmative duties on landowners to protect persons on their premises from criminal acts.

An interesting twist on that general proposition, however, was presented in the case of *Mills v. White Castle Systems, Inc.*, 199 Mich. App. 588, 502 N.W.2d 331 (1992), in which the plaintiff, upon leaving the defendant's premises, was assaulted by several people who had been present and apparently drinking in the defendant's parking lot for over thirty minutes. The plaintiff contended that the defendant was negligent for not removing the group of people from the premises. After lengthy procedural issues were concluded, the appellate court held that the plaintiff presented a sufficient theory of negligence—based on the defendant's failure to evict the unruly persons, regardless of the absence of a duty to provide police protection—to warrant a new trial.

UPDATE

The Michigan Supreme Court revisited the premises liability concepts in *MacDonald v. PKT, Inc.*, 464 Mich. 322, 628 N.W.2d 33 (2001), upholding its prior decisions in *Williams* and *Scott*, and partially overruling *Mason*. In *MacDonald*, a concertgoer was injured when other patrons began throwing sod during a performance by The Ramones. Although PKT, the venue, had instructed the bands to stop playing and admonish the audience to stop throwing sod, the plaintiff suffered a fractured ankle as she moved out of the way of a piece of sod that had been thrown by another patron. The Michigan Supreme Court acknowledged the duty of the defendant merchant to respond to situations that "pose a risk of imminent and foreseeable harm to identifiable invitees." It limited that duty, however, to summoning the police to handle the situation. The court reasoned that to hold otherwise would be to impose the obligation of police protection on private business. The court also rejected the notion that a risk could be foreseeable if there had been prior instances of the behavior, as there had been in this case. Rather, the risk would only become foreseeable as it was unfolding. The court noted that crime, by its very nature, is both "irrational and unpredictable" and would not impose on the defendant the obligation to anticipate crime. The court held that it was not necessary to employ security even if there had been past violence. The duty on the merchant is to act reasonably by summoning the police. The dissent argued that it was appropriate to look at past incidents at the same venue in order to address the foreseeability of a criminal attack.

In an unpublished opinion, the court of appeals pointed out that the *MacDonald* decision is limited to merchants and does not apply to the landlord-tenant relationship. *Cuolahan v. Stamper*, 2004 WL 2534380.

Minnesota

Minnesota decisions in the area of premises security have focused on the issues of special relationships and foreseeability.

In *Errico v. Southland Corp.*, 509 N.W.2d 585 (Minn. Ct. App. 1993), the plaintiff was assaulted in the parking lot of a convenience store, and later contended that the business owner breached a duty to provide security to its customers. The court rejected that contention, specifically concluding that the nature of a relationship between a customer and a convenience store owner does not present the type of special relationship required to impose a duty to provide protection.

However, a special relationship was found to exist in *Erickson v. Curtis Investment Co.*, 447 N.W.2d 165 (Minn. 1989), in which the plaintiff became the victim of a crime in the defendant's commercial parking facility. The court held that the nature of the parties' relationship qualified as a special relationship, comparable to the relationship between a hospital and a patient, or a common carrier and a passenger.

In a case involving the issue of foreseeability, the court dismissed a claim brought by a plaintiff who had been shot following an adult-league basketball game. *Simmons v. City of St. Paul*, 1994 WL 454834 (Minn. Ct. App., August 23, 1994). The plaintiff contended that the defendant was negligent for locking several doors, thereby impeding his attempt to escape. The *Simmons* court concluded that the shooting was an unforeseeable, intervening act.

Courts in earlier decisions, however, have held that while most criminal acts are unforeseeable and intervening acts that would negate a landowner's liability, criminal acts that are deemed reasonably foreseeable will not break the chain of causation. *See, e.g., Hill v. County of Wright*, 400 N.W.2d 744 (Minn. Ct. App. 1987) (jailors should have foreseen that highly intoxicated prisoner would behave in ways dangerous to himself, including an attempted escape resulting in prisoner's injury).

UPDATE

In *Funchess v. Cecil Newman Corp.*, 632 N.W.2d 666 (2001), the Supreme Court of Minnesota once again relied on the concept of whether a special relationship existed between the plaintiff and defendant such that a duty was owed. The court determined that the landlord-tenant relationship was not a special relationship similar to that of guest-innkeeper, and therefore did not impose on the landlord any duty to protect its tenant from criminal attack. The court did, however, consider as a matter of first impression whether the fact that the landlord had installed certain security devices, specifically a security door with a buzzer/intercom system, imposed on the landlord a duty to maintain that security system. The court expressed concern that imposing such a duty might discourage landlords from implementing security measures. In so holding, however, the court pointed out that the landlord had, in addition to the security door, employed a security guard who chased the assailants from the property. The court also pointed out that it was the lock on the decedent's apartment door, rather than the security door to the apartment complex, that was intended to prevent entry into the decedent's apartment.

Mississippi

In *Lyle v. Mladinich*, 584 So. 2d 397 (Miss. 1991), the plaintiff was assaulted in the defendant's night club, and later alleged negligence by the defendant for its failure to provide adequate security. The court held that business owners, while not ensurers of public safety, do have a duty to exercise reasonable care to protect patrons from reasonably foreseeable injury at the hands of other patrons.

In *Kelly v. Retzer & Retzer, Inc.*, 417 So. 2d 556 (Miss. 1982), the decedent was shot and killed in the parking lot of a fast-food restaurant, and surviving family members brought an action against the restaurant, alleging negligent security. Evidence of prior crimes in the parking lot existed. The court affirmed the dismissal of the case, concluding that the security efforts undertaken by the defendant were reasonable, and further finding that the murder was not foreseeable.

This was a case of first impression in Mississippi, and the court cited leading cases from other jurisdictions to support its ultimate findings.

UPDATE

The Mississippi Supreme Court once again declined to adopt the "California Rule" or "totality of the circumstances standard" in *Corley v. Evans*, 835 So.2d 30 (2003), just as it had previously done in *Crain*. In *Corley*, the Mississippi Supreme Court reaffirmed the state's use of the invitee-licensee-trespasser trichotomy in premises cases. Plaintiff Corley had been accidentally shot in the face by a friend while attending a crawfish boil sponsored by defendant Stacy Evans. Corley was an invitee, and as such was owed a duty to be protected from reasonably foreseeable harm. The court noted that defendant Evans had hosted the crawfish boil for a number of years, during which time there had only been one fight. She had employed three security guards at the crawfish boil where the shooting occurred. The court noted that there was no "cause to anticipate" the shooting that injured plaintiff Corley.

In *Simpson v. Boyd*, 880 So.2d 1047 (2004), the Mississippi Supreme Court once again addressed the foreseeability issue. It noted that there are two ways the foreseeability test could be met. The premises owner could have actual or constructive knowledge of the violent nature of the attacker, or the premises owner could have actual or constructive knowledge of "an atmosphere of violence" existing on the premises. While the plaintiff in *Simpson* did provide evidence of several minor criminal violations in and around the premises, it was not enough to prove the atmosphere of violence necessary to give rise to liability.

In *Titus v. Williams*, 844 So.2d 459 (2003), the court upheld summary judgment for the defendants even though there was an atmosphere of violence. The court found that the plaintiff was fully aware of the danger, and in fact had helped to create the danger, which relieved the defendant of any duty.

Missouri

Missouri courts adhere to the general proposition that a landowner or business owner is not liable for criminal acts of third persons, unless the third person is acting under the owner's direction or control or the owner could have reasonably anticipated and guarded against the crime. *See, e.g., Meadows v. Friedman R.R. Salvage Warehouse*, 655 S.W.2d 718 (Mo. Ct. App. 1983). Without the presence of those specific factors, a landowner owes no general duty to protect a plaintiff from the intentional criminal acts of third persons.

Several decisions, however, seem to permit considerable leeway in determining whether a particular crime is reasonably anticipated. In *Madden v. C & K Barbecue Carryout, Inc.*, 758 S.W.2d 59 (Mo. 1988), the plaintiff was kidnapped upon leaving the defendant's restaurant, and later claimed the defendant was negligent for failing to provide reasonable security measures to guard against the occurrence. The Missouri Supreme Court held that a duty to provide security may exist when there is a foreseeable likelihood that particular acts or omissions may cause harm. The court further held that the issue of whether a duty, if owed, was breached, was a question for the jury.

In *Virginia D. v. Madesco Investment Corp.*, 648 S.W.2d 881 (Mo. 1983), the plaintiff was sexually assaulted in a restroom of the defendant's motor hotel, and later alleged that the defendant was negligent for failing to provide adequate security. The court held that the relationship between the parties qualified as the type of special relationship that imposes a duty on the landowner to provide reasonable measures to guard against criminal acts.

However, no such duty was imposed in the case of *Warren v. Lombardo's Enterprises, Inc.*, 706 S.W.2d 286 (Mo. Ct. App. 1986). There, the plaintiff was shot while in the defendant's parking lot, one block away from the defendant's restaurant. In dismissing the complaint, the court held that the defendant owed no duty to provide protection, given the absence of evidence of prior crimes on the premises.

UPDATE

In *Richardson v. Quicktrip Corp.*, 81 S.W.3d 54 (2002), the Missouri Appellate Court overruled *Schelp v. Cohen-Esrey Real Estate Services, Inc.*, 889 S.W.2d 848 to the extent that it was inconsistent with *Madden v. C & L Barbecue Carryout, Inc.*, 758 S.W.2d 59 (1988) and *Becker v. Diomond Parking, Inc.*, 768 S.W.2d 169 (1989). In *Richardson*, a patron sued a convenience store for negligence arising from an incident in which she was raped by an unknown assailant in the store's ladies' room. The court stated that, under *Madden,* a duty would be imposed where a criminal attack was foreseeable given the facts and circumstances of the case. In other words, the court employed the totality of the circumstances approach for determining the duty owed by a business owner to a business invitee to protect the invitee from the criminal acts of unknown third parties.

The court also noted that despite the holdings in *Madden* and *Becker,* many cases in the Missouri Court of Appeals had ignored those cases and followed prior case law. Prior case law indicated that only evidence of recent occurrences of violent crime on the defendant's premises were relevant to determining whether criminal acts on the premises were foreseeable, including *Schelp.* The court further stated that the cases that chronologically followed *Madden* and *Becker,* like *Schelp,* held that evidence of nonviolent crimes on the premises and evidence of violent crimes in the immediate vicinity could not be considered in determining whether violent criminal actions were foreseeable. The court's reexamination in *Richardson* found that, to the extent that these cases were inconsistent with *Madden* and *Becker,* they were overruled. However, the court determined that the totality of the circumstances must be considered.

In *Thompson v. Tuggle,* 183 S.W.3d 611 (App. 2006), the Missouri Appellate Court addressed a case involving the death of a minor child after a gun, owned by the Tuggles, was accidentally discharged. The plaintiff filed suit against the Tuggles and the apartment complex where the Tuggles resided and where the gun was fired. The court reiterated the general rule that landlords are not liable for personal injuries received by a tenant or a tenant's invitees; however, the landlord may be liable if (1) the landlord had knowledge of a dangerous condition not discoverable by the tenant, and the landlord failed to disclose that condition; (2) the injury occured in a common area; or (3) the landlord was responsible for making repairs and negligently failed to do so. Applying the facts of this case, the court found that none of these exceptions applied. The court stated that the Tuggles' ownership of a gun was not a dangerous condition that the apartment complex knew about and failed to disclose, and the accident occurred inside the home as opposed to a common area. Furthermore, there was no knowledge on the apartment complex's part that a person with violent tendencies would have access to the Tuggles' gun. Finally, the court stated that prior criminal activity at the property was irrelevant to the issue of whether the apartment complex had a duty to protect the Tuggles' guest from accidental injuries inside the residence.

Montana

Montana had no cases reported.

UPDATE
There are no updates for this state.

Nebraska

In *K.S.R. v. Novak and Sons, Inc.*, 225 Neb. 498, 406 N.W.2d 636 (1987), the plaintiff, a tenant in the defendant's apartment building, was sexually assaulted in her apartment and later alleged that the defendant was negligent for failing to repair locks on the front door. The lower court granted summary judgment in favor of the defendant, and the plaintiff appealed. The plaintiff had presented evidence of prior crime in the building.

The court reversed the dismissal, holding that the evidence presented raised a question of fact concerning whether the assault on the plaintiff was foreseeable.

The court readily acknowledged that many jurisdictions are expanding landowners' obligations to provide security, stating that it is "now beyond dispute that a landlord, private or public, may have a duty to take reasonable precautionary measures to secure the premises if it has notice of a likelihood of criminal intrusions posing a threat to safety."

UPDATE
In *Knoll v. Board of Regents of the University of Nebraska*, 258 Neb. 1 (1999), the Nebraska Supreme Court addressed the University of Nebraska's liability for severe injuries suffered by a student during fraternity hazing. The court reiterated that a business proprietor is liable for the adverse actions of a third party against an invitee when those actions were reasonably foreseeable to the proprietor. The university argued that the landowner liability theory did not apply because the actions that took place on the university's property were not criminal in nature, but, rather, were simply "horseplay." However, the court stated that a third party's action need not amount to a violation of the criminal law to give rise to liability; such an act may be sufficient even if it is merely accidental.

The university also argued that it owed no duty to Knoll, an invitee, because Knoll had superior knowledge of the danger. Landowner liability is predicated on proof of the possessor's superior knowledge, actual or constructive, of dangers to which the invitee is subjected and of which the invitee is unaware. However, the court found that the "superior knowledge rule" did not apply to this case. It held that an invitee may very well know that the intentionally harmful acts of a third party are foreseeable on the landowner's property. That fact does not obviate the invitee's expectation that the landowner will exercise reasonable care in providing protection. Therefore, the court concluded that based upon the subject fraternity and other fraternities' past history, the subject fraternity's actions against Knoll were foreseeable, and the university owed Knoll a duty to protect.

Nevada

Nevada courts have endorsed the "totality of circumstances" test for evaluating the foreseeability of a particular crime.

In *Doud v. Las Vegas Hilton Corp.*, 109 Nev. 1096, 864 P.2d 796 (Nev. 1993), the plaintiff brought a negligent security action against a casino after he was attacked while entering his motor home that was parked in the casino's parking lot. The court held that a landowner owes a duty to provide adequate security measures to protect patrons when a crime is foreseeable under a "totality of the circumstances" analysis.

Prior similar crimes are among the relevant circumstances considered in determining the foreseeability of a crime. In *Early v. N.L.V. Casino Corp.*, 100 Nev. 200, 678 P.2d 683 (Nev. 1984), an assailant robbed and beat the plaintiff in the restroom of the defendant's casino, and the plaintiff appealed from the lower court's dismissal of his complaint. The appellate court reversed, reasoning that the plaintiff presented sufficient evidence of prior crimes to raise a factual issue regarding foreseeability. The court went on to conclude that a proprietor owes a duty to use reasonable care to keep his or her premises safe for patrons.

Accordingly, when a crime is foreseeable, the landowner owes a duty to provide protection. In *Elko Enterprises, Inc. v. Broyles*, 105 Nev. 562, 779 P.2d 961 (Nev. 1989), the court upheld a jury verdict in favor of the representatives of the decedent who had been murdered in the defendant's hotel. The court held that a review of all relevant evidence suggested that the jury unreasonably concluded that the defendant should have foreseen the shooting, and therefore owed and breached a duty to protect the decedent from the crime.

UPDATE

In *Wood v. Safeway, Inc.*, 121 Nev. 724, 121 P.3s 1026 (2005), the supreme court distinguished from the *Rockwell* case. In *Wood*, the guardian ad litem of a mentally handicapped Safeway store employee brought an action against Safeway and the company that provided janitorial services to the store, seeking to recover for a sexual assault committed on the store employee by the janitorial company's employee. In *Rockwell*, the court stated that they reversed the trial court's ruling because conflicting evidence raised a genuine issue of material fact concerning whether the off-duty guard was acting within the scope of his employment when the shooting occurred. Specifically, the evidence and affidavits produced by the parties conflicted over whether security guards were required to remain in radio contact with the employer and respond to emergency calls when they were off-duty.

Here, the court addressed the foreseeability of the janitor's acts. The court found that the janitor had no prior criminal history, and no complaints of sexual harassment had been submitted to his employer concerning the janitor or any other janitor in the company in ten years. Therefore, under the circumstances of this case, it was not reasonably foreseeable that the janitor would sexually assault the Safeway employee.

New Hampshire

Although New Hampshire courts have held that, as a general rule, landlords do not owe a duty to provide protection from criminal occurrences, an appellate decision has created several exceptions to that proposition.

In *Walls v. Oxford Management Co., Inc.*, 137 N.H. 663, 633 A.2d 103 (1993), the plaintiff was sexually assaulted in her vehicle that was parked on the defendant's premises. The plaintiff, a tenant in the defendant's residential building, alleged that the landlord had a duty to protect her from criminal occurrences. This case was one of first impression in New Hampshire, and the primary issue for the court to address was whether a duty could be imposed on a landlord to provide reasonable protection from criminal acts for residents.

The *Walls* court acknowledged the general rule that landlords owe no such duty, but then proceeded to carve out several notable exceptions. As set forth by the court, a landlord may owe a duty to provide protection under the following circumstances: (1) when a special relationship exists between the parties, such as that between an innkeeper and guest or a common carrier and passenger (the court stated that a landlord-tenant relationship would not be considered a special relationship); (2) when the defendant creates the opportunity for the crime to occur; (3) when there is "overriding foreseeability" of criminal acts; or (4) where the defendant either gratuitously or contractually assumes a duty to provide security.

The *Walls* decision greatly altered the state of the law on premises security cases in New Hampshire, and appears to set the framework for enabling such lawsuits to be presented against landowners.

UPDATE

There are no updates for this state.

New Jersey

New Jersey courts may have the distinction of writing the most scholarly opinions regarding negligent security cases. The decisions are notable for their consideration of the developing law in the various states, the common law rules, and competing policy considerations. One would be well-advised to review the relevant New Jersey cases if handling an appeal or substantive motion that requires knowledge of other states' positions on certain issues.

Private Residential Premises

In *Trentacost v. Brussel*, 82 N.J. 214, 412 A.2d 436 (1980), the New Jersey Supreme Court held that an owner of residential premises could be liable to a tenant for failing to provide adequate security. The court predicated its decision on the theory that the provision of security falls within the implied warranty of habitability. Security, reasoned the court, is vital to the use of the premises and is universally expected by tenants. The court did not elucidate, however, what constitutes adequate security.

Public Authorities

In *Goldberg v. Housing Authority of Newark*, 38 N.J. 578, 186 A.2d 291 (1962), the court held that the defendant was not liable for failing to provide police protection at its housing project. However, the court agreed that liability could be predicated on an alleged breach of duty related to the defendant's proprietary functions. In analyzing the scope of the duty of a private, proprietary landowner, the court stated:

> The question whether a private party must provide protection for another is not solved merely by recourse to "foreseeability." Everyone can foresee the commission of crime virtually anywhere and at any time. If foreseeability itself gave rise to a duty to provide "police" protection for others, every residential curtilage, every shop, every store, every manufacturing plant would have to be patrolled by the private arms of the owner. And since hijacking and

attack upon occupants of motor vehicles are also foreseeable, it would be the duty of every motorist to provide armed protection for his passengers and the property of others. Of course, none of this is at all palatable. The question is not simply whether a criminal event is foreseeable, but whether a duty exists to take measures to guard against it. Whether a duty exists is ultimately a question of fairness. The inquiry involves a weighing of the relationship of the parties, the nature of the risk, and the public interest in the proposed solution.

The court held that a private landowner has no duty to provide police protection. The imposition of such a duty would be unfair, explained the court, because residential landowners would be unaware, prior to a jury determination, of the nature of the specific duty and the acts that would discharge the duty. According to the court, "how can one know what measures will protect against the thug, the narcotic addict, the degenerate, the psychopath and the psychotic?"

In *Lieberman v. Port Authority of New York & New Jersey*, 132 N.J. 76, 622 A.2d 1295 (1993), the New Jersey Supreme Court held that a plaintiff who was robbed, knocked down, and injured in the defendant's bus terminal had a viable cause of action against the defendant for its failure to take "reasonable non-police-protection security measures." The court dismissed the claims that the defendant failed to provide sufficient police protection in the terminal. However, considering that the statutes that created the Port Authority expressly waived sovereign immunity concerning those acts and duties that were akin to those of a private landlord, the court held that liability could be imposed on the defendant in its proprietary function as a business establishment. Among the viable theories of liability are allowing nonbusiness invitees to loiter on the premises and failing to provide reasonably safe premises for invitees. The proprietary, nongovernmental measures that could be actionable are whether the defendant failed to provide better lighting, signs, and security cameras.

In *Bligen v. Jersey City Housing Authority*, 131 N.J. 124, 619 A.2d 575 (1993), the court stated that the defendant, a public housing authority, would not be relieved of liability for its failure to provide safe premises merely because statutes precluded it from raising rents to defray the costs of making the premises safe.

Apportionment of Liability

The case of *Blazovic v. Andrich*, 124 N.J. 90, 590 A.2d 222 (1991), involved a bar fight. The court held that liability among the negligent landowner, the assailants, and the plaintiff could be apportioned. The court reasoned that for purposes of assessing comparative fault, negligence and intentional misconduct were different in degree, not in kind.

Pursuant to New Jersey law, the percentage of negligence assigned to a defendant may affect that party's obligation to satisfy all or part of a judgment.

Stores

In *Butler v. Acme Markets, Inc.*, 89 N.J. 270, 445 A.2d 1141 (1982), which involved a robbery in a parking lot at the defendant's store, the court held that liability could be imposed upon the defendant because there had been prior robbery incidents at the premises and the store employed only one security guard, who spent most of his time inside the store.

UPDATE

Public Authorities

In *Foster v. Newark Housing Authority*, 389 N.J. Super. 60 (N.J. SuperA.D. 2006), Newark Police Detective David Foster, in the course of his duties, was shot three times in an apartment located in a Newark Housing Authority ten-building residential complex. He filed suit against the housing authority, alleging that its negligence permitted his attacker, who was not a tenant, to gain entrance into the building and then into the apartment where the shooting occurred.

Prior to trial, the housing authority filed a notice of motion seeking a ruling that N.J.S.A. 59:4–2, the section of the New Jersey Tort Claims Act (TCA), N.J.S.A. 59:1–1 to 59:12–3, concerned with dangerous conditions of public property, governed the case. The lower court concluded that N.J.S.A. 59:4–2 governed notwithstanding the housing authority's status as a landlord. The lower court also concluded that *L. 1993, c.* 366 §§ 1 and 2, codified as N.J.S.A. 2A:62A-21 to -22 (the "Firefighters' Act"), which abrogated the fireman's rule, does not relieve covered public employees, including police officers, from having to satisfy the requirements of the TCA.

Detective Foster, in turn, argued that when a public entity is a landlord, its responsibility to tenants and visitors is governed by the common law applicable to commercial landlords and not by N.J.S.A. 59:4–2. He cited the following cases for support: *Goldberg v. Housing Authority of Newark*, 38 N.J. 578, 186 A.2d 291 (1962); *Braitman v. Overlook Terrace Corp.*, 68 N.J. 368, 346 A.2d 76 (1975); *Trentacost v. Brussel*, 82 N.J. 214, 412 A.2d 436 (1980); *McGlynn v. Parking Authority of Newark*,

86 N.J. 551, 432 A.2d 99 (1981); *Bligen v. Jersey City Housing Authority,* 131 N.J. 124, 619 A.2d 575 (1993); and *Lieberman v. Port Authority,* 132 N.J. 76, 622 A.2d 1295 (1993).

The court ruled that since *Goldberg* was decided before the TCA was enacted in 1972, L. 1972, c. 45, § 1, it provided no support for Detective Foster's argument. And except for *Bligen,* the other cited cases were inapposite because they did not involve entities covered by the TCA. In fact, *Bligen* actually supported the housing authority since it held that a plaintiff alleging negligence based on a dangerous condition of public property "bears the heavy burden of establishing defendant's liability under the stringent provisions of the Tort Claims Act," and, more specifically, "under *N.J.S.A. 59:4–2.*" *Bligen, supra,* 131 N.J. at 136–37, 619 A.2d 575. Furthermore, the court pointed to the legislature's declaration in the TCA that "public entities shall only be liable for their negligence within the limitations of this act." N.J.S.A. 59:1–2.

In reviewing the lower court's granting of summary judgment in this case, the court discussed the previous four decisions interpreting the Firefighters' Act. In *Boyer v. Anchor Disposal and Sunshiner Maintenance,* 135 N.J. 86, 87–88, 638 A.2d 135 (1994), the court observed in dictum that "because the Legislature has, in effect, abolished the firefighters' rule in New Jersey, L. 1993, c. 366 [N.J.S.A. 2A:62A-21 to -22], this case is probably the last in which this Court will consider an application of the rule." That view, in turn, was shared in dictum by a panel of the court in *James v. Arms Technology, Inc.,* 359 N.J.Super. 291, 326, 820 A.2d 27 (App.Div.2003). But another panel of the court reached a contrary conclusion, holding that the statute did not overturn the common-law rule that a citizen could not be sued by a firefighter or police officer for negligent acts that bring either to a scene and cause personal injury. *Kelly v. Ely,* 336 N.J.Super. 354, 359–61, 764 A.2d 1031 (App.Div.), certif. denied, 167 N.J. 635, 772 A.2d 937 (2001). Then, the third circuit added its voice, predicting that the state supreme court would not follow *Kelly* because the language of the statute was clear. *Roma v. United States,* 344 F.3d 352, 359–62 (3d Cir.2003).

Here, the court found that the police officer was injured at an unlawful incident that arguably resulted, in part, from the housing authority's negligent conduct in failing to provide a working lock for the building's outside door. But since the lower court was obliged to follow *Kelly,* this court did not fault it for dismissing Detective Foster's case, to the extent that it may have done so under the fireman's rule as interpreted by *Kelly.* Under *Kelly,* the housing authority would have been protected by a common-law immunity, and the TCA has been interpreted as providing "that common-law immunities survive the enactment of the [TCA] unless specifically overruled." *Bligen, supra,* 131 N.J. at 131, 619 A.2d 575. But about six months after the lower court ruled, another panel of the court agreed with the third circuit and rejected *Kelly. Ruiz v. Mero,* 385 N.J.Super. 382, 897 A.2d 407 (App.Div.), certif. granted, 188 N.J. 352, 907 A.2d 1012 (2006). Since this court was satisfied that *Ruiz* was correctly decided and that the common-law immunity no longer applied, the Firefighters' Act was found not to be a bar against the instant action.

This court also considered whether the Firefighters' Act is subject to the TCA, or if it provides an entirely separate cause of action. The court concluded that the purpose of the Firefighters' Act was to abrogate the fireman's rule entirely, thereby removing the common-law impediment to suit, and that goal is fully served without reading the Firefighters' Act as exempting the covered officers from the requirements of the TCA. Therefore, the court held that an officer whose negligence suit is permitted by the Firefighters' Act must still comply with all the applicable provisions of the TCA.

Finally, this court dealt with the issue of whether Detective Foster was entitled to a trial pursuant to *N.J.S.A.* 59:4–2. The court firmly stated that a jury could find that the failure to provide a lock for the front entrance of a building was a dangerous condition of the property. *Trentacost, supra,* 82 N.J. at 220–28, 412 A.2d 436. And the court stated that a jury could also find that Detective Foster's injuries were proximately caused by the dangerous condition; that in the context of this case, this was a reasonably foreseeable risk; that the dangerous condition was the result of the public entity's negligence; and that the public entity had notice of the dangerous condition for a sufficient period of time to have corrected it. The only remaining applicable requirement of the TCA to this case was that it be shown that the failure to activate the outer door lock was "palpably unreasonable," meaning "behavior that is patently unacceptable under any given circumstance." *Muhammad v. N.J. Transit,* 176 N.J. 185, 195, 821 A.2d 1148 (2003) (quoting *Kolitch v. Lindedahl,* 100 N.J. 485, 493, 497 A.2d 183 [1985]). Generally, this issue is a fact question for the jury. *Vincitore v. N.J. Sports & Expo. Auth.,* 169 N.J. 119, 130, 777 A.2d 9 (2001). In *Roe v. N.J. Transit Rail Operations, supra,* 317 N.J.Super. at 82, 721 A.2d 302, this court held that the conduct of the public entity defendant could be found to have been palpably unreasonable when it bolted open a gate, thereby inviting the public to enter a known dangerous area where the plaintiff was brutally raped. Similarly, in *Saldana,* 275 N.J.Super. at 488, 646 A.2d 522, this court held that a jury should determine whether the city of Camden was palpably unreasonable because it failed to secure buildings that it owned but had abandoned. Third parties had started fires in one of the buildings, thereby damaging the plaintiffs' adjacent buildings. The *Roe* and *Saldana* cases were found to be analogous to the *Foster* case, and the court perceived no basis for saying that the housing authority was not palpably unreasonable as a matter of law.

Apportionment of Liability

In *Selvaggio v. Burris*, 2004 WL 2563536 (N.J.Super.A.D. Oct. 21, 2004), the plaintiffs' decedent, Peggy Selvaggio, a thirty-three-year-old woman, was shot to death by her ex-boyfriend, defendant Donald Burris, in a Harrah's Casino and Hotel employee parking lot in Atlantic City. At trial, the plaintiffs, Leonard and David Selvaggio, as coadministrators of Peggy's estate, sought punitive damages against Burris; damages for Peggy's injuries; and a wrongful death claim against two of the defendants, Harrah's and Atlantic City. Following the trial, the jury found Burris to be 98 percent at fault as an intentional tortfeasor, and they assessed Harrah's 2 percent responsibility for negligently failing to properly maintain the safety of its parking lot. The jury awarded the plaintiffs $5 million for wrongful death, $588,000 on the survivorship claim, and $7 million on the punitive damage claim against Burris. An amended order of judgment was entered, apportioning nonpunitive damages against Harrah's in the amount of $121,190.50. In this appeal, the plaintiffs and the Association of Trial Lawyers of America (ATLA), as amicus curiae, challenged the apportionment of fault, claiming that the defendants should have been held jointly and severally liable for the nonpunitive damages.

Here, the plaintiffs and the ATLA contended that allowing the jury to apportion between Harrah's negligence and Burris's intentional assault was an error, because Harrah's duty of care to provide security in the parking lot encompassed the obligation to prevent the very harm suffered by the plaintiffs' decedent. The ATLA also contended that the problem with apportionment is that it protects the negligent tortfeasor, and public policy requires that victims not be left uncompensated for the harm that befalls them.

The court agreed with the motion judge and the trial judge that *Blazovic v. Andrich*, 124 N.J. 90 (1991) is dispositive and that apportionment of fault was appropriate under the circumstances of the *Selvaggio* case. The court explained that, generally, "when a plaintiff claims injury from an intentional tort caused by negligent security or supervision, the jury must apportion fault between the negligent and intentional tortfeasor." *Martin v. Prime Hospitality Corporation*, 345 N.J.Super. 278, 286 (App.Div.2001). But where the defendant's responsibility for security encompasses the obligation to prevent the specific misconduct that causes a plaintiff's injuries, the defendant is precluded from relying on apportionment. *Blazovic, supra,* 124 N.J. at 111. Therefore, the court ruled that in order to resolve whether apportionment is appropriate, the trial court must determine whether the intentional tortfeasor's act was sufficiently foreseeable or sufficiently related to the negligent tortfeasor's alleged fault to justify imposing responsibility on the negligent tortfeasor for all the injuries sustained. *Id.* at 112; *Martin, supra,* 345 N.J.Super. at 292. In this case, the court agreed with the trial judge, who, in turn, agreed with the prior finding of the motion judge that Burris's intentional act was not sufficiently foreseeable to preclude apportionment. In reaching his finding, the motion judge noted that the only prior criminal acts that had occurred in the parking lot were petty crimes against property; there was no prior history of physical violence, and Burris's act of violence was unique.

In addition, the court found that the plaintiffs' reliance on *Butler v. Acme Markets Inc.,* 89 N.J. 270 (1982); *Cowan v. Doering,* 111 N.J. 451 (1988); and *Tobia v. Cooper Hosp. Univ. Med. Ctr.,* 136 N.J. 335 (1994) was misplaced. This case was unlike *Butler* because while *Butler* involved a history of similar attacks, Harrah's had no warning that Burris was an assault danger to its employees, much less the decedent. In *Cowan* and *Tobia,* the court found that contributory negligence was not a defense to a mental patient's self-inflicted injury where the defendants' nurses' and doctors' duty of care specifically included the responsibility to protect their patient from foreseeable self-harm. By contrast, this court found that Burris's act, specifically targeting the decedent, was motivated by a personal relationship and, concededly, difficult to predict. As such, Burris's crime was neither sufficiently foreseeable nor related to Harrah's failure of security to justify precluding apportionment.

The court also found equally unavailing ATLA's and the plaintiffs' assertion that the apportionment of fault between negligent and intentional tortfeasors places innocent plaintiffs at a disadvantage because more often than not they go uncompensated or poorly compensated. The court cited *Blazovic* for rejecting this argument, noting that such an analysis "ignores the principle that the parties causing an injury should be liable in proportion to their relative fault." *Blazovic, supra,* 124 N.J. at 110. The court also cited *Steele v. Kerrigan,* 148 N.J. 1, 12 (1997) to reaffirm the holding in *Blazovic*; it noted its unwillingness to follow case law from other jurisdictions that reject the concept that fault should ordinarily be compared between negligent and intentional tortfeasors. Finally, the court observed that following its decision in *Blazovic,* "the 1995 amendments to the Comparative Negligence Act inserted the language 'negligence or fault,' clarifying that the fact-finder must apportion all fault attributable to each party." *Id*. at 11 n. 2 (citing L.1995, c. 140 § 1 [codified at N.J.S.A. 2A:15–5.2]).

Applicability of Workers' Compensation Law

In *Selvaggio v. Burris*, 2004 WL 2563536 (N.J.Super.A.D. Oct. 21, 2004), the defendant also asserted that the plaintiffs' decedent's claim was covered by workers' compensation and, therefore, the cause of action against it for negligence was barred.

Because it was conceded that the decedent's death occurred while in the course of her employment, the court focused on whether it "arose out of" the employment. First, the court stated that in order to meet "arising out of employment" status, an accident must be of such a nature that the risk might have been contemplated by a reasonable person when entering the employment, as incident to it. A risk is incidental to employment when it belongs to or is connected with what a worker has to do in fulfilling his contract of service. *Coleman v. Cycle Transformer Corp.*, 105 N.J. 285, 289 (quoting *Rafferty v. Dairymen's League, Coop. Ass'n*, 16 N.J. Misc. 363, 366 [Dep't of Labor, Workmen's Comp. Bureau 1938]).

The court explained that there are three types of risks: risks "distinctly associated" with the employment, such as an employee's fingers getting caught in a machine; "neutral" risks, such as an employee getting struck by lightning while on the job; and risks that are "personal" to an employee, such as a nonwork-related heart attack suffered while on the job. *Money v. Coin Depot Corp.*, 299 N.J.Super. 434, 437 (App.Div.), certif. denied, 151 N.J. 171 (1997). Risks that are personal to the employee "do not bear a sufficient causative relationship to the employment to permit courts to say that they arise out of that employment." *Howard v. Harwood's Rest.*, 25 N.J. 72, 84 (1957); Larson, *Workman's Compensation Law*, vol. 1, § 7.20. As this court stated in *Howard*, "In these situations, the employment connection with the injury is minimal; it is the personal proclivities or contacts of the employee which gives rise to the harm, so that even though the injury takes place during the employment, compensation is denied." 25 N.J. at 85; *Coleman, supra*, 105 N.J. at 292.

Ultimately, the court found that the *Selvaggio* case is factually similar to *Transactron v. Workers' Compensation Appeals Bd.*, 68 Cal.App.3d 233, 137 Cal. Rptr. 142 (1977). In that case, Sharon Cornelius was working as a receptionist for *Transactron* when, one morning shortly after arriving for work, she saw through a window that her former boyfriend was approaching. She then hid in the women's restroom. When the boyfriend arrived, he asked for Sharon and was told she was in the ladies' room. He then entered the ladies' room and fatally shot her. At trial, an award of compensation was entered for dependency benefits on the ground that a co-employee directed the assailant to the ladies' room. On appeal, the court concluded that the shooting did not arise out of the employment. In support of its holding, the court said:

> [W]here the nature of the employee's duties places her in no particularly dangerous or isolated position, or where the risk of harm is not limited to the place of employment, and where the attack occurs on the premises not because the victim was performing the duties of employment at the time of assault but because she merely was there, and where the nature of employment was not part of an assailant's plan to isolate or trap the victim, the injury does not arise out of the employment. 137 *Cal.Rptr.* at 146; *Id.* at 214.

Similarly, the shooting by Burris was personal to the plaintiffs' decedent and beyond the ambit of the Workers' Compensation Act.

New Mexico

To determine foreseeability and, ultimately, a landowner's duty to protect persons from criminal occurrences on the premises, New Mexico's courts apply a standard that lies somewhere between the "prior similar crimes" and "totality of the circumstances" tests.

In *Pittard v. Four Seasons Motor Inn*, 101 N.M. 723, 688 P.2d 333 (1984), the plaintiff was assaulted by an employee of the defendant's motel, and later alleged various acts of negligence against the defendant. In finding the existence of sufficient evidence that the defendant could have foreseen the crime, the court stated that the specific crime itself need not be foreseeable, but only some "general harm or consequence."

In New Mexico, a duty of protection will also be imposed when a party voluntarily undertakes a duty when none otherwise exists. In addition, the court will generally not find a duty absent a special relationship between the parties. *See, e.g., Rummel v. Edgemont Realty Partners, Ltd.,* 116 N.M. 23, 859 P.2d 491 (N.M. App. 1993).

The apportionment issue was addressed in the case of *Reichert v. Atler*, 117 N.M. 623, 875 P.2d 379 (1994). In this action, the decedent was shot and killed by a patron of the defendant's lounge. The New Mexico Supreme Court upheld the appellate court's reversal of the trial court's entry of judgment against the lounge owner for the full amount of the verdict, holding that the owner's liability must be compared with the liability of the assailant and damages must be apportioned accordingly.

UPDATE

The Court of Appeals of New Mexico held in *Flores v. Danfelser*, 127 N.M. 571, 985 P.2d 173 (1999) that the plaintiffs' negligence claims were barred by the exclusivity provisions of the Workers' Compensation Act, in the absence of any evidence that department officials had actual intent to injure the plaintiff/employee. In this case, the plaintiff, an employee of the New Mexico Human Services Department, was seriously injured by a food stamp recipient who believed she was responsible for reducing his benefits. The assailant pushed his way past the doorway of the public waiting room and went into an area designated for staff offices, where he physically attacked the plaintiff and stabbed her repeatedly. It is interesting to note that unlike similar cases, which often arise out of personal or neutral attacks that happen to occur at the workplace, this attack was directly related to the plaintiff's job as an income support specialist.

The plaintiffs alleged, among other things, that the defendants were aware that security measures at the office were inadequate, and that despite having knowledge of the dangers of allowing public access to the office area where the plaintiff worked, the defendants made a deliberate decision to allow such access. The plaintiffs further alleged that despite recommendations to implement security measures, the defendants failed to take any steps to implement security measures.

The Court of Appeals of New Mexico affirmed the lower court's decision that the plaintiffs' negligence claims were barred by the Workers' Compensation Act, stating that "examination of the Workers' Compensation Act reveals several legislative provisions restricting the right of both employers and employees from pursuing other remedies involving claims arising out of work-related injuries." The relevant inquiry here was not whether the defendants knew or should have known that the plaintiff might be injured by a third party, but whether they had an actual intent to injure her. However, this case was ultimately overruled by *Delgado v. Phelps Dodge Chino, Inc.*, 131 N.M. 272, 34 P.3d 1148 (2001), which held that the exclusivity provisions of the Workers' Compensation Act would not necessarily preclude the decedent's widow from bringing a tort action.

New York

In New York, landowners have been held to owe a duty of providing protective measures to persons upon their premises once it is shown that the landowner had reason to know of the likelihood of a criminal act occurring upon his or her property. *Nallan v. Helmsley-Spear, Inc.*, 50 N.Y.2d 507, 407 N.E.2d 451, 429 N.Y.S.2d 606 (N.Y. 1980). In such instances, a landowner's duty will be to provide reasonable minimal security. The number of instances in which landowners will be found to have had reason to know of the likelihood of a crime occurring upon their premises was greatly expanded when the highest court in the state, the New York State Court of Appeals, rendered its decision in *Jacqueline S. v. City of New York*, 81 N.Y.2d 288, 614 N.E.2d 723, 598 N.Y.S.2d 160 (1993).

In that action, the plaintiff was raped by an unknown assailant in a building that was not equipped with front-door locks. The Housing Authority argued there was insufficient evidence of prior criminal activity in the building, and therefore the Housing Authority could not be held liable for failing to foresee the likelihood of the occurrence. The defendants also contended that the building in question was not covered by subsequent statutory provisions that required all post-1968 multiple dwellings to be equipped with self-locking entrances and with intercom systems. The appellate court reversed the lower court's denial of the defendants' motion for summary judgment.

The New York State Court of Appeals, however, reversed the dismissal of the complaint and, in so doing, greatly expanded the concept of foreseeability. In reaching its decision, the court held that foreseeability can be established by evidence of prior criminal activity in the general vicinity of the building, not just the specific building where the crime in question occurred. The court also held that a landlord's compliance with statutory mandates regarding security does not necessarily mean that the landlord satisfied its common law duty to provide reasonable security measures at its building. The court, accordingly, remanded the case for trial and, following six years of procedural maneuvering, that trial took place in February 1995 in the Supreme Court for the county of New York.

This expansion of the concept of foreseeability in premises security cases by the highest court in New York has had extraordinary ramifications nationwide. The *Jacqueline S.* decision has been cited by dozens of appellate courts in other jurisdictions.

Another decision appears to expand the possibilities of landlord liability for attacks outside the premises. In *Shire v. Ferdiando*, 143 Misc. 2d 650, 540 N.Y.S.2d 964 (Sup. Ct. Suffolk Co. 1995), the decedent was stabbed to death in a parking lot outside a late-night lounge. The lower appeals court found that the lounge operator had no liability because the event occurred off-premises in an area over which the operator had no control. The lounge had the right to authorize its patrons to park in the lot, but that right was shared with others and the lounge did not have the legal right to control access to the lot.

The court held that if the plaintiff could show that criminal attacks on lounge patrons in the parking area were foreseeable, then the operator of the lounge had a duty to take reasonable steps to protect its patrons. Although the parking lot was private property and the lounge operator had legal rights of use under its lease, the court's reasoning appears to suggest that if the owner of a tavern or other public facility is aware that patrons regularly use other areas in connection with their patronage of the facility—such as public streets or vacant lots for which the owner has no legal-use rights—then that owner may have a duty. Of course, one would also assume that the lack of legal control over such off-premises sites would have some impact on the extent of the duty, even though the duty may exist. *See also, Rodriguez v. Oak Point Management*, 205 A.D.2d 224, 618 N.Y.S.2d 772 (1995).

Even with the expanded concepts of foreseeability and duty expressed in the foregoing cases, defendants still have a considerable number of helpful precedents involving particular fact situations, as the following cases indicate.

Plaintiff Must Establish How the Assailant Gained Entry to Building

In *Hendricks v. Kempler*, 156 A.D.2d 425, 548 N.Y.S.2d 544 (N.Y. App. Div. 1989), the second department of the appellate court dismissed a complaint alleging a failure to provide adequate security on the ground that the plaintiff offered no proof concerning how the alleged assailant entered the building. The court stated, "Without some proof as to [how the alleged assailant had] gained entry into the building, it was impermissible for the jury to infer that his presence in the building was attributable to the negligence of the defendant." *See also, Pagan v. Hampton Houses, Inc.*, 187 A.D.2d 325, 589 N.Y.S.2d 471 (N.Y. App. Div. 1992); *Dailey v. Nehring Brothers, Inc.*, N.Y.L.J., July 6, 1988 at 20-21, col. 6, *appeal dismissed*, No. 17-5520, 1989 N.Y. App. Div. LEXIS 15635 (1st Dept. 1989) (reaching same result).

However, the first department of the appellate court has placed a limitation on the above defense. In the case of *Crockett v. New York City Housing Authority*, 592 N.Y.S.2d 26 (N.Y. App. Div. 1993), the court held that because the plaintiff testified that the assailants were not tenants of the apartment building where she was attacked, a triable issue of fact existed concerning whether the assailants gained unauthorized entry into the premises. Thus, there is a split of authority between the first and second departments of the appellate courts, with the latter being more favorable to landlords.

If Plaintiff Was Attacked by a Co-Tenant, the Defendant Landlord Will Not Be Liable

In *Gill v. New York City Housing Authority*, 130 A.D.2d 256, 519 N.Y.S.2d 364 (N.Y. App. Div. 1987), the court held that a landlord has no duty to safeguard a tenant against attack by another tenant. *See also, Simms v. St. Nicholas Ave. Hotel Co.*, 187 A.D.2d 373, 589 N.Y.S.2d 485 (N.Y. App. Div. 1992). This proposition was recently affirmed in the case of *Wright v. New York City Housing Authority*, 208 A.D.2d 327, 624 N.Y.S.2d 144 (N.Y. App. Div. 1995).

If Plaintiff Was Attacked by a Stalker, the Defendant Landlord Will Not Be Liable

When a plaintiff has been stalked by his or her assailant, the courts have held that an alleged failure to provide minimal security cannot be found to have proximately caused the assault on the plaintiff. *Tarter v. Schildkraut*, 151 A.D.2d 414, 542 N.Y.S.2d 626 (N.Y. App. Div. 1989); *Camacho v. Edelman*, 176 A.D.2d 453, 574 N.Y.S.2d 356 (N.Y. App. Div. 1991); *Robinson v. New York City Housing Authority*, 150 A.D.2d 208, 540 N.Y.S.2d 811 (N.Y. App. Div. 1989).

Interestingly, in *Tarter*, the court suggested that expert psychological testimony was necessary to establish that the alleged breach of duty proximately caused the alleged injury. The court stated, "Testimony by plaintiff's expert that the . . . absence of an outside lock was a competent producing cause of the occurrence was not enough to make out a prima facie case . . . since the expert neither demonstrated nor professed knowledge of the particular perpetrator's thought processes." This is certainly an issue that should be litigated in the future. *See also, Salvamoser v. Pratt Institute*, 150 A.D.2d 666, 541 N.Y.S.2d 540 (N.Y. App. Div. 1989) ("Given the criminal behavior which compelled the plaintiff to follow the directions of her assailants, the plaintiff would have been forced up into her apartment whether or not the door[s] in question were locked.")

When the Attack on Plaintiff Commenced off the Premises and Was Completed on Premises, the Landlord Will Not Be Liable

When an assault on the plaintiff is initiated off the defendant's premises but completed on the premises, the defendant landowner will not be liable. *Waters v. New York City Housing Authority*, 69 N.Y.2d 225, 505

N.E.2d 922, 513 N.Y.S.2d 356 (1987); *Salvamoser v. Pratt Institute*, 150 A.D.2d 666, 541 N.Y.S.2d 540 (N.Y. App. Div. 1989); *Parker v. D/U Third Realty Co.*, 141 A.D.2d 301, 530 N.Y.S.2d 137 (N.Y. App. Div. 1988); *see also, Patricia B. v. Brown*, 149 A.D.2d 450, 539 N.Y.S.2d 791 (N.Y. App. Div. 1989).

Unsettled Whether the Defendant Landowner Will Be Entitled to an Offset Based upon the Proportional Share of Fault of the Assailant

In any assault case, it is critical that N.Y. Civ. Prac. L. & R. Article 16 (McKinney 1994) be pleaded as an affirmative defense. Under that statute, a defendant who is found less than 50 percent liable is relieved of joint liability; the defendant's liability is several only and the defendant is thus responsible for only his share of the plaintiff's noneconomic damages. According to David D. Siegel, *New York Practice* 326 (2d ed., West Publishing Co., 1992), Article 16 must be pleaded as an affirmative defense. Such an affirmative defense alleges, in sum, that the plaintiff's injuries were caused by a third person over whom the plaintiff has failed to obtain jurisdiction.

Upon asserting the affirmative defense, it then becomes plaintiff's burden at trial to establish that he or she could not have obtained, even with the exercise of due diligence, jurisdiction over the third-person assailant. In pleading the affirmative defense, the defendant will be entitled to a jury charge, which states that if the jury finds the plaintiff failed to exercise due diligence to obtain jurisdiction over the third person, the jury may consider that third person's share of liability and may apportion liability between the third-person assailant and the defendant/landlord. *Smith v. McCain*, N.Y.L.J. December 2, 1992, p. 24, c.4 (Appellate Term 2d Dep't).

It must be noted, however, that in the case of *Pantages v. L.G. Airport Hotel Associates, Inc.*, 187 A.D.2d 273, 589 N.Y.S.2d 426 (N.Y. App. Div. 1992), the court held that the trial court did not err in refusing to apportion liability. The recitation of the facts and holding in the *Pantages* case is unclear; the court states neither the facts nor the basis for its holding that the trial court "did not err in refusing to apportion liability *among* the three criminal perpetrators." (Emphasis added.) Although the court uses the word "among," a review of the record makes clear that the court rejected the defendant landlord's claim that its liability should have been apportioned according to the liability of the criminal perpetrators, over whom the plaintiff failed to obtain jurisdiction. (The *Pantages* case was thereafter settled and appeal was not pursued.)

The issue of apportionment in favor of a landowner against an assailant was addressed, ironically, during the trial of the previously mentioned case of *Jacqueline S. v. New York City Housing Authority*. The trial judge ruled that, provided the defendant could establish the assailant's identity, the New York City Housing Authority would be entitled to an apportionment of liability against the assailant. For a further discussion of this topic, see Alan Kaminsky, *Premises Security: An Update*, N.Y.L.J. (Aug. 1, 1995).

Defendants Not Liable Where They Provided Reasonable Minimal Security

In *Levya v. Riverbay Corp.*, 206 A.D.2d 150, 620 N.Y.S.2d 333 (N.Y. App. Div. 1994), the court reviewed the security features that were in place at the defendant's cooperative development, and, upon concluding that they satisfied the defendant's obligation of providing reasonable minimal security, dismissed the plaintiff's complaint.

UPDATE

Over the past several years, New York's appellate courts have rendered a series of important decisions that have made it more and more difficult for plaintiffs to establish negligence against a landowner in a premises security lawsuit. Now the courts seem equally intent on limiting a plaintiff's likelihood of establishing that any such negligence on behalf of a landowner was a substantial factor in causing a crime victim's injuries. The appellate courts have recently addressed causation issues where an assailant appears to have specifically targeted the victim and where the assailant's means of entry onto the premises remains unknown or there is a question as to whether it can be attributed to the defendant's negligent or inadequate security.

Consider the defendant-friendly cases of *Ramos v. 1199 Housing Corp.*, 6 A.D.3d 416, 774 N.Y.S.2d 346 (2nd Dep't 2004) and *Flores v. Dearborne Mgmt.*, 24 A.D.3d 101, 806 N.Y.S.2d 478 (1st Dep't 2005). *Ramos* was a wrongful death action against a building owner and security company, arising out of the murder of the plaintiff's decedent in her apartment. Prior to the assailant's apprehension, the defendants' motion for summary judgment was granted because "the plaintiffs adduced no factual support for the contention that the assailant was an intruder who gained entry to the building by virtue of the alleged negligence of [the defendants]." Even after the assailant's identity was known and he pleaded guilty to the crime, the plaintiffs failed to show on their motion to vacate the prior order that the newly discovered evidence would produce a different result. There was still no evidence that negligent maintenance or inadequate security enabled an intruder to gain access to the building, thus it could not be found that the defendants' conduct constituted a proximate cause of the murder.

Meanwhile, in *Flores*, the Appellate Division, First Department, found that the owner of an apartment building was not liable for a tenant's death, regardless of any negligence in building security, when her assailants' intentional conduct was the sole proximate cause of her death. The plaintiff's decedent was shot execution-style during a robbery, and the evidence showed that her murder was the result of a planned crime, incident to the intended murder of a specific target in the apartment. "In particular, the perpetrators . . . planned in advance to seize a particular woman to gain entry to an apartment, execute one of the residents . . . and leave with any money they could find." Besides the plaintiff's decedent, five others were similarly executed. The court found that "such intentional conduct was, as a matter of law, the sole proximate cause of the decedent's death."

The First Department used similar reasoning in *Buckeridge v. Broadie*, 5 A.D.3d 298, 774 N.Y.S.2d 132 (1st Dep't 2004), in which the plaintiff was injured during a robbery while working as a handyman in the defendant's house. The plaintiff claimed that the defendant was negligent when he let the (disguised) robbers into his house and that the crime was foreseeable because of several robberies at a nearby grocery store. However, the record was devoid of any proof of prior criminal incidents at the defendant's house, and nearby grocery store robberies were found insufficient to place the defendant on notice that his house was likely to be robbed. The court held that the "intentional criminal act at issue was an unforeseeable, intervening force which severed the causal nexus between the alleged negligence . . . and the . . . injury." Moreover, the plaintiff's injury was "the result of an . . . act of sophisticated armed robbers . . . who targeted defendant and his home in advance."

In *Perez v. McFarlane*, 18 A.D.3d 232, 794 N.Y.S.2d 359 (1st Dep't 2005), a tenant who was assaulted in her apartment failed to establish that the defendants' negligence or inadequate security caused an intruder to gain entry to the building. The First Department found that the plaintiff's claim that an intruder gained access to the premises through a window in an adjacent garage office (left open on two occasions several months earlier) was "unsupported and speculative." Therefore, the court held that absent any proof, "the claim that defendants' negligence or inadequate security measures permitted the intruder to gain entry [was] insufficient to defeat defendants' motion for summary judgment."

New York's appellate courts also reached similar decisions in *Raghu v. 24 Realty Co.* 7 A.D.3d 455, 777 N.Y.S.2d 487 (1st Dep't 2004) and *Alvarez v. Masaryk Towers Corp.*, 15 A.D.3d 428, 789 N.Y.S.2d 727 (2nd Dep't 2005). In the cases of *Raghu* and *Alvarez*, a tenant and a guest, respectively, were robbed and shot in buildings owned by the respective defendants. Both plaintiffs alleged negligent security. In these two cases, the defendants satisfied their initial burdens with evidence that the building door locks and intercom systems were operable. Additionally, the landowner in *Raghu* submitted affidavits from tenants who witnessed the decedent allow his attackers into the building, while the landowner in *Alvarez* used testimony from its security guard that the subject door was locked during the ninety minutes preceding the assault. The plaintiffs failed to raise triable issues of fact as to whether their attackers were intruders who entered the building through negligently maintained entrances. The plaintiffs would not prevail at trial because they could not prove that negligent security by the landowners was a proximate cause of their injuries, and accordingly, the complaints against the landowners were dismissed.

In a premises security case not involving an apartment building, the First Department held that an alleged violation of New York City law (dimmer-than-required lighting at a bank's outdoor ATM) did not render the bank defendant liable in a personal injury action because the assault was not shown to be foreseeable. In this case, *Coronel v. Chase Manhattan Bank*, 19 A.D.3d 310, 798 N.Y.S.2d 41 (1st Dep't 2005), a patron of the bank's outdoor ATM brought a personal injury action after being shot during an attempted robbery. In light of the court's determination of unforeseeability, the plaintiff's claim that the ATM's lighting was "very dim," with some bulbs on and some bulbs off, in violation of the Administrative Code of the City of New York § 10–160(a)(6), was found insufficient to defeat the defendant's summary judgment motion. There was no evidence that the dim lighting was a proximate cause of the attempted robbery and assault.

These trends are evident outside of New York City as well. In *Browning v. James Properties, Inc.*, 32 A.D.3d 1160, 821 N.Y.S.2d 696 (4th Dep't 2006), the Fourth Department granted the defendants' motion for summary judgment and dismissed the plaintiffs' complaint. Significantly, the defendants established that there was no history of violent crime in the building and that the building's doors were secure (automatic locks, deadbolts, an intercom system, and peepholes, all operable at the time of the crime). The plaintiffs presented evidence of one violent crime in proximity to the subject building, but the court ruled that they failed to raise a triable issue of fact as to whether "crime had demonstrably infiltrated the premises" or whether the defendants should have otherwise foreseen the risk. Thus, the defendants' duty to protect against third-party criminal activity had not arisen.

On the other hand, New York's appellate courts are inclined to give plaintiffs a chance to prove their case at trial when a triable issue of fact is raised as to whether negligence by the defendant proximately caused the plaintiff's injuries. In *Venetal v. City of New York*, 21 A.D.3d 1087, 803 N.Y.S.2d 609 (2nd Dep't 2005), a fifteen-year-old tenant who was raped at gunpoint by an unidentified assailant on her building's rooftop brought a negligence action against the building's owner, the New York City Housing Authority, alleging inadequate security. Specifically at issue was the foreseeability of harm to tenants from the criminal conduct of third parties and whether the tenant's assailant was an intruder who gained access to the building because of a defect in a door lock.

The court noted that although evidence of prior criminal activity may establish the element of foreseeability, there is no requirement that the prior criminal activity be at the precise location of, or of the same type as, the present crime. *Jacqueline S. v. City of New York*, 81 N.Y.2d 288, 614 N.E.2d 723, 598 N.Y.S.2d 160 (1993). In *Venetal*, the crime statistics on which the plaintiff relied showed that "more than seventy felonies, including murder, forcible rape, arson, assault, and burglaries with forced entries, were committed during the two years prior to the date plaintiff was raped [and] demonstrate[d] that [plaintiff's housing project] suffered from an extensive history of violent criminal activity." Notice of the housing project's history of criminal activity was established by the superintendent's testimony that police reports were submitted to the building's manager. Moreover, the plaintiff testified that keys from one apartment building were able to open the doors to other buildings in the housing complex. Evidence of a security lapse was substantiated by the superintendent, who admitted that when the door locks become worn, keys from one building's lock can fit in another building's lock. The superintendent also testified that he was aware of complaints from tenants regarding this issue and conceded that if this were true, it would violate the defendant's policy (which was to have different locks for each apartment building and building keys that are restricted to tenants of the particular building).

The Second Department found that this testimony supported the inference that the assailant was an intruder, "particularly when viewed in light of the plaintiff's testimony that her unidentified assailant, who told her that he lived in the housing complex and did not attempt to shield his identity, offered to open the locked exterior door for her." Thus, the court held that the evidence presented raised a triable question of fact as to whether the plaintiff's assailant was an intruder who gained access to the building through a negligently maintained entrance. Accordingly, the defendant landowner's motion for summary judgment was denied.

Similarly, the court in *Mayer v. 486 Associates, Inc.*, 35 A.D.3d 404, 825 N.Y.S.2d 724 (2nd Dep't 2006) held that a tenant who was sexually assaulted in the defendant's building should be permitted to conduct discovery with respect to an assault committed by the same perpetrator who struck in another building owned by the same owners. The location of the other building was found to be "sufficiently proximate to that of the subject building and the circumstances surrounding that incident may be relevant to the foreseeability of the sexual assault at the subject building."

In the same vein, in *Washington v. Montefiore Med. Ctr.*, 9 A.D.3d 271, 780 N.Y.S.2d 322 (1st Dep't 2004), a wrongful death action against a building lessee and a security firm arising from a worker's stabbing at the leased premises, the First Department upheld denial of the defendants' motions for summary judgment, because, among other issues, fact issues remained as to "whether defendants' negligence, if any, was a substantial cause of the decedent's harm." In this case, the court found that evidence of prior incidents on the premises, including one in which the decedent's assailant was removed for harassing female staff, "raised triable issues as to the adequacy of the measures taken to secure the premises against predation by intruders." Specifically, evidence regarding the adequacy of the security response when the decedent's attacker was seen loitering on the premises shortly before the attack was needed to resolve the issue of causation.

As the recent case law suggests, a plaintiff's initial burden in premises security litigation has become increasingly high. To defeat a landowner's motion for summary judgment, a plaintiff must show that the landowner's negligent security was the proximate cause of the crime. To do this, a plaintiff must show that the crime was reasonably foreseeable, that the attacker was an intruder, that the intruder gained access to the premises due to the negligence of the defendant, and that the victim was not the target of a planned attack. If the plaintiff fails to meet his or her burden of proof as to causation, courts are inclined to grant summary judgment to defendant landowners.

North Carolina

North Carolina courts hold that landowners have a duty of "ordinary care" toward business invitees upon their premises. Although this duty does not ordinarily extend to protecting invitees from intentional criminal acts of third persons, such a duty of protection has been imposed in cases where the relationship of the parties suggests it is warranted. North Carolina decisions continue to expand the situations that warrant imposition of the duty. In *Sawyer v. Carter*, 71 N.C. App. 556, 322 S.E.2d 813 (1984), a convenience store owner was found to owe such a duty to its customer.

Foreseeability remains the essential factor in determining whether a duty to protect a business invitee from criminal acts of third persons will be imposed on a particular owner in a particular case. The standard for determining crime's foreseeability is the "totality of the circumstances" test.

In the leading case of *Foster v. Winston-Salem Joint Venture*, 303 N.C. 636, 281 S.E.2d 36 (1981), in which the plaintiff was assaulted in the parking lot of the defendant's shopping mall, the court held that the absence of prior similar crimes on the premises was not dispositive on the foreseeability issue. Similarly, the *Sawyer* court, in upholding a dismissal of the complaint, nevertheless concluded that foreseeability must be evaluated by considering all relevant evidence, and not just evidence of prior crimes on the premises.

The proximate cause issue was squarely addressed by the Court of Appeals for the Fourth Circuit in the case of *Crinkley v. Holiday Inns, Inc.*, 844 F.2d 156 (4th Cir. 1988). In *Crinkley*, the plaintiffs had been viciously beaten by assailants who forced entry into a hotel room. The plaintiffs presented evidence that the hotel did not have adequate security, and the trial resulted in a verdict for the plaintiffs. On appeal, the defendant's contentions included an assertion that the judgment should be reversed because the plaintiffs presented no evidence that the crime could have been prevented, even if the additional security measures discussed by the plaintiffs' security expert had been in place. The court rejected that argument, holding that the "stringent rule of proximate causation" sought to be applied by the defendant was not the law in North Carolina. Rather, the court held that proximate cause can be inferred from a link between specific security deficiencies and an assault upon a guest. Accordingly, North Carolina does not require a strict finding that the crime would not have occurred had additional security measures been in place before a court will impose liability on a landlord.

Following a lower court's dismissal of a negligent security claim in the case of *Abernethy v. Spartan Food Systems, Inc.*, 103 N.C. App. 154; 404 S.E.2d 710 (1991), the appellate court ordered a new trial. The plaintiff in the case had been attacked in the defendant's restaurant. The court held that a jury could conclude that the store manager should have foreseen the occurrence and the imminent danger to his customers. The court therefore imposed a duty to provide protection on the defendant.

These and other premises security decisions suggest that North Carolina is continuing to liberalize situations in which landowners may face liability for crimes committed on their premises.

UPDATE

In the same vein as *Cummings, supra*, the Court of Appeals of North Carolina noted that where an independent contractor is a specialist in his field, an employer is not liable for injuries arising from dangerous conditions that are open and obvious to the contractor. *Schrimsher v. Red Roof Inns, Inc.*, 149 N.C. App. 221, 223, 560 S.E.2d 386 (2002). In this case, the defendant hotel was not liable for the plaintiff's murder, which occurred on the hotel premises while the plaintiff, an off-duty police officer, was working as an independent contractor security guard.

The court found that the plaintiff had left the door through which the gunman entered unlocked, thus creating the "open and obvious" dangerous condition himself. Further, the

> decedent's knowledge of appropriate security measures, including the effect of allowing the lobby door to be unlocked at nighttime, was equal to or superior than the knowledge of defendant. . . . Indeed, decedent was hired by defendant to prevent the very kinds of criminal acts from which decedent died.

Evidence that the defendant's employee left the door open on other occasions, but not on the night in question, raised a "mere conjecture." 149 N.C. App. at 223. Thus, with an insufficient foundation for a verdict, the directed verdict in favor of the defendant was proper.

Over the past several years, North Carolina's appellate courts have also found triable issues of fact in a number of cases. For example, in *Holshouser v. Shaner Hotel Group*, 134 N.C. App. 391, 518 S.E.2d 17 (1999), a waitress on her way into work at a Holiday Inn in Winston-Salem was grabbed and raped by an unknown assailant just outside the hotel premises. Distinguishing *Hoisington, supra*, the Court of Appeals of North Carolina held that a genuine issue of material fact existed as to whether a contract for the provision of security services imposed a duty on the defendant security company and guard to protect the plaintiff, an employee of the defendant hotel operator. In *Hoisington*, the security contract was interpreted as not imposing a duty, whereas in *Holshouser* the contract was found to be ambiguous as to duty, and thus it should be presented to a jury. Accordingly, summary judgment for the defendant security company and guard was improper.

The court in *Connelly v. Family Inns of Amer., Inc.*, 141 N.C. App. 583, 540 S.E.2d 38 (2000) addressed the question of which incidents of prior criminal activity should be considered as bearing on the issue of foreseeability. Victims of an armed robbery at the defendant motel alleged inadequate security based on the door to their motel room through which the robbers entered, which contained only a push lock on the doorknob and no chain or deadbolt. Rejecting the plaintiffs' argument for a rule that prima facie liability of negligence is established where a motel's door lock system fails to prevent minimal effort intrusions, the court turned to the issue of foreseeability.

The plaintiffs presented evidence of approximately 160 prior criminal incidents, 100 of which the court found relevant as bearing on the issue of foreseeability. The crimes were analyzed according to location, type, and number, and were found to be sufficiently proximate, similar, and numerous to raise a triable issue of fact as to the foreseeability of the attack upon the plaintiffs. Of course, the injury does not end on the question of foreseeability—"establishing a duty on the claim of negligence here is contingent upon notice to the proprietor of that criminal activity." 141 N.C. App. at 590.

The court found that the plaintiffs' evidence fulfilled the requirement of notice, given that many of the prior criminal acts had occurred "so close" to the motel where they were assaulted. 141 N.C. App. at 591. The court therefore concluded that there was a triable issue of fact as to whether the defendants should have reasonably foreseen that their guests might be exposed to injury by the criminal acts of third parties.

The case of *Miller v. B.H.B. Enterprises, Inc.*, 152 N.C. App. 532, 568 S.E.2d 219 (2002) involved a bar patron who sued a bar owner for injuries he sustained when he was assaulted by an intoxicated, off-duty bouncer after being ejected from the premises for his own disorderly behavior. The Court of Appeals of North Carolina addressed whether it was foreseeable that the bouncer would assault and injure the patron when the manager and two on-duty bouncers left them together just outside the premises. Given the evidence, particularly the mutual intoxication and an earlier encounter between the plaintiff and the bouncer, the court affirmed the denial of the defendant's motion for a directed verdict, ruling that the jury could have reasonably found that it was foreseeable that the bouncer might assault and injure the plaintiff if left outside in a "perilous position." 152 N.C. App. at 541. The court also held that the third-party bouncer's intervening criminal actions did not entirely supersede the bar owner's negligence.

North Dakota

North Dakota had no cases reported.

UPDATE

In *Azure v. Belcourt Pub. Sch. Dist.*, 681 N.W.2d 816 (N.D. 2004), a teacher who was injured when she attempted to break up a fight between students brought a negligence action against the school district, alleging that it had failed to maintain a safe environment. The dispositive issue in this case was whether the school district had a duty to provide a safe environment for Azure, an employee not of the district but of the Bureau of Indian Affairs. On appeal to the Supreme Court of North Dakota, the plaintiffs argued that the lower court improperly concluded that the school district did not have control over the lunchroom where the injury occurred, and therefore did not owe a duty to provide a safe environment for Azure. The plaintiffs improperly relied on premises liability law, however, because they failed to plead their case as such. In order for the plaintiffs to establish a duty, they had to establish a special relationship between the school district and Azure, which the court found that they failed to do. Therefore, the district court's grant of summary judgment in favor of the defendant was affirmed.

Ohio

In Ohio, the foreseeability of a crime will now be determined by considering the totality of all the circumstances, instead of an assessment based on prior similar acts. Even with this apparent expansion of situations in which a landowner may be found liable for failing to foresee a crime, Ohio courts rarely find landlords negligent in premises security cases.

In the leading case of *Reitz v. May Co. Dept. Stores*, 66 Ohio App. 3d 188, 583 N.E.2d 1071 (1990), the Ohio Court of Appeals rejected the "prior similar acts" test and adopted the "totality of the circumstances" standard for considering the issue of a crime's foreseeability. The court reasoned that other criminal activity at or near the location of the business could certainly be probative evidence concerning whether additional crimes may occur. Nevertheless, the court affirmed the dismissal of the plaintiff's case, holding that there was still no evidence to suggest that the department store had reason to foresee an assault on the plaintiff that was committed in the defendant's parking lot.

The *Reitz* court further stated that courts must be mindful that "businesses are not insurers of the safety of their customers," and that "criminal behavior by third persons is not predictable." With that understanding, the court emphasized that the totality of the circumstances must be somewhat overwhelming before a business will have a duty to protect persons from the criminal acts of others.

In *Hickman v. Warehouse Beer Systems, Inc.*, 86 Ohio App. 3d 271, 620 N.E.2d 949 (1993), the Ohio Court of Appeals had an opportunity to reconsider the criteria for assessing the foreseeability of a crime. In *Hickman*, the decedent's estate brought an action against the liquor store where the decedent was shot and killed. The court acknowledged that the test for considering the foreseeability of the shooting was the "totality of the circumstances," and then concluded that the shooting was not foreseeable because no prior crimes involving personal violence occurred on the premises. The *Hickman* court was not impressed with uncontroverted evidence of prior burglaries and theft at the premises, and was equally unimpressed with the expert's affidavit that declared a liquor store owner should foresee criminal occurrences. Citing the criteria set forth in *Reitz*, the court concluded its opinion by saying the totality of the circumstances was not "somewhat overwhelming." The court refused to impose a duty to provide protection on the defendant.

A dismissal of the complaint was also affirmed in *Lovett v. Rogers Community Auction, Inc.*, No. 91-C-35, August 10, 1993, 1993 WL 307602 (Ohio Ct. App. _____, 1993). In *Lovett*, two children at a flea market engaged in a dispute, resulting in one child shooting the other with a loaded BB gun that had just been purchased from a vendor at the market. The court concluded that the defendant could not have foreseen the occurrence, and so dismissed the complaint.

The "totality of the circumstances" test was also applied in *Allison v. McDonald's Restaurants*, No. 63170, 1993 WL 453689 (Ohio Ct. App., Nov. 4, 1993), in which the plaintiff was abducted and raped while a customer at a McDonald's restaurant. In this case, however, the court considered evidence of hundreds of prior crimes around the location to be "somewhat overwhelming," and concluded that the specific crime committed on the plaintiff could be considered foreseeable. Accordingly, the dismissal of the case by the lower court was reversed.

A dismissal was also reversed by the Ohio Court of Appeals in *King v. Lindsay*, 87 Ohio App. 3d 383, 622 N.E.2d 396 (1993). In *King*, the plaintiff was assaulted on a dance floor at a bar located just off the Ohio State University campus, following a football game at the university. The court considered all relevant circumstances—such as the likelihood of violence on a Saturday night following a football game, the defendant's failure to have bouncers strategically stationed, and prior violence upon the premises—and concluded that the assault could be considered as foreseeable by the defendant.

The rationale expressed by the Ohio courts for replacing the "prior similar acts" test with the "totality of the circumstances" criteria was to prevent a situation in which a landowner would be automatically immune from liability for the first criminal act occurring on its premises. The first crime victim, accordingly, is not precluded from recovery. However, the more liberal policy for assessing foreseeability has still resulted in strict application by the courts. The requirement that the overall circumstances be "somewhat overwhelming" before a crime will be considered foreseeable is a very difficult burden for a plaintiff to overcome.

UPDATE

While Ohio courts today are more likely to use the "totality of the circumstances" test, there are instances where these courts will also rely on the "prior similar acts" test to determine foreseeability.

In *Whisman v. Gator Inv. Props, Inc.*, 149 Ohio App. 3d 225 (1st Dist. 2002), a patron of a bar was injured when the bartender broke up a fight between the patron and another person. The court declined to follow the totality of the circumstances test and relied on the prior acts test. Here, the court held that a business owner has a duty to warn or protect invitees when it knows or should have known of a substantial risk of harm that is reasonably foreseeable (i.e., past instances of prior similar acts) even though in this case the court did not find that this duty was breached.

In *Williams v. Prospect Mini Mar*, No. 2002-L-084, 2003 WL 21000932 (Ohio App. 11th Dist. May 2, 2003), the court held that a business owner does not have a duty to keep an adjoining parking lot safe for customers when the business owner neither exercises control over the parking lot nor owns the parking lot. *See also Krause v. Spartan Stores, Inc.*, 158 Ohio App. 3d 304 (6th Dist. 2004), where the court applied the totality of the circumstances test but held that a business owner has no duty to protect customers from criminal acts of third parties unless the act was foreseeable and the business owner was in possession and control of the premises. Here, the assault in the parking lot was not foreseeable because there was only one similar assault that occurred three years earlier.

Oklahoma

In Oklahoma, a business owner has a duty to warn a customer of, or protect a customer from, criminal acts of third persons when the owner knows or has reason to know that the criminal acts are occurring or are about to occur. *Taylor v. Hynson*, 856 P.2d 278 (Okla. 1993). In *Taylor*, the plaintiff was the victim of a racial assault that occurred in the drive-through lane of a fast-food restaurant. Apparently, the assailants had been inside the restaurant earlier, and were acting in a "harassing" manner while there. The trial court dismissed the complaint and the appellate court upheld the dismissal. However, the Oklahoma Supreme Court reversed, holding that the facts were such that the case qualified as an exception to Oklahoma's general rule that a merchant is under no duty to protect patrons from criminal acts.

The court explained that evidence showed the defendant knew or should have known that the attack was going to occur, and that a question of fact existed concerning whether it acted reasonably under the circumstances.

UPDATE

In *Spencer v. Wal-Mart Stores, Inc.*, 203 Fed. Appx. 193 (10th Cir. Okla 2006), a case where a patron was struck by a vehicle while walking through a store parking lot, the court distinguished the case from the prior case of *McClure v. Group K Enterprises, Inc.*, 977 P.2d 1148 (Okla. Civ. App. Div. 4 1999). In *McClure*, the plaintiff was struck in the head by a flying beer bottle while dancing in a nightclub. The issue was whether a reasonable jury could find that the defendant knew or should have known the beer bottle would be thrown at the plaintiff. The plaintiff introduced evidence of the defendant's knowledge of similar incidents involving thrown bottles and argued that the defendant continued to provide alcohol to patrons who posed an inherent risk of violence. Also, the defendant did not enact policies prohibiting patrons from bringing bottles onto the dance floor. The court found that a jury could find that the defendant "created the danger" and therefore should have known the incident was about to occur. *Id.* at 1151–2.

The court distinguished *McClure* from *Spencer v. Wal-Mart*. In *Spencer*, the plaintiff was a patron of Wal-Mart who was struck by a vehicle while walking through a parking lot. The court noted that the defendant in this case did not provide the third party with the vehicle and did not impair the third party's judgment by offering him alcohol. Also, there was no evidence of prior hit-and-run assaults or of the defendant enacting certain security measures to reduce that type of crime. The court held that the business did not have a duty to protect its invitees from the criminal act of a third party who struck the patron in a hit-and-run assault occurring in its parking lot, and there was no evidence that enacting certain security measures would reduce the incidences of this type of crime. The court also found that

> even assuming Wal-Mart had actual knowledge of the facts . . . no reasonable jury could conclude a landowner should know a crime is about to occur under these circumstances. To hold Wal-Mart liable for the criminal act committed in its parking lot in this case would make it an insurer for virtually any criminal act that occurred in its parking lot, a theory of liability the Oklahoma Supreme Court has consistently rejected. *Id.* at 200

Oregon

In *G.C. v. Kaiser Foundation Hospital, Inc.*, 306 Ore. 54, 757 P.2d 1347 (1988), the plaintiff brought an action against the defendant/hospital relative to a sexual assault committed by an employee of the hospital upon the patient/plaintiff. The various causes of action included allegations that the hospital should be liable under a theory of respondeat superior, as well as under theories of strict liability and implied contract. The court held that the hospital would not bear civil liability for the intentional acts of the assailant, concluding that such acts were clearly outside the scope of the individual employment with the defendant. The court emphasized that there was no basis to conclude that the assailant's acts were in furtherance of his employment and, therefore, the doctrine of respondeat superior was not applicable. As an aside, the court seemed to suggest that the doctrine of respondeat superior may be applicable in other assault cases, such as where a bouncer commits an assault in relation to his employment.

In *Estate of Buchler v. State of Oregon* (Ore. Sup. Ct., 1993), the plaintiffs brought an action against the state for damages caused by an escaped prisoner. Subsequent to his escape from prison, the assailant shot and killed the decedent. In dismissing the complaint, the court held that there was no evidence to suggest that the state knew or had reason to know of the specific danger presented to the decedent by the prisoner. The court further rejected the plaintiffs' allegations of negligence predicated on a failure-to-recapture or failure-to-warn theory.

The *Buchler* decision also went into considerable detail in addressing earlier controlling decisions that had more liberal interpretations of the concept of "foreseeability."

UPDATE

In *McPherson v. State of Oregon*, 2007 WL 258427 (only the Westlaw citation is currently available), tenants who were assaulted by an escaped convict brought a negligence action against their landlord. Bertha McPherson had been doing her laundry when an escaped convict entered the stand-alone laundry shed and repeatedly raped and assaulted her. The convict also restrained and assaulted McPherson's teenage son. The plaintiffs each brought an action alleging that the defendants were negligent in failing to provide safe premises.

The defendants moved for summary judgment, which was granted by the trial court. The trial court stated that there was no evidence that the defendants could have reasonably foreseen the harm that befell the plaintiffs. The court of appeals reversed.

The court of appeals determined that a landlord has a common-law duty to take reasonable steps to protect tenants in common areas from reasonably foreseeable criminal acts by third parties. Although no bright line rule exists to determine whether the plaintiff's harm was foreseeable, the court of appeals reviewed the specific facts and determined that a reasonable juror could find that the defendants breached their duty to avoid foreseeable harm to the plaintiffs. These facts indicated that the defendants should have known that the apartment complex was in a high crime area, that a tenant had been threatened by a person with an ax, that there was vandalism and trespass in the laundry facility area, and that it was understood among landlords that laundry facilities should have windows or peepholes—in this case, the laundry shed had neither. As such, the case was reversed and remanded.

Pennsylvania

In Pennsylvania, the courts adhere to the common law rules. In *Feld v. Merriam*, 506 Pa. 383, 485 A.2d 742 (1984), the court held that the owner of a residential apartment building has no duty to provide security in the common areas of the building. In reversing the lower court decision upholding the imposition of liability, the court stated:

> The Superior Court viewed the imposition of this new duty as merely an extension of the landlord's existing duty to maintain the common areas to be free from the risk of harm caused by physical defects. However, in so holding that court failed to recognize the crucial distinction between the risk of injury from a physical defect in the property, and the risk from the criminal act of a third person. In the former situation the landlord has effectively perpetuated the

risk of injury by refusing to correct a known and verifiable defect. On the other hand, the risk of injury from the criminal act of third persons arises not from the conduct of the landlord but from the conduct of an unpredictable independent agent. To impose a general duty in the latter case would effectively require landlords to be insurers of their tenants' safety: a burden which could never be completely met given the unfortunate realities of modern society.

The court held that absent an agreement or voluntary undertaking to provide security, an owner of residential premises is under no duty to provide security.

The case was remanded for a new trial to determine whether there had been a voluntary or contractual undertaking to provide security and, thoughtfully, the court stated the basis for imposing liability in the event such an undertaking was found. According to the court, negligence—not inadequacy—is the key:

> A tenant may rely upon a program of protection only within the reasonable expectations of the program. He cannot expect that a landlord will defeat all the designs of felonry. He can expect, however, that the program will be reasonably pursued and not fail due to its negligent exercise. If a landlord offers protection during certain periods of the day or night a tenant can only expect reasonable protection during the periods offered. . . . A tenant may not expect more than is offered. If, for instance, one guard is offered, he cannot expect the same quality and type of protection that two guards would have provided, nor may he expect the benefits that a different program might have provided. He can only expect the benefits reasonably expected of the program as offered and that that program will be conducted with reasonable care.

UPDATE

In *Estate of Mickens v. Stevenson*, (2002) 57 Pa. 287, the court held that the defendant, an owner and operator of a bar, was not liable in negligence for the murder of a patron by another customer because no special relationship existed between the defendant and the patron. In *Mickens*, the decedent, Lisa Mickens, and Vaughn Stevenson went to the Showboat bar in Pennsylvania. As the Showboat was closing, Stevenson and the decedent went to another bar called American Legion Post. In the parking lot of the American Legion, Stevenson shot and killed Mickens.

The court held that the Showboat bar was not liable to the plaintiffs for the death of Mickens. The plaintiffs did not produce evidence to establish that Stevenson was served alcoholic beverages at the Showboat while he was visibly intoxicated. Furthermore, when Mickens was killed, she and Stevenson were nowhere near the Showboat bar, but instead had moved to the parking lot of the American Legion. The court concluded that, based on the evidence, the defendant did not owe a duty to Mickens to protect her from the actions of Stevenson.

Conversely, in *Rosa v. 1220 Uncle's Inc.*, (2001) 51 Pa. 89, the court held that a bar was liable for damages that a patron suffered during an assault by another patron. In *Rosa*, the court determined that the bar owed a duty to its patron from the actions of a third party because one of its own bartenders had been the victim of a robbery the year before. The plaintiff was attacked and robbed in a bathroom at the defendant's establishment. The court determined that the owner of the bar had notice that violence could occur in his establishment, and therefore he had a duty to warn or protect the plaintiff from such harm.

Rhode Island

Rhode Island had no cases reported.

UPDATE

In *Martin v. Marciano*, (2005) 871 A.2d 911, a guest of a party who was struck in the head by a baseball bat brought an action against the property owner and the assailant. In *Martin*, the plaintiff had been attending a high school graduation party hosted by the defendant. The defendant had been anticipating a large party, and she proceeded to provide alcohol to underage guests.

The court held that a party host who makes alcohol available to underage guests has a duty to take reasonable steps to protect guests from injury caused by other guests. The court determined that it was generally foreseeable that one of the underage guests could become the victim of an attack while attending the defendant's party. As such, the defendant had a duty to protect her guests from unreasonable harm by other guests and third parties.

South Carolina

The duty of protection owed by a residential building owner to a tenant was addressed by the South Carolina appellate courts in the case of *Zitricki v. Balcor Property Inc.*, 411 S.E.2d 317 (S.C. 1994). In *Zitricki*, the decedent was murdered by an assailant who gained entry into her apartment by prying open a glass door. The South Carolina Supreme Court upheld a dismissal of the case, rejecting the plaintiff's contention that the landlord breached its duty of providing protection to the decedent against the assault.

The *Zitricki* court refused to extend the duty of protection that may be placed on store owners and innkeepers to the landlord in the case at bar, holding that apartment buildings, unlike "places of general resort, are not open to the public, and, as such, criminal activity may not necessarily be foreseeable by the landlord." In support of its holding, the court cited *Cooke v. Allstate Management*, 741 F. Supp. 1205 (S.C.O.S.C. 1990).

A duty of protection, however, has been imposed, albeit narrowly, upon store owners in situations where the underlying criminal occurrence was denied to have been foreseeable.

In *Callew v. Yarborough Eats d/b/a Hardees*, 442 S.E.2d 216 (S.C. 1994), the plaintiff was injured during an altercation that took place in the drive-through lanes of the defendant's restaurant. The court rejected the plaintiff's contention that the defendant breached its duty of having to provide protection from the criminal assault, holding that the particular occurrence was not foreseeable. In reaching that conclusion, the court considered such factors as the nature of the defendant's business, the fact that the restaurant did not serve alcoholic beverages, and the absence of similar prior occurrences at the premises.

Similarly, in *Munn v. Hardees Food Systems*, 274 S.C. 529, 266 S.E.2d 414 (1990), where the plaintiff was killed during an altercation upon the defendants' premises, the court dismissed the complaint, holding that the occurrence was "spontaneous" in nature and, therefore, could not have been foreseen by the defendants.

The Supreme Court of South Carolina has also rejected negligence actions against school districts on the grounds of governmental immunity. In *Clyburn v. Sumter County School District #17*, 451 S.E.2d 885 (S.C. 1994), the plaintiff was attacked by a nonstudent on a school bus and brought an action for personal injuries against the school district. The court affirmed a dismissal of the case, holding that the actions of the school district were not "grossly negligent" and, accordingly, under governmental immunity statute, the school district could not be held liable for the student's injuries.

Generally, liability for criminal occurrences will only be imposed upon South Carolina landlords in very limited circumstances. The South Carolina Supreme Court has held that store owners are generally not charged with the duty of protecting customers against criminal acts of third persons, but the intervening criminal act may not always relieve the store owner of liability for his or her negligence. *Shipes v. Piggly Wiggly St. Andrews, Inc.*, 269 S.C. 479, 238 S.E.2d 167 (1977).

UPDATE

In *Jackson v. Swordfish Investments, LLC* (2005) 365 S.C 608, the court held that a landlord had no duty to protect patrons from criminal acts of third parties that occurred inside the leased premises. In *Jackson*, a nightclub patron was shot multiple times by an assailant inside the nightclub. The nightclub was owned by Swordfish, who leased the premises to Upton Management. Swordfish arranged for security in the common areas and charged its tenants for the cost of maintaining the security. The tenants, including Upton, failed to pay for the costs of the security, and Swordfish discontinued the security in the common areas.

On the night in question, there were two altercations. A male patron was escorted from the club. Later, that patron reentered the club and began shooting. The plaintiff was shot multiple times.

The trial court granted Swordfish's motion for summary judgment. The court determined that Swordfish had no duty to protect the plaintiff from the criminal acts of third parties because the area had been leased to another entity, and Swordfish did not control or possess the property. Furthermore, although Swordfish had agreed to provide security to maintain the common areas, it never agreed to provide security inside the club. As such, Swordfish did not breach its duty to secure the common areas, and the motion for summary judgment was upheld.

South Dakota

South Dakota has adopted the "totality of the circumstances" test for assessing the foreseeability of a crime.

In *Small v. McKennan Hospital*, 403 N.W.2d 410 (S.D. 1987), after the decedent was abducted from a hospital parking lot and murdered, her estate alleged negligence by the hospital. The complaint was dismissed by the lower court, which concluded the incident was not foreseeable because no prior similar acts on the premises had been reported.

The appellate court reversed the dismissal and remanded for trial, taking the opportunity to reject the "prior similar acts" test for determining foreseeability and applying the "totality of circumstances" criteria. The court concluded that incidents of prior criminal activity in the parking lot, while not similar to the crime in the case, were sufficiently significant to raise a question of fact under the "totality of the circumstances" standard about the crime's foreseeability.

UPDATE

South Dakota continues to use the "totality of the circumstances" test first used by the supreme court in *Small v. McKeannan Hospital*, 403 N.W.2d 410 (S.D. 1987) to determine foreseeability of criminal activity.

In *Rowland v. Log Cabin*, 658 N.W.2d 76 (S.D. 2003), a patron sued a bar for negligence after being bitten in the face by another patron's dog. The court cited the rule from *Small* that "the duty to foresee a risk of harm is dependent upon all the surrounding facts and circumstances and may require further investigation or inquiry before action is taken." Accordingly, the supreme court held that a question of fact existed as to whether the attack was reasonably foreseeable to the bar, precluding a summary judgment declaring that the bar did not breach duty of care.

Tennessee

Prevailing Tennessee case law makes winning a negligent security case against a landlord or store owner extremely difficult. Several recent decisions have rejected arguments that underlying crimes were foreseeable, including cases that presented evidence of prior crimes on the premises.

In *Gray v. McDonald's*, No. CV-00234, 1993 WL 453887 (Tenn. Ct. App. Nov. 3, 1993), *aff'd*, 874 S.W.2d 44 (Tenn. 1994), a decedent had been shot and killed while waiting in the restaurant's drive-through lane. The court dismissed the complaint, holding that the shooting was not foreseeable.

The same result was reached in *Kelton & Williams v. Park Place Center*, No. CV-00207, 1993 WL 415637 (Tenn. Ct. App., Oct. 12, 1993), in which unknown assailants shot the plaintiffs in the parking lot of the defendants' shopping mall. Even though the plaintiffs presented evidence of prior criminal acts on the premises, the court held that such evidence was insufficient to establish that the defendants owed a duty to provide protection. The court based its finding on a determination that no evidence suggested the defendants knew or should have known the particular crime was imminent.

The Tennessee Supreme Court addressed the same issues in *Speaker v. Cates Co.*, 879 S.W.2d 811 (Tenn. 1994). In that case, the decedent's former roommate murdered him in the defendants' apartment complex. The estate brought a negligence action against the defendants, alleging that the decedent's request to have a new lock placed on his door put the defendants on notice of the pending danger. Although the plaintiff presented evidence of prior criminal acts committed on the premises, the court dismissed the complaint, concluding that the evidence failed to suggest that the defendants could have foreseen the specific crime.

UPDATE
In *Z Gem Company v. Dollar Rent-A-Car*, 406 F.Supp.2d 867 (Tenn. 2005), rental car patrons were assaulted and robbed by a third party while returning a rental car. The court found that the assault and robbery of the rental car patrons when they returned the rental car was not foreseeable. As such, it did not give rise to the rental car's company duty to protect the patrons from the crime committed by a third party. The rental car company had assessed security of the location upon assuming ownership, and the only previous incident of criminal activity on the premises had been the theft of two vehicles.

In analyzing the case, the court followed the rule established in *McClung v. Delta Square Ltd. Partnership*, 937 S.W.2d 891, 894 (Tenn.1996) regarding a business's duty to protect customers from criminal acts of third parties. In contrast to *McClung*, the plaintiffs in *Z Gem* did not cite multiple incidents of crime at the defendants' location or in the immediate vicinity. Because the plaintiffs could not establish essential elements of their negligence claim, the defendants' motion for summary judgment was granted.

Texas

In Texas, the nature of the duty, if any, owed by an owner of premises to one who comes upon the premises is unsettled. If the case involves a business establishment, the courts tend to rely on the common law rules regarding the duties of businesses to their invitees, innkeepers to their guests, and common carriers to their passengers. *See, e.g., Castillo v. Sears, Roebuck & Co.*, 663 S.W.2d 60 (Tex. Ct. App. 1983); *Kendrick v. Allright Parking*, 846 S.W.2d 453 (Tex. Ct. App. 1992); *Walkoviak v. Hilton Hotels Corp.*, 580 S.W.2d 623 (Tex. Ct. App. 1979). But if the case involves a private residential landlord, the common law rule—that no duty to provide security exists—may be circumvented.

In *Nixon v. Mr. Property Management Co., Inc.*, 690 S.W.2d 546 (Tex. 1985), a young girl was dragged into a vacant apartment and raped. The Texas high court held that the landowner breached a specific ordinance that imposed a duty to board up the vacant apartment. Considering the breach of the statutory duty, the court held that the landowner could be held liable. In a concurring opinion, the court was criticized for failing to abandon the common law rules and to adopt a less restrictive standard—a general duty of ordinary care under the circumstances without regard to the classification of the landowner or the person who comes upon the premises. According to the concurring opinion, the fact that the rape took place in an apartment complex that had an extensive crime history was also sufficient to require the defendant to provide security.

Although the *Nixon* case adhered to the common law rules, such rules were not discussed in the notorious case of *Berry Property Management, Inc. v. Bliskey*, 850 S.W.2d 644 (Tex. Ct. App. 1993), in which a rape victim was awarded $16 million against a landowner. In *Berry*, the court held that even apart from a breach of statute, a landowner may be held liable for failing to provide adequate security. In reaching its decision, the court did not even discuss the *Nixon* case, which leads to the inescapable conclusion that the *Berry* court deliberately skirted the restrictive holding of *Nixon*. Although a writ of error was issued for an appeal to the Texas Supreme Court, the case was settled before the appeal was taken.

Another way parties avoid the *Nixon* case is by relying on contract principles. In *Blaustein v. Gilbert-Dallas Co., Inc.*, 749 S.W.2d 633 (Tex. Ct. App. 1988), the assailant entered the plaintiff's apartment by using a key. The plaintiff previously asked the landlord to change the locks and, under the lease, the landlord had an affirmative duty to do so. The failure to change the lock could result in the imposition of liability on the landlord.

The particular lease provision in *Blaustein* is congruous with Section 92.153 of the Texas Property Code, which also imposes an affirmative duty on the landlord to change or rekey a "security device" (not just a door lock) at the request of a tenant. Although the statute does not require that the request be in writing, it does provide that a lease may require that a request be in writing. (The *Blaustein* decision does not discuss whether the lease provision in that case contained a clause requiring that the request be in writing.)

In *Benser v. Johnson*, 763 S.W.2d 793 (Tex. Ct. App. 1988), the plaintiff was raped in her apartment by an assailant who entered through her window. She alleged that the window latch was defective. In affirming the finding of liability against the defendant, the court relied on the previously mentioned statute, as well as Section 92.052 of the Texas Property Code, which requires that a landlord repair or remedy a condition if (1) the tenant makes a proper request according to the statute, (2) the tenant is not delinquent in paying rent, and (3) the condition materially affects the tenant's physical health or safety.

Foreseeability

The general rule regarding foreseeability is set forth in *Nixon* and in *Blaustein*, where the courts noted that the test for foreseeability is whether a person of ordinary intelligence and prudence should have anticipated the danger to others created by the alleged negligence. The *Nixon* court held that evidence of previous crimes on or near the premises raises a fact issue concerning the foreseeability of criminal activity. The following cases have also discussed the foreseeability issue.

In *Berly v. D & L Security Services*, 876 S.W.2d 179 (Tex. Ct. App. 1994), a store employee was shot and killed. In the action against the company that had provided security to the store, the court held that foreseeability could be established without prior gun-shooting incidents at the store. The incidence of prior crimes involving force and violence sufficed to establish foreseeability.

In *Ronk v. Parking Concepts of Texas, Inc.*, 711 S.W.2d 409 (Tex. Ct. App. 1986), a business invitee who leased a parking space on a month-to-month basis was attacked in the parking lot. The case was dismissed on the ground that the evidence was insufficient to establish that the crime was foreseeable. Although numerous thefts and burglaries previously took place in the parking lot and the adjacent building, only one assault had occurred, and that crime involved two persons at a party who came to blows over a woman.

On the ground that the plaintiff submitted no affidavit of a security expert, the *Ronk* court distinguished the case from *Allright, Inc. v. Pearson*, 711 S.W.2d 686 (Tex. Ct. App. 1986). *Allright* involved an armed robbery and car theft in a multilevel parking garage. The court held that a triable issue of fact existed about whether the attack was foreseeable, based on the expert's affidavit. The court stated, "It was reasonably foreseeable that a person bent on robbery could enter, hide on upper levels, and lay in wait for persons coming in, whether or not such incidents had occurred in the past."

The *Ronk* decision was criticized as too restrictive in *Garner v. McGinty*, 771 S.W.2d 242 (Tex. Ct. App. 1989), in which the court held that a business invitor owes a duty to protect invitees when the invitor knows, or has reason to know from his or her past observations, that the business is likely to attract crime. The *Garner* court also held that the defendant's installation of security devices was not, by itself, evidence that the defendant had notice that criminal activity posing a danger to invitees was likely to occur. The court explained that a lack of prior similar incidents does not necessarily preclude a finding of foreseeability and a resulting duty to protect business invitees, because the test for determining foreseeability is the "totality of the circumstances."

The court noted, however, that at best, "the evidence cumulates to show a reason to know that criminal activity might occur. That, however, is not sufficient to create a duty to take precautions against harm intentionally inflicted on invitees."

In *Eastep v. Jack-in-the-Box, Inc.*, 546 S.W.2d 116 (Tex. Ct. App. 1977), the court held that the defendant, a restaurant proprietor, need not know that its patrons are violently disposed before the court can impose liability. Instead, the proprietor need know only of "a sequence of conduct sufficiently long to enable the proprietor to act for the patron's safety." The court held the defendant restaurant liable for failing to ask four intoxicated individuals to leave the premises, and for failing to call the police when those persons started cursing and harassing the plaintiff's group.

Causation

In *East Texas Theatres, Inc. v. Rutledge*, 453 S.W.2d 466 (Tex. 1970), the court found no evidence that the person who injured the plaintiff by throwing a bottle from the balcony of a theater was among a group of unruly individuals who were previously throwing paper cups from the balcony. Therefore, the plaintiff could not establish that the defendant's failure to oust the disorderly patrons caused the plaintiff's injuries.

In *Yarborough v. Erway*, 705 S.W.2d 198 (Tex. Ct. App., Houston, 14th Dist., 1985), the plaintiff accompanied an assailant out of the bar, where the two intended to resolve their dispute. The plaintiff was stabbed. The court held that the alleged breach of duty—the defendant's failure to provide adequate security—did not cause the attack. According to the court, had the plaintiff "not voluntarily accompanied [the assailant] outside, even when he alone thought [the assailant] might want to fight, it is probable no injury would have occurred. *See Boss v. Princes's Drive-Ins*, 401 S.W.2d 140 (Tex. Ct. App. 1966)."

Tenants' Employees and Independent Contractors

A landlord may be liable to a tenant's employee to the same extent as the landlord may be liable to a tenant. Also, a landlord may owe such a duty to an independent contractor if the landlord exercises control over the contractor. *Exxon Corp. v. Tidwell*, 867 S.W.2d 19 (Tex. 1993); *O'Neill v. Startex Petroleum, Inc.*, 715 S.W.2d 802 (Tex. Ct. App. 1986) (employee of lessee gas station has viable cause of action against lessor for injuries employee sustained in an armed robbery, because lessor maintained control over products that could be sold and retained title to products until time of sale, and because lessor had to approve changes to premises). In a case involving a lease that expressly stated the lessor had no right to direct or control the management of the premises, the court held that an employee could not sue the lessor. *Daniels v. Shell Oil Co.*, 485 S.W.2d 948 (Tex. Ct. App. 1972).

Liability of Out-of-Possession Lessor

To impose liability on an out-of-possession lessor, a court or jury must find that the lessor had specific control over the safety and security of the premises, rather than a more general right of control over operations. As stated by the court in *Exxon Corp. v. Tidwell*, 867 S.W.2d 19 (Tex. 1993), the "focus should be on whether the [lessor] had the right to control the alleged security defects that led to [plaintiff's] injury." The court stated that in the absence of a right to control the premises, no corresponding duty exists.

Notably, the *Exxon* decision rejected the concept that a lessor's actual exercise of control over the operation of the premises, regardless of whether the operations had anything to do with security, could form the predicate for finding liability against the lessor. Instead, the extent of control over security forms the basis for imposing liability on an out-of-possession lessor. The case is enigmatic, for it seems to suggest that even if the lessor voluntarily controlled the security of the premises—having no right or duty to do so under a lease—the lessor would not be liable to a crime victim. The result in *Exxon* may be explained by the fact that the case involved gas stations, around which an entire and distinct body of case law has developed. Nevertheless, this matter will certainly be the subject of future litigation.

Agent for Majority Owner of Condominium

In *Siegler v. Centeq Realty, Inc.*, 874 S.W.2d 304 (Tex. Ct. App. 1994), the defendant Centeq Realty, Inc. was the agent of the majority owner of the condominium development, and Centeq's president exercised majority voting power at the condominium board meetings. The court held that such control was sufficient to raise a triable issue of fact concerning whether Centeq exercised control over the condominium development and, therefore, could be held liable for failing to provide adequate security to prevent the plaintiff's kidnapping from the condominium's garage. Unfortunately, the case contains no discussion of the duty owed—whether it arises from statute, contract, or some other source—nor did the *Siegler* court even discuss the *Nixon* case.

Off-Premises Assault

In *LaFleur v. Astrodome-Astrohall Stadium Corp.*, 751 S.W.2d 563 (Tex. Ct. App. 1988), the court held that a defendant landowner cannot be held liable for an assault that occurs on adjacent property the defendant neither controls nor has a right to control.

In *Castillo v. Sears, Roebuck & Co.*, 663 S.W.2d 60 (Tex. Ct. App. 1983), the plaintiffs were threatened while inside the defendant's store, and then were attacked outside the store. No store employees witnessed the confrontation. The complaint against the store and the mall owners was dismissed because those parties lacked knowledge of the crime and because the store was not the type of place that would attract or provide a climate for criminal activity.

Parking Lots

In *Kendrick v. Allright Parking*, 846 S.W.2d 453 (Tex. Ct. App. 1992), the court held that a triable issue of fact existed in the parking lot case because, notwithstanding the defendant's employee's denial of knowledge, the plaintiff testified at her deposition that the employee was only fifteen to twenty feet away when she was attacked and the employee looked at her immediately before the attack. Additionally, the applicable policy and procedure manual urged parking lot attendants to be vigilant about intruders and to call police about suspicious activities. Finally, an expert's affidavit helped the plaintiff meet her burden of proving that the attack was foreseeable.

In *Walkoviak v. Hilton Hotels Corp.*, 580 S.W.2d 623 (Tex. Ct. App. 1979), the court held that a triable issue of fact existed about whether the defendant hotel provided adequate security in its parking lot, where the plaintiff was assaulted and robbed during a convention. The court noted that the police were called to the hotel twice during the previous twelve months, due to robberies near the hotel. One incident involved a hotel guest, and the other involved a person who was assisted into the hotel after the crime occurred. The court considered this evidence sufficient to impose a duty on the hotel to ascertain the security measures necessary to protect its guests. Notably, the hotel had a policy of deploying extra security guards during conventions, but failed to do so on this occasion. *See also, Allright, Inc. v. Pearson*, 711 S.W.2d 686 (Tex. Ct. App. 1986); *Ronk v. Parking Concepts of Texas, Inc.*, 711 S.W.2d 409 (Tex. Ct. App. 1986).

Restaurants and Taverns

In *Yarborough v. Erway*, 705 S.W.2d 198 (Tex. Ct. App. 1985) (which is also discussed above in the section on causation), one patron bumped into another in the defendant's bar and the two exchanged words. They agreed to step outside, and the plaintiff was stabbed. A jury held the assailant only 35 percent liable, the bar 50 percent liable, and the plaintiff 15 percent liable. Liability was imposed on the bar because its workers failed to ascertain that the assailant was intoxicated, throw him out of the bar, and call the police. The court reversed the judgment and dismissed the complaint against the defendant bar owner. The court noted that the bar was a neighborhood tavern, the patrons knew each other, and no history of violence at the bar existed. Additionally, the court found that the defendant did not have sufficient time to prevent the assault on the plaintiff. The court stated, "It is not reasonable to say the management should have foreseen the danger when [plaintiff] and those around him could not."

In *Polk v. Rhinestone Wrangler & K.C.O., Inc.*, 774 S.W.2d 799 (Tex. Ct. App. 1989), the plaintiff stated, in opposition to the defendant's motion for summary judgment, that he had been to the defendant's bar on many occasions and that fights occurred 60 percent of the times he was there. Not surprisingly, the court held that a triable issue of fact existed about whether the bar provided adequate security to the plaintiff. *See also, Eastep v. Jack-in-the-Box, Inc.*, 546 S.W.2d 116 (Tex. Ct. App. 1977).

Security Guard Companies

As a general rule, a plaintiff who is injured by a third person has no cause of action against an independent security company that guards the premises where the plaintiff was injured. However, in the case of *Midkiff v. Hines*, 866 S.W.2d 328 (Tex. Ct. App. 1993), the plaintiff was permitted to maintain a direct action against a security company. Although not noted in the court's decision, the security company did not raise a "lack of privity" defense because the company was intertwined with, and controlled by, the owner of the premises (defendant Hines), and the owner and security company were jointly defended by the same law firm. Plaintiffs will probably attempt to use this case as a basis for circumventing the "lack of privity" defense. If the case is so cited, the defense lawyer must demonstrate that the *Midkiff* court was not asked to address this issue.

Also important in this decision is the court's reliance on evidence that the security company was negligent for not learning about police reports of aggravated robbery, assault, burglary, theft, and kidnapping in the area, and its reliance on expert testimony that a uniformed guard would have been a visible deterrent that would have prevented the crime.

UPDATE

Fitzgerald v. Patel, 2000 WL 547017 (Tex.App.—Austin) involves a woman who rented a room at a hotel. She invited three friends over and four male acquaintances. Three of the women left, leaving plaintiff

Megan Fitzgerald alone with the four men. Throughout the evening, the individuals were consuming alcohol and various illegal drugs. One of the four men was playing with a gun, and the slide on the gun seemed to jam. The gun discharged and shot Fitzgerald in the head, killing her. The four men fled. When the other three women returned to the room, they discovered Fitzgerald's body.

In its analysis, the court focused on *Timberwalk Apartments v. Cain*, 972 S.W.2d 749 (Tex. 1998), wherein the court held that a person who controls a premises has a duty to use ordinary care to protect invitees from criminal acts of third parties if he knows or has reason to know of an unreasonable and unforeseeable risk of harm to the invitee. However, a landowner has no duty to protect people on his property from criminal conduct whenever crime might occur. In *Fitzgerald*, the hotel established that it could not foresee the risk of harm to the plaintiff and consequently had no duty to protect her from, or warn her of, the acts of another invited guest in the same room.

Utah

In *Hunsaker v. Utah and Gas-A-Mat*, 870 P.2d 893 (Utah 1993), the plaintiff was abducted from the service station where she worked as a cashier and was murdered. The complaint against the service station alleged that it breached its duty of care owed to the plaintiff. The court upheld the dismissal of the complaint, concluding that this action was barred by the state workers compensation statute.

UPDATE

In determining foreseeability, the court still follows the holding in *Rees v. Albertson's, Inc.*, 587 P.2d 130, 133 (Utah 1978) that the trier of fact should determine whether the injury was foreseeable and proximately caused by the alleged negligent conduct. In *Mackay v. 7-Eleven Sales*, 995 P.2d 1233 (Utah 2000), the parents of a minor passenger brought a negligence claim against a store. They sought recovery for injuries sustained by the passenger when the intoxicated minor driver of the truck in which the passenger was riding caused a rollover accident. The store had unlawfully sold beer to the driver's friend. The trial court granted the store's motion for summary judgment and dismissed the case, ruling that it was not the store but the consumption of alcohol by the driver that was the proximate cause of the plaintiff's injuries. The supreme court reversed, holding that there was a genuine issue of material fact as to whether the injuries sustained by the passenger were reasonably foreseeable and proximately caused by the store's negligence.

Vermont

Vermont had no cases reported.

UPDATE
There are no updates for this state.

Virginia

Virginia courts limit landowners' obligations to provide protection from criminal occurrences by applying the "prior similar acts" standard for determining foreseeability.

In *Wright v. Webb*, 234 Va. 527, 362 S.E.2d 919 (1987), the plaintiff was assaulted in the defendant's motel parking lot, and later alleged that the defendant failed to supply proper security to guard against the occurrence. The Virginia Supreme Court held that, under the "prior similar acts" rule, the landlord owed no duty of protection to the plaintiff, despite reports of prior dissimilar crimes on the premises. The court concluded that a business owner does not have a duty to protect a guest from crime, unless the owner knows that a crime is occurring or is about to occur. The court found no such imminent probability of harm under the facts of the case.

UPDATE
In *Aldrich v. McDonald's Restaurants of Virginia, Inc.*, 24 Va.Cir.11 (Va. Cir. Ct. 1990), the plaintiff moved to strike the defendant's demurrer to the amended motion for judgment, in which it was alleged that the plaintiff suffered personal injuries as a result of the negligence of certain employees of a McDonald's restaurant in Sterling, Virginia. The court held that *Wright v. Webb*, 234 Va. 527 (1987) provided a very narrow exception to the general rule that a business invitor whose method of business does not attract or provide a climate for assaultive crimes does not have a duty to take measures to protect an invitee against criminal assault. This exception was found to apply when: (1) the business invitor knows that criminal assaults against persons are occurring or are about to occur (2) on the premises (3) which indicate an imminent probability of harm to an invitee.

Here, the allegations of the amended motion for judgment did not indicate that the manager knew that the plaintiff was going to be assaulted on the McDonald's premises. It was alleged that the assault occurred outside the door of the restaurant, and there was no allegation that the place where the manager was told the assault would occur or where the assault did occur was a part of premises owned or possessed by the defendant. Nor did the court believe that it could be fairly inferred from the alleged facts that the area of the threatened attack and/or the actual attack was on the defendant's premises. This was true particularly in light of the allegations of paragraph 24 of the amended motion for judgment that a shopping center surrounds the subject McDonald's restaurant.

In *Thompson v. Skate America, Inc.*, 261 Va. 121 (Supreme Court of Virginia 2001), the court considered whether the trial court had properly sustained demurrers to a motion for judgment, where the plaintiff, a business invitee, alleged that a minor, also a business invitee, intentionally injured him while on the business owner's premises.

On March 12, 1999, Thompson and Bateman (both minors) were both patrons and invitees of Skate America, a commercial skating rink in Hanover County. "On several prior occasions, Bateman had caused disturbances, arguments and fights" at Skate America and "was a known trouble maker, consistently disobeyed the rules of [Skate America] and generally was a menace to . . . patrons of the skating rink." On several prior occasions, "Bateman had been ejected from Skate America by its employees," and he "had been banned from reentry to Skate America on multiple occasions and was under such a ban" on March 12, 1999. At closing time, Thompson and Bateman were waiting on Skate America's premises for their parents to pick them up. "Without . . . provocation, Bateman struck [Thompson] in the back of [his] head with a roller skate, fracturing [his] skull, causing severe and permanent damage, extensive hospitalization and medical expense and grave emotional damage."

The issue in this case was whether the factual allegations in Thompson's motion for judgment were sufficient, as a matter of law, to establish that Skate America had a duty of care to protect Thompson from the injuries caused by Bateman such that a jury could find it liable for those injuries. See *Burns v. Johnson*, 250 Va. 41, 44 (1995). "In Virginia, [the courts] adhere to the rule that the owner or occupier of land ordinarily is under no duty to protect an invitee from a third person's criminal act committed while the invitee is upon the premises." *Gupton v. Quicke*, 247 Va. 362, 363 (1994). However, the court has recognized that certain "special relationships" may exist between particular plaintiffs and defendants, either as a matter of law or because of the particular factual circumstances in a given case, which may give rise to a duty of care on the part of the defendant to warn and/or protect the plaintiff against the danger of harm from the reasonably foreseeable criminal acts committed by a third person. The court has also recognized examples of such necessary special relationships that arise as a matter of law to include a common carrier and its passengers, an employer and its employees, an innkeeper and its guests, and a business owner and its invitees. *See Klingbeil Management Group Co. v. Vito*, 233 Va. 445, 448 (1987).

Here, a special relationship was found to exist between Skate America, a business owner, and Thompson, its invitee. Accordingly, the dispositive question in this case was whether that special relationship also gave rise to a duty of care on the part of Skate America to protect Thompson from the danger of harm from the criminal act of Bateman.

In *Wright*, the first instance in which this court directly addressed the special relationship between a business owner and an invitee, it held that despite the existence of a special relationship, the business owner does not owe a duty of care to protect its invitee unless it "knows that criminal assaults against persons are occurring, or are about to occur, on the premises which indicate an imminent probability of harm to [its] invitee." *Wright*, 234 Va. at 533, 362 S.E.2d at 922. The court further held that for the duty to be imposed, there must be "notice of a specific danger just prior to the assault." *Id.*

The court found that the significant factor that distinguished the *Thompson* case from *Wright*, and from other similar cases, with respect to the question whether Skate America owed Thompson, its invitee, a duty of care to protect him from criminal assaults on its premises, was that here it was alleged that a specific individual was known to Skate America to be violent and to have committed assaults on other invitees on its property in the recent past. While in *Wright* and other cases, the court declined to "impose liability for negligence based solely upon . . . a background" of prior criminal activity on the defendant's premises or in its vicinity by unknown persons (234 Va. at 533), here the circumstances were quite different. Indeed, the allegations in Thompson's motion for judgment plainly stated that Skate America had specific knowledge of Bateman's propensity to assault its other invitees, had intervened to inhibit that behavior in the past, and had taken steps to avoid a recurrence of that behavior. Thus, taking these allegations as true on demurrer, the court was of the opinion that the allegations regarding Bateman's presence on Skate America's premises were sufficient to state a claim that Skate America was on notice—specifically, that Thompson was in danger of being injured by Bateman in a criminal assault. The "imminent probability" of that harm, as characterized in *Wright*, is merely a heightened degree of the "foreseeability" of that harm, and the court was of the opinion that the specific allegations concerning the knowledge Skate America had of Bateman's prior violent conduct satisfied the necessary degree of foreseeability.

Similarly, these allegations raised the fair and just inference that the magnitude of the burden on Skate America to guard against Bateman's act was negligible, inasmuch as Skate America need only to have enforced the ban it was alleged to have imposed on Bateman. The consequences of placing that burden on Skate America were equally negligible, for it was obviously in the best interest of any business owner to exclude from its premises a person it knew had disrupted its business in the past and who was likely to do so in the future. Thus, the court held that the invitee had sufficiently alleged that the owner had a duty to protect the invitee from a minor's criminal assault.

In *Taboada v. Daly Seven, Inc.*, 271 Va. 313 (Supreme Court of Virginia 2006), a hotel patron filed a common-law and statutory negligence claim against a hotel after the patron was assaulted and shot by a third party in the hotel's parking lot. This case presented an issue of first impression—what duty of care is owed by an innkeeper to a guest for injuries caused by a third party?

At approximately 2:00 A.M. on March 27, 2003, Ryan Taboada and his family arrived at the Holiday Inn Express seeking lodging for the night. Taboada registered as a guest at the hotel and was assigned a room. Taboada then returned to his vehicle in the hotel's parking lot where his wife and two children were waiting and began to unload the family's luggage. Derrick W. Smith, who was not a guest at the hotel, approached Taboada and demanded money from him. Smith then, immediately and without provocation, began to fire a weapon at Taboada. Taboada was wounded eight times, suffering severe bodily injuries. Smith took a wristwatch from Taboada's seven-year-old son and stole the family's vehicle; Taboada's infant daughter was still in her car seat in the vehicle at the time. Police apprehended Smith, recovered the vehicle, and rescued the infant, who was not physically harmed.

In Virginia, the duty of care owed by an innkeeper "to take reasonable precautions to protect the persons and property of [his] guests" is defined, and the innkeeper's liability is limited by Code § 35.1–28. In summary, the duties prescribed and the limits of monetary loss provided for in that statute relate to the provision of adequate locks on doors and windows, and are principally directed to the prevention of the loss of personal property of the guest. *See* Code § 35.1–28(B)-(D). However, as relevant to the issues raised in this appeal, Code § 35.1–28(E) makes plain that the duties prescribed, and the limitation of liability afforded, by the statute do not "change or alter the principles of law concerning a hotel's liability to a guest . . . for personal injury." Thus, with respect to the specific facts of this case, the duty of care owed to Taboada by Daly Seven with respect to protecting him from injury as the result of a criminal assault by a third party is not governed by the provisions of the statute, but remains governed by the common law. *See Couplin v. Payne*, 270 Va. 129, 136, 613 S.E.2d 592, 595 (2005); *Boyd v. Commonwealth*, 236 Va. 346, 349, 374 S.E.2d 301, 302 (1988).

The general rule in Virginia is that there is no common-law duty for an owner or occupier of land either to warn or to protect an invitee on his property from the criminal act of a third party. *Yuzefovsky*, 261 Va. at 106, 540 S.E.2d at 139. "There are narrow exceptions to this rule," but the application of those exceptions "is always fact specific and, thus, not amenable to a bright-line rule for resolution." *Id.* However, before an exception to the general rule can apply so as to impose a potential duty upon the owner of land, the facts "must establish that there is a special relationship, either between the [owner of land] and the [invitee] or between the third party criminal actor and the [owner of land]." *Id.* at 107, 540 S.E.2d at 139. The relationship between innkeeper and guest has long been recognized by the common law as constituting just such a special relationship. *See*, e.g., *Yuzefovsky*, 261 Va. at 108, 540 S.E.2d at 140; *Skate America*, 261 Va. at 129, 540 S.E.2d at 127; *Holles v. Sunrise Terrace, Inc.*, 257 Va. 131, 136, 509 S.E.2d 494, 497–98 (1999); *A.H. v. Rockingham Publishing Co.*, 255 Va. 216, 220, 495 S.E.2d 482, 485 (1998); *Klingbeil Management Group Co. v. Vito*, 233 Va. 445, 448, 357 S.E.2d 200, 201 (1987).

Thus, the establishment of the necessary special relationship is the threshold requirement for the application of an exception to the general rule of nonliability in these cases. Even though the necessary special relationship is established so as to create a potential duty on the defendant to protect or warn the plaintiff against criminal conduct of a third party, there is no liability when the defendant neither knows of the danger of an injury to a plaintiff from the criminal conduct of a third party nor has reason to foresee that danger. In short, the special relationship does not make the defendant an insurer of the plaintiff's safety. *See Rockingham*, 255 Va. at 220–21, 495 S.E.2d at 485.

Although this court had previously addressed questions of liability for injuries caused by third parties involving property owners who were innkeepers, the plaintiffs in those cases were regular business invitees on the property and not guests of the innkeepers. *See*, e.g., *Wright v. Webb*, 234 Va. 527, 529, 362 S.E.2d 919, 920 (1987) (patron of adjoining business using parking on innkeeper's property by permission); *Alpaugh v. Wolverton*, 184 Va. 943, 945, 36 S.E.2d 906, 907 (1946) (patron of restaurant located in innkeeper's property). In contrast, this case presented the opportunity to address directly the question of what duty of care an innkeeper owes to a guest as a result of that special relationship for injuries caused by the criminal conduct of a third party while on the innkeeper's property.

In the absence of prior case law in Virginia concerning the special relationship of innkeeper and guest with regard to injuries suffered by criminal acts of a third party, the trial court looked for guidance in prior cases involving other special relationships between owners of land and either invitees or tenants. The trial court principally chose *Yuzefovsky*, which involved the recognized special relationship of a landlord and tenant, for guidance. The court was of the opinion, however, that the nature of the landlord-tenant relationship was not congruent with the relationship of innkeeper and guest. Additionally, the court was unpersuaded by the analogy of the landlord-tenant relationship in this case, because, unlike a landlord, an innkeeper is in direct and continued control of the property and usually maintains a presence on the property personally or through agents. Thus, "while a lessee may be expected to do many things for his own protection," an innkeeper's guest is not as well situated to do so. *Crosswhite v. Shelby Operating Corp.*, 182 Va. 713, 715, 30 S.E.2d 673, 674 (1944).

In *Kirby v. Moehlman*, 182 Va. 876, 30 S.E.2d 548 (1944), a premises liability case involving an innkeeper and guest, the court observed with regard to the common definition of negligence that "negligence is a relative term and the degree of care in fact should be greater or less commensurate with the circumstances." *Id.* at 884, 30 S.E.2d at 551 (quoting *Eastern Shore of Va. Agric. Assoc. v. LeCato*, 151 Va. 614, 619, 144 S.E. 713, 714 [1928]). In a similar vein, as observed in *Rockingham*, even though the necessary special relationship is established with regard to a defendant's potential duty to protect or warn a plaintiff against criminal conduct, the defendant is not held to be the insurer of the plaintiff's safety, but, rather, it must be established that "the danger of a plaintiff's injury from such conduct was known to the defendant or was reasonably foreseeable." 255 Va. at 220, 495 S.E.2d at 485.

Consistent with these basic principles, this court has long recognized that some special relationships impose an elevated duty of care on the property owner. One such special relationship is that of common carrier and passenger. *See, e.g., Hines v. Garrett*, 131 Va. 125, 137, 108 S.E. 690, 693–94 (1921); *Virginia Ry. & P. Co. v. McDemmick*, 117 Va. 862, 870, 86 S.E. 744, 747 (1915); *see also Wright*, 234 Va. at 532, 362 S.E.2d at 922 ("a business invitee does not entrust his safety to a business invitor to the same extent a passenger does to a common carrier"). Imposing an elevated duty of care upon the carrier is justified essentially because the passenger entrusts his safety to the carrier, who alone knows the condition of his vehicle and the dangers of the neighborhoods and environs through which the routes of travel may lie. This imbalance of knowledge and control warrants imposition of a duty on a common carrier "to protect its passengers against violence or disorderly conduct on the part of its own agents, or other passengers and strangers, when such violence or misconduct may be reasonably expected and prevented, yet it is not liable to an action for damages when it is not shown that the company had notice of any acts which justified the expectation that a wrong would be committed." *Virginia Ry. & P.*, 117 Va. at 870, 86 S.E. at 747; *see also Norfolk & Western Ry. v. Birchfield*, 105 Va. 809, 822, 54 S.E. 879, 884 (1906).

The court reasoned that, like a passenger, the guest of an innkeeper entrusts his safety to the innkeeper and has little ability to control his environment. The guest relies on the innkeeper to make the property safe and to use his or her knowledge of the neighborhood in taking the reasonably necessary precautions to do so. In this regard, it is reasonable for the law to impose upon the innkeeper, as on the common carrier, a duty to take reasonable precautions to protect his guests against injury caused by the criminal conduct on the part of other guests or strangers, if the danger of injury by such conduct is known to the innkeeper or reasonably foreseeable. Indeed, Code § 35.1–28(A) supports the conclusion that such a duty rests upon the innkeeper, although under subsection (E) of that statute, the parameters of that duty are a matter of common law. The court has held that neither the innkeeper nor the common carrier is an absolute insurer of the guest's or the passenger's personal safety. *See, e.g., Crosswhite*, 182 Va. at 716, 30 S.E.2d at 674 (innkeeper); *Norfolk & Western*, 105 Va. at 821, 54 S.E. at 883 (common carrier). Nonetheless, the court has held that the duty of care imposed on common carriers is an elevated duty that requires them " 'so far as human care and foresight can provide . . . to use the utmost care and diligence of very cautious persons; and they will be held liable for the slightest negligence which human care, skill and foresight could have foreseen and guarded against.' " *Norfolk & Western*, 105 Va. at 821, 54 S.E. at 883 (quoting *Connell v. Chesapeake and Ohio Ry. Co.*, 93 Va. 44, 55, 24 S.E. 467, 468 [1896]). Given the nature of the special relationship between an innkeeper and a guest, the court held that it imposes on the innkeeper the same potential elevated duty of "utmost care and diligence" to protect a guest from the danger of injury caused by the criminal conduct of a third person on the innkeeper's property.

Daly Seven argued that in *Wright*, the court extended the application of the duty of care previously applied in common carrier cases "to business invitors in general," and, thus, the liability for negligence in the latter cases is imposed only when a business invitor "knows that criminal assaults against persons are occurring, or are about to occur, on the premises which indicate an imminent probability of harm to an invitee." 234 Va. at 533, 362 S.E.2d at 922. The court's decision in *Wright*, however, involved a business invitee and not a guest of the hotel, and for that reason alone was not authority for Daly Seven's broad contention. Moreover, in *Wright*, the court specifically noted that in a prior common carrier case, *Hines v. Garrett*, 131 Va. 125, 108 S.E. 690 (1921), it had recognized "the high degree of care a common carrier owes its passengers and, therefore, a carrier's duty to protect passengers from criminal acts of third persons which are reasonably foreseeable." *Wright*, 234 Va. at 532, 362 S.E.2d at 922. The court went on to hold that *Hines* was inapplicable in *Wright* "because a business invitee does not entrust his safety to a business invitor to the same extent a passenger does to a common carrier." *Id.*

In commenting on three other common carrier cases, the court noted that implicit in all of them "is the element of notice of a specific danger just prior to the assault." *Id.* at 533, 362 S.E.2d at 922. It then stated that, in the context of a business owner and invitee special relationship, the court would not impose liability for negligence based solely on a background of previous criminal activity on the owner's property. *Id.* Here, the court did not retreat from its holding in *Wright*; it is simply not applicable to the potential duty of care owed to a guest as a result of the special relationship of innkeeper and guest. And, in the context of that special relationship, the court equated "notice of a specific danger" with the concept of a reasonably foreseeable danger, not with the degree of knowledge of criminal assaults that indicate "an imminent probability" of harm. *See Skate America*, 261 Va. at 130, 540 S.E.2d at 128 ("imminent probability" of harm is a heightened degree of foreseeability).

Having determined that the special relationship of innkeeper and guest recognized by the common law imposes a duty of "utmost care and diligence" to protect the guest against reasonably foreseeable injury from the criminal conduct of a third party, the court then reviewed the allegations of the amended motion for judgment to determine whether Taboada had adequately pled a cause of action under that standard. *See Sanchez v. Medicorp Health Sys.*, 270 Va. 299, 303, 618 S.E.2d 331, 333 (2005).

Limiting its consideration only to whether the facts alleged in the amended motion for judgment were sufficient to survive Daly Seven's demurrer, the court held that those allegations, if proven, would be sufficient to permit a trier of fact to find that Daly Seven had breached its duty of care. Taboada alleged that, over a three-year period immediately prior to the attack upon Taboada, Daly Seven's employees had contacted police ninety-six times to report criminal conduct, including robberies, malicious woundings, shootings, and other criminally assaultive acts. As a result of these repeated incidents, Daly Seven had been advised by police that "its guests were at a specific imminent risk for harm to their persons from uninvited persons coming into or upon its property." These allegations were found to be sufficient to support a reasonable conclusion that Daly Seven knew its property was located in a high-crime area, and that Daly Seven was on notice that its guests were in danger of injury caused by similar criminal acts of third parties. These allegations sufficiently supported the further conclusion that the injury to Taboada from the criminal act of the third party was reasonably foreseeable.

Washington

Under applicable common law in Washington, a private person does not have a duty to protect others from criminal acts of third persons. *Hutchins v. 1001 Fourth Ave. Assoc.*, 116 Wash. 2d 217, 802 P.2d 1360 (1991).

However, Washington courts recognize an exception to that rule in cases where a special relationship exists between the parties. Examples of special relationships include those between school districts and students, *McLeod v. Grant County School Dist. No. 128*, 42 Wash. 2d 316, 255 P.2d 360 (1953); innkeepers and their guests, *Miller v. Staton*, 58 Wash. 2d 879, 365 P.2d 333 (1961); common carriers and their passengers, *Hutchins* (cited above); and business establishments and their customers, *Hutchins* (cited above).

The above examples suggest a fairly broad application of the "special relationship" doctrine. However, once the doctrine is applied, the nature of the duty owed may be fairly narrow.

Washington courts have also extensively addressed the issue of foreseeability. The *McLeod* decision has been widely cited for the proposition that a specific criminal act itself need not be foreseeable. Rather, according to the *McLeod* court, "the question is whether the actual harm fell within a general field of danger which should have been anticipated."

In applying a "field of danger" test, the courts have considered whether the specific criminal act is within the scope of hazards covered by the duty imposed upon the defendant. *Rikstad v. Holmberg*, 76 Wash. 2d 265, 456 P.2d 355 (1969).

Expanding on that proposition, a 1994 decision held that to overcome a motion for summary judgment, a plaintiff must establish that a defendant knew or should have known of the risk that resulted in the occurrence of the harm. *J.N. v. Bellingham School District*, 74 Wash. App. 49, 871 P.2d 1106 (1994).

UPDATE

In *Fuentes v. Port of Seattle*, 119 Wash.App. 864 (Court of Appeals of Washington 2004), Nathalie Fuentes, while waiting in her car at the Seattle-Tacoma (SeaTac) International Airport's pick-up drive for passengers, was injured when her car was carjacked. The carjacker was fleeing Port of Seattle police after they caught him breaking into a car in the airport parking garage. Fuentes sued the Port of Seattle, alleging that it failed to provide adequate police and/or security for the safety of invitees at the airport. The trial court granted summary judgment for the Port of Seattle.

The general rule in Washington is that a person owes no duty to prevent criminal harm to third parties. *Hutchins*, 116 Wash.2d at 220, 802 P.2d 1360. This rule was tempered, however, in *Nivens*, where the court held that "a business owes a duty to its invitees to protect them from imminent criminal harm and reasonably foreseeable criminal conduct by third persons." *Nivens*, 133 Wash.2d at 205, 943 P.2d 286.

The parties disputed the duty of care the Port owed to Fuentes. The Port asserted that the trial court erred when it determined that Fuentes was an invitee. The Port argued that Fuentes was a licensee and, therefore, was owed only an intermediate duty of care. The court reasoned that Fuentes was at the airport to pick up passengers disembarking from an airplane, and as such, although she herself was not an airline passenger, her purpose for being at the pick-up drive was connected to airport business. The Port of Seattle provided the pick-up drive, where Fuentes was at the time of the carjacking, for the specific purpose for which she was there. The record did not support the Port's assertion that Fuentes was a licensee because she exceeded the Port's invitation by remaining too long on the pick-up drive. Thus, the court found that the trial court did not err in finding that Fuentes was entitled to the status of an invitee, and as such, the Port owed a duty of reasonable care for Fuentes's safety.

Fuentes asserted that genuine issues of material fact existed that should have precluded summary judgment on the issue of foreseeability. But Fuentes offered no evidence that the Port knew of carjackings at the airport pick-up drive in the past. Instead, to support her assertion that the carjacking was foreseeable, Fuentes marshaled evidence of criminal activity in the SeaTac garage provided for suit against the Port by an airport patron, Soheila Motamed, who had been assaulted in the garage in December 1996. In that case (*Motamed v. Port of Seattle* [King County Cause No. 97-2-30521-7- KNT]), Motamed alleged that the Port was on notice of criminal activity in the garage and that police patrols of that facility were inadequate. To support Motamed's claim, she presented as evidence a 1995 report stating that, as of 1994, "a passenger at Seattle-Tacoma International Airport is more likely to be victim of a crime tha[n] at any other comparable airport in the United States." She also presented testimony from several police officers that the garage had a problem with car prowlers.

The court found that even if the Motamed assault had established a pattern of violent crime in the airport garage, it would not be dispositive of a pattern of crime at the airport pick-up drive. The kind of knowledge required before a duty to protect arises is knowledge from past experience that there is a likelihood of conduct that poses a danger to the safety of patrons. *Nivens*, 133 Wash.2d at 204, 943 P.2d 286. A history of car prowlers working the unoccupied cars parked in the airport garage did not create foreseeability of kidnapping or carjackings of occupied cars at the airport's pick-up drive. Fuentes also provided 1997 and 1998 crime statistics documenting crimes at the SeaTac Airport, but those statistics were found to disclose neither violent crimes at the pick-up drive nor carjackings anywhere on the airport grounds. Because Erickson's carjacking of Fuentes's car was so highly improbable as to be beyond the range of expectability, the court found that the carjacking was unforeseeable as a matter of law and, accordingly, held that the Port owed no duty to Fuentes.

West Virginia

West Virginia had no cases reported.

UPDATE
There are no updates for this state.

Wisconsin

At one time, the Supreme Court of Wisconsin was at the forefront of premises security law, with its 1979 decision in the case of *Peters v. Holiday Inns*, 89 Wis. 2d 115, 278 N.W.2d 208 (1979). The *Peters* court fully addressed the various aspects of a negligent security case against a hotel for an assault committed on a guest, and wrote an insightful decision holding that hotel operators, and perhaps all business owners, may be under a duty to provide appropriate security measures to protect their patrons from certain criminal acts.

According to the *Peters* court, the degree of care that must be exercised varies in relation to the attendant circumstances, including the prevailing industry standards, the community's crime rate, and the peculiar security problems posed by the building's design. The particular circumstances may require various safety features, such as closed-circuit television, security patrols, or dead bolts and chains. The court further stated that hotel security cases require a plaintiff "to prove the innkeeper's failure to exercise ordinary care commensurate with the circumstances," and noted that such cases usually are not appropriate for summary judgment consideration.

Following that landmark decision, Wisconsin courts have revisited the issues related to premises security cases, and routinely hold that a landowner is not under a duty to provide protection unless the underlying crime was foreseeable.

In *Pfeifer v. Petcoff*, 175 Wis. 2d 622, 502 N.W.2d 282 (Wis. Ct. App. 1993), the plaintiff tenant was assaulted by a former tenant who entered the premises apparently because he still had his key and the locks had not been changed. The court found that the defendant did not owe a duty to prevent the harm, because the defendant could not have reasonably foreseen the crime.

Similarly, a court dismissed a negligent security case on the issue of foreseeability in *Gallun v. Soccer USA Inc.*, 184 Wis. 2d 401, 516 N.W.2d 789, 1994 WL 133053 (Wis. Ct. App., April 19, 1994). There, the plaintiff sued the defendant after discovering that a maintenance employee of the defendant had placed a video camera in the women's locker facility. The court concluded that the defendant could not have foreseen the employee's actions and, therefore, dismissed the claim for emotional injuries.

UPDATE

In *H. K. Mallak, Inc. v. Fairfield FMC Corp.*, 209 F.3d 960 (U.S.C.A. 7th Cir. 2000), a hotel guest and his employer sued a hotel operator for damages for personal injuries and property loss arising after a guest held them at gunpoint and stole more than $1 million in diamonds. The United States District Court for the Eastern District of Wisconsin granted summary judgment for the operator on the employer's property claim, 33 F.Supp.2d 748, and dismissed the guest's claim with prejudice. The court of appeals held that the Wisconsin statute limiting hotel liability did not apply to preclude recovery for theft occurring before the guest received the required notice.

This diversity case required the court to construe a Wisconsin statute designed to protect what the common law quaintly called "innkeepers"—today's hotels and motels—from potentially astronomical liability for theft of property stored by guests in their rooms. The thieves here were either exceptionally lucky or they knew only too well who their target was. As he stepped into his room for the first time, with more than $1 million in diamonds wrapped around his body, salesman Eshagh Kashimallak was assaulted by masked men and stripped of his valuable inventory. Kashimallak and his employer, H. K. Mallak, Inc. ("Mallak") sued Fairfield FMC Corp., the owner of the hotel, seeking respectively damages for personal injuries and property loss.

The Wisconsin Hotelkeeper's Liability statute § 254.80 provides that a hotelkeeper who fulfills certain obligations will not be held liable for a guest's loss of jewelry, precious metals, or gemstones. Also relevant is § 254.81, which addresses the hotelkeeper's duties once property is tendered to it: Every guest and intended guest of any hotel, upon delivering to the hotelkeeper any baggage or other property for safekeeping, elsewhere than in the room assigned to the guest, shall demand and the hotelkeeper shall give a check or receipt, to evidence the delivery. No hotelkeeper shall be liable for the loss of or injury to the baggage or other property of a hotel guest, unless it was delivered to the hotelkeeper for safekeeping or unless the loss or injury occurred through the negligence of the hotelkeeper.

There is a dearth of case law in Wisconsin construing § 254.80, and so, as a federal court sitting in diversity, the court reviewed the statute to decide whether Wisconsin law supports Mallak's right to recover on this record. The parties agreed that the leading decision was the eighty-two-year-old ruling in *Busley v. Hotel Wisconsin Realty Co.*, 166 Wis. 294, 164 N.W. 826 (1917), which construed the predecessor to § 254.80. In *Busley*, as in *Mallak*, the parties had stipulated that the innkeeper had complied with the applicable statutory notice requirements. An additional stipulation provided that the loss in question occurred either through the theft or the gross negligence of the innkeeper's servants. The court thus had only to consider what was the extent of the innkeeper's liability for the loss of property delivered to him, when that loss occurred without any negligence on his part. The *Busley* court held that the statute did not eliminate the innkeeper's liability for loss caused by the theft or gross negligence of himself or his servants, although § 1726 of the statute in question limited liability to ten dollars for packages placed under the care of the cashier under the predecessor to § 254.81, § 1725a. The innkeeper argued that the ten-dollar limitation of liability applied to the loss of money and jewelry, but the court disagreed. Noting that § 1725, the predecessor to § 254.80, was limited to "money, jewelry and articles of gold or silver manufacture," the court stated that "it never was the legislative intent to limit an innkeeper's liability to ten dollars for the contents of a package of goods described in section 1725. For the loss of such a package, caused by the gross negligence of himself or his servants, the value thereof is the true measure of damages." 164 N.W. at 828.

As such, the court read *Busley* to indicate that, at a minimum, the notice and delivery provisions of the predecessors to § 254.80 did not suffice to protect an innkeeper from liability for its own gross negligence or that of its employees and that this rule was consistent with the general understanding in the area. The court stated that the following decisions, however, all indicated in one way or the other that the statutory limitations found in laws like Wisconsin's (a) do not relieve the hotelkeeper from liability based on acts of its own employees, and (b) merely modify the duty of the insurer that the common law otherwise imposed on innkeepers, replacing it with a negligence regime. *See, e.g., Shifflette v. Lilly*, 130 W.Va. 297, 43 S.E.2d 289, 293–94 (1947) (holding that a similar statute requiring the deposit of jewelry in the office and the posting of notices did not relieve the innkeeper of the general duty to exercise due care in providing honest servants and in taking reasonable precautions to protect the person and property of guests); *Rockhill v. Congress Hotel Co.*, 237 Ill. 98, 86 N.E. 740, 741–42 (1908) (Illinois statute did not apply to a case involving the theft of a handbag containing valuables and jewelry, where the loss occurred by the negligence of the porter or servants of the hotel); *Shamrock Hilton Hotel v. Caranas*, 488 S.W.2d 151, 153 (Tex.Civ.App. 1972) (a statute limiting hotel liability did not apply to a case alleging that loss occurred through the negligence of the hotel); *Kutbi v. Thunderlion Enterprises, Inc.*, 73 Or.App. 458, 698 P.2d 1044, 1048 (Or.App.1985) (a summary judgment was considered improper in a case where a plaintiff alleged negligence and gross negligence, through knowledge of a lost master key for the area where the plaintiff was staying and through loss of the key, where jewelry was stolen from the plaintiff's room; the innkeepers' law only modified the common-law rule of strict liability). In a case dealing with the checkout process, rather than the check-in process, a New York appellate court found that a hotel was not entitled to summary judgment where a departing guest's tote bag, containing jewelry and other valuables, was snatched away from her while she sat in a livery cab in the hotel's driveway. *See Penchas v. Hilton*

Hotels Corp., 198 A.D.2d 10, 603 N.Y.S.2d 48 (App.Div.1993). Under those circumstances, notwithstanding the hotelkeepers' liability laws, the hotel continued to have a duty to exercise reasonable care to protect its guests from injury at the hands of third parties who were not hotel employees, and to protect them from the criminal acts of third parties. *Id.* at 49–50.

In the court's view, in light of the cases mentioned above, it thought that a Wisconsin court would likely follow a similar rule for a guest who was subjected to a criminal act during the process of checking in. Just as the provisions for notice and a safe are no longer useful for a guest who has checked out, such provisions cannot help a guest who has not even penetrated the interior of his room and had a chance to use them. Even if the prediction about Wisconsin law is wrong, however, and Wisconsin gives absolute protection to hotels that have the proper notices posted in the rooms (no matter where or when the crime occurs), the court was confident that Wisconsin would not extend the protection of the statute to the case of an inside job, as may have been the case in *Mallak*. The court did not find a single jurisdiction that would go so far, and there was no reason to think that Wisconsin would become such an outlier.

Wyoming

Wyoming courts appear to be fairly restrictive in evaluating situations that may create liability for crimes committed on business owners' premises.

In *White v. HA, Inc.*, 782 P.2d 1125 (Wyo. 1989), the plaintiff was shot outside a bar following an altercation with another bar patron. The complaint alleged the defendant breached its duty to provide protection to the plaintiff. The lower court dismissed the case, and the plaintiff appealed.

In upholding the dismissal, the court refused to extend situations in which a bar owner will be held liable for criminal occurrences. The court concluded that the defendant could not have foreseen the shooting.

However, the court acknowledged the following limited instances in which a tavern owner might face liability for criminal acts:

- When a tavern owner serves liquor to a minor, *McClellan v. Tottenhoff*, 666 P.2d 408 (Wyo. 1983)
- When a person is injured by someone whose behavior should alert the tavern owner that danger is imminent, *Mayflower Rest. Co. v. Griego*, 741 P.2d 1106 (Wyo. 1989)

In addition, the court reaffirmed the leading case of *Fisher v. Robbins*, 78 Wyo. 50, 319 P.2d 116 (1957), which held that to recover damages a plaintiff must show an original disturbance putting the defendant on notice of danger; a relationship between the disturbance and violence; an opportunity for the defendant to act; the defendant's allowing the act to occur; and the defendant's failure to give the plaintiff reasonable protection.

UPDATE

In *Rader v. Sugarland Enterprises, Inc.*, 149 P.3d 702 (2006), where a bar patron brought a negligence action against a bar owner for injuries sustained in a fight outside the bar with other customers, the Supreme Court of Wyoming held that the bar owner did not owe a duty to the bar patron. The patron was beaten and injured by other customers outside the bar after he was asked to leave following an altercation between his wife and other women on the dance floor; the customers had played no part in the original altercation inside the bar, and the patron had no contact with the customers in the bar, so there was no way the bar owner could foresee that an altercation involving the patron's wife and other women on the dance floor would lead to the customers' attack on the patron outside, and there was no nexus between the altercation on the dance floor and the customers' attack on the patron outside.

The court began with an analysis of its ruling in *Fisher v. Robbins*, 78 Wyo. 50, 319 P.2d 116 (1957). The disturbance, in order to attract the attention of the bar owner, must be more than a battle of words. It must be action, threats of action, or some type of demonstration. *Fisher*, 319 P.2d at 120; *White v. HA, Inc.*, 782 P.2d 1125, 1129 (Wyo.1989). At the heart of this cause of action is notice and foreseeability of some impending danger to a business invitee and the business's ability to avert the danger. The court reasoned that bars and taverns, by their very nature, involve alcohol, loud and animated conversations, and spontaneous actions and reactions to normally innocuous words and events; given those realities, the court had been reluctant, and declined now, to broaden tavern owner liability beyond what it had ruled in *Hanna v. Cloud*, 9, 889 P.2d 529 (Wyo.1995) or *White*, namely that the "duty to protect a third party from danger, above and beyond the general landowner duty to provide reasonably safe premises to all invitees, arises when the disturbance in the bar is sufficient to alert the tavern keeper that there is imminent danger of injury to a third party," and that "proof of defendant's actual or implied knowledge of impending danger to his invitees and that he had reasonable opportunity to avert [that danger] is indispensable to entitle plaintiff to recovery." *White* at 1129 and 1131.

Applying the three-part burden of proof test set forth in *Hanna*,[2] the court concluded that the plaintiff's evidence failed on each part of the test. The plaintiff, however, pointed to a brief excerpt of the court's opinion in *Fisher*, where the court said, "Even conceding that under some circumstances it might be of little importance whether those engaged in an argument were the same persons who became involved in later violence. . . ." *Fisher*, 319 P.2d at 123. The plaintiff argued, therefore, that the defendants did not have to be part of the original disturbance to alert the bar owner. The court acknowledged that one could hypothesize a scenario where the subsequent combatants were not direct participants in the earlier disturbance and the bar owner would be liable; however, the court also said in *Fisher* that if it were not shown that the later violence was connected with, precipitated by, or resulted in some manner from an earlier manifestation of danger, it cannot be said that the injury occurred because of the defendant's negligence in failing to suppress the trouble or avert the danger indicated by that manifestation. The hazard that required the defendant's action must be shown to be the same danger that resulted in the plaintiff's injury. No matter how ominous a condition or a situation becomes, if it is not the forerunner of acts that cause the plaintiff injury, it cannot be made the basis for his recovery. *Fisher*, 319 P.2d at 123–24.

Thus, in the *Rader* case, the connection between the argument involving the four ladies and the subsequent attack by Sutherland and Taylor was too tenuous to impose a duty upon Sugarland to anticipate that such an attack would occur. In fact, the sophistry of Rader's argument was best illustrated by Rader himself. In his deposition testimony, he stated that the attack by Taylor and Sutherland came as a complete surprise. He further testified that there was no prior hostility between him and Taylor and Sutherland. Nevertheless, Rader asserted that despite his own inability to predict the assault, Sugarland should have anticipated this surprise attack by two men who were not involved in the dance-floor incident. The court held that it could not find a breach of a duty where, as here, there was an unprovoked assault by two men who played no part in the initial disturbance and exhibited no hostility toward Rader prior to the attack.

---

[2]In order for a plaintiff to establish liability against a bar owner, one or more of the following must have been present: (1) a disturbance that did attract or should have attracted the tavern keeper's attention; (2) the lapse of a reasonable amount of time between the attracting disturbance and the subsequent tortious act on the injured invitee by the other invitee, within which time period the tavern keeper had the opportunity to avert the impending danger or subsequent tortious act; and (3) a relationship between the attracting disturbance and the subsequent tortious act. *Hanna* at 532.

ABOUT THE AUTHOR

Alan Kaminsky is a partner with the firm of Lewis, Brisbois, Bisgaard & Smith, LLP, in New York, where he serves as co-chair of the firm's General Liability Practice Team. Alan specializes in defending landowners, law enforcement and security providers, and businesses and corporations against high-profile personal injury actions. Alan has obtained over fifty defense verdicts in trials involving claims of inadequate security brought on behalf of wrongful death, sexual assault, and other crime victims, and other claims of negligence. Many of Alan's cases have been cited by appellate courts in New York and other jurisdictions, including the preeminent premises security case of *Jacqueline S. v. the City of New York*, in which he served as lead trial lawyer. Alan also consults on major cases on a national basis, and served as the National Coordinating Defense Counsel for all civil litigation resulting from the Columbine school shootings and the Atlanta day-trader shooting cases.

Alan has written extensively on the topic of premises security. He is a contributing author to many legal publications and is the editor of *A Complete Guide to Lead Paint Poisoning Litigation*, published by the American Bar Association. Alan has been a guest speaker at dozens of national conventions, including programs presented by the American Society for Industrial Security, the CPCU Society, the Defense Research Institute, the International Council of Shopping Centers, and the American Library Association. He has also served as chair for a series of programs sponsored by the New York State Bar Association and regularly lectures to insurance companies, trade groups, and business associations.

Alan is a graduate of New York University and of Hofstra University School of Law, where he served as the research editor for the Law Review. Alan is admitted to the New York and New Jersey state and federal courts. He is a member of the American Bar Association, the New York State Trial Lawyers Association, the Bronx County Bar Association, and the New York State Bar Association.

Your comments are welcome. Alan Kaminsky can be reached at Lewis, Brisbois, Bisgaard & Smith, 199 Water Street, New York, New York 10038, telephone (212) 232-1340, or by e-mail at kaminsky@lbb slaw.com.

TABLE OF CASES

INDEX